Dynamic Social Studies for Constructivist Classrooms

Inspiring Tomorrow's Social Scientists

EIGHTH EDITION

George W. Maxim

West Chester University

PEARSON

Merrill
Prentice Hall

Upper Saddle River, New Jersey
Columbus, Ohio

Library of Congress Cataloging-in-Publication Data

Maxim, George W.
  Dynamic social studies for constructivist classrooms : inspiring tomorrow's social
scientists / George W. Maxim.—8th ed.
      p. cm.
  Rev. ed. of: Dynamic social studies for elementary classrooms. 7th ed. c2003.
  Includes bibliographical references and index.
  ISBN 0-13-171270-5 (pbk)
  1. Social sciences—Study and teaching (Elementary)—United States. 2.
Interdisciplinary approach in education—United States. 3. Effective teaching—United
States. I. Maxim, George W. Dynamic social studies for elementary classrooms. II. Title.
  LB1584.M378 2006
  372.83'044—dc22   2005007011

Vice President and Executive
  Publisher: Jeffery W. Johnston
Senior Editor: Linda Ashe Montgomery
Senior Editorial Assistant: Laura Weaver
Senior Development Editor: Hope Madden
Senior Production Editor: Mary M. Irvin
Design Coordinator: Diane C. Lorenzo
Photo Coordinator: Valerie Schultz

Production Coordination and Text Design:
  Lea Baranowski, Carlisle Publisher Services
Cover Designer: Ali Mohrman
Cover Image: Images.com
Production Manager: Pamela D. Bennett
Director of Marketing: Ann Castel Davis
Marketing Manager: Darcy Betts Prybella
Marketing Coordinator: Brian Mounts

This book was set in Souvenir by Carlisle Communications, Ltd. It was printed and bound by Courier
Kendallville, Inc. The cover was printed by Coral Graphic Services, Inc.

Photo Credits: AP Wide World Photos, p. 2; Anthony Magnacca/Merrill, pp. 9, 32, 97, 148, 169, 185, 208, 219,
227, 238, 296, 329, 370, 379, 436; Scott Cunningham/Merrill, pp. 38, 90, 110, 158, 269, 281, 312, 323, 332, 355,
383, 391, 425; Silver Burdett Ginn, pp. 46, 260, 336; Barbara Schwartz/Merrill, pp. 58, 67; KS Studios/Merrill,
pp. 61, 347; Paul Conklin/PhotoEdit, p. 82; Bruce Johnson/Merrill, p. 137; Dan Floss/Merrill, p. 181; Anne
Vega/Merrill, pp. 204, 350; Patrick White/Merrill, pp. 251, 447; PH College, p. 406.

Pearson Education Ltd.
Pearson Education Singapore Pte. Ltd.
Pearson Education Canada, Ltd.
Pearson Education—Japan

Pearson Education Australia Pty. Limited
Pearson Education North Asia Ltd.
Pearson Educación de Mexico, S.A. de C.V.
Pearson Education Malaysia Pte. Ltd.

PEARSON
Merrill
Prentice Hall

10 9 8 7 6 5 4 3 2 1
ISBN: 0-13-171270-5

*Dedicated to Martha Drobnak
and Deb Preston for being
sensitive, kind, caring, and funny.*

Educator Learning Center: An Invaluable Online Resource

Merrill Education and the Association for Supervision and Curriculum Development (ASCD) invite you to take advantage of a new online resource, one that provides access to the top research and proven strategies associated with ASCD and Merrill—the Educator Learning Center. At *www.educatorlearningcenter.com*, you will find resources that will enhance your students' understanding of course topics and of current educational issues, in addition to being invaluable for further research.

HOW THE EDUCATOR LEARNING CENTER WILL HELP YOUR STUDENTS BECOME BETTER TEACHERS

With the combined resources of Merrill Education and ASCD, you and your students will find a wealth of tools and materials to better prepare them for the classroom.

Research

- More than 600 articles from the ASCD journal *Educational Leadership* discuss everyday issues faced by practicing teachers.
- A direct link on the site to Research Navigator™ gives students access to many of the leading education journals, as well as extensive content detailing the research process.
- Excerpts from Merrill Education texts give your students insights on important topics of instructional methods, diverse populations, assessment, classroom management, technology, and refining classroom practice.

Classroom Practice

- Hundreds of lesson plans and teaching strategies are categorized by content area and age range.
- Case studies and classroom video footage provide virtual field experience for student reflection.
- Computer simulations and other electronic tools keep your students abreast of today's classrooms and current technologies.

LOOK INTO THE VALUE OF EDUCATOR LEARNING CENTER YOURSELF

A four-month subscription to Educator Learning Center is $25 but is **FREE** when packaged with any Merrill Education text. In order for your students to have access to this site, you must use this special value-pack ISBN number **WHEN** placing your textbook order with the bookstore: 0-13-218483-4. Your students will then receive a copy of the text packaged with a free ASCD pincode. To preview the value of this website to you and your students, please go to *www.educatorlearningcenter.com* and click on "Demo."

Preface

Bringing the social studies curriculum to life for elementary and middle school students will encourage them to become informed, caring citizens who will make a difference in our world. *Dynamic Social Studies for Constructivist Classrooms: Inspiring Tomorrow's Social Scientists* is a guide, tool, and reference to help you inspire your students. You'll come away from reading it with a clear vision of the most effective and creative ways to teach social studies and motivate your students to become social scientists.

This brief, manageable text helps teachers breathe life into social studies teaching, illustrating the creation of a dynamic social studies classroom with its constructivist framework, key instructional approaches, literacy-based pedagogy, text sets, activities, and classroom vignettes.

MODELING CONSTRUCTIVIST TEACHING

Constructivism is the most advocated approach for social studies instruction and the most meaningful methodology for engaging students in their own learning. Building on the fundamental principles of constructivism, this text provides the most comprehensive presentation of constructivist classroom applications in the field.

New!
- Part 3: Constructivist Approaches to Classroom Instruction presents three entire chapters devoted to constructivist teaching covering the learning cycle, cooperative learning, and inquiry and problem solving, modeling a clear and effective foundation for constructivist social studies teaching.
- Chapters on Young Historians, Young Geographers, and Young Political Scientists provide fresh perspectives on and insight into stimulating social studies teaching, capturing what it means to teach children to be social scientists through a constructivist approach.

EMPHASIZING CREATIVE TEACHING IN TODAY'S CLASSROOM

You'll be escorted through model social studies classrooms, discovering how masterful teachers address the realities of contemporary classrooms to engage and motivate students.

New! • NCSS coverage will help you integrate the National Council for the Social Studies Standards in your teaching.

New! • Literacy connections to social studies teaching are designed to help you better prepare your future social scientists and help you plan for an integrated curriculum.

New! • Chapter openings present illustrative classroom examples identifying one major theme for each chapter and demonstrating how it translates into classroom practice.

• Authentic classroom samples share children's artwork and writing, illustrating the responses you can expect to receive from your own students when you are successful at motivating and engaging them in social studies learning.

PROVIDING DYNAMIC INSTRUCTIONAL TOOLS

Beginning with the sound philosophical approach of constructivism, the text offers many practical examples of classroom instruction and includes creative tools to assist you in bringing this framework to life in your own classroom.

New! • *Text Sets* in every chapter help you engage students in social studies through quality children's literature. These features offer readers an annotated collection of five or six books to use in classrooms to integrate social studies themes and topics, helping readers establish the strong connection between language arts and social studies concepts.

• *Inside an Active Classroom* features throughout chapters help you develop background knowledge and provide you with a bank of activities to take into your classroom.

ADDRESSING THE NEEDS OF PRE-SERVICE TEACHERS AND PROFESSORS

The new edition presents a streamlined, applied approach because university students and professors have a limited amount of time and need to focus on the most effective presentation of practices and sound research.

• Written in a readable, relaxed style, the text engages the reader.

• The manageable size and reduced price make the text a perfect fit for today's students, who have limited budgets, and today's professors, who have limited time.

• Supplements available to professors include an online Instructor's Manual with test bank and PowerPoint® presentations.

New! • A Companion Website is available for coursework and includes self-assessments, web links, advance organizers, and a Syllabus Manager for professors. This CW is designed to engage users, encourage reflection and practice, help readers gauge their understanding of text concepts, and provide professors with meaningful technological integration.

ACKNOWLEDGMENTS

I would like to thank the reviewers of the manuscript for their suggestions and insights: Ernest Barnett, Northern Kentucky University; Karen Ivers, California State University, Fullerton; Deborah C. Johnson, Holy Family; Carolyn Riley, Northern Illinois University; and Saundra Wetig, University of Nebraska at Omaha.

Brief Contents

Contents

Part I

FOUNDATIONS OF INSTRUCTION

Chapter 5 *Young Political Scientists: Future Citizens in Action 208*

Part III

CONSTRUCTIVIST APPROACHES TO CLASSROOM INSTRUCTION

Chapter 6 *The Learning Cycle: Teacher Scaffolded Social Constructivism 260*

**Part
IV**   **KEY ORGANIZATIONAL DECISIONS**

Dynamic Social Studies:
The Subject You Will Teach

WHAT DOES DYNAMIC SOCIAL STUDIES LOOK LIKE?

Mrs. Holzwarth's fourth graders in Upper Darby, Pennsylvania, were about to wind up a thematic unit on their state when Naisha brought in a newspaper story about Maryland having recently adopted the monarch butterfly as its state insect. "Does Pennsylvania have a state insect, too?" inquired several interested youngsters. That was all it took to launch Mrs. Holzwarth's class into one of the most enjoyable social studies learning adventures it had ever tackled.

The students got the ball rolling by looking up information in various books and pamphlets; they found a state flower, a state song, a state tree, a state nickname, and various other state symbols, but no official "state bug." The children suggested that they should write to the president of the United States to see if they could have one, but Mrs. Holzwarth explained that since this was a state matter, they should direct their query to their district legislators in Harrisburg, the state capital.

Before they did so, however, the class decided to conduct a regular democratic election to determine what insect would be the most suitable state symbol. Several insects were nominated and each nominee became the subject of careful study. The students explored the pros and cons of an assortment of bugs such as the praying mantis, dragonfly, ladybug, and grasshopper. After weighing the advantages and disadvantages of each, a class vote settled the matter: the firefly was their selection. Why? One reason was that the scientific name, *Photuris pennsylvanica,* closely resembled the name of their state. Students also liked the fact that the soft glow of hundreds of these insects dotted their backyards on warm summer evenings, and they spent many a summer night running around catching these elusive "lightning bugs." (The children had been taught that to catch a firefly and let it walk all over their hands for a while is "okay" but to hurt the insect in any way is very wrong.)

After the vote, the students were not quite ready to drop the matter. They agreed to write a letter to their two state representatives informing them of their actions and asking how they might make their actions official. Both lawmakers were extremely impressed with the children's civic energy and arranged to visit Mrs. Holzwarth's classroom to answer the children's questions and personally thank them for their interest in state issues. The awestruck youngsters listened intently as the legislators discussed the process of introducing a law in the state legislature and advised the students how they might proceed with their project. The children learned that their next step would be to persuade other legislators to support their cause. Undaunted, these 26 children wrote more than 250 letters—203 to the House, 50 to the Senate, and 2 to the governor and his wife. The children also learned that they needed popular support from voters in their area, so they canvassed their neighborhoods and shopping malls until they obtained more than 2,100 signatures.

To interest others in their work, the students printed more than 600 luminous bumper stickers proclaiming "Firefly for State Insect." They also kept up their letter-writing campaign, asking legislators to vote YES when the bill came onto the floor. The children were invited to Harrisburg for the House Government Committee hearings on their bill and went to the state capital armed with banners on the side of the bus. Instead of the time-honored bus trip favorite, "Ninety-nine Bottles . . . ," the children repeatedly sang an original song they wrote especially for this occasion:

Oh firefly! Oh firefly!
Please be our state bug.
Photuris pennsylvanica,
You'll fly forever above.
Oh firefly! Oh firefly!
You light up so bright.
It's fun to see such a pretty sight.
Oh firefly! Oh firefly!

Imagine the thoughts of the children as they arrived in Harrisburg to be met by television crews and reporters from the major news services. The hearing itself was held according to established decorum, the children testifying about fireflies for about 2 hours. The committee reported its unanimous support of the bill to the House of Representatives, and eventually the bill passed the House by a vote of 156 to 22. Next, the Senate passed the firefly bill by an overwhelming vote of 37 to 11. When the governor finally signed the bill (Act 59), the children were again in Harrisburg to watch the institution of a new state law. *Photuris pennsylvanica* officially took its place alongside the whitetail deer, ruffed grouse, and Great Dane as official state animals.

For Mrs. Holzwarth's class, this "happening" was much more than an exercise in choosing a state insect. It was an authentic, purposeful learning experience in which the children took direct political action and participated in meaningful legislative processes. They learned about petitioning and writing letters to their representatives, and they saw firsthand how government works. One child noted, "Now we have something to tell our grandchildren." Another, when asked if she would like to get another law passed, blurted, "Darn right! I'd like a law against homework. Homework gives you pimples!"

(As an aside, I recently heard of a group of fourth graders in another Pennsylvania school district who replicated this adventure by voting for the chocolate chip cookie as the official "State Cookie." They diligently followed the process used by Mrs. Holzwarth's class, but the bill died in committee. One of the legislators liked oatmeal/raisin cookies better!)

Social studies can be the single most exciting subject in the elementary school, for no other subject helps guide children through the fascinating world around them with such strength and power. Children come to school deeply curious about their surroundings, and social studies provides an ideal setting for their innate drive to explore and investigate. Social studies teachers understand that elementary school children are the most eager of all learners and that there seems to be a "natural social scientist" living within each. Therefore, their social studies classrooms are richer in variety, richer in stimulation, and richer in challenge than we might find for any other subject.

Good social studies teachers—the "Mrs. Holzwarths" of our world—bring an aura of distinction to their social studies classrooms; they obviously enjoy their work and value the lives they touch. There are no secret recipes or die-cast molds that might help us duplicate these special individuals; each is one of a kind. They know and love our nation and hold bright hopes for its future. Their sense of democratic values influences everything they do in their classrooms. These teachers know that young children are our future, and the way they live and learn today becomes the way they will live and learn tomorrow. They expertly handle with keen insight and skill all the subtle professional tasks of a social studies program, and their instructional choices are based on a maze of complicated decisions. They subscribe to Mattioli's (2004) observation that, "Teaching is a complex, non-routine and responsive endeavor. . . . As teachers, we have to be constantly aware of what we are doing in the classroom, why we are doing it and why we are doing it the way we are doing it. Teaching is not like Nike. It's not 'Just Do It'" (p. 8). Teachers, in order to make a difference in the lives of our nation's young citizens, must have considerable professional knowledge and skills.

The physical setting is important, as are the materials used to carry out social studies instruction, but a teacher's professional skills blended together with outstanding personal qualities are the most vital ingredients of good social studies programs. Personal and professional behaviors dictate the tone of the environment and make a lasting impact on the students, on their families, and on society. Few individuals are more significant in the lives of elementary school children than their parents, close relatives, and teachers. As Risinger (2002) so convincingly stated, "Although this may sound corny or naïve, I believe that teaching social studies is more than a job . . . even more than a profession: It's a mission, a calling" (p. 231). For that reason, elementary school social studies teachers should be among the finest people we know. Being a fine person does not in itself guarantee success in teaching. A superior teacher must also possess a set of professional skills founded on sound theoretical and research-based principles.

Successful teachers welcome the challenge of creating marvelous social studies classrooms and look to sound theory as the basis for their instruction. They deliberately build their programs on their best knowledge of whom they are teaching, what they are teaching, and how they are teaching. Successful social studies teachers have what it takes, in spirit and skill, to tailor their classrooms to fit the children who come to them. They demonstrate, without timidity, that they would rather be challenged than safe and bored.

It's a good idea to acquire this can-do spirit early in your career, for succeeding in risky situations may be a more powerful indicator of would-be greatness than any other single personality trait. Those who take risks seem to have a high degree of self-confidence, a distinctive quality of outstanding social studies teachers. As I once heard, having a strongly positive sense of self-worth is worth 50 IQ points. So work hard, dream a lot, and muster up the grit to establish a point of view. However, risks cannot, and should not, be taken unless your fundamentals are solid. Good social studies teachers never take risks blindly; their decisions are based on a strong foundation of knowledge and skill. Build that foundation in social studies education and take your risks there, for it is the one area of the elementary school curriculum that most openly invites the ideas and dreams of adventurous and creative teachers.

WHAT DO YOU REMEMBER ABOUT SOCIAL STUDIES?

Do you remember a "Mrs. Holzwarth" from your elementary school days? Think back to the time when you were an elementary school child. What memories do you have of a social studies teacher doing the things you liked, but also the things you didn't like? Make a list of both kinds of experiences. Share the list with your classmates, perhaps by constructing a group chart listing positive and negative experiences under their appropriate headings. What kinds of memories did most students have? I enjoy doing this activity on the first day of a semester with my classes. It is instructive both for my students and for me. Although I hesitate to describe this category first, the "dislike" category usually includes such memories as reading pages 79 to 81 in the text and writing answers to the questions at the end of the section (while the teacher corrected the weekly spelling tests), listening to the teacher drone on about how a cotton gin works (without benefit of a picture or model), being required to memorize facts about the early explorers of North America (where they came from, when they left their homeland, the date they arrived here, and where they explored), or copying "research reports" directly from the encyclopedia. After generating a list of 15 to 20 "dislikes" such as these, I ask the students to suggest one-word descriptions that best sum up those types of instructional practices. "Boring," "deadly," "dull," "mind-numbing," and "humdrum" are some of the expressions I remember.

Unfortunately, when their elementary school days had been filled with inconsequential classroom experiences like these, young adults tend to underestimate the hard work that goes into effective social studies instruction: "Is that all there is to it? Why, anybody can teach social studies to elementary school kids! Who can't tell them to take out their textbooks? Read a few pages? Answer the questions at the end of the section? Why does anyone need to take a college methods course to learn to do something so simple?" When faced with such an accusation, the best way to cope is to admit its validity. Anybody *can* tell children to take out their textbooks to read a few pages. And, yes, it's true that anybody *can* ask them the questions printed at the end of a reading selection. The indictments are true, but there is one thing wrong—they miss the whole point of elementary school social studies education. Social studies is not meant to be taught that way; if it were, it's indeed true that there is no point in taking this course.

In contrast to the "dislike" category, the "like" category usually includes memories such as: "Writing our own classroom constitution and holding elections," "Making travel brochures to interest students from other states to visit our state," "Using milk cartons to build a frontier town," "Role-playing a historical figure for a pageant of great people who lived during the Civil War," "Taking a field trip to the seashore to study the shells that washed up," "Cooking venison stew as we read the book, *Sign of the Beaver*," "Hearing a Peace Corps volunteer tell of her experiences in Ethiopia," "Making a large mural of the rainforest," "Taking food and clothing to a homeless shelter," "Learning about the history and origin of the families of everyone in the classroom," "Performing a skit about an African naming ceremony," and "Making a large dragon as part of a Chinese New Year celebration." When asked to suggest one-word descriptions to best sum up these experiences, students regularly come up with words like "fun," "exciting," "interesting," "lively," "rewarding," "active," and "instructive." I bring closure to the activity by asking my students to think about these questions: "Which set of words would you want others to use to describe *your* social studies program? What will you need to know or be able to do for that to happen?"

The resulting discussion usually draws out questions about the professional know-how required to carry out social studies programs that are fun, exciting, interesting, lively, rewarding, and active, but at the same time, instructive. Some worry that using "fun-type" programs all the time might create serious classroom management problems: "I'd like my social studies class to be fun and exciting, but I'm worried that the children will lose control." "Won't children think of the 'fun' activities as 'play time' and just fool around in class, not learning anything?" They worry that an enjoyable program reduces social studies to a series of insignificant events that most often end up in hard-to-handle behavior problems.

Others are concerned that being strictly serious about the content can do just the opposite—result in a dull and boring fact-filled social studies program: "How do you get across the important social studies content without being run-of-the-mill or ordinary?" "How can you teach content without communicating to the children that we think they're unskilled or ignorant?" They fear that "serious-type" social studies programs can become trivial and tedious for both the teacher and the children and are prone to provoke resentment and hostility in the children. In essence, the question becomes, "How can I make social studies fun and still maintain control over what the children do and understand?" One of the most significant challenges social studies teachers face is, on one hand, helping children acquire the knowledge, skills, and values that help prepare them for constructive participation in a democratic society, and, on the other hand, organizing and conducting lessons that offer a blend of pleasure, intrigue, variety, active involvement, and excitement.

Back in 1933, John Dewey addressed this dilemma and offered some sage advice that remains relevant today. In speaking to the serious–fun dichotomy of social studies instruction, Dewey (1933) said that when either is used exclusively, "Play degenerates into fooling and work into drudgery" (p. 286). Dewey recommended a program in which a balance between seriousness and fun is maintained to help promote learning. That is, teachers should build a participative approach that takes the best elements from both extremes and blends them to their needs and those of their students. The philosophy of this text echoes Dewey's view: When learning is fun, students become more interested and open to acquiring new knowledge. As a result, they see social studies as an important and fulfilling part of their lives and will strive for serious learning.

We continue to build this spirit to know and do when we honor students' ideas and offer them opportunities to create their own understandings. This is not a traditional notion of social studies instruction, one that simply views learning as a one-way transfusion of information from teacher to students. An appropriate social studies classroom helps children look on their world as a never-ending mystery. For many of you, facilitating such a program may require a radical shift in thinking. However, to start you on your way to acquiring a sound plan for teaching social studies, it is important to examine carefully these four fundamental questions:

What is social studies?

Why is social studies important?

What are the major goals of social studies instruction in the elementary school?

What is *dynamic* social studies?

WHAT IS SOCIAL STUDIES?

Your first stop on the road of attaining the know-how considered necessary for making content and methodological decisions in elementary school social studies classrooms is to acquire a clear understanding of the subject you will be teaching. Although social studies has been part of the elementary school curriculum for decades, it is not an easy subject to describe. A meaningful description usually begins by examining the difference between two potentially confusing terms: *social science* and *social studies*.

First, it is instructive to define *social science* by breaking it down into its two component parts: "social" refers to human society and its members while "science," derived from the Latin word "scientia," means knowledge. So, the term *social science* refers to several multifaceted disciplines that seek knowledge about societies and the relationships of individuals within societies. Whether you're interested in learning about the cultures of the Andes, their activities and customs, how their governments work, or about their extraordinary past, you will need to consult a particular branch

Young children learn social studies by living it.

of scientific knowledge called a *social science*. *Social studies*, on the other hand, is the title for the school subject that provides for a systematic study of the social sciences in a coordinated, integrated fashion. Social studies helps students acquire the knowledge, skills, and values necessary to make informed and reasoned decisions as active citizens in a culturally diverse, democratic nation, and interdependent world. To more completely understand the relationship between the social sciences and social studies, each will be discussed in the following sections.

The Social Sciences

Six major social sciences contribute the knowledge and processes that form the supportive backbone of most elementary school social studies programs: geography, history, political science, anthropology, sociology, and economics. Research is the major activity for social scientists from these disciplines; they use various methods to assemble facts and construct theories, such as carrying out field investigations, living and working among people being studied, examining historical documents and records, preparing and interpreting maps, administering tests and questionnaires, and conducting interviews and surveys. The work associated with each discipline varies greatly, but specialists in one discipline often find their research overlaps with work being done in another.

Geography

Geographers study people and places, the natural environment, and the capacity of the earth to support life. They ask questions about places on the Earth and their relationship to the people who live in them. The first task in geography is to locate places, describing and explaining their physical characteristics (climate, vegetation, soil, and landforms) and their implications for human activity. Geographic inquiry continues by exploring the relationships that develop as people respond to and shape their physical and natural environments. It permits us to compare, contrast, and comprehend the world's regions and their various physical and human features and patterns. This knowledge helps us to manage the world's resources and to analyze a host of other significant problems in terms of the spaces they occupy and how these spaces interact with each other on the Earth's surface.

History

Historians systematically research, analyze, and interpret the past. They use many sources of information in their research, including interviews, government and institutional records, newspapers and other periodicals, photographs, film, diaries, and letters. Historians usually specialize in a certain country or region or a specific time period. Some function as biographers, collecting detailed information on individuals. Others are genealogists, interested in tracing family histories. Some help preserve or study archival materials such as artifacts or historic buildings and sites. History is a principal social science discipline contributing to social studies but is not itself considered by many to be a "true" social science because the processes of empirical research are not used rigorously in historical study. This is not to fault the efforts of historians, but only to indicate that they are handicapped in their abilities to control or reproduce the phenomena they are studying, as scientists do. Instead, historians must reconstruct events of the past from surviving evidence, and resulting interpretations are not always accurate. For example, interpretations change as historians develop more sophisticated techniques of examining evidence and accumulate different kinds of evidence. Consider that, in the 1920s, many historians argued that the first large constructions in the world were the Egyptian pyramids. This contention was disproved in the 1960s with the introduction of carbon-14 dating, which indicated that northern European monuments such as Stonehenge were constructed earlier than most of the pyramids. As we enter the 21st century, powerful new methodologies, many using computers, may offer historians the rigorous processes that a true science demands. But for now, history is treated as a discipline wavering somewhere in the murky region between the sciences and the humanities. This is why you may see references to social studies as "history and the social sciences."

Civics (Political Science)

Political scientists study the origin, development, and operation of political systems and public policy. The emphasis of civics inquiry has been to examine the structure and functions of government—how people get power, what their duties are, and how they carry out their duties. Political scientists conduct research on a wide range of subjects such as the relationship between the United States and other countries, the political life of nations, the politics of small towns or a large metropolis, or the decisions of the U.S. Supreme Court. Political scientists approach their subject through analyses of political institutions or policies and by means of detailed examinations of the day-to-day workings of contemporary governments. Depending on the topic, political scientists take polls, conduct public opinion surveys, analyze election results, interview public officials, examine the speeches of politicians, study the actions of legislators and judges, and probe the beliefs and personalities of political leaders.

Anthropology

Anthropologists study people to find out about their physical, social, and cultural development. They examine the total pattern of human behavior and its products particular to a special group, including language, tools, beliefs, social forms, art, law, customs, traditions, religion, superstitions, morals, and occupations. Anthropologists usually concentrate in one of four specialties: archaeology, sociocultural anthropology, linguistic anthropology, or biological-physical anthropology. Archaeology is the scientific study of earlier civilizations carried out by recovering and examining material evidence of the past, such as skeletal remains, fossils, ruins, implements, tools, monuments, and other items from past human cultures, in order to determine the history, customs, and living habits. Sociocultural anthropology is the study of customs, cultures, and social lives in settings that vary from nonindustrialized societies to modern urban centers. Linguistic anthropology examines the role of language in various cultures. Biological-physical anthropology studies the evolution of the human body and analyzes how culture and biology influence one another. Most anthropologists specialize in one region of the world. Because of this immense scope of study, anthropology has often been described as a universal discipline, one that comprehensively studies cultures by looking at all aspects of their existence.

Sociology

Sociologists study society and social behavior by examining groups and social institutions such as the family, government, religion, business, or school. Sociologists investigate the values and norms of groups to discover why group members behave as they do. They study how groups form, how they operate, and how they change. Sociologists organize their study of groups around many questions, such as, "What kinds of groups do people form in any given society?" "What are the expectations of each group member?" "What problems do the group members face?" "How does the group control its members?" To answer these questions, sociologists may visit a particular group, observe what the people in that group do, interview group members, or even live with a group for a short time to understand more completely its nature. The results of a sociologist's research aid educators, lawmakers, administrators, and others interested in resolving social problems and formulating public policy.

Economics

Economists study the production, distribution, and consumption of goods and services. They describe the ways economics affects all of our lives. From youngsters who save their allowance for a special toy, to college students who must scrape together enough money for tuition, through newlyweds who apply for a mortgage as they buy their first home, all people face situations where they attempt to satisfy unlimited wants with limited resources. Referred to as the *scarcity concept*, it is from this idea that a family of economics emerges. Because of scarcity, humans have attempted to find ways to produce more in less time with less material, by which specialization of labor was developed. From specialization has emerged the idea of interdependence, a reliance of people upon one another that necessitates monetary, transportation, and communication systems. From interactions of these factors, a market system developed through which buyers and sellers produce and exchange goods or services. Finally, governments, responsible for controlling segments of the market system, ensure the welfare of all their citizens. Information about the economy, including the study of taxation, consumer economics, and economic policy, helps one assess pressing issues of the day.

The Social Science/Social Studies Connection

To help differentiate between the terms *social science* and *social studies*, we must travel back in time to 1916 when waves of Europeans had already arrived on the shores of America ready to fuel a newly industrialized economy. In the midst of an era of unprecedented social transformation in our growing young nation, the National Education Association (NEA) searched for new approaches to teaching that could effectively educate and assimilate these millions of immigrants and their children. Up to this time, the major purpose of elementary school education was to teach the 3Rs—reading, 'riting, and 'rithmetic. There were no social studies classes in elementary schools; teachers were advised to nurture young citizens by reading stories that stressed such virtues as courage, honesty, fairness, and obedience. Tales of George Washington and the cherry tree, Ben Franklin and his kite, and other exemplary deeds were read to the children. In effect, story reading could be considered an informal instructional approach to history, as students learned about the virtuous deeds of important people from the past through instructive stories. However, the informality ended with the story reading, for afterward the teacher made sure that the information contained in these stories was "learned by heart and, when forgotten, learned and learned again." The following statement, written by two historians at the turn of the century, furnished support for those educational practices:

> In its effect on the mind, American history is distinctly to be commended. The principal reasons for the study of history are that it trains the memory . . . exercises the judgment and sets before the students' minds a high standard of character. In all these respects, American history is inferior to that of no other country. The events which are studied and should be kept in memory are interesting in themselves and important to the world development. (Channing & Hart, 1903, p. 1)

The National Education Association (NEA) established various study committees to examine whether this strong emphasis on factual memorization should remain the central priority of schooling in a "new age," or whether the penetrating voice of emerging, "progressive" educators should be recognized. Look how the following proposal for change in history instruction differs from the quote you just read:

> The one thing that [history] ought to do, and has not yet effectively done, is to help us to understand ourselves and our fellows and the problems and prospects of mankind. It is this most significant form of history's usefulness that has been most commonly neglected . . . . It is high time we set to work boldly . . . to bring our education into the closest possible relation with the actual life and future duties of . . . those who fill our public schools. (Robinson, 1912, p. 134)

The NEA established a special committee to study which of these contrasting philosophies might be more useful in addressing the dual processes of assimilating immigrants into a new society and preparing an industrial workforce. After careful reflection, the committee suggested that the school curriculum and teaching strategies should be brought more in tune with contemporary society. Supported by the work of leading educators such as Francis Parker and John Dewey, the NEA proposed that the work of our schools was to guarantee social efficiency by educating students to understand and resolve social problems; readying students for the job market in a changing world of business and industry; and developing in students practical skills related to health, hygiene, and nutrition. The committee recommended that school subjects should be practical.

To help achieve practical learning, the special NEA committee proposed a brand new school subject—*social studies*—as the major vehicle to help accomplish these social education goals. Making this proposal was a bold move. Never before had a school subject called social studies existed—not in the United States or anywhere else in the world. The only thing that was known was that this completely new subject would be responsible for promoting the idea of "social efficiency" in a rapidly changing society. The NEA (1916) envisioned social studies as "the subject matter related directly to the organization and development of human society, and to individuals as members of social groups" (p. 5). The "subject matter" for this new school subject was to be drawn from the most influential social sciences of the time—history, geography, and civics—and blended together as one school subject for the purpose of helping children understand our American heritage and acquire the skills and sensitivities basic to constructive participation in our nation's democratic society. (It has now expanded to include the six social disciplines described earlier.) Thus, we can think of social studies as an amalgamation of content and processes from the six major social sciences.

Defining the Term *Social Studies*

What could prevent such a deceptively simple idea from becoming immediately embraced by the educational community? An answer to that question was as difficult to arrive at in 1916 as it is today, for over the years splinter groups have presented conflicting views of what this new subject called *social studies* should be. According to some, their efforts have come up empty, for they are said to have constructed nothing more than an endless maze of ambiguity, inconsistency, and contradiction. Finn (1988) elaborates on this point: "The great dismal swamp of today's school curriculum is not reading or writing, not math or science, not even foreign language study. It is social studies, a field that has been getting slimier and more tangled ever since it changed its name from history around 1916" (p. 16).

Students in social studies methods courses often become confused when they learn of the years of deep internal conflict: "After all these years, why can't social studies educators agree on the nature of this school subject?" To gain some perspective on this question, you must understand that, as with every sensitive educational issue, attempts to reshape social studies are sparked by experts holding strong opinions about how students learn best and what knowledge, skills, and values are most important for active citizenship participation. Such disagreements cannot be quickly resolved; years of controversy, disagreement, and debate are to be expected (see Figure 1–1).

FIGURE 1–1
A Search for Identity

After decades of carefully and patiently gazing at a clouded tangle of puzzle pieces, however, an intelligible, practical image of social studies has begun to materialize. Out of the hazy mist, razor-sharp patterns are now taking shape. The leading professional association for social studies educators, the National Council for the Social Studies (NCSS) (1993b), helped bring about harmony by aggressively addressing the nature of social studies and ultimately approving the following definition:

> Social studies is the integrated study of the social sciences and humanities to promote civic competence. Within the school program, social studies provides coordinated, systematic study drawing upon such disciplines as anthropology, archeology, economics, geography, history, law, philosophy, political science, psychology, religion, and sociology, as well as appropriate content from the humanities, mathematics, and natural sciences. The primary purpose of social studies is to help young people develop the ability to make informed and reasoned decisions for the public good as citizens of a culturally diverse, democratic society in an interdependent world. (p. 3)

With this NCSS initiative, social studies can now be defined and set apart as a viable school subject. (If you would like to impress your professor, you might like to visit the NCSS website provided at the end of this chapter and order a T-shirt with the entire definition printed on the back!) Clearly, the definition (1) has affirmed citizenship education as the primary purpose of social studies instruction, (2) presented an argument for integrated content from the social sciences and other disciplines (expanded from political science, history, and geography), (3) emphasized the need for higher-order thinking skills as opposed to memorization of facts, (4) focused on the need for multicultural understandings, and (5) stressed decision making and personal responsibility as important characteristics of good citizens. We will thoroughly examine these fundamental attributes throughout the remainder of this chapter.

WHY IS SOCIAL STUDIES IMPORTANT?

From the start of public schooling in the United States, the major purpose of elementary education has been to teach children the basic skills of reading, writing, and arithmetic. But, following the NEA's 1916 initiative, social studies took its important place in the curriculum for the primary purpose of helping prepare our nation's youth for constructive participation in society. Today, it is accepted that our schools must do more than help prepare children with competencies in the "three Rs"; to become effective citizens, they must also possess the knowledge, skills, and civic virtues necessary to become active participants in the world of the 21st century. The survival of our democratic society depends on citizens who care for their country and for humanity itself. Will our students receive an education that cultivates the moral grit to stand up and cry out for the protection of our nation's future or one that minimizes civic responsibility and respect for the legacies and principles of our families, neighborhoods, and national communities? How will our future citizens measure the purpose and quality of life in our nation? The Children's Defense Fund, an organization with a solid reputation for social advocacy, commented on the impact of schools in responding to our nation's increasingly diverse society:

> A thousand years from now, will civilization remain and humankind survive? Will America's dream be alive, be remembered, and be worth remembering? Will the United States be a blip or a beacon in history? Can our founding principle "that all men are created equal" and "are endowed by their Creator with certain inalienable rights" withstand the test of time, the tempests of politics, and become deed and not just creed for every child? Is America's dream big enough for every fifth child who is poor, every sixth child who is Black, every seventh child who is Latino, and every eighth child who is mentally or physically challenged? (1996, p. xi)

Participatory Citizenship

These questions are not new. Social studies educators have asked variations of these questions for years. From the first colony at Plymouth Rock to our bustling communities today, educators and community leaders have debated the best way to fulfill their responsibility to educate America's young citizens. Every generation has experienced deep concern about how to place in its children's collective hands the trust and understanding required to protect peace and freedom and how to teach its youngsters tolerance, cooperation, and the skills of living together in a diverse, democratic society and an increasingly interdependent world. As a nation, we have situated social studies instruction at the core of this responsibility because we are a proud people, a democratic republic of more than 290 million citizens, each of whom is part of a unique political venture. We prize our political processes, our institutions, our shared heritage, and our freedom. To preserve and protect this prized inheritance, we call upon our schools to fully prepare our youngsters as good citizens—individuals possessing the knowledge, skills, and attitudes required to participate in and maintain a democratic nation. We want our future citizens to respect our past as a democratic society and recognize the rich contributions of all groups who have made modern America a free and powerful nation. We want students to take active roles as champions of freedom who stand up and cry out for the rights and responsibilities of citizenship. We want students to speak with their voices, actions, and votes for the improvement of the quality of life in our families, neighborhoods, nation, and world. The NCSS (2002), in its position statement on citizenship education, recommends that the overriding purpose of social studies should be to provide students with the education required to guard and protect their cultural inheritance, to ready students for the most important duty they will be entrusted with in the new millennium—accepting the post that Thomas Jefferson called the *office of citizen:*

> The National Council for the Social Studies believes that a primary goal of public education is to prepare students to be engaged and effective citizens. NCSS has defined an effective citizen as one who has the knowledge, skills, and attitudes required to assume the "office of citizen" in our democratic republic.

The preservation of our democracy depends upon a system of education that prepares its young people to accept responsibility in society, but today's social commentators say we are failing that test. They sadly lament the growing apathy of today's adult citizens, describing our nation as being comprised of "civic couch potatoes" (Tyack, 1997). Submerged in public apathy, these apathetic individuals reject such basic citizenship responsibilities as volunteering in civic or public arenas (PTA, town council, organizations that feed and clothe the poor), helping solve such real problems as eliminating drug abuse and homelessness, writing letters to the editor, deliberating and debating public policy, working for public interest groups, and voting.

Martin Rochester (2003) tells us that in ancient Greece the word *idiot* referred to an individual who took no interest in public affairs, and he is discouraged that more and more young Americans seem to qualify as idiots in that sense. They are uninterested in political and civic life and have descended into "know-nothingism" and "do-nothingism." To produce fewer idiots, Rochester believes we need to stress the importance of a common base of useful information, skills, and attitudes requisite for producing future citizens to be trustees of our democratic community. As teachers of future citizens, how can we help young adults resist social indifference and accept full responsibility as stakeholders in our democratic nation?

Preparing students to participate in the political, social, and economic affairs of our democracy and to live together as good citizens in a drastically different world of the future requires a social studies program with citizenship education at its heart. A program centering on participatory citizenship must be made a regular part of school life to help students establish the sense of personal responsibility and accountability that forms a solid foundation to participate as adults in public life. Teachers must provide opportunities for students to go beyond the simple acquisition of facts; they must offer situations where learners use what they know to reason, analyze, create, and evaluate. The NCSS Task Force on Early Childhood/Elementary Social Studies (1989) suggests:

> For children to develop citizenship skills appropriate to a democracy, they must be capable of thinking critically about complex societal problems and global problems. Teachers must arrange the classroom environment to promote data gathering, discussion, and critical reasoning by students. Another important aspect of citizenship is that of decision maker. Children must acquire the skills of decision-making, but also study the process that occurs as groups make decisions. . . . Children need to be equipped with the skills to cope with change. (p. 16)

A significant responsibility of social studies teachers, then, is to offer a sound program that promotes the knowledge, skills, and attitudes necessary for young people to make informed and reasoned decisions for the public good.

WHAT ARE THE MAJOR GOALS OF ELEMENTARY SCHOOLS SOCIAL STUDIES INSTRUCTION?

As a democratic nation, citizens are expected to be both knowledgeable and thoughtful, able to make informed decisions based upon national ideals and principles. These requirements of democratic citizenship place tremendous demands on our schools:

How can our nation's schools teach patriotism in an open society? Several professional organizations have issued position statements describing goals delineating precisely how that question might be addressed throughout all levels of schooling, and the NCSS Task Force on Early Childhood/Elementary Social Studies (1988) has compiled a list specifically for the elementary school grades. The NCSS task force suggests that the traditional skills of reading, writing, and computing are necessary but not sufficient for young citizens to participate or even survive in a world demanding the kinds of independent and cooperative problem solving required to deal with complex social concerns. Therefore, for the elementary school, the following goals have been identified to help children accomplish what other subjects cannot help them achieve. The specialized social studies goals are divided into three broad areas:

Knowledge. Social studies instruction should develop in students a rich and accurate store of information about the world at large and the world at hand, the world of the past and the world of the future. This knowledge base will provide the necessary foundation for emerging reflective thought. Even though elementary school children have difficulty with time concepts, they must develop a rich store of knowledge about their country's *history. Geography* is equally difficult, but social studies provides continuing opportunities for children to understand the relationships of people with their environment. Concepts from *anthropology* and *sociology* provide understanding of how the multiplicity of cultures within society and the world has developed. Children need to recognize the contributions of each culture and to explore its value system. Knowledge from *sociology, economics*, and *political science* allows children to understand the institutions within the society and to learn about their roles within groups.

Skills. The skills that are primary to social studies are those related to maps and globes, such as understanding and using locational and directional terms. Skills that are shared with other parts of the curriculum but may be most powerfully taught through social studies include communication skills such as writing and speaking; research skills such as collecting, organizing, and interpreting data; and reading skills such as reading pictures, books, maps, charts, and graphs.

Values and Beliefs. The early years are ideal for children to begin to understand core civic principles, or core democratic values (i.e., justice, individual rights, truth, the common good, equality of opportunity, and diversity), especially in terms of the smaller social entities of the family, classroom, and community. Children can also develop, within the context of social studies, positive attitudes toward knowledge and learning and develop a spirit of inquiry that will enhance their understanding of their world so that they will become rational, humane, participating, effective members of a democratic society.

Effective social studies teaching, then, begins with a clear understanding of the subject's unique instructional goals. In general, the goals include the categories of knowledge, thinking skills, and democratic values and beliefs. *Knowledge* does not refer to a predetermined collection of facts for students to memorize, but to understandings that students construct by connecting new learning to their previous experiences in and out of school. The *democratic values and beliefs* are drawn from various sources, but especially from the Declaration of Independence and the United States Constitution with its Bill of Rights. These beliefs form the basic principles of our democratic society. Elementary school social studies programs also prepare students to tie together knowledge with beliefs and values using *thinking skills*, such as acquiring and processing information to investigate problems and making well-informed decisions that are defensible according to democratic principles.

WHAT IS DYNAMIC SOCIAL STUDIES?

The goals for social studies education in the elementary school years reflect the aim of social studies education in general, but the environment within which these goals are achieved is much different for these youngsters than for any other level of schooling. These children come to school with a high degree of natural energy, curiosity, and imagination. They are adventurous, curious, eager to learn, energetic, always in motion, loud, and emotional. Elementary school children are also great socializers and are eager to fit in. Consequently, they like group activities and projects. These are but a few of the characteristics that lead elementary school teachers to establish a one-of-a-kind, developmentally appropriate learning environment for their young learners.

If the young people of our democratic nation are to grow into effective citizens, then social studies must be delivered in a developmentally appropriate way during the elementary years. Knowledge, skills, and attitudes necessary for informed and thoughtful participation in society require an active, engaging, enjoyable, and rewarding system of instruction that results in meaningful and substantial learning. I like to call an approach to carry out this mission *dynamic social studies* largely because it places students in a classroom environment that encourages them to rediscover the "young social scientists" within. Much as adult social scientists, they hold a powerful desire to answer questions about their world and are captivated by spectacular phenomena of their social surroundings. One of the greatest joys of practicing adult social scientists, for example, is to answer a question with the words, "I don't know," because it is exciting to discover the unknown. Not knowing is the fuel for their furnace; their joy is in the challenge of finding out something new. And, if the truth is told by my social scientist friends, most would keep doing what they do even if they weren't paid for it. Isn't that just like the natural curiosity of childhood?

We encourage and support this sense of wonder when we open children's minds to the creative spirit that floods the social sciences. Just think about the deep sense of wonder our youngsters display as they operate on their world like young social scientists: a "geographer" bends down to study the effect of sand sifting through her fingers; an "economist" helps determine how the class will obtain the money necessary to buy a sapling for the school playground; a "political scientist" petitions the principal for a new piece of playground equipment; an "anthropologist" leafs through an old yearbook and marvels at the hairstyle and clothing differences; a "historian" watches and listens as a senior citizen augments stories of World War II with fascinating memorabilia. These children have not attained the educational credentials required of practicing social scientists. However, they are curious enough about their social world to act on their interests. That is the basic premise of this text: Children are curious about their world and strive to seek answers to their questions so they can obtain knowledge about their wondrous social environment. Anyone who has ever observed children in their private "child's world" must conclude that they are doers and thinkers—in other words, natural social scientists.

The model of dynamic social studies that will play a major role in describing the teacher's role and in shaping the remainder of this text is shown in Figure 1–2. It is simple, but the model brings together in a clear way the major components of dy-

FIGURE 1–2
Dynamic Social Studies

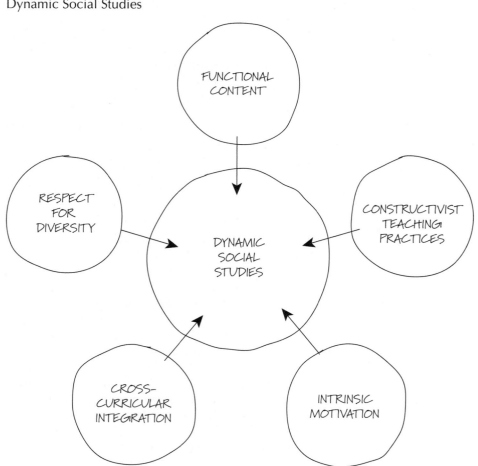

namic social studies instruction. The model has five components, each of which must be in place for effective learning to take place: functional content, constructivist teaching practices, intrinsic motivation, cross-curricular integration, and respect for diversity.

Functional Content

Social scientists must be informed, for their investigations do not spring forth from a knowledge vacuum. Social scientists launch their investigations from a complete and organized knowledge base related to the problems they want to solve. When they encounter a new phenomenon that cannot be explained in terms of their organized knowledge base, social scientists become energized to seek new information that might alter or replace their "trusty framework." Think about how this works: The unanticipated discovery of what was going on with Maryland's state insect fueled Mrs. Holzwarth's students' strong interest in learning how to propose one for Pennsylvania. In this case, the youngsters were not completely fulfilled with simply accepting information at face value.

Content knowledge in dynamic social studies programs is not treated merely as facts to be ingested and memorized, but as a base of operation through which questions or problems are explored and confronted. If students are satisfied to merely store the information and retrieve it for others, they could not be considered "young social scientists." If children are to become explorers and questioners rather than passive acceptors of information, they must know enough about something to raise questions, discover something new, or solve a problem. Therefore, dynamic social studies instruction does not stop with the *what* of the social sciences, but continues on with the *how* of the social science disciplines. Students who are learning about geography, for example, must not only have knowledge of geography, but also experience how geography works and what geographers do.

The hardest lesson for beginning teachers, though, is to learn that telling is not teaching; told is not taught. Those who consider teaching as information transmission ignore the paramount role of the learner in learning. Students will not learn content if they cannot attach meaning to it. Therefore, if children are going to develop the skills appropriate for active citizenship in a democracy, they must be capable of thinking about complex social problems in a classroom environment that promotes decision making and problem solving. Thinking and content are clearly inseparable in dynamic social studies programs.

The most basic responsibility of dynamic social studies teachers, then, is to select *functional content*, or a meaningful knowledge core that furnishes the information necessary to become aware of, identify, and solve problems. This component can be thought of as the background of subject area content that spurs the questioning mind and allows one to solve problems or do original work. A firm knowledge background spurs questions, and these questions, in turn, provide the context for obtaining more knowledge.

Curriculum Scope and Sequence

Think for a moment about all the social studies knowledge you have learned over the years. Some, like the name of the 17th president of the United States or the major exports of Bolivia, may have been long forgotten, but there is probably more that you remember to this day and feel every child should know, too. What five specific facts or understandings do you feel are indispensable for today's youth? Write them down. Compare your list with your classmates. Should children learn about important people like Benjamin Franklin, Confucius, or Harriet Tubman, or important places like the Gobi Desert, the Fertile Crescent, or the rainforests of the Amazon? What about important things like pueblos, railroads, or the Great Wall of China, or events such as the Battle of Bull Run, the rise of Christianity, or the discovery of Mohenjo-Daro? Did anyone list significant ideas such as Henry Ford's assembly line, Hinduism, or the Bill of Rights? When we ask the question, "What content from the social science disciplines should be selected for our social studies program?" we are dealing with the *scope* of the program, or *what* will be taught. This is but one critical question when considering the makeup of the social studies curriculum. The second important question is, "*When* is the most developmentally appropriate time to teach the selected content?" Answers to this question create the *sequence*, or order, in which the content is treated.

Content may be ordered in several possible ways, but the most traditionally popular method has been the *expanding environment approach.* No one knows exactly how this system came into existence, but beginning in the 1930s, Lucy Sprague Mitchell (1934) started the ball rolling by proposing that children's understandings of their world developed through a series of stages, beginning with an awareness of what is near and moving to that which is far away—beginning with the "here and now" of their lives and gradually expanding their environments. Mitchell described growth in understanding one's social environment much like the ripples that radiate out after throwing a pebble into a pond. The first ripple can be considered knowledge gained about one's body and the physical characteristics of the immediate surroundings (crib, play area, room, house); the next ripple includes knowledge of the home, family, friends, relatives, and other significant people in the environment; and the next focuses on the classroom, school, and other familiar environments such as the street, neighborhood and the homes of friends and relatives. As the child matures, constant investigations open up new environments, so succeeding ripples spread out to the community, the state, the United States, the hemisphere, and the world. Mitchell suggested that social studies content should be organized with respect to this natural progression: Begin with the self, home, and school in grade 1, then widen to the neighborhood in grade 2, to the community in grade 3, and systematically outward to the state in grade 4, United States in grade 5, and the Western hemisphere or world in grade 6. In the 1930s, when social studies was becoming firmly entrenched in our schools, the overwhelming pattern of content selection became the expanding environment approach. Likewise, when textbook companies began to publish their first social studies textbooks, the overwhelming scope and sequence pattern was this approach.

Social studies educators favor the "I Like Me" self-concept emphasis early in the expanding environment approach because it is important that children feel good about themselves before they can be expected to learn anything academically. The idea is that if we start early, we can reduce the likelihood that children's self-concept will become fueled by negative influences. Self-concept can be nurtured in warm classrooms with warm teachers. If we have those things, we maximize the chance that children will grow in a positive direction both intellectually and emotionally. The charming example in Figure 1–3 is a free-form poem written in a social studies program that focused on helping children acquire a positive self-concept and learn to participate as members

FIGURE 1–3
Self-Concept Poem

of a compassionate classroom society. The teacher took deliberate steps to encourage children to be positive, to smile, and to feel special. The inspiring poem was Algonquin Patee's heartwarming expression of what that classroom did for him—being unconditionally accepted and loved for one's good (and maybe not-so-good) attributes!

Paul Hanna (1963) reaffirmed the concept of expanding environments in an article so influential that his name is most closely associated with the expanding environment approach today. In 1983, the NCSS organized a Task Force on Scope and Sequence to study whether the expanding environment approach remained suitable for contemporary times. The task force reaffirmed the merit of the expanding environment approach (Figure 1–4), and it remains the overwhelming favorite among social studies curriculum developers and textbook publishers today.

A dynamic social studies program, then, must provide for consistent and cumulative learning from kindergarten through the middle school years. Content is extended and enriched at each grade level, as students build upon knowledge and skills already learned while receiving preparation for that which is yet to come.

Scattered throughout this text are text set boxes. Text sets are groups of books across a variety of reading levels designed to support the study of a variety of social studies themes. For example, Ms. Trammell, a first grade teacher, put together a *Families* text set. She searched for books that supported the theme and listed them according to topic and reading level. Because of the developmental level of her children, Ms. Trammell sought out, in particular, picture books. Teachers of older children often add three other categories: biographies, chapter books, and nonfiction books. These books hold the potential of supporting student learning more than any single text by offering a variety of reading material.

Likewise, teachers are finding that most students are not helped when schools rely on the same social studies textbook for every student. They are convinced that this "one-size-fits-most" approach fails horribly if the goal is achievement for all students. To help you become ready for your place in such a dramatically new social studies classroom situation, you will be presented with several text set examples and asked to think about how you would organize text sets in your own classroom. In addition to these examples, you will also want to read more information on creating and arranging text sets in your language arts and/or reading methods text.

National Curriculum Standards

Over the years, the expanding environment approach has experienced unparalleled recognition as the principal force influencing content selection in social studies, but recommendations associated with reform movements in education now have added rigorous standards for both curricular content and assessment. This all began in the mid-1980s when education in general was placed under the microscope because of reports such as *A Nation at Risk* (National Commission on Excellence in Education, 1983). *A Nation at Risk* fired volleys of criticism at our nation's schools with searing commentaries such as, "If an unfriendly foreign power had attempted to impose on America the mediocre instructional performance that exists today, we might well have viewed it as an act of war" (p. 9). For social studies in particular, standardized test

FIGURE 1–4
Expanding Environment Scope and Sequence

Kindergarten—Awareness of Self in a Social Setting

Providing socialization experiences that help children bridge their home life with the group life of school.

Grade 1—The Individual in Primary Social Groups: Understanding School and Family Life

Continuing the socialization process begun in kindergarten, but extending to studies of families (variations in the ways families live, the need for rules and laws).

Grade 2—Meeting Basic Needs in Nearby Social Groups: The Neighborhood

Studying social functions such as education, production, consumption, communication, and transportation in a neighborhood setting.

Grade 3—Sharing Earth-Space With Others: The Community

Focusing on the community in a global setting, stressing social functions such as production, transportation, communication, distribution, and government.

Grade 4—Human Life in Varied Environments: The Region

Emphasizing the region, an area of the earth defined for a specific reason; the home state is studied as a political region where state regulations require it.

Grade 5—People of the Americas: The United States and its Close Neighbors

Centering on the development of the United States as a nation in the Western Hemisphere, with particular emphasis on developing affective attachments to the principles on which the nation was founded; Canada and Mexico also studied.

Grade 6—People and Cultures: The Eastern Hemisphere

Focusing on selected people and cultures of the Eastern Hemisphere, directed toward an understanding and appreciation of other people through development of such concepts as language, technology, institutions, and belief systems.

Grade 7—A Changing World of Many Nations: A Global View

Providing an opportunity to broaden the concept of humanity within a global context; focus is on the world as the home of many different people who strive to deal with the forces that shape their lives.

Grade 8—Building a Strong and Free Nation: The United States

Studying the "epic of America," the development of the United States as a strong and free nation; emphasis is on social history and economic development, including cultural and aesthetic dimensions of the American experience.

Source: Task Force on Scope and Sequence. (1984). In search for a scope and sequence for social studies. *Social Education, 48* (4), 376–385.

TEXT SET 1

Theme: Families

Donald Crew's **Bigmama's** (HarperTrophy) takes children on a journey back to a summer during the 1940s to visit the rural home of his "Bigmama" (mama's mama) in Cottondale, Florida. After a train ride of 3 days and 2 nights, the children inspect every inch of the house, barn, backyard coop, pond, sugar cane pit, and boat. To their delight and satisfaction, they see that everything is "still the same." Crews lovingly portrays the extended family and the idea of family togetherness.

Vera B. Williams's **A Chair for My Mother** (HarperTrophy) is the story of Rosa, a young girl who lives in an apartment with her hard-working mother and grandmother. After their apartment is destroyed by a fire, Rosa, her mother, and grandmother save their coins until they can afford to buy a really comfortable chair for all to enjoy. When the jar is finally full, they go searching for and find the perfect chair. This marvelous picture book captures the heartwarming spirit of a loving family.

Cynthia Rylant's **When I Was Young in the Mountains** (Dutton) is a tender story of her childhood days living in the Appalachian Mountains. The book offers vivid scenes describing the pleasures of mountain living. A brave adult is needed to take you to the outhouse on dark scary nights. Other scenes include getting baptized in the local swimming hole, taking baths in the kitchen, and sharing loving family times.

scores of students from the United States were compared with students from other industrialized nations. These reports indicated that America's students did not have the knowledge required to make informed decisions about issues that affect them, their families, and their communities. One of the first reports specifically dealing with social studies was titled *What Do Our 17-Year-Olds Know?* The coauthors, Diane Ravitch and Chester E. Finn, Jr. (1987), reported the results of the first nationwide academic assessment of American 17-year-olds. In history, the national average for correct answers to basic history questions was 54.5 percent. The authors pointed out that if we approach this percentage from the commonly accepted view that 60 percent is the dividing line between passing and failing, our American students are in serious trouble.

Richard Paxton (2003) provided a historical perspective of these formal and informal surveys designed to measure students' social studies knowledge. The surveys produced some fascinating results. For example, 14 percent of America's teens identified Abraham Lincoln as our country's first president. The same percentage said that our country celebrates its independence from France each July 4, 11 percent named John Adams, our second president (succeeding Abe Lincoln?) as the composer of *The Star-Spangled Banner*, while 9 percent believed it was Betsy Ross! In response to these results, some argued that it was the responsibility of social studies

Barbara Joosse's **Mama, Do You Love Me?** (Chronicle) describes an Inuit mother who loves her daughter, no matter what. As if testing her mother's love, an Inuit child asks her mother over and over, "Mama, do you love me?" She comes up with many intriguing and playful questions for her mother: What if I broke the ptarmigan eggs? What if I threw water at our lamp? The story goes on with the child's questions and the mother's reassurances. Despite all the challenges, mother assures her daughter that she will love her forever and for always because she is her "Dear One."

Eve Bunting's **The Wednesday Surprise** (Clarion) is a warm and loving story about a devoted granddaughter and her successful efforts to teach her grandmother to read. Every Wednesday evening Anna's grandmother comes to take care of her while both of her parents work. Grandma and Anna have fun each week cooking hot dogs, eating ice cream, and reading together. They also are planning a surprise for Dad's birthday. Dad thinks he has received all his presents, but Grandma stands up and gives him an unexpected birthday surprise. Anna, who is only 7, has taught grandmother to read.

TRY THIS

These books form a text set appropriate for the scope of first grade social studies programs that are based on the expanding environment approach. In small groups, it would be instructive for your class to put together a text set of four or five books for the content normally covered at the other grade levels. Share them in class.

programs to move "back to the basics" and teach essential elements of lasting knowledge children need to do well on achievement tests.

By 1990, in reaction to this considerable educational faultfinding, President George Bush brought together our nation's governors to discuss national educational policy and to determine what might be needed to improve our schools. Their discussions were summarized in the well-known *America 2000*, six national goals for public education. Goal 3, the most noteworthy of all, stated,

> By the year 2000, American students will leave grades 4, 8, and 12 having demonstrated competency over challenging subject matter including English, mathematics, science, history, and geography; and every school in America will ensure that all students use their minds well, so they may be prepared for responsible citizenship, further learning, and productive employment in our modern society. (U.S. Department of Education, 1991, pp. 5–6)

A great deal of attention was given to *America 2000*, prompting our nation's leading professional organizations to develop instructional standards, statements of what all students should know and be able to do at the completion of their education, in various subject areas for their fields. In addition, most states created their own content standards and new measures to promote assessment. Initiating a search of your state's department of education website should help access its social studies standards. As far as professional standards are concerned. NCSS, was quick to establish a task force to define what the standards should be for social studies. The central questions guiding members were: "What will students be taught?" "How will students be taught?" "How will student achievement be evaluated?" Using the questions as a guide, the task force worked for over one year before publishing *Curriculum Standards for Social Studies: Expectations of Excellence* (NCSS, 1994).

The social studies curriculum standards are expressed as 10 thematic statements that each begin with these identical words: "*Social studies programs should include experiences that provide for the study of. . . .*" For example, the first thematic strand reads, "Social studies programs should include experiences that provide for the study of *culture and cultural diversity.*" When presented in list form, this thematic strand is preceded by a roman numeral and shortened thusly, *I Culture.* Similarly, each of the 10 themes that serve as organizing strands for the social studies curriculum are listed in the same way:

  I Culture

  II Time, Continuity, and Change

  III People, Places, and Environments

  IV Individual Development and Identity

  V Individuals, Groups, and Institutions

  VI Power, Authority, and Governance

  VII Production, Distribution, and Consumption

  VIII Science, Technology, and Society

  IX Global Connections

  X Civic Ideals and Practices

Each of these thematic strands is comprehensively explained in a separate chapter of the standards document (see Figure 1–5 for a condensed version). Then, in separate chapters for each of three school levels (early grades, middle grades, and high school), performance expectations and two or three examples of classroom activities are put forward. For example, the performance expectations for the first theme, Culture, are as follows (NCSS, 1994):

Social studies programs should include experiences that provide for the study of culture and cultural diversity, so that the learner can:

a. explore and describe similarities and differences in the ways groups, societies, and cultures address similar human needs and concerns;

b. give examples of how experiences may be interpreted differently by people from diverse cultural perspectives and frames of reference;

c. describe ways in which language, stories, folktales, music, and artistic creations serve as expressions of culture and influence behavior of people living in a particular culture;

d. compare ways in which people from different cultures think about and deal with their physical environment and social conditions; and

e. give examples and describe the importance of cultural unity and diversity within and across groups. (p. xiii)

FIGURE 1–5
Curriculum Standards for Social Studies

Ten Thematic Strands

Ten themes serves as organizing strands for the social studies curriculum at every school level (early, middle, and high school); they are interrelated and draw from all of the social science disciplines and other related disciplines and fields of scholarly study to build a framework for social studies curriculum design.

I Culture

Human beings create, learn, and adapt culture. Human cultures are dynamic systems of beliefs, values, and traditions that exhibit both commonalities and differences. Understanding culture helps us understand ourselves and others.

II Time, Continuity, and Change

Human beings seek to understand their historic roots and to locate themselves in time. Such understanding involves knowing what things were like in the past and how things change and develop—allowing us to develop historic perspective and answer important questions about our current condition.

III People, Places, and Environments

Technological advancements have ensured that students are aware of the world beyond their personal locations. As students study content related to this theme, they create their spatial views and geographic perspectives of the world; social, cultural, economic, and civic demands mean that students will need such knowledge, skills, and understandings to make informed and critical decisions about the relationship between human beings and their environment.

IV Individual Development and Identity

Personal identity is shaped by one's culture, by groups, and by institutional influences. Examination of various forms of human behavior enhances understanding of the relationships between social norms and emerging personal identities, the social processes which influence identity formation, and the ethical principles underlying individual action.

V Individuals, Groups, and Institutions

Institutions exert enormous influence over us. Institutions are organizational embodiments to further the core social values of those who comprise them. It is important for students to know how institutions are formed, what controls and influences them, how they control and influence individuals and culture, and how institutions can be maintained or changed.

VI Power, Authority, and Governance

Understanding of the historic development of structures of power, authority, and governance and their evolving functions in contemporary society is essential for the emergence of civic competence.

VII Production, Distribution, and Consumption

Decisions about exchange, trade, and economic policy and well-being are global in scope and the role of government in policy making varies over time and from place to place. The systematic study of an interdependent world economy and the role of technology in economic decision making is essential.

VIII Science, Technology, and Society

Technology is as old as the first crude tool invented by prehistoric humans, and modern life as we know it would be impossible without technology and the science which supports it. Today's technology forms the basis for some of our most difficult social choices.

IX Global Connections

The realities of global interdependence require understanding of the increasingly important and diverse global connections among world societies before there can be analysis leading to the development of possible solutions to persisting and emerging global issues.

X Civic Ideals and Practices

All people have a stake in examining civic ideals and practices across time, in diverse societies, as well as in determining how to close the gap between present practices and the ideals upon which our democracy is based. An understanding of civic ideals and practices of citizenship is critical to full participation in society.

Source: Nickell, P. (1995). Pullout feature: Thematically organized social studies. *Social Studies & The Young Learner, 8,* 1–8. © National Council for the Social Studies. Reprinted by permission.

Following a presentation of each standard and associated performance expectations, the chapters describe classroom activities to illustrate how the standards and performance expectations can be applied. For example, to meet performance expectations a, b, and d, the experiences of Carlene Jackson are recounted. Before the first day of school, Jackson examined her class list and inferred from the children's surnames that her class was a rich mix of cultural backgrounds—Mexican, Vietnamese, Korean, African American, and European American. By the end of the first month of school, Jackson and her students decided to study and compare how families meet their basic needs of food, clothing, and shelter in five places: their community; Juarez, Mexico; Hanoi, Vietnam; Lagos, Nigeria; and Frankfurt, Germany. Throughout the unit of study, Jackson and her students read books, looked at photos and slides, watched videos, and talked to speakers from their designated cities. The students honed their reading, writing, speaking, and map-reading skills. They created a chart summarizing the data they collected. You can request a copy of the Curriculum Standards for Social Studies (Bulletin 89) by writing or phoning the National Council for the Social Studies or visiting the NCSS website:

National Council for the Social Studies
8555 Sixteenth Street
Suite 500
Silver Spring, MD 20910
(301) 588-1800
www.ncss.org

As with most breaks from long-established practices, the standards movement has brought forth glowing arguments of support as well as blistering criticisms. In speaking of the advantages of standards, Resnick says, "standards and assessments [will] help bring about better student outcomes—a different quality and higher level of student achievement" (O'Neil, 1993, p. 17). In effect, standards had become "images of excellence" for their proponents.

Supporting this "image of excellence" was the No Child Left Behind Act of 2001 (No Child Left Behind), a landmark in educational reform signed into law by President George W. Bush in 2002. President Bush described this law as the "cornerstone of my administration." He declared that since our children are our future, "Too many of our neediest children are being left behind." Under No Child Left Behind, each state must measure every public school student's progress in reading and math in each of grades 3 through 8 and at least once during grades 10 through 12. By school year 2007–2008, assessments (or testing) in science are to be underway. These assessments must be aligned with state academic content and achievement standards and are designed to help provide parents with objective data on where their children stand academically.

Howard (2003) agrees that improved student performance is a worthy goal, but disapproves of the "high stakes" assessments (both positive and punitive) associated with the legislation. In some states, for example, teachers and administrators get financial rewards when their students meet or exceed the standards (positive) while in others an entire educational staff can be removed and the school reopened with a completely different faculty and administration (punitive). According to Howard, because social studies has not been included as an area of assessment in No Child Left Behind, the targeted assessments nevertheless have a significantly harmful impact on social studies:

> One of the consequences is to diminish the role of social studies, especially in elementary classrooms, artificially narrowing the school's curriculum [by increasing the time spent on the subjects with the most pressure to do well—reading, writing, and math—and eventually science], and treating social studies as a 'second-class' and 'at risk' discipline. (p. 285)

Mattioli (2004) decries the "second class" status for social studies that many have feared and suggests that social studies has more importance as a basic subject in the elementary school curriculum now than ever before:

> What is more basic than giving students the knowledge and skills to function in, care for, and nurture our democratic nation? What is more basic than teaching children about their personal power to impact change in their own lives, this country and the world? What is more basic than teaching a child to value justice, equality and fair play? What then is more basic than citizenship education? What is more basic than social studies? (p. 7)

No Child Left Behind appears to create a situation in stark contrast to a recommendation from the NCSS Task Force on Early Childhood/Elementary Social Studies that, given the importance of social studies in the elementary school, *20 percent of the school day*, which includes reading/language arts, science, mathematics, and the arts, be devoted to social studies instruction.

We cannot tell right now how the standards movement will influence social studies in our nation's elementary schools. Will the movement reduce the role of social studies in the curriculum? Will the pressures of high-stakes testing force teachers to emphasize the acquisition of factual knowledge rather than decision making about important issues? Or will the movement offer the strong guidance and leadership required to prepare students for active citizenship in a participatory democracy? I cannot answer those questions right now, but as this book goes to print, there appears to be an increasingly hostile response against high-stakes testing that dominates the standards movement today.

Constructivist Teaching Practices

Many theories of learning and teaching have been proposed during the past 50 years, but the constructivist viewpoint has convincingly burst to the forefront today and will serve as the model for dynamic social studies. Constructivism isn't new, radical, revolutionary, or unheard-of. Jean Piaget and Lev Vygotsky developed the theories to support constructivism almost 70 years ago. John Dewey advocated an instructional system we now call constructivism back at the turn of the 20th century; Jerome Bruner did the same a few decades later.

Constructivist instruction is a child-centered approach that focuses on knowledge construction, not knowledge reproduction. Constructivism emphasizes that students interpret new objects and events by trying to alter or modify existing mental

Thematic Strand II Time, Continuity, and Change
TOPIC: The Civil War

Jim Murphy's **The Boys' War: Confederate and Union Soldiers Talk About the Civil War** (Clarion, 1990) engages young readers in actual letters, diaries, and oral histories to tell of the youngest soldiers' experiences during the Civil War.

Russell Freedman's **Lincoln: A Photobiography** (Clarion, 1987) received a Newbery Medal, an award seldom given to a work of nonfiction. Freedman did a masterful job putting together this photobiography with as much information about the Civil War as about Lincoln himself.

Jean Fritz's **Stonewall** (Putnam, 1979) reveals the odd habits and routines of the man who stood like a stone wall at the battle of Manassas and became a great leader in spite of his idiosyncrasies.

Paul Fleischman's **Bull Run** (HarperTrophy, 1993) uses short (often only two page) chapters of alternating positions to tell the stories of 16 people heading for the battle of Bull Run. Each has a different purpose for being there, and Fleischman lets each of them address us before the battle. After the battle, some of them talk to us again.

Learning in constructivist classrooms is carried out through cooperative relationships among the students and between the teacher and students.

Patricia Beatty's **Charley Skedaddle** (Morrow, 1987) tells the story of Charley, a young teenager who longs to experience the glory of battle. He eventually joins the Union Army to avenge his brother's death and to get away from the harsh Bowery of New York City. Charley does not find his courage during the first battle, and he "skedaddles" or deserts to the mountains of Virginia. There his courage is tested again when an old woman needs his help.

Patricia Polacco's **Pink and Say** (Philomel, 1994) is a picture book based on a true story of two young men, one white and one black, who meet after a bloody battle. Their different loyalties soon come to an end as Pink carries Say to his own home nearby where Pink's mother is surviving in the ruins of a plantation. While the boys hide in the cellar, Pink's mother is murdered by raiders and the boys are captured as they attempt to rejoin their units. Say is taken to Andersonville prison and Pink is hanged. It is interesting that Say was Polacco's own great-great-grandfather.

TRY THIS

As either an individual or group project, select any of the remaining thematic strands of the social studies standards and put together a text set of five books for it. Annotate each book as I have done for each selection above.

structures that had formed as a result of their previous life experiences. For that reason, each student's view of the world differs from others because of the personal and distinctive nature of those experiences. Constructivist learning takes place within a classroom environment that offers the child authentic, experience-based activities—that is, tasks with real-world relevance and utility.

Social studies educators generally recommend constructivist practices, including discovery learning in real-world environments, peer interaction, hands-on activities, and student tasks that challenge existing concepts and beliefs. Constructivist teachers are flexible; sometimes they present knowledge, but more often they are collaborators and facilitators. Teachers in constructivist, dynamic social studies classrooms do not commit themselves to any single method as the exclusive "right way to teach." They realize that there are many ways to unlock the mysteries of their subject matter and that the heart of solid social studies instruction is balance and proportion. Sometimes, as *collaborators* in social constructivist situations, they will "bring the action to the children," demonstrating, assisting, and explaining to help their students construct new knowledge or refine skills. At other times, as *facilitators* in cognitive constructivist situations, they will guide as children initiate the action, supporting students emotionally and intellectually as they independently strive to explain a puzzling question or problem.

Content knowledge is a necessary component of constructivist teaching, but not sufficient in itself. Knowing how the social sciences work is the "something extra" of dynamic social studies instruction. Historians, for example, must not only understand the historical information uncovered by others, but also know where the information comes from, what kinds of questions to ask about the information, and how to investigate their questions. Bruner (1960) advised:

> To instruct someone in [a] discipline is not a matter of getting him to commit results to mind. Rather, it is to teach him to participate in the process that makes possible the establishment of knowledge. We teach a subject not to produce little living libraries on the subject, but rather to get a student to think . . . for himself, to consider matters as a historian does, to take part in the process of knowledge-getting. Knowledge is a process, not a product. (p. 72)

Without consideration of the processes and the content of the disciplines, students are left with the impression that anything they are told or read about in their textbooks is true, a sad commentary for a subject area responsible for preparing students to assume the office of citizen of the United States.

Intrinsic Motivation

The third component of the dynamic social studies model is intrinsic motivation, or an internal impulse that provokes us to action or keeps us absorbed in certain activities. For example, in recent months I have learned how to play fantasy sports on the Internet. I am not addicted to the game as I understand many are, but I love drafting teams, trading players, and fighting for league championships (yes, I've won a few). I participate in fantasy sports not because someone has told me I must, but because it brings me pleasure. Certainly, the T-shirts that come with league championships are a special reward for doing well, but I enjoy the competition whether or not it results in a championship or a T-shirt. To me, the activity is pleasurable and worthwhile in and of itself. What activities do you engage in on a regular basis simply because you enjoy doing them? Intrinsic motivation is what leads you to action and keeps you engaged in those activities.

I engage in some activities that are not so enjoyable, but I do them anyway because they bring me things I do enjoy. Washing my car is an example. It's not something I would freely choose to do during my free time because I don't particularly like doing it. However, my family and I do appreciate a clean, shiny automobile. The motivation to wash my car is the same as it is for mowing my lawn or shoveling the snow from my driveway. It is called *extrinsic motivation* because the drive to do these chores does not come from within; the activities themselves are not enjoyable, but the rewards are—a shiny car, a clean yard, and a clear driveway. A child who searches several trade books to find out how it might have felt to leave home at the age of 12 to work as an apprentice in Colonial America because he or she is genuinely interested in finding out is intrinsically motivated. Meanwhile, the child who researches the topic just to get a good grade is extrinsically motivated. The interest, enjoyment, and satisfaction is in the work itself when one is intrinsically motivated; when one is extrinsically motivated, the driving force is outside pressure or reward.

No activity in itself is intrinsically motivating. Fantasy sports are important to me, but I'm sure there are some of you who would rather watch paint dry than play fantasy sports. The same is true for any other activity; it can be motivating only to a particular person at a particular time. What are some factors influencing whether we enjoy doing something, or whether students will become intrinsically motivated to learn? Following are several suggestions that can guide you in your efforts to promote student motivation in dynamic social studies programs (Amabile, 1989; Ormrod, 1999):

- *Interest.*   Students are more motivated by something that has captured their interest than by something with no perceived value.
- *Pleasure.*   Students become more involved when they are enthusiastic and excited about the subject matter or classroom activities.
- *Competence.*   Students will seek out activities and persist longer at them if they feel they are capable of accomplishing tasks successfully and when they feel in control of their lives. The more confident children feel, the more likely they are to begin a task and see it through to completion.
- *Self-determination.*   Students will become more intrinsically motivated when they are working on something for their own reasons, not someone else's.

Having children work for an expected reward appears to make students less likely to take learning risks or approach a task with an experimental or pleasurable attitude. In addition, setting up competitive situations where students lock horns with one another for some desirable reward or other form of recognition tends to undermine intrinsic drive. Lastly, although classroom assessment can serve as an intrinsic motivator when it is perceived as a valid measure of course objectives, all too often the focus is turned away from the intrinsically enjoyable aspects of learning. As a result, students often become overly tense and suffer test anxiety.

To summarize, students are more likely to exhibit a high level of intrinsic motivation when they find the subject matter they are studying to be interesting, when they like what they're doing, when they feel they are capable of accomplishing a task, and when they believe they have some control over the learning situation. Ormrod (1999) suggests, however, that it is important to note that students' intrinsic motivation for social studies learning emerges slowly over a period of time, especially if students have previously been accustomed to receiving extrinsic reinforcement for their efforts. In these situations, she advises, you might want to slowly increase their focus on the intrinsic rewards of learning while gradually weaning your students from an overdose of external reinforcement.

Cross-Curricular Integration

In an effort to make their students' education more authentic and worthwhile, dynamic social studies teachers often challenge the traditional practice of teaching each elementary school subject separately—in other words, isolating reading, spelling, writing, math, science, and social studies into separate blocks of time with little connection to one another. Dynamic social studies teachers have become particularly critical of this arrangement since the limited number of hours in the school day prevents all subjects from receiving equal treatment. In fact, most teachers spend the bulk of their day teaching the basic skills subjects such as reading, writing, spelling, and math. The content subjects (science and social studies) have traditionally been the disciplines most likely to be shoved to the end of the day and, if time runs out, postponed or forgotten about altogether. If social studies is somehow squeezed into the end of the day, the children are often led through a quick oral reading of a textbook section and a brief question-answer recitation period "just to get it in." To remedy these lopsided practices, dynamic social studies teachers are seeking ways to connect, or integrate, all the subjects commonly taught in the elementary school curriculum. By bringing together the various subject areas and relating the content to a central theme, teachers can effectively and efficiently use the allotted time during a busy school day and create interesting and challenging learning opportunities. To that end, dynamic social studies brings together, or integrates, the various areas of the school curriculum into a wholly unified program where learning experiences cut across all subjects. Dynamic social studies provides the obvious connection between the arts, humanities, and physical sciences. For example, consider all the cross-curricular experiences possible on a trip to the dairy farm:

Read *The Milk Makers* by Gail Gibbons (New York: Simon & Schuster, 1985), *Milk from Cow to Carton* by Aliki (New York: HarperCollins, 1992), *What a Wonderful Day to Be a Cow* by Carolyn Lesser (New York: Knopf, 1995), and *Cows in the Parlor: A Visit to a Dairy Farm* by Cynthia McFarland (Colchester, CT: Atheneum, 1990). **(Literature)**

Talk about the trip before, during, and after taking it. **(Language Arts)**

Sing *Old MacDonald Had a Farm* and *The Farmer in the Dell*. **(Music)** Establish rules for the trip. **(Political Science)**

Talk about appropriate group behavior. **(Sociology)**

Figure out how much the trip will cost. **(Math/Economics)**

Illustrate the two types of cows seen on the farm—Holsteins and Jerseys. **(Art)**

Construct an experience story of the field trip. **(Reading/Writing)**

Construct an informational chart about cows with illustrations and appropriate captions, such as "Cows are milked twice a day" or "Cows have four stomachs." **(Science)**

Observe daily activity on the dairy farm. **(Geography)**

Arrange clothes and props for a dairy farmer in a dramatic play area. **(Creative Dramatics)**

Make cottage cheese and/or butter. **(Science/Health/Nutrition)**

Print the caption "Foods Made From Milk" across the top of a large sheet of paper. Have the children display appropriate foods by cutting pictures from magazines or drawing their own. **(Science)**

Collect different types of food containers. Place all in a large box. The children sort the containers representing dairy products from the other types of food containers. **(Math)**

All of these concepts, skills, and strategies (and more) emerged within the context of a trip to the dairy farm, yet the whole experience was labeled social studies. That is because social studies is usually a central element in the development of cross-curricular learning experiences and serves as the "core' to pull everything together. Elementary schools around the country are moving toward the idea of integrating the curriculum, and dynamic social studies appears to be at the center. Berg (1988) answers the question, "Where does social studies fit into cross-curricular integration?" with this perceptive response:

> Right in the middle! A major goal of the social studies is to help students understand the myriad interactions of people on this planet—past, present, and future. Making sense of the world requires using skills that allow one to read about the many people and places that are scattered about the globe; to use literature to understand the richness of past events and the people who are a part of them; to apply math concepts to more fully understand how numbers have enabled people to numerically manage the complexity of their world. The story of humankind well told requires drawing from all areas of the curriculum.

Howard (2003), in offering a recommended course of action to remedy the "clear and present danger [of] a standards-based era" (p. 286), suggests designating social studies as the most important discipline in our schools. If that happens at the elementary school level, Howard suggests, social studies should be integrated with the other subjects. Without these measures, Howard argues, social studies is in danger of having a seriously diminished role in the elementary school curriculum.

NCSS (1993a) has supported the integrative aspect of social studies instruction with this statement from its influential position statement, *A Vision of Powerful Teaching and Learning in the Social Studies*:

> . . . social studies teaching integrates across the curriculum. It provides opportunities for students to read and study text materials, appreciate art and literature, communicate orally and in writing, observe and take measurements, develop and display data, and in various other ways to conduct inquiry and synthesize findings using knowledge and skills taught in all school subjects. . . . Particularly in elementary and middle schools, instruction can feature social studies as the core around which the rest of the curriculum is built. (p. 217)

By integrating subject areas with themes having a social studies focus, students become involved in activities and experiences that are both purposeful and meaningful.

Respect for Diversity

Have you ever been involved in a situation where you had more difficulty doing something than anyone else? Dancing? Playing a musical instrument? Dribbling a basketball? Speaking a foreign language? Ice skating? Maybe you were the only one who had problems. How did you feel? How would you have felt if *every* day when you came to school you were the only one who couldn't perform certain tasks that others completed with relative ease? What kind of "treatment" or "special help" would you need to keep you coming to school each day?

Creating a context for learning in dynamic social studies classrooms starts with genuine respect for the cultures of all learners.

Now consider if you have ever been involved in a situation where you were able to do something more easily and quickly than anyone else. How did you feel then? What could be done in school to keep you from becoming miserably bored? What could be done to best help you work toward fulfilling your unlimited potential?

Like any of us who have been in these situations, all children come to school with varied strengths and limitations and form unique collections of distinctive talents and abilities. Some children stand out because they are exceptional performers; others face certain challenges that require special services to help them reach their potential. Teachers achieve quality in the dynamic social studies program when they deliver the best for each youngster and make the most of their time with everyone in their classrooms. Effective teachers adapt instruction to meet the special needs, talents, and interests of all their students; the quality of their dynamic social studies programs is distinguished by a keen awareness and consideration of each youngster as a distinct individual, including those whose backgrounds or exhibited needs are not shared by most others. These children may exhibit specific developmental disabilities, speak a home language that does not match the school's, come from diverse cultural or ethnic backgrounds, or possess unique gifts and talents. Whatever the circumstance, the field of elementary school social studies education should be consistently responsive by offering appropriate experiences to fully develop their native capabilities.

Inside an Active Classroom

Gerald, a fourth grader, was turned off to school. He achieved well below grade level, rarely responded to his teacher's questions, could barely print legibly, and was seldom included in activities by his peers. Although his teacher accepted Gerald and valued him as a person of worth, he rarely assigned him a useful role in group projects.

One day, Gerald and three other members of his group were involved in an origami project in which they were required to read and follow illustrated directions showing how to fold an 8-inch square piece of paper several times until it turned into a cup. Two of Gerald's partners were high-achieving students, one was an average student overall but extremely gifted as a problem solver, and then there was Gerald.

Qing Yu, the highest achiever, was the best reader in class and was assigned the group role as "reader/clarifier." Qing Yu was responsible for reading the directions aloud to her group as clearly as possible. Darnell, the other high achiever, was the group manager. He was responsible for making sure everyone stayed on task and had the necessary materials. Felice, the average achiever/top problem-solver was there to help out if anyone experienced difficulty completing the task. Gerald, reacting as he normally did, drew away and went to work on his own. The three others tried their best but became completely lost in the directions. They followed each other along a path of confusion.

At the same time, alone and overlooked, Gerald had successfully completed seven of the eight steps and was about to finish the last. However, his attention was unexpectedly sidetracked as he heard Qing Yu call to the teacher, "Help! We're lost!"

Not paying attention to Gerald, the teacher addressed the troubled students. As the teacher suggested that the students go back to the beginning, reread the directions more carefully, and study the illustrations, Gerald made the last fold and clutched a cup ready for service. But no one noticed, and the confusion continued. As the teacher stood near and offered encouragement, Gerald slowly slipped the cup below his desk out of sight of everyone (assuming someone might actually want to see it) and waited until it was time to move on to something else.

At the heart of this topic is a concern about equity and fair treatment for groups that have traditionally experienced discrimination because of race or ethnicity, language, gender, or exceptionality. Because of the wide range of diversity in contemporary society, all teachers must become instructionally effective with diverse groups of students. There are at least three arguments why this charge is especially meaningful for social studies teachers (Winitzky, 1991):

The first is that these issues should be of major concern to every citizen, that it is incumbent upon us as citizens to work toward the public good by trying to ameliorate these problems. . . . The second argument is that Americans have a strong belief in the power of education as the route to later success in life—economically, politically, and culturally. . . . Finally, many believe that we really have no choice. We simply live in a [diverse] world, and our schools should reflect that aspect of modern life. (pp. 126–127)

Children in today's schools come from an enormous range of backgrounds, languages, and abilities. To meet their educational needs, dynamic social studies teachers must derive instruction from our pluralistic society as well as our membership in a global community.

As an example of how cultural awareness can work in dynamic social studies classrooms, Rosee Arya asked her young children to identify what they considered to be the most important characteristic they could use to define themselves. She offered them several examples of characteristics that were descriptive of her: female, ex-athlete, teacher, and mother. Then, in pairs, Ms. Arya had the students share stories about when they felt especially proud to be associated with the characteristic. Next, the students were asked to write and illustrate a short story that explained the characteristic they selected. Amy, proud of her Jewish background, used it to define herself. Then, because this activity took place in early December, she told the story of Hanukkah, which is also referred to as "The Festival of Lights." See Amy's story in Figure 1–6.

Despite differing conceptualizations of multicultural education, there are three common principles that offer a basis for its implementation in dynamic social studies programs: (1) Each student must have equal opportunity to reach her or his full potential, (2) Each student must be ready to play a part in both a multicultural society and interdependent world, and (3) The social studies program must be student-centered and inclusive of the backgrounds, needs, and experiences of each student.

AFTERWORD

At the roots of a democracy are knowledgeable and thoughtful citizens. Of course, they have many other qualities, too, but high on the list of behavior for democratic citizens is thinking for themselves. Democracy requires individuals who can search for and examine the facts whenever they must make up their minds about important issues. These issues might relate to one's personal life or to complex international concerns; regardless, the protection of our freedoms lies in the hands of rational people. Such skills must be learned during the early years with a dynamic social studies curriculum that offers meaningful experiences to all. All youngsters must find something to excite their interest and stimulate their thinking. A one-dimensional approach to social studies instruction cannot do this. We fail our children with our narrowness; if our myopic view of teaching has caused them to feel stupid or to be bored, we have lost. Learning for an informed citizenry is too important to be thought of as something that everyone must do in any single way. The danger to our future is great when we restrict the adventuresome, can-do spirit of childhood.

Therefore, dynamic social studies programs must employ various teaching strategies and promote functional thinking skills. The probing, wondering mind of

FIGURE 1–6
Lower-Grade Personal Story

Amy L.
The BAd Gise
SaiD YOU CAN't
PRAy To 9od. You
hAve To PRAy To us
not 9od. And The
BAd reckt Their HOUES

But thAt WAs not
nice. And A
Little Kid found
Some oel. And
The LigHt StAd
for eight DAYs.

childhood must be freed. Our society of tomorrow starts in your classroom today. The complexities of the 21st century may dictate a quality and quantity of education far different than we can currently imagine. You must take your emerging view of what social studies is and constantly search for ideas that help construct new roles for teachers in a new century. In addition to what we have considered up to this point, one of the most helpful ways of keeping up with current trends is to review the activities and publications of professional organizations.

The largest and most influential professional organization for social studies educators is the National Council for the Social Studies (NCSS). The council publishes several publications of interest to social studies teachers. *Social Education*, the primary journal, publishes articles focused on philosophical, theoretical, and practical classroom applications for K-12 instruction. *Social Studies and the Young Learner*, a separate journal for elementary school teachers, offers articles primarily concerned with teaching strategies. The NCSS also periodically publishes how-to pamphlets that offer in-depth suggestions for implementing specific instructional strategies such as using creative dramatics or current affairs programs in the social studies classroom. You should also become familiar with *The Social Studies*, a journal not associated with any particular professional organization. It deals with classroom practices on the K-12 level and contains a wealth of articles describing ideas for classroom use and stimulating thought on philosophical issues. The relevant addresses follow.

National Council for the Social Studies
8555 Sixteenth Street
Silver Spring, MD 20910
(301) 588-1800
www.ncss.org

The Social Studies
1319 Eighteenth Street, NW
Washington, DC 20036
www.periodicals.com/Heldref.html

REFERENCES

Amabile, T. M. (1989). *Growing up creative*. New York: Crown.

Berg, M. (1988). Integrating ideas for social studies. *Social Studies and the Young Learner, 1*, unnumbered pull-out feature.

Bruner, J. (1960). *The process of education*. New York: Vintage.

Channing, E., & Hart, A. B. (1903). *Guide to the study of American history*. Boston: Ginn and Company, 1.

Children's Defense Fund. (1996). *The state of America's children: Yearbook 1996*. Washington, DC: Author.

Clark, D. C., & Cutler, B. C. (1990). *Teaching*. New York: Harcourt Brace Jovanovich.

Dewey, J. (1933). *How we think*. Boston: D. C. Heath.

Finn, C. E. (1988, May). The social studies debacle among the educationaloids. *The American Spectator*, 15–16.

Hanna, P. R. (1963). Revising the social studies: What is needed? *Social Education, 27*, 190–196.

Hirsch, Jr., E. D. (1987). *Cultural literacy: What every American needs to know*. Boston: Houghton Mifflin.

Howard, R. W. (2003). The shrinking of social studies. *Social Education, 67*, 285–287.

Mattioli, D. (2004). The power of one: Making a difference in a changing world. *Social Education, 68*, 7–8.

Mitchell, L. S. (1934). *Young geographers*. New York: John Day.

National Commission on Excellence in Education. (1983). *A nation at risk: The imperative for educational reform*. Washington, DC: Author.

National Council for the Social Studies. (1981). Essentials of the social studies. *Social Education, 45*, 163–164.

National Council for the Social Studies. (1993a). A vision of powerful teaching and learning in the social studies: Building social understanding and civic efficacy. *Social Education, 57*, 213–223.

National Council for the Social Studies. (1993b). Definition approved. *The Social Studies Professional, 114* (January/February 1993), 3.

National Council for the Social Studies. (1994). *Curriculum standards for social studies: Expectations of excellence* (Bulletin 89). Washington, DC: National Council for the Social Studies.

National Council for the Social Studies. (2002). Creating effective citizens. *Social Education, 65*, 319.

National Council for the Social Studies Task Force on Early Childhood/Elementary Social Studies. (1989). Social studies for early childhood and elementary school children preparing for the 21st century. *Social Education, 54*, 16.

National Education Association. (1916). *The social studies in secondary education. Report of the Committee on Social Studies, Bulletin 28*. Washington, DC: Bureau of Education.

Ochoa-Becker, A. S. (2001). A critique of the NCSS curriculum standards. *Social Education, 65*, 165–168.

O'Neil, J. (1993). On the new standards project: A conversation with Lauren Resnick and Warren Simmons. *Educational Leadership, 50*, 17–23.

Ormrod, J. E. (1999). *Human learning*. Columbus, OH: Merrill.

Paxton, R. (2003). Don't know much about history—never did. *Phi Delta Kappan, 85*, 264–273.

Peterson, P., & Knapp, N. (1993). Inventing and reinventing ideas: Constructivist teaching and learning in mathematics. In G. Cawelti (Ed.), *Challenges and achievements of American education* (pp. 134–157). Alexandria, VA: Association for Supervision and Curriculum Development.

Ravitch, D., & Finn, C. (1987). *What do our 17-year-olds know?* New York: Harper & Row.

Risinger, C. F. (2002). Two different worlds: The dilemma facing social studies teachers. *Social Education, 66*, 231–233.

Robinson, J. H. (1912). *The new history*. New York: Macmillan, 17–18, 134.

Rochester, M. (2003). The training of idiots. In J. Leming, L. Ellington, and Cathleen Porter-Magee, *Where did social studies go wrong?* Retrieved from: http://www. edexcellence.net/foundation/publication.cfm?id=317

Tyack, D. (1997). Civic education—What roles for citizens? *Educational Leadership, 54*, 22–24.

U.S. Department of Education (1991). *America 2000: An education strategy*. Washington, DC: Author.

Winitzky, N. (1991). Multicultural and mainstreamed classrooms. In R. I. Arends, *Learning to teach* (pp. 125–156). New York: McGraw-Hill.

Diversity in the Classroom:
The Children You Will Teach

WHAT DOES DIVERSITY IN THE CLASSROOM LOOK LIKE?

St. Guadalupe:	"Knock, Knock!" (Child pretends to knock on a door.)
Rainbow:	"Who is it?"
St. Guadalupe:	"St. Guadalupe."
Rainbow:	"What do you want?"
St. Guadalupe:	"I want a color."
Rainbow:	"What color?"
St. Guadalupe:	"Rojo!"

In this game, one child is chosen to be St. Guadalupe and another is chosen to be Mother-of-Color, or Rainbow. All of the other children are assigned color names, each one assigned by Rainbow. (You could use English color names only, or create an opportunity to teach Spanish color names: *rojo* = red, *verde* = green, *azul* = blue, *amarillo* = yellow, *negro* = black, or *blanco* = white.) All the colors belong to Rainbow, and they line up behind her, across the play space from St. Guadalupe. St. Guadalupe's area is designated as home base. St. Guadalupe then initiates the dialogue listed previously. When St. Guadalupe calls our a color, all the children assigned that color name must attempt to reach home base without being tagged by St. Guadalupe. If they reach home base safely, they get ready to go again. Those who are caught help St. Guadalupe tag other players until everyone, including Rainbow, is captured. Then the game is over.

The children in this second-grade classroom were playing a game called *Los Colores* (Colors), a group game well known to Spanish-speaking children (Perez, 1993). Their teacher, Maria Quinones, selects games from various cultures as a vehicle to teach children that, despite many fundamental differences, cultures are alike in many ways. In fact, this game is much like the popular childhood game you may have played, Red Rover. Ms. Quinones believes that if we focus on children's likenesses—their common bonds—then they will be able to celebrate their differences with pride.

WHAT IS MULTICULTURAL EDUCATION?

Ms. Quinones includes multicultural experiences as an integral part of her classroom program, establishing an all-inclusive learning environment that nurtures mutual trust and respect for all people. She operates with a strong conviction that children who are equipped with a knowledge of an appreciation for the glorious diversity among people will more likely be wise citizens who respect our nation's rich variety of cultures, heritages, abilities, and interests.

Ms. Quinones recognizes that tourist approaches to learning about human diversity, although often carried out with the best of intentions, rarely broaden children's understanding of people and cultures. *Tourist approaches* are characterized by putting special activities or projects into the school day only when a cultural holiday or special observance comes up, such as performing a dragon dance only during the Chinese New Year, reading a book about Amelia Bloomer only during Women's History Month, teaching a unit on Mexican Americans only during early May (Cinco de Mayo), reading books about important African Americans only during the month of February, or playing the dreidel game only during Hanukkah. Certainly, those events are important and should be rendered a special place in dynamic social studies programs, but limiting a multicultural program to such singular, isolated events does not embody the true multicultural spirit. We must explore more deeply the likenesses and differences among all of us so that children learn ways to be more tolerant of people unlike themselves and to recognize that it is healthier to accept difference rather than to steer clear of it. Teachers who believe that cultural awareness should be part of the child's education must plan to incorporate multicultural activities into the mainstream social studies curriculum. Tourist-type experiences might make students a bit more aware of the world around them, but genuine understanding comes from all that children do during the day and throughout the school year.

Educators today recommend doing away with the tourist approach and infusing multicultural content into the broad curriculum. The primary goals of infusion are to

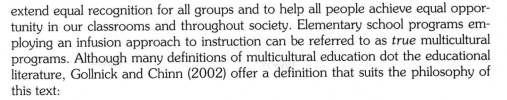

extend equal recognition for all groups and to help all people achieve equal opportunity in our classrooms and throughout society. Elementary school programs employing an infusion approach to instruction can be referred to as *true* multicultural programs. Although many definitions of multicultural education dot the educational literature, Gollnick and Chinn (2002) offer a definition that suits the philosophy of this text:

> *Multicultural education* is the educational strategy in which students' cultural backgrounds are used to develop effective classroom instruction and school environments. It is designed to support and extend the concepts of culture, diversity, equality, social justice, and democracy in the formal school setting. (p. 5)

Multicultural was once a term that considered differences, including cultural differences, as handicaps. The goals of many ensuing educational programs were designed to assist diverse students conform to majority standards and mainstream cultural expectations. Now, however, multiculturalism accepts cultural diversity as a resource rather than a handicap, and has been expanded to include groups based on exceptionality, gender, and class as well as language and culture. Teachers who employ practices that affirm and respect the cultures of students look upon the students' cultures as strengths rather than handicaps. They are known as *culturally responsive* teachers. Cultural responsiveness means being sensitive to and capable of functioning in a culturally diverse environment.

Cultural Responsiveness

The cultural, racial, and ethnic composition of our schools has become increasingly diverse and, as you would expect, mirrors the changing nature of American society. To provide effective and successful classroom instruction, culturally responsive teachers must understand and commit to practices that confirm and build upon the cultures and strengths of our children. Knowledge of a culture's value system and its expectations for its children can provide information that enhances the development of effective classroom interactions and instructional practices. Some long-established models of education tend to overlook the ways cultural conditions can influence the lives of children; therefore, they operate with a conviction that there is "one best path for all." The belief that a singular approach is applicable to all cultural groups, however, tends to render education practically useless to all but the most assimilated groups.

A rich storehouse of information provides insight into what teachers can do with children in a culturally responsive classroom. However, before we examine these recommendations, it must be noted that the cultural group labels used to organize this chapter are merely social constructions that cannot embrace the life of any single individual. For example, a person might be "Caucasian," but also French, Southerner, farmer, Roman Catholic, hearing impaired, female, and lower-middle class. Each person's group memberships include race, ethnic group, region, occupation, religion, disabled or nondisabled, gender, and social class. Many aspects of one's life are shaped by membership in many groups, making this Caucasian female a much different person than an intellectually gifted Asian American male doctoral student from a large Eastern city who grew up in a crowded high-rise apartment, or a female Navajo physician whose family makes its home in a pueblo in the desert Southwest. Groups can be defined along many different lines, and everyone is a member of an assortment of groups, each of which creates its own culture—the knowledge, rules, values, and traditions that guide its members' behavior.

Membership in any specific group may reflect certain tendencies and likelihoods of expected behavior. For example, Hmong families from Laos and the mountains of Vietnam tend to have many children. Another example is that students of low-socioeconomic status (SES) tend to exhibit lower levels of school achievement than those with high SES. However, such tendencies do not tell you about *individual* students. Banks (1993) clarifies: "Although membership in a gender, racial, ethnic, social-class, or religious group can provide us with important clues about an individual's behavior, it cannot enable us to predict behavior. . . . Membership in a particular group does not determine behavior but makes certain types of behavior more probable" (pp. 13–14).

All of this is not meant to confuse you, but only to emphasize that the children you teach are not just Haitian, not only female, nor just wheelchair bound. They are uniquely complex individuals who have become who they are through the interaction of many intricate genetic and environmental factors. The labels we choose to describe the groups they belong to are not meant to stereotype, only to provide insight into the best practices for dynamic social studies instruction.

WHY IS MULTICULTURAL AWARENESS IMPORTANT?

Although a majority of Americans currently are of European descent, since 1980 the number of Americans identified as ethnic minorities, a term frequently used to refer to people receiving unequal or discriminatory treatment, has been steadily increasing. As a matter of interest, some predictions estimate that by the year 2020, about half the population of the United States will come from groups traditionally labeled *minority*: African American, Asian American, Native American, and Latino or Hispanic. As this trend continues to spiral, it is obvious that significant changes in the makeup of our school population will follow. Our nation's growing diversity has important ramifications for all educators, but it should be of special significance for those concerned with social studies. That is where the foundation of tolerance and understanding begins.

Cultural and Ethnic Diversity

As a nation, we pride ourselves on our cultural, ethnic, and religious diversity. We are of many colors, speak many languages, and observe many different customs and traditions. All of us contribute to our nation's rich and wonderful diversity, whether our ancestors are Ukrainian, Polish, German, African, Swedish, Inuit, Sioux, Jewish, Korean, English, Puerto Rican, Mexican, Irish, Algonquin, French, Brazilian, Japanese,

Italian, Russian, Cuban, Seminole, Lithuanian, Spanish, Scottish, Australian, or Chinese. In the past, the term *melting pot* (or crucible) was popularly used to characterize how to deal with our nation's diversity, especially as it was applied to "Americanizing" foreign immigrants.

Melting pot was the term selected to label the approach some believed stood the best chance of successfully blending together varied groups of immigrants into a new American culture:

> America is God's great Crucible, a great Melting Pot where all races of Europe are melting and reforming! . . . Germans and Frenchmen, Irishmen and Englishmen, Jews and Russians—into the Crucible with you all! God is making the American. . . . The real American has not yet arrived. He is only in the Crucible, I tell you—he will be the fusion of all races, the coming superman. (Zangwell, 1909, p. 37)

Proponents of the melting pot idea believed that all ethnic groups possessed strengths and that, as the "Crucible of America" fused them into a single amalgamation, a new and greater culture would be cast. The melting pot, then, was not meant to destroy cultural diversity per se, but to combine the strengths of many cultures into something new and unique: " . . . the new emerging American culture must be built not on the destruction of the cultural values and mores of the various immigrant groups but on their fusion with the existing American civilization. . . . In the burning fires of the melting pot, all races were equal—all were reshaped, and molded into a new entity" (Krug, 1976, p. 12).

The public school system of the time mirrored the melting pot ideals to the extent that diversity in the educational process was not highly accepted. Stearns (1996) comments: "It remains true that the American educational tradition . . . opted largely for a single cultural standard, to which all minority groups were expected to bow" (p. 23). A student cast in the mold of middle-class values was the fundamental goal of the educational tradition. Immigrants as well as members of the working class were instilled with "appropriate American middle-class standards" about such habits as personal grooming, punctuality and diligence at work, and political correctness.

Cultural Pluralism

Today, our nation and its schools have done away with the idea of a single "American" culture emerging from a great melting pot. Cultural pluralism is the philosophy that now describes how all the parts of society contribute to an American whole. The United States is viewed as a multitude of cultures, each with its own distinctively rich uniqueness that contributes to the larger culture. Instead of a melting pot, our society has been likened to a salad bowl, pizza, mosaic, or patchwork quilt where each culture retains its own individuality but yet contributes to the design of the whole. The foundation of social studies instruction is based on this idea of cultural pluralism—becoming sensitive to and respecting the contributions of each group to society in general.

Cultural Identification (Ethnicity)

All individuals belonging to a group—whether an ethnic group, religion, peer group, or family—have a culture, or a system of behaviors, beliefs, customs, and attitudes.

Culture is reflected in the group's artwork, literature, language, clothing, inventions, and traditions. Cultural differences are widespread, in both the overt (clothing, hairstyle, language, naming ceremonies) and the subtle (how one speaks to an elder). Culture consists of all the accepted and patterned ways of a group's behavior. It is a body of common understandings, the sum total of the group's ways of thinking, feeling, and acting.

Cultures have similar needs but often choose to satisfy them in dissimilar ways. For example, let us look into a need that all cultures have in common—food. All groups must eat food to survive; that's a given. Everybody eats, but what we eat, how we eat, where we eat, and when we eat are determined by our culture. The basic ingredients, the way food is preserved, the way it is prepared, the amount served at a meal, the way the meal is served, and the tastes we enjoy vary depending on our cultural background. Cultural practices for food preparation and consumption are incredibly varied. Some groups, for example, acquire protein from various animal sources—cows, pigs, horses, dogs, cats, mice, snakes, or beetle grubs. Other groups eat no meat, poultry, or fish—"nothing with a face." Some groups may reject certain foods because of their values and beliefs: Muslims and Orthodox Jews do not eat pork, Hindus do not eat beef, some East Africans find eggs unfit for human consumption, and some Chinese do not drink milk. While we share physiological need for food with other humans, the food we eat and the pleasure we derive from eating certain foods are rooted in our cultural beliefs. As Confucius once said, "A man cannot be too serious about his eating, for food is the force that binds society together."

What foods do you think of as multicultural? Are they foods from other countries, like *Deok* (traditional Korean rice cakes), *Dodo* (a Nigerian fried plantain or banana), or *Won ton* (Chinese dumplings)? Are they foods from different regions of the United States like smoked salmon (Northwest), collard greens and grits (Southeast), Navajo fry bread (Southwest), or New England clam chowder (Northeast)? Your college roommate may eat stir-fried dishes daily yet be in awe of your fondness for spaghetti and meatballs. Each of our cultural backgrounds and life experiences shape the way we think of food.

In our contemporary global community connected by the Internet, cellular phones, and convenient travel, it is easy to network with a broader variety of people and learn about their culture. Returning to our food theme, for example, 25 years ago it would have been difficult to imagine going to a major league ballpark and eating anything other than a hot dog, peanuts, or popcorn. I recently went to a game and was still able to buy this traditional food, but found that it's not unusual to find nachos, suchi, stir fry, chili, tacos, pizza, or an assortment of pastas and salads. Whether we choose to compare and contrast food, religion, holiday customs, clothing styles, or any other of the array of cultural traits, the unique beliefs and behaviors of any distinct culture provide its members with a feeling of group identity (ethnicity). See Figure 2–1.

Ethnicity, then, entails a deep feeling of personal attachment to a cultural group and greatly influences the standards its members use to judge themselves and others. It involves beliefs about what is worthwhile, satisfying, or important. Strong feelings of ethnicity determine the ways we think, feel, and act. Sometimes, cultures become

FIGURE 2–1
Cultural Diversity

MORRIE TURNER

Source: Turner, M. (1980). *Social studies and the young learner, 5,* 2. © National Council for the Social Studies. Reprinted by permission.

convinced that their own behaviors and beliefs are the proper and best ways of thinking and acting. A characteristic found in most cultures, this phenomenon is referred to as *ethnocentrism,* or the tendency to view one's own culture as the absolute center of everything and the standard against which all others are judged. Although it is proper to deeply revere one's own culture, ethnocentrism carried to an extreme makes it impossible to view another culture objectively through its "cultural lens." In so doing, it prevents one culture from understanding, coexisting with, or appreciating another. Cultural insularity often results, a condition especially worrisome today in light of the need for interdependence among countries and the importance of establishing positive ties among all cultural groups.

All children come to school with a strong ethnic identity, whether their identities are typical or extreme. The teacher must accept and respect students' ethnic identities and use them to form the starting point for all that goes on in the classroom. It is correspondingly essential that the children maintain their own ethnicity and recognize the importance of learning about and valuing the ethnicity of the other children in their classroom. By demonstrating an appreciation for and recognizing the children's ethnic identities, teachers help establish a bond between themselves and their students as well as among the students. For this reason, an essential ingredient of effective teaching in social studies is to value and praise ethnic identity, to regard all children and their families with dignity and respect.

TEACHING IN CULTURALLY DIVERSE SETTINGS

To work effectively with the diverse populations that now typify our nation's schools, teachers must use extra planning time to ensure that instruction accurately reflects the true makeup of the school population. If that extra effort is not made, multicultural programs can often turn into *culturally assaultive* experiences instead of culturally responsive ones. To explain what it means to be culturally assaultive, pretend

for a moment that you are a young child, the only "non-Indian" child in your classroom. You are about to learn some very interesting things about your ethnicity during Thanksgiving time. As you politely enter the room and approach a place to sit
in the circle with your classmates, your teacher begins the following discussion:

> "Who knows what kind of houses non-Indians live in? Yes, that's right. They live in square
> houses with red tile roofs. Who lives in these houses? Mother and father and sister and
> brother. Yes, that's right. Grandmother? No, they don't live with their grandmothers, like
> we do. They send their grandmothers away to special places called retirement homes.
> Why? I don't know.
>
> "Next week, during Thanksgiving, we'll have a unit on non-Indians. We'll all make a
> non-Indian town out of clay. It's called a *suburb.* Can you say *suburb?* Non-Indians sleep
> in separate rooms, and they have little houses to keep their cars in.
>
> "Now this is a non-Indian hat." The teacher pulls out a Pilgrim's hat. "Non-Indians
> wore these when they first came to our land." (Clark, DeWolf, and Clark, 1992, p. 5)

Clearly, the authors paint a clear picture of how discourteous and offensive culturally assaultive teaching can be. It has no place in dynamic social studies classrooms.
In its place, we must use *culturally responsive teaching.* Gay (2000) defines culturally responsive teaching as responding to the students' cultural knowledge, experiences, and performance styles to make learning more appropriate and effective; it
teaches to and through the strengths of our diverse student population. In more detail,
Gay (2000) describes culturally responsive teaching as having these characteristics:

- It acknowledges the legitimacy of the cultural heritages of different ethnic
  groups, both as legacies that affect students' dispositions, attitudes, and
  approaches to learning and as worthy content to be taught in the formal
  curriculum.
- It builds bridges of meaningfulness between home and school experiences as
  well as between academic abstractions and lived sociocultural realities.
- It uses a wide variety of instructional strategies that are connected to
  different learning styles.
- It teaches students to know and praise their own and each others' cultural
  heritages.
- It incorporates multicultural information, resources, and materials in all the
  subjects and skills routinely taught in schools. (p. 29)

The overall goal of culturally responsive education is to gradually and cumulatively
empower students with the knowledge, skills, and attitudes needed to understand and
appreciate racial, cultural, and ethnic diversity. The following steps are suggested as
ways to infuse multicultural education into existing social studies programs:

1. *Know your community.*   If you plan to turn your classroom into a place
where cultural responsiveness is a reality, start with a focus on the cultural groups
represented by the school population. The students, community, and families your
school is serving should be the primary starting point for culturally responsive programming, but this is a daunting prospect for many teachers. Many teachers are at
a disadvantage because they do not live, nor have they ever lived, in the community

where they teach. In most instances, they have not been in their students' homes nor have they been active in community activities. It is no easy task to incorporate cultural knowledge into one's teaching, so how does a teacher begin to learn about other cultures? Gollnick and Chinn (2002) explain:

> Using the tools of an anthropologist or ethnographer, we could observe children in classrooms and on playgrounds. We can listen carefully to students and their parents as they discuss their life experiences. We can study other cultures. We can learn about the perspectives of others by reading articles and books written by men and women from different ethnic, racial, socioeconomic, and religious groups. Participation in community, religious, and ethnic activities can provide another perspective on students' cultures. (p. 320)

The knowledge you uncover about the community in which you teach and about the rich cultural backgrounds of the families served by your school should help you make the content you are teaching more meaningful by making their own experiences the center of the educational process.

2. *Seek family support.* A prerequisite for meeting the needs of all families is the belief in their dignity and worth. Researchers have found that "to the extent that the home culture's practices and values are not acknowledged or incorporated by the school, parents may find that they are not able to support children in their academic pursuits even when it is their fervent wish to do so" (Florio-Ruane, 1989, p. 169). Be especially willing to listen as well as talk to the parents of your students, and make sure that they understand your program's goals. Find out what they would like their children to learn about their own culture and other cultures. To teach multiculturally requires starting where students are. By finding out where the children are, you may find that the values and expectations of some families may differ markedly from your own. For example, Islamic parents could be puzzled about why the school celebrates Christian holidays and never Islamic holidays. Celebrate diversity by incorporating appropriate content into the curriculum, but first know the viewpoints of the families served by the school.

3. *Give equal attention to all groups.* Social studies classrooms must reflect the diversity of cultures, whether or not the school population itself is diverse. Instructionally, the curriculum must incorporate information about many cultures and intergroup relations. The amount of specific content about various cultures will vary but recognition of the culturally pluralistic nature of the nation must be reflected in all classroom experiences. Regardless of how assimilated the students in your classroom might be, it is your responsibility to ensure that they understand cultural diversity and know the contributions of members of minority as well as dominant groups.

Teachers with a multicultural perspective know that, because they cannot possibly offer equal treatment to the hundreds of microcultures in this country, they must begin by developing an understanding of and sensitivity and respect for the various cultures of the families served by the school community. In urban Los Angeles or El Paso, a teacher could start with the Mexican-American culture, and in rural Lancaster County, Pennsylvania, a teacher would find it beneficial to start with the Amish culture. In other areas of the country, schools should focus on the character of the groups represented in the community. These cultures should become an integral part

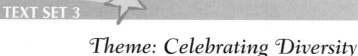

Theme: Celebrating Diversity

Cynthia Rylant's **Appalachia: The Voices of Sleeping Birds** (First Voyager) is a wonderful story of the people of Appalachia told by an author who lived there. The story and illustrations bring this incomparable countryside alive for young readers and help them to understand one of the most unique cultures in the United States.

Diane Hoyt-Goldsmith's **Hoang-Anh: A Vietnamese-American Boy** (Holiday House) is a photo essay about the life of the youngest son in a family of Vietnamese boat people now living in San Rafael, California. His father is a fisherman and his mother works in a beauty parlor. Hoyt-Goldsmith describes the family's emigration to the United States and weaves many details about Vietnamese history, customs, folklore, and family life into the photo essay.

Bryan Collier's **Uptown** (Henry Holt), a Coretta Scott King Illustrator Award winner, helps young readers discover the pulsating world of Harlem, as seen through the eyes of one little boy who lives there. The lucid details of life in Harlem are clearly detailed in Collier's wonderful illustrations—from the legendary Apollo Theater to chocolate-colored brownstones, from weekend shopping on 125th Street to summer basketball games on the playground.

of social studies, expanding the standard curriculum with diversity and multiple perspectives. As the students begin to realize they are important members of a school where diversity is valued, the curriculum can examine sensitive issues and topics from the perspective of various ethnic and cultural groups, such as Chinese Americans, Irish Americans, African Americans, Puerto Ricans, Catholics, Southern Baptists, Caucasian males, or Jewish women. Cultural diversity must be infused into the social studies program and become the lens through which the pluralistic nature of our nation can be focused.

4. *Fill your room with fascinating things.*   Think about all the curriculum materials in your room. Multiethnic dolls, pictures, and study prints from different parts of the world, crayons that match in degree of skin tone, examples of Japanese calligraphy, tortilla presses, kimonos, cowboy boots, nesting dolls, chopsticks, bongo drums, serapes, and tie-dyed cloth from Africa fascinate children and encourage interest in people.

5. *Invite visitors into your room.*   Having people from the community who are willing to come to your class and share something of their culture is a splendid addition to a multicultural program. Resource people can demonstrate a special craft or talent, read or tell a story, display and talk about an interesting artifact or process of doing something, share a special food or recipe, teach a simple song or dance, or help children count or speak in another language. If you arrange for visits from different people throughout the year, your children will begin to respect and value all cultures.

Dorothy and Thomas Hoobler's **We Are Americans: Voices of the Immigrant People** (Scholastic) offers a chronological history of people from all over the world who eventually became Americans. Filled with detailed information and poignant personal narratives (oral histories, diaries, letters), the book tells the comprehensive story of the shifting patterns of immigration through the centuries.

Guy Garcia's **Spirit of the Maya: A Boy Explores His People's Mysterious Past** (Walker) tells the heart-warming story of Kin, a 12-year-old Lacando'n boy living in Palenque, Mexico, who is descended from the ancient Maya. After his grandfather shows him a book about Pacal, a Mayan boy who became king in 615 A.D. when he, too, was 12, Kin eagerly accompanies his father to the site of Pacal's tomb where he explores the ancient Mayan temples and pyramids built by his ancestors more than a thousand years ago. For the first time in his life, Kin realizes the richness of his heritage.

TRY THIS

It would be fun and instructive for each student in your class to visit the library to find one good children's book about her or his culture. Celebrate the diversity in your classroom by presenting a brief book talk (patterned after my short reviews) and a few sample illustrations or photos from each book.

6. *Draw from the vast resources of the arts.* The arts offer one of the most valuable sources from which to draw suitable multicultural experiences for music, art, and literature. The arts know no cultural boundaries. The common expressions of human feeling found in these art forms can be used effectively to develop children's capacities to identify with other groups and other societies—indeed, the totality of human civilization. The arts provide ways of giving students an opportunity to try on a situation—to know its logic and feeling—even though it is remote to the lives of the school population.

It is never too early to introduce young children to the arts of various cultures. Songs, rhymes, and chants evoke pleasure and enthusiasm from the very young in kindergarten and first-grade classrooms. Stories, pictures, books, arts and crafts, stage plays, puppets, dance, and other forms of creative expression add zest to the early grades. Children of all ages can visit museums or displays, especially those associated with specific ethnic groups. Seeing the beautiful handmade crafts (pottery, silver and turquoise jewelry, and baskets) of the Hopi and Zuni, for example, helps students understand important aspects of these cultures. Take your children to musical events having distinct cultural characteristics—African chants, Yiddish folk tunes, Scottish bagpipe music, or Eastern European polkas. Invite guest speakers to demonstrate their special arts techniques, such as Amish quilt making, Inuit soapstone carving, Cajun music, or Plains Indian pictographs. Read, tell, or dramatize

Teachers must select learning experiences that are accurate in their portrayal of today's diverse cultures.

stories of various cultures. For instance, these books provide outstanding examples of the many ways people from various cultures celebrate December holidays: *The Miracle of the Potato Latkes* by Malka Penn (Holiday House), *The Angel of Olvera Street* by Leo Politi (Scribner's), *The Gifts of Kwanzaa* by Synthia Saint James (Albert Whitman and Company), and *Christmas Around the World* by Emily Kelly (Carolrhoda Books). Children should be helped to understand that the arts reflect culture and that one cannot fully appreciate the value of any art without some understanding of the cultural matrix from which it grew. Conversely, one cannot fully appreciate a culture unless one values the creative efforts of its members.

All social studies programs have the responsibility to provide quality educational experiences that help children become compassionate individuals who feel comfortable with their identities and sense their unity with other people. We must create positive environments where children learn to accept others with cultural differences and begin to develop the skills of living cooperatively in a culturally diverse nation.

Language Diversity in the Classroom

Hand-in-hand with the rich diversity of cultures enjoyed in the United States is a grand assortment of languages and dialects. Changing populations and an influx of immigrants from Asian and Hispanic/Latino nations have produced a situation where more than 200 languages are now spoken in the United States (Arends, 1991). Although this is a fascinating circumstance, it has resulted in significant challenges for the education of our nation's youth. These challenges, however, are not new. Concerns about the goals and purposes of educating non-English-speaking students date back to the Revolutionary War, when school was taught in any of 18 languages spoken by the colonists, including English, German, Scottish, Irish, Dutch, French, Swedish, Spanish, and Portuguese. As the colonies eventually blended into a new nation, however, English became the dominant language in public education. The freedom to use other languages has become a matter of unrelenting conflict since that time.

Although there has been evidence of the sporadic use of languages other than English in our schools, the widespread use of bilingualism, or teaching in two languages, did not occur until the 1960s. The civil rights movement brought attention to discriminatory practices throughout society, including children whose first language was not English. From the 1960s into the 1980s, federal court decisions ruled that schools are required to offer quality programs to enable students to participate successfully in all-English classrooms.

Currently, our nation's changing demographics require a new look at the needs of children from homes where English is not the first language. Campbell (1996) reports that since 1970 the United States has experienced massive immigration similar to the levels that occurred from 1890 to 1910. At least 10 million immigrants have come to live in this country during the past three decades. Well over 70 percent of these new immigrants are Hispanics/Latinos from Mexico, El Salvador, Guatemala, Nicaragua, and Honduras, and a great number are Southeast Asians from Vietnam, Cambodia, Laos, Korea, Japan, and China. Settlement patterns indicate that 80 percent of these immigrants settled mainly in 10 states, chief among them California, Texas, and Florida. As teachers, we must be aware of how these changing demographics will influence the student composition of our classrooms into the next millennium:

> By the year 2050, the present percentage of Latinos in the U.S. population will almost triple; the Asian population will more than triple; African Americans will increase about 3 percent; the non-Hispanic white population will drop from 76 percent to 53 percent. (U.S. Census Bureau, 1990)

It is unwise to use only English in the classroom—in effect, to ask students to give up their family's language. Crawford (1992) describes the effect of this practice on children:

> To devalue a minority child's language is to devalue the child—at least, that's how it feels on the receiving end. The longtime policy of punishing [Hispanic/Latino] students for speaking Spanish is an obvious example. While such practices are now frowned upon, more subtle stigmas remain. Children are quick to read the messages in adult behavior,

such as a preference for English on ceremonial occasions or a failure to stock the school library with books in Chinese. . . . Whatever the cause, minority students frequently exhibit an alienation from both worlds. Joe Cummins calls it bicultural ambivalence: hostility toward the dominant culture and shame toward one's own. (pp. 212–213)

An alternative to submersion in English is bilingual teaching—that is, using two languages as vehicles of instruction. The primary goal of bilingual programs is not to offer instruction in English per se, but to teach children in the language they know best and to reinforce their understandings through the use of English. Grant and Gomez (1996) explain:

The core curriculum in public school bilingual classrooms is the same as that for any other classroom. The only significant curricular difference is the focus on language development (ESL and the appropriate native language) and attention to the cultural heritage of the targeted language minority group. Besides teaching language, science, math, social studies, art, and music, bilingual teachers must facilitate language learning in everything they do. They are concerned with how best to teach non-English speaking students the full range of subjects while developing native and [English language] skills. (p. 118)

If you visited an elementary school social studies classroom with a bilingual program, you would likely see an English-speaking teacher and a teacher or aide fluent in a native language. Their preferred teaching approach follows Scarcella's (1990) preview/teach/review format. In this design, the content of the lesson is previewed in English, the body of the lesson is taught in the student's native language, and then the lesson is reviewed in English. This approach is often used when two teachers—one English-speaking teacher and one fluent in the native language—collaborate in a team-teaching effort. In addition to Scarcella's preview/teach/review format, Freeman and Freeman (1993) recommend the following guidelines for bilingual instruction:

1. *Environmental print.* Children learn to recognize words written in both English and their native language when they see print in a number of environmental contexts—magazines, newspapers, telephone books, menus, food packages, street signs, days of the week, classroom posters, labels, nametags, charts, bulletin boards, and other interesting sources. Words should be printed both in English and the children's native language.

2. *Culturally conscious literature.* Classroom use of multicultural literature written in the students' native language helps strengthen cultural values and beliefs. Quality books are now being written for children in a number of languages and are becoming increasingly available throughout the United States. For example, Carmen Lomas Garza's bilingual book *Family Pictures: Cuadros de Familia* (Children's Book Press) is an authentic portrayal of what it is like to grow up in a Mexican American family in South Texas (Rosalma Zubizerreta authored the Spanish version). If you cannot afford to purchase a number of like books, parents or other members of the community might be willing to lend books written in the children's native language. Having a parent or other volunteer come to school and read from these books adds respect and appreciation for the native language.

3. *Language buddies.* Learning a second language is enhanced greatly when students are paired up with English-speaking classmates who speak the native lan-

Respect for each child's culture and language promotes children's genuine acceptance of themselves as successful learners and as valued classmates.

guage fluently. English proficiency is promoted by the classmate's careful explanations, modeling, and assistance with new words.

Bilingual education, like all dimensions of multicultural education, is based on a commitment to school success for all of our nation's children. A bilingual curriculum should provide students with educational opportunities that are meaningful, compassionate, and challenging to develop the full range of oral and written language necessary to function in school and as a citizen in our democratic society.

Educating Exceptional Children

Nearly every day, you will come into contact with individuals who fall into one or more categories of exceptionality. Exceptional people include individuals with disabilities as well as gifted individuals. Anyone who has spent time with children knows that there are many ways they are all alike and some ways they stand apart from one another. It is important to keep this perspective in mind, for children with disabilities are similar in many ways to children without disabilities. Wolery and Wilbers (1994) clarify:

> All children share needs for food and shelter, for love and affection, for affiliation with others, for opportunities to play and learn, and for protection from the harsh realities of their environments. All children deserve freedom from violence, abuse, neglect, and suffering.

All children deserve interactions and relationships with adults who are safe, predictable, responsive, and nurturing. All children deserve opportunities to interact with peers who are accepting, trustworthy, kind, and industrious. All children deserve . . . educational experiences that are stimulating, interesting, facilitative, and enjoyable. (p. 3)

Despite these commonly shared needs, children with disabilities are different from children without disabilities. Wolery, Strain, and Bailey (1992) explain: "They need environments that are specifically organized and adjusted to minimize the effects of their disabilities and to promote learning of a broad range of skills. They need professionals who are competent in meeting the general needs of . . . children and are competent in promoting learning and use of skills important to the specific needs of children with disabilities" (p. 95).

In addition to sharing a set of basic needs, all children go through similar stages of development. Although the timing will not be exactly the same for each, children all around the world move through predictable patterns of motor development (they will walk before they run), language development (they will babble before they speak in sentences), cognitive development (they will want to explore their surroundings with their hands and fingers before they try to read a book for information), and social-emotional development (they will scream to get their own way before they ask permission for things). Chandler (1994) explains that children with special needs may develop at a rate different from that of more typical children, but the sequence of development remains the same:

For example, we know that children learn to sit before they stand, stand before they walk. This sequence is the same whether a child is nine months old or three years old. If three-year-old Amanda is unable to walk, we consider her a child with special needs. However, our knowledge of child development still tells us that she first needs to sit, and then stand, before she can walk, even though her development of these skills is delayed. Again, understanding typical development provides the information needed to teach and care for the child with special needs. (p. 21)

Despite the fact that children are similar in many ways, some children with exceptionalities will exhibit characteristics not quite like most others. An estimated 10 to 12 percent of all children in the United States fall into the children with disabilities category; they deviate far enough from the typical in at least one respect that an individualized school program is required to address their needs. Who are these children with disabilities? Public Law 101-476, the Americans With Disabilities Act of 1990, defines children with disabilities as those:

A. With mental retardation, hearing impairments including deafness, speech or language impairments, visual impairments, including blindness, serious emotional disturbance, orthopedic impairments, autism, traumatic brain injury, other health impairments, or specific learning disabilities; and B. who, by reason thereof, need special education and related services.

The Concept of Inclusion

Much effort these days is being directed toward inclusion. Inclusive classrooms operate with a conviction that students with disabilities have a right to be brought together into regular classrooms with their nondisabled peers. An educational system for all students is a major focus of our nation's schools for several reasons. First, state and federal laws mandate, support, and encourage it. Second, some parents of children with special needs were troubled that their children were required to attend separate programs. They viewed these programs as a form of segregation. Third, educators, parents, and children have had rewarding experiences in inclusive environments.

Despite these strong points, not everyone is sold on the idea of inclusion. First, not all parents want their children with disabilities taken from their special programs. They believe their children are best served in separate special education facilities. Second, many teachers feel inadequately prepared to provide for the special disabilities brought to their classrooms. Third, some people think the great cost of inclusion outweighs its benefits.

Federal Legislation

Despite these opposing positions, inclusion is currently an established educational reality. The movement was initiated with Public Law 94-142 (the Education for All Handicapped Children Act), signed into law in 1975 and implemented in the fall of 1978. It was a valuable outcome of the many social efforts during the early 1970s to prevent the segregation of any child from regular classrooms, whether because of special needs or race. Specifically, Public Law 94-142 made free public education mandatory for all children older than age 5 who were identified as having special needs. Such education was to take place within a "least restrictive environment." A least restrictive environment was defined as a place where the same opportunities as those available to any other child are offered to children with special needs. Those children include students who need special attention to overcome conditions that could delay normal growth and development, distort normal growth and development, or have a severe negative effect on normal growth and development and adjustment to life.

A comprehensive educational, medical, sociocultural, and psychological evaluation by a multidisciplinary team determined the extent of a child's disability. From there, possible remediation strategies were proposed. Schools did this by scheduling a meeting with the prospective teacher, the child's parents, a representative from the school district (usually a special educator), and a member of the assessment team. All information about the child was shared, and a personalized education plan, the individualized education program (IEP), unfolded.

In 1990, Public Law 101-476 amended Public Law 94-142 in several very important ways. First, the legislation clarified what parents could demand for their children with disabilities. It reinforced the idea that all children with disabilities between the ages of 3 and 21 should receive a free and appropriate public education in a least restrictive environment (LRE) with their nondisabled peers. In addition to expanding and clarifying special education services for children with disabilities, the legislation replaced the title of PL 94-142 (Education for All Handicapped Children Act) with a new one (Individuals With Disabilities Education Act, or IDEA). Although the change may seem insignificant to some, IDEA communicated a monumental message. By replacing the term *handicapped* with *individuals with disabilities*, Congress declared

TABLE 2–1
Examples of Person-First Language

Use . . .	Do not use . . .
• person with a disability	• disabled or handicapped person
• individual without speech	• mute, dumb
• child who is blind or visually impaired	• blind child or "the blind"
• student who is deaf or hearing impaired	• deaf student or "the deaf"
• boy with paraplegia	• paraplegic
• girl who is paralyzed	• paralyzed girl
• individual with epilepsy	• epileptic
• student who has a learning disability or specific learning disability	• slow learner, retarded, learning disabled
• person with a mental disability, cognitive impairment	• crazy, demented, insane
• child with a developmental disability	• mentally retarded
• child with a congenital disability	• birth defect
• child who uses a wheelchair	• wheelchair-bound child

that professionals should think of children with special needs as children first rather than focusing on their disabilities. In addition, IDEA was noted for its use of "person-first" language; this means that the person is emphasized first, the disability second. Examples of appropriate person-first usage appear in Table 2–1.

To extend this idea of appropriate terminology, persons without disabilities should be referred to as *nondisabled* rather than *normal* or *able-bodied*. The word *handicap* should be used only in reference to a condition or physical barrier ("The stairs are a handicap for Nina," or "Erwin is handicapped by the inaccessible bus").

Teaching Children With Disabilities

Although an awareness of appropriate terminology helps, our desire to include children with disabilities in all aspects of social studies classroom life must also be based on our own feelings toward and understandings of children with disabilities. How would you feel, and what would you do, for example, in each of the following situations?

• Sarah has a convulsion and you are the only adult around.
• Alejandro is lost and cannot hear you calling him.
• Jessica seems unable to sit still; she constantly interrupts other children in class.

It might surprise you that the way most people choose to "deal" with problems like these is to avoid them. How many of us tend to steer clear of children with disabilities because we feel inadequate or insecure? You cannot take this approach as a teacher of elementary school children today. You must replace your feelings of inadequacy by confronting your uncertainties and replacing them with confidence based upon accurate knowledge. To effectively implement the spirit of inclusion, all professionals must learn something about how it operates; doing so may alleviate many fears and make those involved in the process feel more secure. The following suggestions are general and should be adjusted in consideration of each unique situation.

1. *Learn about each specific disability.* You have a good start toward understanding children with disabilities if you know about child development. After all, children with disabilities are, first of all, children. It is important to know that children with disabilities are more like other children than they are different from them. Therefore, your first step in working with children with disabilities is to establish a framework with a solid understanding of child development.

When a child with developmental disabilities enters your classroom, take time to meet and get to know something about him or her. You might invite the family to visit your classroom, or find it instructive to visit the child at home. Whatever the choice, you will need a great deal of background information about the child. Other sources of background information include past teachers or other specialists who have previously cared for the child.

Certainly, it is not possible to know everything about all the exceptionalities you will meet during your teaching career, but you will have to learn a lot about each as you encounter it. That is why the relevant public laws stipulate that a team of specialists must be involved in the formulation of each IEP. However, you should become familiar with the ways one can accept, understand, and become sensitive to the needs of every child. To help in this regard, search through many professional journals, books, and videotapes available through professional organizations or publishers of special education materials. Get to know each child well.

Once you gather basic information about a specific disability, you have taken the first step in working with a child. Solit (1993) uses the case of Marie to describe how this knowledge background fits into the total scheme of planning a program for children with disabilities:

> The teacher learns that Marie has a moderate hearing loss, with no developmental or cognitive delays. Marie wears hearing aids. The audiologist taught the teacher how to check the hearing aid to ensure it is working. The teacher learns that the hearing aid will make sounds louder, but it will not necessarily clarify speech. The parents explain that Marie uses American Sign Language to communicate. The [principal] decides to find a volunteer who can sign to Marie, communicate with the teacher, and also be a role model for Marie. The teacher also receives release time to attend sign language classes.
>
> The audiologist explains how to adapt the classroom environment so there are less auditory distractions for Marie. The teacher learns that many aspects of the program do not need to change because Marie will benefit from the high quality . . . classroom that is already in place. (p. 133)

2. *Maximize interactions between children with disabilities and nondisabled children.* It is important for children living in a pluralistic society to develop relationships with children who experience a wide range of disabling conditions. That way, children will learn to accept differences at an early age. You can help in this regard by giving simple explanations about a child's disability when she or he comes to your classroom. Youngsters are curious; they want to know about a new child and will be satisfied with a short, open, honest explanation. ("Russell's legs don't work well, so he needs a wheelchair.") Encourage the children with disabilities to share their strengths. For example, Russell can help another child in a project that involves the use of his hands (such as building a diorama or drawing a picture) while nondisabled learners may assist Russell with his special needs. In his classroom, for example, Russell regularly joins his classmates on the playground for recess. One of their favorite games is kickball. To play, Russell selects a "designated kicker" to kick the ball for him; after it is kicked, he speeds around from base to base in his wheelchair. Social acceptance and cooperation help support students with diverse abilities.

3. *Individualize your program.* Start where the child is and plan a sequential program to encourage him or her to build one skill upon another. Visit classrooms where children with disabilities have been successfully included. Look for ways teachers individualize their instruction. How is peer interaction stimulated? Are parents involved in the classroom activities? Are peer questions about a child's disability answered openly and honestly?

4. *Assess your classroom environment.* Helping children with special needs feel comfortable in your classroom involves some critical considerations. Overall, the inclusive classroom should contain the same materials and activities suggested for general social studies programs but enhance these offerings with opportunities to meet the needs of children with disabilities. It helps to include photographs or pictures of people with disabilities participating with nondisabled people on the job or in a variety of other activities. Be sure the learning materials are accessible to all children. Some children will need Braille labels to help them locate things while others may require ramps to move from one area to another. Whatever the case, be sure to explain to the other children why these special adaptations have been made: "This ramp helps Francine get to the top level when she is in her wheelchair." Invite adults with disabilities to share their special talents and interests with your children. In short, the classroom should offer a safe environment where all children feel accepted, whatever their capabilities or limitations. Despite the fact that some adjustments must be made, each child should be enabled to gain skills and understanding in all areas and to reach his or her full potential.

5. *Choose books that help children learn about and appreciate exceptionality.* Many good children's books offer information about disabilities, explain difficulties youngsters with disabilities often encounter, and tell stories about people who serve as positive role models for children with disabilities. Marc Brown's *Arthur's Eyes* (Little, Brown), for example, tells of how a little boy learns to cope with teasing about his new eyeglasses. Ada B. Litchfield's *A Button in Her Ear* (Whitman) explains deafness and how hearing aids help children with hearing losses. Lucille Clifton's *My Friend Jacob* (Lothrop) portrays a relationship between a young boy and his older friend with a learning disability. Maxine B. Rosenberg's *My Friend Leslie* (Lothrop) is a photographic essay of a young girl with multiple disabilities.

Literature can be an important path to understanding and acceptance. This point can be illustrated clearly through this episode from the life of Helen Keller (1920), who lost her sight and hearing after a fever at the age of 19 months. The following high point in Keller's life occurs when her teacher, Anne Sullivan, places the hand of her then-7-year-old pupil under the spout of a pump:

> We walked down the path to the well-house, attracted by the fragrance of the honeysuckle with which it was covered. Someone was drawing water and my teacher placed my hand under the spout. As the cool stream gushed over one hand she spelled into the other the word water, first slowly, then rapidly. I stood still, my whole attention fixed upon the motions of her fingers. Suddenly I felt a misty consciousness as of something forgotten—a thrill of returning thought; and somehow the mystery of language was revealed to me. I knew then that "W-A-T-E-R" meant the wonderful cool something that was flowing over my hand. That living word awakened my soul, gave it light, hope, joy, set it free! (pp. 23–24)

Keep many types of stories available and use them to promote questions, conversations, and empathy for children with developmental disabilities.

Inclusion involves changes in attitudes, behaviors, and teaching styles. Plan your inclusive social studies program to fit your children's needs. No single chapter in a textbook can hope to give you a complete idea of the responsibilities involved in doing so, but if you truly want to be a standout teacher, you must begin with sensitivity to the world of all children.

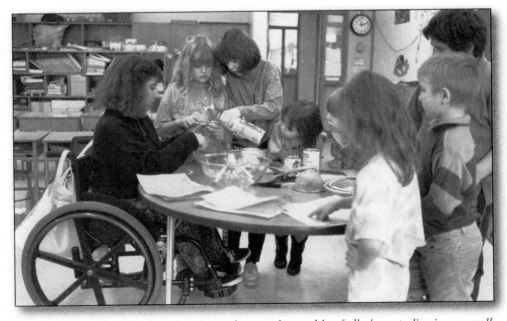

Social studies classrooms must be among the most honorable of all places to live in—a small society filled with understanding and appreciation for all.

Theme: Books About Children With Disabilities

C. S. Adler's **Eddie's Blue-Winged Dragon** (Putnam) is a first-person fantasy told by Eddie, an 11-year-old boy who attends a regular school but struggles to communicate clearly because of his cerebral palsy. Darrin, the school bully, immediately begins to harass him. Eddie buys a brass dragon that seems to have some powers to help him through his problems. After overcoming other challenges and intolerance by teachers and students alike, Eddie finally gains his self-respect by winning a school speech contest, speaking about his cerebral palsy.

Mary Riskind's **Apple Is My Sign** (Houghton Mifflin) is a historical novel about a 10-year-old boy who returns to his parents' apple farm for the holidays after his first term at a school for the deaf in Philadelphia. This touching story effectively portrays the special circumstances in the lives of children with hearing impairments.

Helen Keller's **Story of My Life** (Bantam Books) is an awe-inspiring autobiography written by Helen Keller when she was a 20-year-old student at Radcliffe University. Left deaf and blind at 19 months old by scarlet fever, she learned to read (in several languages) and even speak, eventually graduating with honors from Radcliffe in 1904. Accomplishing all of this is indeed

Gifted Children

Exceptionally talented or bright children were given little special attention in elementary schools prior to the 1970s. The general consensus was that these youngsters could do well with little or no help; their superior intelligence and advanced skills guaranteed success in whatever they chose to do. Sparse information, at best, described the specific needs of gifted students. To single out and offer special planning for these youngsters was considered by many to be elitist. "Why," people wondered, "should we channel extra money and resources into education for the gifted when they can learn so well on their own?" However, educators have now begun to realize the importance of accommodating gifted children's needs and agree that every child deserves a developmentally appropriate education, not just 'average' children and children with learning disabilities.

How will you know when you have an exceptionally gifted youngster in your class? What gifts and talents characterize this unique population? One way to begin answering these questions is to examine your children for exceptional characteristics:

1. *Verbal skills.*   Do they use advanced vocabulary, spontaneously create stories, modify language to the level of the person being spoken to, explain complex processes, influence the behavior of others, and exchange ideas and information fluently?

2. *Abstractions.*   Do they retain easily what they have heard or read?

3. *Power of concentration.*   Are they attentive to features of a new environment or experience? Do they become totally absorbed in an activity? Are they alert and observant? Do they respond quickly?

impressive, but the added challenge of overcoming her disabilities at a time when women faced many social barriers makes this story truly extraordinary.

Berniece Rabe's **Margaret's Moves** (Scholastic) is a story about a 9-year-old girl with spina bifida, who is confined to a wheelchair. She tries to earn money for a new, lightweight, faster "sportsmodel" chair so that she can speed around and keep up with her athletic brother.

Betsy Byars's **Summer of the Swans** (Puffin) gives readers insight on living and dealing with a child with mental impairment. Sara Godfrey is a young girl who lives in West Virginia with her aunt, an older sister, and brother, Charlie. Sara is having the worst summer of her life. She doesn't like the way she looks or acts, and she can't understand Charlie's neediness. This all changes when Charlie wanders off one night and Sara frantically searches for him.

TRY THIS

Read Betsy Byars's *Summer of the Swans.* Observe a classroom where a child with a mental impairment is learning. Take notes summarizing the behaviors of the child and the kinds of instructional strategies the teacher employs. Compare Charlie's behaviors and needs with the child you observe.

4. *Intellect.* Can they carry out complex instructions, focus on problems and deliberately seek solutions, store and recall information easily, memorize well and learn rapidly, and explain ideas in novel ways? Are they curious? Do they ask questions? Did they master academics at an earlier age? Do they have multiple interests and know about many things of which other children are unaware?

5. *Behavior.* Are they sensitive to the needs and feelings of other children and adults? Do they have strong feelings of self-confidence and influence others?

It makes sense for teachers of gifted children to follow the guidelines for establishing a personalized curriculum as described for children with disabilities. No single method will work with all gifted children; individual strengths and interests dictate varieties of approaches. As we consider special approaches, however, above all else, we must not remove childhood from the lives of gifted elementary school youngsters. The gifted youngster is a child first and should be treated like other children. Most 8-year-olds, for example, have similar interests whether they are gifted or not, but gifted children often show greater interest in digging deeper into something. Like their peers, gifted first graders will enjoy playing with airplanes and trucks but, while their peers may stop there, gifted youngsters will want to investigate them in more detail (e.g., how high airplanes fly or how diesel engines differ from gasoline engines).

The goal of working with gifted students is not to separate them from their classmates with materials and activities only they can use; rather, it is to provide enrichment and acceleration experiences within the classroom for all children. We must allow gifted students to grow to their fullest by building on their interests and talents in developmentally appropriate ways. Some general suggestions follow.

1. Gifted students require faster-paced instruction for skills- and content-based learning so they can move more rapidly through the curriculum.

2. Gifted students require more frequent use of inquiry and independent research projects that encourage independent learning.

3. Gifted students require more advanced materials—higher-level reading materials, computers, self-directed learning packets, and other more highly complex sources that allow students to explore topics in depth.

4. Gifted students require the reorganization of subject matter content so it allows them to explore issues across curricular areas and promotes higher-order thinking skills.

Multiple Intelligences and Talents

Children differ from the time they enter this world and grow increasingly more unique as they mature through childhood. They differ in physical appearance, emotional makeup, interests, likes, dislikes, and a myriad of other characteristics. They differ, also, in the way they learn. Any teacher with a deep interest in children can tell you that it is easy to see the degree to which their minds differ from one another and how important it is that teachers take these individual differences seriously. Observant teachers find that as children experience challenging and varying environments at school, they begin to demonstrate more specific kinds of intelligences and emerging talents. Although teachers have informally recognized these differences among children for years, formal theories of different kinds of intelligences are fairly new. One of the most recognizable of these theories has been the *theory of multiple intelligences*. This theory of human intelligence, developed by psychologist Howard Gardner (1983), suggests there are at least eight distinctive ways by which people learn about the world. He labels each of these ways a discrete intelligence:

- *Logical-mathematical intelligence.* Children with this strength are good problem solvers. They quickly discover logical patterns and enjoy numbers and counting. They appreciate principles of cause and effect. These students are curious, enjoy making predictions, and ask endless streams of questions. This intelligence is most often associated with scientific and mathematical thinking.

- *Linguistic intelligence.* Children with this strength are endowed with a mastery of language. They love the sound and rhythm of words and enjoy listening to, reading, and making up stories, poems, jokes, and riddles. They learn new vocabulary or a second language easily. These children are good at expressing themselves with words and are sensitive to the different functions of language.

- *Musical intelligence.* Children with this strength enjoy producing or listening to music and appreciate various forms of musical expressiveness. You will find them singing, humming, and moving with a constant stream of musical actions.

- *Visual-spatial intelligence.* Children with this strength can manipulate and create mental images to solve problems. They can draw and paint superbly, enjoy building things with a variety of construction materials, and have an easy time interpreting and constructing maps and models.

- *Bodily-kinesthetic intelligence.*   Children with this strength can coordinate their bodily movements and handle objects skillfully. They dance, run, jump, throw, catch, and climb better than their age mates. They enjoy making things with their hands and manipulate objects with great dexterity. These children want to move all the time.

- *Interpersonal intelligence.*   Children with this strength are outgoing and tuned into other people's feelings and emotions. They can recognize the moods and feelings of others, empathize with them, and respond appropriately. They understand other people and work effectively with them. These children appear to be "natural leaders."

- *Intrapersonal intelligence.*   Children with this strength are inner-directed. They understand things about themselves—their own strengths, weaknesses, and motivations. These children appear quiet and often prefer working alone. They have great confidence in their own ability to get things done.

- *Naturalist Intelligence.*   Children with this strength recognize flora and fauna, make other consequential distinctions in the natural world, and use their ability in hunting, farming, and the biological sciences.

Traditional schooling has heavily favored the verbal-linguistic and logical-mathematical intelligences, so Gardner suggests that we must modify our teaching approaches to better meet the needs of all students. The role of teachers is to identify their students' learning strengths and to help them learn through a variety of strategies such as puppetry, literature, model making, classroom demonstrations, songs, dance, plays, and group work.

Dynamic social studies teachers attempt to use as many of these intelligences as possible in the materials and activities they select for their students. By doing so, it is possible for each child to experience success in ways that build on individual strengths and also encourage strengths in new areas. These goals are achieved when teachers offer discovery activities that require children to solve problems, question and reason, or work with numbers (logical-mathematical intelligence). Children read a story, write down ideas in a journal, or dramatize a social studies event (linguistic intelligence). Children dance, march, and move in other creative ways to music, sing, or design a musical instrument (musical intelligence). Students examine pictures and study prints, paint a diorama, or map the route from their community to a location under study (visual-spatial intelligence). They make a model of something with their hands or play physically active games (bodily-kinesthetic intelligence). Children work together in cooperative groups, solve problems together, or share ideas freely (interpersonal intelligence). Students are given opportunities to express their own unique ideas and emotions, spend time alone planning how to approach a specific learning situation, or pursue their personal interests through individualized learning experiences (intrapersonal intelligence). And, they form connections with nature, posing their own questions and pursuing their own answers about the intriguing mysteries and challenges of the outdoor world (naturalist intelligence).

Gardner insists that all eight intelligences are required for individuals to function productively in society. Therefore, teachers should consider each discrete intelligence as being equally important while building children's learning opportunities. Provide occasions to experiment with writing, to explore attractively displayed books, to participate in creative dramatics, to participate in group discussions, to sing songs and move rhythmically, and to explore the outdoor environment. Build on children's interests and incorporate projects and activities that include multi-intelligence experiences.

It is important to observe children carefully to discover the kinds of intelligences they favor as they work and play. Students often do particularly well in one area and exhibit no outstanding ability in the others. As areas of strength are revealed, build on them in a responsive and supportive way. Naturally, every daily social studies lesson will not lend itself to the use of each intelligence, but all should be in plain sight regularly throughout the school year. All children should be given many opportunities to flaunt their intelligence, whether approaching and solving problems, participating in hands-on activities, taking part in individual or group projects, or uncovering and recalling information. Each child has special strengths and deserves the opportunity to use them in a nurturing, supportive environment. Dynamic social studies instruction requires the selection of activities that work across a great number of children's intelligences.

Gender

The image each of us acquires about our masculine or feminine characteristics and the various behaviors and attitudes normally associated with them is called *gender identity*, or *gender typing*. Like most other aspects of child development, gender identity emerges from dynamic interactions of biological and environmental forces. For example, there are unquestionably basic genetic and physiological differences between males and females; biology sets the stage for gender identification. However, biology alone does not determine gender-specific behavior. From birth, many families begin to show their children in subtle ways exactly what it means to be masculine or feminine. For example, little girls are most often dressed in something pink and frilly, whereas boys are routinely clad in blue. Boy babies are commonly referred to by such terms as "big" or "tough," whereas girls are quite often described as "pretty" or "sweet." From these early days on, choices of toys, clothing, and hairstyles supplement verbal messages to influence gender identity.

Through such environmental power, children perfunctorily acquire a gender frame of reference that explains what it means to be a boy or girl. This happens at about the age of 2; from that point on, children work hard to fit into their gender roles. By age 5 or 6, they have already learned much of the stereotypical behavior of their gender. "Appropriate" behaviors are reinforced throughout the early years of life by internalizing the attitudes and responses of such environmental influences as family, relatives, peers, and the media. In other words, little girls who are rewarded for playing with dolls, read books about girls playing with dolls, and see girls playing with dolls on television will be more likely to play with dolls than with trucks. Likewise, little boys who have similar experiences with trucks will be more likely to play with trucks than with dolls. It would seem, then, that if gender-specific behaviors are influenced by such environmental phenomena, children raised in bias-free environments would not exhibit a preference for stereotypically gender-specific toys. However, a phenomenon referred to as *developmental sexism* seems to crop up despite our most systematic attempts to shape a nonsexist environment. This means that young children grow to be enormously sexist in their perception of gender roles and choice of play activities—most boys choose to engage themselves as cowboys while girls play house—even if they have been brought up in a nonbiased environment.

This concept of developmental sexism is supported by Kohlberg's (1992) idea of *gender constancy*. That is, children learn early in life that they permanently belong to a category called "boy" or "girl"—their gender cannot change. Once children grasp the concept that they cannot be transformed from girl to boy and back again, they organize the world into "girl" or "boy" categories and become powerfully attached to their gender. I remember watching one warm spring day as Teddy, a kindergartner, proudly skidded around the playground on his sister's outgrown pink roller skates. "You're a-a gir-l! You're a-a gir-l!" chanted his friend Johnny in sing-song fashion. Each time Johnny finished his melodic rhyme, Teddy angrily retorted, "No, I'm not! No, I'm not!" but Johnny persisted: "You're a girl 'cause you have pink roller skates. You're a-a gir-l!" Johnny continued his taunts until Teddy was reduced to tears. Such a strong attachment to one's gender continues to grow through the early elementary grades, cementing the peer solidarity that influences behaviors compatible with society's expectations for males and females.

Gender-role stereotypes seem to be markedly decreasing in our elementary schools, but they continue to be a problem. Although books appear to be more fair and inclusive than in the past, Sadker, Sadker, and Klein (1991) believe that teachers prefer to read the books they grew up with; many of these older books represent highly traditional gender roles. Therefore, even today, the influence of sexist books can be found in some classrooms.

In addition to problems with books, Sadker and Sadker (1986) suggest that girls are shortchanged during classroom interactions. Elementary school teachers ask boys more questions, give them more precise feedback, criticize them more frequently, and give them more time to respond. The teacher's reaction may be positive, negative, or neutral, but the golden rule appears to be that boys get the most attention from teachers in elementary school classrooms.

Additionally, the American Association of University Women (AAUW) has reported

[T]here is clear evidence that the educational system is not meeting girls' needs. Girls and boys enter school roughly equal in measured ability. In some measures of school readiness, such as fine motor control, girls are ahead of boys. Twelve years later, girls have fallen behind their male classmates in key areas such as higher-level mathematics and measures of self-esteem. (1992, p. 2)

Although most of the research into gender bias in schools has been centered on the unfair treatment of girls, Campbell (1996) cautions that,

> It is boys who lack role models for the first six years of schooling, particularly African American, Latino, and Asian boys. While young, European American girls benefit from their female-centered primary school experience, children of color—particularly boys— fail. It is boys who encounter the most conflicts and receive the most punishments in school and most often get placed in special education and remedial programs. (p. 113)

Gender stereotyping can be tied to many influences and conditions, but teachers must take a positive role in recognizing bias and replacing it with equitable expectations for all children. This means eliminating one's own biases of gender-associated behavior and stereotyped notions about gender roles. This can be done by providing males and females with appropriate instruction and by avoiding gender-role stereotyping. Some guidelines to avoid sexism in teaching follow.

1. *Avoid stereotyping masculine and feminine roles.*   Examine ways you might be limiting the options open to boys and girls. During class discussions, for example, many teachers attempt to reason with young children to create more objective attitudes about gender roles. When a child says, "Only boys can grow up to be truck drivers," teachers are tempted to reply, "That's not true. Women can be truck drivers, too." This approach often fails. The young child's way of classifying the world into male and female is new and not open to exceptions. A child may even become upset that the teacher fails to see the world in the same light and defend his or her case even more strongly. We can compound the problem, therefore, by trying to reason with a child. This presents us with an interesting dilemma: We want children to experience a nonsexist world, but they tend to resist our efforts of objectivity. What can we do?

First, let the children know you understand and accept their unique system of trying to make sense of the world. Their willingness to come to you and share their excitement about new discoveries should always be accepted with openness and sincerity. You do, however, have a responsibility to help them understand that choices should be open to each person, regardless of gender. In responding to the truck driver comment, you might say, "I know you've never seen a woman truck driver before, so it's hard to understand that women can drive large trucks, too." However, trying to reason with a child through comments such as, "It's okay for women to be truck drivers, too. Many women are very good at driving large trucks," often elicits a response such as, "Well, they shouldn't be!"

Stereotyping should be avoided at all costs. This advice extends not only into how females are featured, but also into whether men are depicted in traditionally male roles and careers.

2. *Use gender-free language whenever possible.*   Through words and actions, teachers assume the position of a positive role model. Be sensitive to your choice of masculine terms to refer to all people; for example, *police officer* replaces *policeman*, *firefighter* replaces *fireman*, and *mail carrier* replaces *mailman*. If your children use terms such as fireman frequently, begin a discussion with a comment such as, "Saying the word *fireman* makes it sound like only men fight fires. Do you think that's true?" Then introduce the word *firefighter* and point out that men and women (and boys and girls) can do the same kinds of jobs. Additionally, be aware of how actions can convey ideas of gender-role coequality. For example, the children may learn to interpret gender roles less rigidly if they see their teachers, male and female, displaying characteristics typically associated as either masculine or feminine—for example, being assertive and forceful or sensitive and warm depending on the situation.

3. *Make sure your classroom materials present an honest view of males and females.* Just as you lead young children toward understanding the idea of equality through your words and actions, the activities and materials you choose for your classroom should resist gender stereotyping. Books like *Heather Hits Her First Home Run* by Phyllis Hacken Johnson (Lollipop Power Books) and Charlotte Zolotow's *William's Doll* (Harper & Row) are sensitive books that address stereotypes. *William's Doll* portrays a situation many little boys face:

> William would like a doll so he could play with it like his friend Nancy does with her doll. At the very thought of a little boy with a doll, his brother and friend call him creep and sissy. William's father buys him a basketball and a train, instead of a doll. William becomes a very good basketball player and he enjoys the train set, but he still longs for a doll. Finally, when William's grandmother comes for a visit, she buys him a doll and explains to his father that having a doll will be good practice for him when he grows up and has a real baby to love. (Raines & Canady, 1989, p. 50)

Teachers who wish to build a good classroom collection of gender-fair books will need to look for books that show children and other people engaged in a variety of activities, regardless of gender.

A program offering opportunities for both sexes to participate in positive classroom experiences should transcend obsolete sex-role expectations such as boys taking the lead when mathematics skills are required, and girls when sewing or cooking are needed for a project. Encourage the boys to wash the art table after completing a salt-and-flour relief map and the girls to hammer the nails needed to hold together a model clipper ship. If this doesn't happen freely, discuss the situation with your children. Say, "I notice that in most social studies projects the boys build the model. This seems to exclude the girls. Why do you think that is happening?" Invite equal access to activities by encouraging children to engage in a wide range of experiences that are free of gender stereotypes.

4. *Balance the contributions of men and women in the social studies program.* All students should be exposed to the contributions of women as well as men throughout history. Students are being cheated of a wealth of information about the majority of the world's population when women are not included as an integral part of the curriculum. Banks (1994) suggests that women can be virtually ignored in written history. Citing the Montgomery, Alabama, bus boycott of 1955 as an example, Banks maintains that most textbook accounts emphasize the work of men such as Martin Luther King, Jr., and Ralph D. Abernathy, or organizations headed by men, but virtually ignore the work of women. He uses the memoirs of Jo Ann Gibson Robinson, president of the Women's Political Council of Montgomery, as an example. The Council was started in 1946 to "provide leadership, support, and improvement in the black community and to work for voting rights for African Americans" (Banks, 1994, p. 6). The Council received numerous complaints concerning bus driver offenses against African Americans who were asked to give up their seats on crowded buses to whites. On December 1, 1955, Rosa Parks was arrested for refusing to give up her seat. Disgusted by such hostile encounters with bus drivers, the Council distributed leaflets that called for a boycott of city buses. Referring to Rosa Parks, Robinson's leaflet read in part: This woman's case will come up on Monday. We are, therefore, asking every Negro to stay off the buses Monday in protest of the arrest and trial. Don't ride the buses to work, to town, to school, or anywhere else on Monday (Garrow, 1987).

Although most textbook accounts credit King and Abernathy for the Montgomery bus boycott, plans to end bus segregation with a boycott were actually instituted 2 years earlier, in 1953, by Robinson's Council. The Parks case in 1955 just happened to be the right time to implement the boycott. The situation seems to be improving in recent years, but the work of historically significant females such as Jo Ann Gibson Robinson still must find its way into our nation's textbooks. This does not mean we must sit back and wait for that day; it will take a great deal of scholarly effort to uncover their stories, but the experiences of women from all walks of life must be highlighted in the social studies curriculum.

Schools that foster positive gender roles will help children value the likenesses and differences in themselves, thereby taking an important step toward alleviating the damage resulting from long-ingrained patterns of sexism in our society. It is this unconditional positive regard for children that lies at the heart of social studies education.

Social Class

The term used by the U.S. Bureau of the Census and by sociologists to describe the variations of wealth and power among individuals and families is *socioeconomic status* (SES). SES is normally determined by studying such economic factors as occupation, income, and level of education. Of all the forms of inequality affecting our children's education, SES could be the most powerful; it frequently surmounts the effects of race and gender. For example, although upper-SES Hispanics share customs and traditions with low-SES Hispanic/Latino families, they will be more likely to interact with upper-SES families of other ethnic groups than they will with Hispanic/Latino families at other class levels.

Research over the past 20 years has indicated a number of strong relationships between SES and school performance. A consistent connection is that low-SES students of all ethnic groups exhibit lower average standardized test scores, receive lower grades in school, and leave school earlier than high-SES students. Several factors explain the lower school achievement of low-SES students, such as poor health care for mother and child, limited resources, family stress, interruptions in schooling, and discrimination. Garcia (1991) cautions that research in this area is meager, but lists other explanations for lower achievement among low-SES children:

1. *Low expectations—low self-esteem.*   Low-SES students often speak ungrammatically, come to school in old or dirty clothing, frequently are poorly groomed, and are often confused by the school's punishment and reward systems. Since most teachers find it difficult to identify with these characteristics, they often conclude that low-SES students are not good at schoolwork. They have reduced expectations for low-SES students, thereby contributing to phenomena called the *self-fulfilling prophecy* (tending to behave as others expect) and the *looking-glass self* ("I am what I think you think I am"). When teachers associate such reduced expectations with socioeconomic status, discriminatory practices surface and low-SES students are denied access to equal educational opportunity.

2. *Learned helplessness.*   Some children from low-SES homes come to school from communities where dropout rates of 50 percent are not uncommon. Since their relatives and friends leave school early, many low-SES students are not motivated to go on. However, poor but stable families often value education and prepare their students well for school, viewing school as the best place to end their cycle of poverty. Teachers must understand that poverty is not the child's fault. Their challenge as teachers is to help low-SES students overcome the effects of poverty.

3. *Resistance cultures.*   Teachers, especially in inner-city schools serving poor Hispanic/Latino American, African American, or Native American families, will find that some children come to school as part of a "resistance culture," members of which oppose upper- and middle-SES values, including school. This opposition can take the form of willfully breaking school rules, minimizing the value of achievement, and attaching more importance to manual rather than mental work. Students who accept any characteristics considered "middle class" or "white," including behaviors that would make them successful in school, are thought of as "selling out" their minority or peer group. To address this challenge, teachers must interact with the minority groups represented in the school population to determine the most effective instructional experiences for their children.

4. *Tracking.*   A significant factor contributing to poor academic performance among low-SES students is that they are usually placed in low-ability groups or classes, where they are taught differently. Teachers see these children as less able academically and often use teacher-dominated strategies calling for lots of worksheets, rote memorization, and passivity. Additionally, less-experienced or less-successful teachers are generally assigned to the low-ability groups. After reviewing the research on the effects of tracking, Gamoran (1992) has concluded that "grouping and tracking rarely add to overall achievement in a school, but they often contribute to inequality. . . . Typically, it means that high-track students are gaining and low-track students are falling further behind" (p. 13).

What can be done? Slavin (1987) suggests that tracking in elementary schools must be stopped because teachers often fail to match students' needs with instruction. Tracking will continue to have no positive effect on achievement until teachers use it to provide specialized instruction to children having specific needs: "For ability grouping to be effective at the elementary level, it must create true homogeneity on the specific skill being taught, and instruction must be closely tailored to students' levels of performance" (Slavin, 1987, p. 323).

Therefore, since ability grouping rarely contributes to positive academic achievement, it should be eliminated or curtailed. If it is used, students should be grouped according to skills they need, and, when instruction is completed, the group should be disbanded.

AFTERWORD

Good social studies teachers always impress me with how affectionately they talk about the special moments they have shared with their students. They prize the look on children's faces when they learn something new, the excitement shown by parents as their children make progress during the year, just being with children and sharing a common bond of affection, and the children's unspoiled enthusiasm. Such experiences revitalize teachers and can strengthen their commitment to the profession. Many teachers find great joy in the candid individual expressions that mark each child's uniqueness: "Henry came up to me holding his finger as if it were hurt. When I asked him what was the matter, he replied, 'An elephant bit my finger,' and then turned and walked away!"

These are the special moments of satisfaction awaiting a teacher of elementary school children. You will find extraordinary joy, affection, excitement, and personal satisfaction as you meet challenges each day.

Children thrive under good teachers who delight in children being who they are. These teachers adapt the social studies classroom to meet every child's cultural, linguistic, and individual needs. This includes providing the child with the time, opportunities, resources, understanding, and affection to achieve the important goals of social studies education. To affirm individual differences, teachers must eliminate bias from the elementary school environment. Every child must know he or she is appreciated and respected by the teacher and needs experiences that reflect an understanding and appreciation for individual and cultural differences. These experiences are not only memorable and pleasurable, but they also last a lifetime—they help make our world.

REFERENCES

Alwin, D., & Thornton, A. (1984). Family origins and schooling processes. Early versus late influence of parental characteristics. *American Sociological Review, 49,* 784–802.

American Association of University Women. (1992). *How schools shortchange girls.* Washington, DC: Author.

Arends, R. I. (1991). *Learning to teach.* New York: McGraw-Hill.

Banks, J. A. (1993). Multicultural education: Characteristics and goals. In J. Banks & C. McGee Banks (Eds.), *Multicultural education: Issues and perspectives* (pp. 2–26). Boston: Allyn & Bacon.

Banks, J. A. (1994). Transforming the mainstream curriculum. *Educational Leadership, 51*, 4–8.

Campbell, D. E. (1996). *Choosing democracy: A practical guide to multicultural education*. Upper Saddle River, NJ: Merrill/Prentice Hall.

Chandler, P. A. (1994). *A place for me: Including children with special needs in early care and education settings*. Washington, DC: National Association for the Education of Young Children.

Clark, L., DeWolf, S., & Clark, C. (1992). Teaching teachers to avoid having culturally assaultive classrooms. *Young Children, 47*, 5.

Crawford, J. (1992). *Hold your tongue: Bilingualism and the politics of English only*. Reading, MA: Addison-Wesley.

Florio-Ruane, S. (1989). Social organization of classes and schools. In M. Reynolds (Ed.), *Knowledge base for beginning teachers* (pp. 163–172). Oxford: Pergamon.

Freeman, D. E., & Freeman, Y. S. (1993). Strategies for promoting the primary languages of all students. *The Reading Teacher, 46*, 552–558.

Gamoran, A. (1992). Is ability grouping equitable? *Education Leadership, 50*, 11–17.

Garcia, R. L. (1991). *Teaching in a pluralistic society: Concepts, models, and strategies*. New York: HarperCollins.

Gardner, H. (1983). *Frames of mind: The theory of multiple intelligences*. New York: Basic Books.

Garrow, D. J. (1987). *The Montgomery bus boycott and the women who started it: The memoir of Jo Ann Gibson Robinson*. Knoxville: The University of Tennessee Press.

Gay, G. (2000). *Culturally responsive teaching: Theory, research, & practice*. New York: Teachers College Press.

Gollnick, D. M., & Chinn, P. C. (2002). *Multicultural education in a pluralistic society* (6th ed.). New York: Macmillan.

Grant, C. A., & Gomez, M. L. (1996). *Making schooling multicultural: Campus and classroom*. Upper Saddle River, NJ: Prentice Hall.

Jones, E., & Derman-Sparks, L. (1992). Meeting the challenge of diversity. *Young Children, 47*, 12–17.

Keller, H. (1920). *The story of my life*. Garden City, NY: Doubleday.

Kohlberg, L. (1992). In G. R. Lefrancois, *Of children*. Belmont, CA: Wadsworth.

Krug, M. (1976). *The melting of the ethnics*. Bloomington, IL: Phi Delta Kappa.

Perez, J. (1993). Viva la differencia. *First Teacher, 14*, 24–25.

Perez, S. A. (1994). Responding differently to diversity. *Childhood Education, 70*, 151–153.

Public Law 101-476, October 30, 1990, Stat. 1103.

Raines, S. C., & Canady, R. J. (1992). *Story s-t-r-e-t-c-h-e-r-s: Activities to expand children's favorite books*. Mt. Ranier, MD: Gryphon House.

Sadker, D., & Sadker, M. (1986). Sexism in the classroom: From grade school to graduate school. *Phi Delta Kappan, 68*, 512.

Sadker, M., Sadker, D., & Klein, S. (1991). The issue of gender in elementary and secondary education. In G. Grant (Ed.), *Review of research in education*. Washington, DC: American Educational Research Association.

Sadker, M., Sadker, D., & Steindam, S. (1989). Gender equity and educational reform. *Educational Leadership, 46*, 44–47.

Scarcella, R. (1990). *Teaching language minority students in the multicultural classroom*. Upper Saddle River, NJ: Prentice Hall.

Slavin, R. E. (1987). Ability grouping and achievement in elementary schools: A best-evidence synthesis. *Review of Educational Research, 57*, 293–336.

Solit, G. (1993). A place for Marie: Guidelines for the integration process. In K. M. Paciorek (Ed.), *Early childhood education 94/95*. Guilford, CT: Dushkin Publishing.

Stearns, P. N. (1996). Multiculturalism and the American educational tradition. In C. A. Grant & M. L. Gomez (Eds.), *Making schooling multicultural: Campus and classroom* (pp. 17–33). Upper Saddle River, NJ: Merrill.

U.S. Bureau of the Census. (1990). *Current population reports. Series P-20*. Washington, DC: U.S. Government Printing Office.

U.S. Office of Education. (1977). *Education of handicapped children*. Federal Register (part 2). Washington, DC: Department of Health, Education and Welfare.

Wolery, M., Strain, P. S., & Bailey, D. B. (1992). Reaching potentials of children with special needs. In S. Bredekamp & T. Rosegrant, *Reaching potentials: Appropriate curriculum and assessment for young children, Vol. 1*. Washington, DC: National Association for the Education of Young Children.

Wolery, M., & Wilbers, J. S. (Eds.). (1994). *Including children with special needs in early childhood programs*. Washington, DC: National Association for the Education of Young Children.

Wolfle, J. (1989). The gifted preschooler: Developmentally different but still 3 or 4 years old. *Young Children, 44*, 42.

Woolfolk, A. E. (1995). *Educational psychology*. Boston: Allyn & Bacon.

Zangwell, I. (1909). The melting pot (A Play). Quoted in D. M. Gollnick & P. C. Chinn (1983), *Multicultural education in a pluralistic society*. St. Louis: Mosby.

Young Historians:
Coming Face to Face With the Past

WHAT DOES HISTORY LOOK LIKE?

Eleven-year-old Heather exploded into her house after school shouting, "I can't wait to start it. This is going to be so cool!" The "it" Heather was so excited about was a history assignment to make a family tree showing key family members and their relationships to her. Heather's teacher, Olivia Svensson, felt the project would highlight the diversity of her classroom as her young historians explored their family roots.

To begin the family tree project, Ms. Svensson read to her fifth graders Ann Douglas's book, *The Family Tree Detective: Cracking the Case of Your Family's Story* (Maple Tree Press). Appropriate for children 9 to 12 years old, the book explains in clear and interesting terms how students can get started researching their family trees through interview techniques, data collection and storage, and ways to present the family story once it is put together.

Ms. Svensson was careful not yet to overwhelm her students with examples of family trees filled with details—names, dates and place of birth. She explained that it is more helpful to "draw in the students by taking advantage of their natural curiosity. I like to start by showing them personal artifacts and photographs from the past, or teach them games from years gone by. If children find that family history is fun, they will be eager to plunge in."

Acting on her own advice, Ms. Svensson used her personal family history as a model. She showed family artifacts and photos, referring to the family members from the past as her "ancestors." She located on a large world map where her ancestors came from, described some unique family traditions, and shared a favorite family heirloom: "I remember when I was a child your age how I loved to go through my mom's hope chest. She had filled it with all kinds of mementos from as far back as my great-grandparents. The chest contained memorabilia like photographs, clothing, and

83

old toys, as well as school items like report cards and special projects. Each keepsake had special importance for my mom and our family. The items may not have been worth much money, but they were important to our family in other ways."

Then, holding up a fine-looking doll for all to see, Ms. Svensson continued: "Here is a story to illustrate my point. This is my great-grandmother Julia's doll. It is a porcelain doll that was made in Sweden during the 1890s. The doll was given to my great-grandmother in 1903 when she was just 7 years old. After her oldest sister got married and moved away, the doll became Julia's best friend. Years later, after Julia married, her own daughters loved to play with the doll so much that sometime during the 1930s, my great-grandmother Julia sadly put the broken doll into a box. In time Julia's two daughters, Karin and Olga, raised their own families and everyone seemed to have forgotten about the broken doll in the box. It wasn't until after my great-grandmother Julia's funeral in 1972 that my mother, Emma, found the box of doll parts, and questions about its history came flooding out. She brought the box home and showed it to me, explaining what she uncovered about the doll's history. My mom was broken hearted that she had never before seen the mislaid doll and that she had never heard it's story from any of her ancestors. Carefully, she placed the tattered cardboard box containing the damaged doll into her hope chest. Years later, I had the doll restored, and now it proudly sits in a child's rocker in my living room. I make sure that my family knows the story of great-grandmother Julia's doll and of its place in our family's history."

Next, Ms. Svensson showed the students her family tree, tracing the generations involved in her story of the porcelain doll. Using Ms. Svensson's family tree as a model, the children were then assigned to complete their own family trees. Ms. Svensson passed out to each child a sheet of paper with a drawing of a tree covered with stategically placed apples (see Figure 3–1). She directed each child to write her or his complete name near the top of the tree trunk; and their siblings' names beneath theirs on the trunk. Next, the children were to take the family tree charts home and fill in each apple with the names and birthplaces of parents, grandparents, and great-grandparents. Again, using her own family tree as a model, Ms. Svensson demonstrated how to complete the assignment. To culminate the project, students were asked to bring to school a family artifact ("special family treasure") and tell a story of its significance to their families.

As an important note, teachers like Ms. Svensson realize that family tree assignments can be extremely difficult for children whose families have been touched by adoption, divorce, death of a parent, and blended families. The very idea of a family tree can raise questions of belonging, relatedness, divided loyalty, confusion, and embarrassment. As a result, many youngsters may struggle with fitting, or even refusing to fit, their various familial associations into the standard format of a family tree. Some children may be satisfied to include only their current family in family trees. Others will think only about their birth-family members. Ms. Svensson anticipated these possibilities, so she made sure to telephone the parents of children who might have difficulties before she sent home the family tree charts. The parents were appreciative of her consideration. One set of adoptive parents encouraged their daughter to research her birth family, while a blended family refused its child permission to participate in the family tree project. Students and their families have a right to choose how they want to construct their family tree, as they often have a few different options. If their

FIGURE 3–1
Family Tree

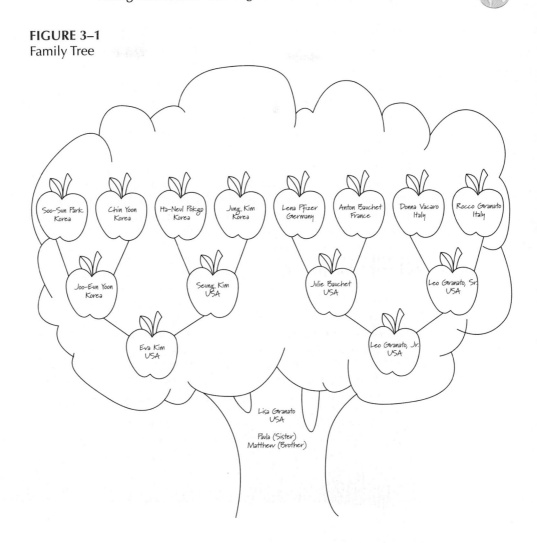

parents are divorced and students now have a stepparent(s), they may want to make two trees, or only half a tree (Mom's side, for example). You might also give them the option of including "common law" marriages, boyfriends, or girlfriends.

Ms. Svensson went on to explain: "All of your families come from other countries and have interesting stories to tell. We will learn about your families by interviewing them just like newspaper and television reporters do!" Ms. Svensson clarified that interviewing is a good way to learn new information and that most interviews are based on who, what, when, where, and why questions. Together, the students came up with a list of five possible questions that might help them better understand their families. Ms. Svensson recorded the students' suggestions on the chalkboard:

Where did your family originally come from?
Why did your family come to the United States?

When did your family move to the United States?
What are some favorite holidays/games/foods/activities your family enjoys?
What are some customs unique to your culture or family?
Do you have a favorite family story that you would like to share?

Children shared the results with each other upon completion of their research project. They compared their family trees and noticed how the structure of each tree was the same, but the composition differed in each case. To summarize, the children talked about why family trees are important for preserving family history. The family trees were displayed in the classroom during the autumn open house.

Next, the students took turns presenting their family artifacts and reading from a "museum card" the story of each artifact's family significance. Heather, the energized student from the start of this example, carried out a great deal of detailed research about her family and read this report about a Confederate Army brass spur that she brought in as her artifact.

My branch of the Campbell family migrated to the New World in 1839. Magnus Campbell came to Charleston, South Carolina, from Inverness, located in the Scottish Highlands. He stayed in Charleston for about a year. He then joined his older brother Brendan who had lived near Atlanta since 1828. Magnus Campbell was a farmer, and he had seven children, including three boys who were in the Confederate Army. One of these, Robert Campbell (1834–1865) was in the Confederate Infantry. He was killed at the Battle of New Hope Church, near Atlanta. Robert had three children—a girl who died as an infant, another girl, and a boy. Robert's son, Keith Harvey Campbell (1864–1947), was my great-great-grandfather.

Likewise, 23 of the 24 students came to the front of the class, presented a family artifact, and read about its significance from a "museum card." Many children had artifacts from World War II, while others brought items such as sports memorabilia, childhood toys, and family photographs. The class sat spellbound as each artifact was shared, and students asked spontaneous questions about each.

To bring the experience to a smooth close, Ms. Svensson led a discussion of how learning about other families and their traditions is not only interesting but rewarding as well. She told of a time when something she learned about another family's traditions became a part of her own life: "When I was a little girl, we lived next door to a family who came to this country from Italy. Among many other things, I learned of a traditional custom where Italian families name their first-born son after his father's father (the baby's paternal grandfather). My husband and I named our first son Michael because that was the name of his father's father. Even though both my husband and I have our roots in Sweden, we chose to name our son just like many Italian families do!" The class enjoyed sharing the interesting things they had learned about their own families and talking about what they had learned about their classmates. One of the greatest benefits of this experience, Ms. Svensson says enthusiastically, is the sense of community it builds in the classroom.

Ms. Svensson bases her overall approach to teaching history on a conviction that this subject is not restricted to memorizing "who did what to whom, when, and where" or to an outline of chronological events commonly found in textbooks. She believes history can be found in hope chests, museums, and newspapers. It can be found in a box of old receipts; in games children play; in stories people tell; in paintings, clothes, tools, furniture, books, letters, and diaries. Wherever we look, we can find clues to our past. Ms. Svensson wants her students to know that history is not just a list of names and dates, but a story that tells of life in other times.

Unfortunately, not all children experience history like Ms. Svensson's students. When asked to share their feelings about history, many children echo Henry Ford's sentiment that history is "bunk." They don't like history because they say it is boring. Ms. Svensson, however, helps to steer clear of this aversion to history by meeting the goals of historical study in a much more inspired way. Her young historians learn history, but the part they like best is the "story" of history. Ms. Svensson's history is today's history.

The National Standards for History (National Center for History in the Schools, 1996) reinforces Ms. Svensson's convictions. This influential document proclaims history—along with literature and the arts—as the most enriching studies in which elementary school students can be engaged, because "History connects each child with his or her roots and develops a sense of personal belonging in the great sweep of human experience" (p. 2).

WHAT IS HISTORY?

Simply put, *history* is regarded as a *narrative* (story or description) of the past. Anything that has a past has a history—and a story. People who study the past to determine what happened, how it happened, and why it happened are called *historians*. Connecting these two thoughts, I like to refer to elementary school students engaged in getting to the bottom of the mysteries of the past as *young historians*. Young historians, like all historians, look at the past as a puzzle to be solved. They ask questions of the past and look for answers in the evidence left by people who lived before them.

Historians, then, study the past by examining the objects and documents that have somehow survived the years. The approach they use is commonly referred to as the *historical method*, which generally entails three separate responsibilities: (1) locating pertinent information about a past event, (2) examining the informational sources for accuracy, and (3) organizing this information into a well-constructed historical narrative.

To assemble information about the past, historians seek out evidence from many sources, both written and nonwritten. Written sources include books, journals, almanacs, letters, diaries, songs, speeches, poems, court records, cookbooks, traveler's reports, advertisements, memoirs, government publications, land surveys, account books, and campaign slogans. They include gravestones, old calendars, posters, maps—anything with writing on it. However, written sources go back only to about 3000 B.C. when the Sumerians developed a pictographic type of writing known as *cuneiform*. Writing made it possible for people to keep records, write poems and stories, or inscribe a treaty—all potential sources of information for historians. History before the development of writing is called *prehistory*.

Nonwritten sources include *physical artifacts*, such as tools, weapons, jewelry, machines, toys, uniforms, masks, utensils, furniture, momuments, buildings, clothing, photographs, statues, or cookware; *visual images*, such as photographs, video, paintings, sculpture, and cave drawings; and *oral and audio histories*, such as a culture's oral tradition—stories such as folktales and myths that have been passed down from generation to generation by word of mouth and live interviews or audio recordings.

Written and nonwritten clues that were produced at the same time an event took place are called *primary sources*. Evidence communicated by someone at another time who did not witness the actual event is called a *secondary source*. For example, a videotape of Martin Luther King delivering his famous "I Have a Dream" speech is considered a primary source, while a magazine story describing the speech is a secondary source. Secondary sources include, but are not limited to, textbooks, encyclopedias, websites, informational books, and newspaper or magazine articles that do not give firsthand accounts. Clearly, primary sources are much more helpful to historians. Good historians, however, combine the use of a wide range of primary sources with a careful inspection of useful secondary sources to explain an event from the past. That is a goal for teaching our young historians, too.

Are you a good historian? Read the following sources of historical evidence. Decide which can be classified as primary sources and which as secondary sources. Be careful; some of these can be tricky!

A. Looking at pictures of Korean artifacts depicted in the book *Things Korean* by O-Young Lee (Tuttle)

B. Studying a photo of John F. Kennedy, Jr. (John-John) saluting as JFK's casket passes by

C. Reading a diary kept by Pvt. Andrew Bates, a soldier in the Union Army

D. Looking up information about the Cherokee nation in the *World Book Encyclopedia*

E. Reading the text of a speech delivered by Elizabeth Cady Stanton at a women's rally in Seneca Falls, New York, on July 19, 1848, recognizing the need for women's rights

I'm sure you selected the primary sources as B, C, and E. As a good historian, you will certainly know what kinds of sources are available to you and where you can find exciting sources that can help make history come alive.

The historical method begins with a historian's attempt to use primary and secondary sources to unlock mysteries about the past. But, because no evidence from the past is self-revealing—the evidence can't talk or communicate directly—it is open to interpretation. Therefore, we say history is *subjective*. A historian studies the evidence, examines it for accuracy, and then pieces it together to the best of her or his ability as a written narrative. Because this is an extremely delicate process, our views of history are constantly changing as new findings are uncovered and revised interpretations of old evidence are made. Take, for example, the story of Heinrich Schliemann.

When Schliemann was a young boy, he enjoyed listening to and reading all kinds of stories. Among his favorites were Greek myths and legends. The gods and goddesses were most interesting to Heinrich, particularly in stories where they took sides with the Greeks during the Trojan War (around 1250 B.C.). Historians first learned about the Trojan War from the *Iliad* and the *Odyssey*, two of the best-known epic poems of all time. Homer, a blind Greek poet, is thought to have composed these poems about 750 B.C., about 500 years after the fall of Troy. It is said he based his poems on oral stories that had been passed down through the generations.

When Schliemann was growing up, most historians believed that Homer's story of Troy's burning was just a myth. Because the story mixed the exploits of gods and goddesses with those of human heroes, it seemed to have no authentic historical base. But Heinrich Schliemann was not convinced; he thought Troy really existed. Schliemann had an opportunity to test his conviction when, as an adult, he visited a location in northwestern Asia Minor to investigate stories of buried cities that matched Homer's description of Troy. After much searching, he eventually found a huge mound of earth close to the Aegean Sea, an area where the ancient city of Troy was believed to have once stood. Schliemann dug into the earth and discovered that the site had been the location of several cities, each built upon the other as the previous city had been destroyed—nine separate cities altogether. Archaeologists rushed to the site and used their special methods and equipment to study the area. To Schliemann's surprise and joy, they found that charred wood and other evidence suggested that the city of Troy actually did stand at this location. Archaeologists believed that the Troy made famous by Homer was the city found in the seventh layer of Schliemann's mound. By pursuing a lifelong interest that began during his childhood, Schliemann showed that Homer's great epic poems were more than fiction; they had a real historical base.

New challenges to historical events confront established views and add controversy to any historian's story of the past. Was Christopher Columbus a heroic explorer or a liar and a crook? Did John Hancock help organize the Boston Tea Party to protest lack of representation or because British taxes threatened his tea business? Did the redcoats really fire the first shot at Lexington? Did Edwin Stanton, Secretary of War at the time of Lincoln's assassination, actually plot to kill President Lincoln? Was Mary Todd Lincoln bright, vivacious, and politically astute, or was she high strung, hot tempered, and not especially sold on the concept of honesty? Our views of history constantly shift as the interpretation of new and old evidence disputes the legitimacy of earlier explanations. To function gainfully in dynamic social studies classrooms, young historians must understand and make use of the strategies considered a part of the historical method.

Young historians become engrossed in personal research when learning materials and activities are tailored to their individual needs and interests.

Why Is History Important?

Of all the disciplines that comprise today's social studies, history appears to spawn greater reaction to its nature and worth than any other. "Why bother with history?" some seem to ask dismissively, while others argue that history is so important it should be the central subject in our schools. See Figure 3–2.

Despite these mixed messages, one of the most hopeful signs in social studies education during the past decade has been the widespread and growing support for more history in our schools. Not the kind that demands memorizing a bunch of facts, but the history that makes the past seem real—the history that captivates young historians and activates them to weave together various pieces of information in the best tradition of a storyteller. Taking on the role of young historian helps students recognize their place in history, realizing that their lives will be part of a yet unrecorded history.

The most often stated reason for including history as a central part of social studies is that, by studying the past, our young citizens will be better prepared to judge the present and the future. To help clarify this point, it might be instructive to think about what response you might offer for these two questions: What is prerequisite to understanding any present social condition? What is prerequisite to effectively making decisions about the future? To many, the answer to both questions can be given with a single word, "Knowledge." Should knowledge be the key, there is only one

FIGURE 3–2
Quotes About History

Kierkegaard:

Life must be lived forward, but understood backward.

David Ben Gurion:

Anyone who believes you can't change history has never tried to write his memoirs.

George Santayana:

Those who cannot learn from history are doomed to repeat it.

Winston Churchill:

History will be kind to me for I intend to write it.

Henry Ford:

History is more or less bunk.

Laurel Thatcher Ulrich:

Well-behaved women rarely make history.

Mark Twain:

To arrive at a just estimate of a renowned man's character one must judge it by the standards of his time, not ours.

Maya Angelou:

History, despite its wrenching pain, cannot be unlived, but if faced with courage, need not be lived again.

Oscar Wilde:

Anybody can make history. Only a great man can write it.

place to find it—in the past. Why? I once heard it said that the future is unknown, the present is momentary, and everything else is history. Where else but the past does one come across the knowledge needed to understand and confront great issues? The experiences of other times enlighten us with the knowledge required to figure out solutions to present and future challenges.

The National Center for History in the Schools (1996) supports these views with the argument that knowledge of history is the precondition for political intelligence:

> Without history, a society shares no common memory of where it has been, of what its core values are, or of what decisions of the past account for our present circumstances. Without history, one cannot undertake any sensible inquiry into the political, social, or moral issues in society. And without historical knowledge and the inquiry it supports, one cannot move to the informed, discriminating citizenship essential in the democratic processes of governance and the fulfillment for all our citizens of the nation's democratic ideals. (p. 1)

What Should Students Know or Be Able to Do?

History must be an important part of the educational experience for every child. To make history more appealing for our young historians, instruction must focus on finding answers to the question, "How did things get this way?" Barbara Wisdom (a great name for a teacher, don't you agree?), a fifth-grade teacher, recounted, "We used to teach about the westward movement in the United States by giving the students a lot of names and dates and places and battles. We tried to make the ingestion of these facts more appetizing by periodically spicing them up with projects such as building prairie schooners and making a lot of quilt squares. But there was simply not enough time in the school year to cover every aspect of the westward movement and still teach all the other historical topics that were part of our fifth grade Historical Survey of the United States curriculum."

This year, instead, Ms. Wisdom put away the quilt squares and ditched the old westward movement unit altogether. Instead, she set off her social studies program in a small, but personable, way by asking her students to question their parents about familial ancestors who had left their homelands, either willingly or otherwise, to settle in the United States. Instead of centering instruction solely on the pioneers of the 1800s, Ms. Wisdom is using the theme of migration to study the movement of people through several eras and locations, including the pioneers of the west. This approach makes use of themes, such as *migration*, *patriotism*, or *revolution*, that cover several periods and places. "What we do in history now," explains Ms. Wisdom, "is more along the lines of getting students to think critically about why people do what they do and less along the lines of learning hundreds of facts about any single period in time. Once we select a theme, we must carefully decide on high interest experiences that help students look at the world of the past in new ways and 'turn them on' to history. With themes, we don't have to hurry to get through the gold rush by the middle of June."

Although memorizing names and dates is not the overriding purpose of history instruction, important facts and concepts are an important part of any history program. The reason is obvious: We can't teach our children how to think as young historians unless they have something worth thinking about. The argument that we can teach students how to understand the world of the past without conveying to them the events and ideas that have brought it into existence is a weak argument. One reason why history is so tricky to teach is that students are not interested in learning facts unless those facts are embedded in challenging or engaging contexts, but they cannot comprehend the contexts without knowing the facts.

The National Center for History in the Schools (1996) establishes a strong case for knowledge as an important basis for rational thought:

> Children's study of history rests on knowledge of facts, dates, names, places, events, and ideas. In addition, true historical understanding requires students to engage in historical thinking: to raise questions and to marshal solid evidence in support of their answers; to read historical narratives and fiction; [to go beyond the facts presented in their textbooks and examine the historical record for themselves]; to consult historical documents, journals, diaries, artifacts, historic sites, and other records from the past; and to do so imaginatively—taking into account the times and places in which these records were created and comparing the multiple points of view of those on the scene at the time. (p. 14)

With this important perspective, the National Center for History in the Schools (1996) developed a set of content standards considered suitable for an educated citizenry, the National Standards for History. The standards have made explicit the knowledge goals that all students should have the opportunity to acquire through the K-4 social studies curriculum. The Standards Committee recommends that, to bring history alive, historical study should be centered on four topics, or themes, under which eight standards are distributed (see Figure 3–3). Because most educators agree that young children learn history best when it's introduced within the familiar context of the expanding environment approach—home, school, neighborhood, community, and so on—the National Center advises that history instruction in grades K-4 should encompass the following four topics:

- Living and working together in families and communities, now and long ago
- The history of students' own state or region
- The history of the United States
- The history of peoples of many cultures around the world

IN GENERAL, HOW SHOULD HISTORY BE TAUGHT?

Although the National Standards for History pinpoint the content for a K-4 social studies program, the National Center for History in the Schools (1996) does not ignore the important matter of instructional methodology. The group stresses that teachers should bring history alive primarily by using "stories, myths, legends, and biographies that capture children's imaginations and immerse them in times and cultures of the recent and long-ago past" (p. 3).

Teachers can greatly enhance history instruction through the use of good literature. A generous supply of elementary-level historical fiction, biographies, and

FIGURE 3–3
Standards in History for Grades K-4

Overview	
Topic 1:	**Living and Working Together in Families and Communities Now and Long Ago**
Standard 1:	Family Life Now and in the Recent Past; Family Life in Various Places Long Ago
Standard 2:	History of Students' Local Community and How Communities in North America Varied Long Ago
Topic 2:	**The History of the Students' Own State or Region**
Standard 3:	The People, Events, Problems, and Ideas That Created the History of Their State
Topic 3:	**The History of the United States: Democratic Principles and Values and the Peoples From Many Cultures Who Contributed to Its Cultural, Economic, and Political Heritage**
Standard 4:	How Democratic Values Came to Be, and How They Have Been Exemplified by People, Events, and Symbols
Standard 5:	The Causes and Nature of Various Movements of Large Groups of People Into and Within the United States, Now and Long Ago
Standard 6:	Regional Folklore and Cultural Contributions That Helped to Form Our National Heritage
Topic 4:	**The History of Peoples of Many Cultures Around the World**
Standard 7:	Selected Attributes and Historical Developments of Various Societies in Africa, the Americas, Asia, and Europe
Standard 8:	Major Discoveries in Science and Technology, Their Social and Economic Effects, and the Scientists and Inventors Responsible for Them

Source: National Center for History in the Schools. (1996). *National Standards for history.* Los Angeles, CA: Author.

special reference works is related to history. Teachers should work with their school media specialists to identify the titles of books that may be used to energize history learning. Such books should be displayed appealingly, used regularly, and discussed as a part of the regular classroom instructional routine.

The Standards document recommend that, "In addition to stories, children should be introduced to a wide variety of historical artifacts, illustrations, and records that open to them first-hand glimpses into the lives of people in the past: family photos; letters, diaries, and other accounts of the past obtained from family records, local newspapers, libraries, and museums; field trips to historical sites in their neighborhood and community; and visits to 'living museums' where actors reenact life long ago" (p. 3). In addition, instruction about the past is supported by the sensory images of history offered through laserdiscs, videotapes, films, and filmstrips. Special experiences pump life into history. Such experiences include field trips to museums and historical sites, historical craft and model-building experiences, National History Day projects, and the experiences of constructing an oral history of some local "big event." When students are properly prepared for such special history learning experiences, the depth of understanding gained more than justifies the extra effort required.

Historical Narratives

The notion that historical narratives have an important role to play in history education has been widely accepted for a long time. Actually, narratives can be regarded as the lifeblood of an elementary school history program. You will recall that *historical narratives* are chronicles of real events that connect in such a way as to tell a story. Narratives have the power to reveal the motives and intentions, values and ideas, the hopes, doubts, fears, strengths, and weaknesses of people who have lived before us.

Three major types of narratives, *historical fiction*, *biographies*, and *folk literature*, dramatize and humanize the sterile facts of history for us. They transport young historians to the past and enable them to more clearly understand that today's way of life is a continuation of what people did in the past, that the present will influence the way people live in the future. A history textbook tells; a quality piece of literature not only tells but also has the power to evoke emotion. Textbooks keep students in the classroom; compelling stories from good books transport them to new and exciting worlds filled with individual heroism and epic events, bringing forth feelings rarely connected with textbook passages—compassion, humanness, misfortune, happiness, awe, and grief. Darigan, Tunnell, and Jacobs (2002) elaborate: "If history is indeed the story of ourselves, then [a] limitation of history textbooks is that people are missing! The best one-word definition of history is, in fact, 'people.' Without human beings, whose emotions and actions influence the times, there is no history" (p. 271). This fundamental value of historical narratives, by itself, should make them a valued part of the social studies program. Ravitch (1978) laments the gradual displacement of quality literature with textbooks based on the expanding environment approach during the early to mid-1900s:

> Until expanding environments managed to push historical material out of the social studies curriculum children in the early grades in most public schools learned about . . . myths, biographies, poems . . . fairy tales, and legends. The story of Robinson Crusoe and the study of Indian life were particular favorites. Stories about explorers, pioneer life, American heroes . . . , and famous events in American history were the staples of the first three grades. The line between historical literature and general literature was virtually nonexistent. Teacher guides emphasized the importance of telling stories. (p. 38)

Young historians need to be exposed to a wide variety of historical narratives, but exposure to good literature is only half the story. If students are going to function as true young historians in the classroom, they must have a chance to write their own narratives in addition to reading those written by others. Actually, this is not that hard for them to do, as most elementary school children are natural storytellers. Just take some time to listen carefully to their casual conversations, and you will hear youngsters spinning yarns about what is happening in their lives and describing the importance of those events. Their narratives may be about the past or present, and sometimes they venture into the uncertainty of their future as well. Like historical narratives, young people's narratives include stories of successes, dreams, and heroism as well as of sadness and pain. Narratives bring to light the "stuff" of history—the important incidents, events, and accomplishments that help to illuminate both the past and the present.

Using Historical Narratives Written by Others

Let's look more closely now at integrating the use of historical fiction, biographies, and folk literature into the social studies program. In addition, we can include the use of textbooks as a type of historical narrative, since they, too, provide accounts of past events written by authorities in the field.

Historical Fiction   Historical fiction is a category of realistic stories that are set in the past. The facts are accurate, but the characters are fictional, although they sometimes interact with actual historical figures. Historical fiction offers children opportunities to vicariously experience the past by entering into a convincingly true-to-life world of people who have lived before them. By being transported to the past through the vehicle of literature, students enter into the lives of the historical figures and, through mental imagery, become moved to attach emotion to their condition.

It is easy to see how good historical fiction makes history seem real. Note how Patricia Beatty brings to life a young boy's struggles in her book, *Charley Skedaddle* (1987). The story is set during the Civil War when 12-year-old Charley Quinn, a member of the Bowery Boys (the toughest street gang in New York City), vows revenge for his brother's death at Gettysburg and plans to enlist in the Union Army. One day, he sees Con, an old friend, as Con is marching along a street in New York City with other soldiers of the Union Army:

> "Take me along with you, Con, please!"
> For a moment the man's face twisted and thought, then he boomed, "Sure, Charley. Why not? I got five day's cooked rations with me. Ye can share 'em."
> A short man with brown sideburns and a dark face in the ranks next to Con said, "He's only a shirttail kid, Con."
> "No matter, Jem Miller. The Army's got uses for kids. Ye keep up with us men, Charley, ye hear. Ye let go of me now."
> "I'll keep up, you bet." As Charley trotted past the Bowery Boys, he waved his hat and shouted, "I'm off to join the Army!"

Unfortunately, when the horrors of war became a reality and he sees his best friend killed, Charley becomes terrified. He "skedaddles" away from the Union Army. Eventually, though, while still a deserter, an act of courage far from the battlefields

Children's trade books hold a wealth of fascinating information about the past. An abundance of good books in a fitting classroom center helps bring history to life.

proves to Charley that he's not the coward he thought himself to be. Beatty brings the Civil War to life for elementary school students by telling about its horrors through the experiences of someone who thinks of life the same way they, as 12-year-olds, do.

Mildred D. Taylor is an African-American author who has written with great sensitivity and understanding about racial injustice in rural Mississippi during the 1930s. *Mississippi Bridge* (Bantam Skylark) is a tale based on a true story told to Taylor by her father. It centers on the Logan family and their determination to fight racial injustice. The story opens with Jeremy Simms, a 10-year-old white child, watching from the porch of the general store as the weekly bus from Jackson splashes through a heavy rainstorm to stop at the store. His neighbors, Stacey Logan and his sister Cassie, are there to see their grandmother off on a trip. Jeremy's friend, Josias Williams, is taking the bus to a new job. But Josias and the Logans are black; black people can't ride the bus if that means there won't be enough room for white people to ride. When several white passengers arrive at the last minute, Taylor describes the injustice that unfolds as the driver sends Josias and Stacey's grandmother off the bus. The author's words make it impossible not to attach deep emotions to the event:

> Josias stood. He picked up his bundle of clothes and he give up his seat. He took himself some slow steps to the front of the bus. I moved over to the door waiting to say my spell to him, but he still ain't got off. He stopped hisself right front of that driver and he gone

to pleading. "Please, boss . . . I got to get to the Trace t'day. Please, boss. I done got my ticket. I done made all my plans. Folks spectin' me. I got t' go on this bus!"

"Nigger, I said you gettin' off."

"Boss, please . . . . "

That bus driver, he ain't give Josias chance to say no more. He jerked Josias forward to the door, put his foot flat to Josias's backside, and give him a push like Josias wasn't no more 'n a piece of baggage, and Josias, he gone sprawling down them steps into the mud. The bus driver, he throw'd Josias's bundle after him, his ticket money too. (1992, p. 31)

Shortly after this episode, the bus skids off the bridge and all are drowned. The nightmare changes the lives of the townspeople forever.

A teacher's obvious interest in and use of historical fiction strengthens the appeal of the past. Suddenly, through story, the magnitude of humanity's accomplishments is revealed, arousing the reader's imagination and interest.

If written well, historical fiction offers children fuller understandings of human problems and human conditions. To be considered for social studies programs, well-written historical fiction should be selected by using the following guidelines:

1. It must tell an interesting story. The book should "set the reader on fire."

2. It should be accurate and authentic. The historical period should be so precisely described that the people within the book "walk right into the room."

3. It should reflect the spirit and values of the times. The stories cannot be made to conform to today's ethical values, such as contemporary points of view concerning women and minorities.

4. It should contain authentic language. The spoken words should give the flavor of how people actually talked.

5. It should provide insight into today's problems. Putting the conditions of women and minorities into historical context is a prime example.

Biographies Biographies are much like historical fiction in that they are based on documented information, but rather than telling stories of fictional characters, biographies are stories of the lives of real people. The work of Esther Forbes offers an excellent comparison of a biography and historical fiction. In 1942, Forbes won the Pulitzer Prize for her adult biography, *Paul Revere and the World He Lived In*. While she was researching the book, she uncovered many fascinating anecdotes about the responsibilities of Boston's young apprentices. As a result, she wrote a book for children, *Johnny Tremain* (Houghton Mifflin); it won the Newbery Medal in 1944. The book is about a fictional silversmith's apprentice to Paul Revere who lived in Boston in the days leading to the American Revolution. A skilled craftsperson, Johnny becomes one of the best at his trade. But a practical joke backfires, and Johnny's hand becomes maimed for life. Johnny then becomes involved in pre-Revolutionary War activities. The book captures nearly every student's interest and remains one of the most popular works of historical fiction to this day.

In recent years, there has been a nationwide interest in teaching and learning values, or ideals that citizens agree distinguish right from wrong and good from bad. Reading about heroes has been an important part of this interest because heroes embody the values we seek out in real life. Heroes are brave, compassionate, loyal, tolerant, and fair. They are willing to stand up for what they believe. And, for children, biographies of exemplary heroes provide superb models of citizenship. Heroes are special people; their behavior seems to invite emulation. Children need heroes because heroes inspire them to similar rightness. In contrast to the past, however, when heroes could do no wrong, modern biographies show their human side, informing young historians about their weaknesses as well as their strengths. Children relate more closely to heroes when they can accept them as real people, complete with doubts, discouragement, mistakes, conflict, and frustration.

The best biographies for young historians characterize their subjects as true-to-life, neither extraordinarily gushing with praise nor disgraceful and humiliating. Jean Fritz has been especially effective in creating remarkably true-to-life portraits of famous figures. In Fritz's (1979) absorbing biography, *Stonewall*, she characterizes the controversial Confederate general Thomas "Stonewall" Jackson as a hard-working but underachieving young cadet at West Point:

> But however determined he was, no one watching him struggle would have guessed that Tom ("The General" as they called him) could have survived four years at West Point. Indeed, he could hardly get through a recitation. When called on to answer a question or solve a problem, Tom sweated so profusely his classmates joked that one day he would drown them all. (p. 26)
>
> But, Jackson's determination to succeed served him well.
>
> Inch-by-inch Tom pulled himself through. Near the bottom of his class at the end of his first year (fifty-first in a class of seventy-two), he rose to seventeenth by the end of his senior year, and his classmates, who had grown fond of him, said it was a pity there wasn't a fifth year at West Point. Tom would have graduated top man. (p. 26)

By examining Stonewall Jackson's character at various points throughout the story, students learn to appreciate one of the nation's most brilliant and heroic leaders as well as one of its oddest heroes. Likewise, the best biographies are intimate and memorable, presenting as fairly as possible accurate information within a frame of human emotion.

A "master biographer" whose works serve as excellent resources for elementary school students is Russell Freedman. Freedman reacted strongly against the "I cannot tell a lie" stories that were fashionable in earlier times and replaced them with a more objective treatment of historical figures in his books. In *Lincoln: A Photobiography* (1989), for example, Freedman contrasts the physical differences between Lincoln and Douglas as they prepared for one of their famous debates:

> The striking contrast between Douglas and Lincoln—The Little Giant and Long Abe, as reporters called them—added color and excitement to the contests. Douglas was Lincoln's opposite in every way. Barely five feet four inches tall, he had a huge round head planted on massive shoulders, a booming voice, and an aggressive, self-confident manner. He appeared on the speakers' platform dressed "plantation style"—a navy coat and light trousers, a ruffled shirt, a wide-brimmed felt hat. Lincoln, tall and gangly, seemed plain in

---

TEXT SET 5

Theme: Presidential Biographies

John B. Severance's **Thomas Jefferson: Architect of Democracy** (Clarion) is an impressive biography of America's third president. It chronicles Jefferson's life and career from his early education through his positions as author of the Declaration of Independence, governor of Virginia, ambassador to France, U.S. vice president and president, and finally as founder of the University of Virginia.

David A. Adler's **Picture Book of Dwight David Eisenhower** (Holiday House) is a complete biography of our nation's thirty-fourth president. Illustrated with interesting photographs, the book highlights Ike's Kansas childhood, love of sports, West Point career, marriage, family life, military service in World War I, leadership in World War II, accomplishments as president, and death.

Betsy Harvey Kraft's **Theodore Roosevelt: Champion of the American Spirit** (Clarion) offers a spirited look at our nation's 26th president. Written in an engaging manner, the book pulls from quotes, political cartoons, period photos, and journal entries to provide a fascinating glimpse into the public and private life and the wide range of accomplishments of a major figure in American history. A popular president, a champion of women's and working-class rights, and a devoted husband and father, Roosevelt claimed near the end of his life that "No man has had a happier life than I have led."

---

his rumpled suit, carrying his notes and speeches in an old carpetbag, sitting on the platform with his bony knees jutting into the air. (pp. 58–59)

The same guidelines used for selecting historical fiction apply to biographies. Be sure the story is a well-researched, carefully documented account of the person's life with fast-moving narrative and a clear, readable writing style.

Katrina Probst uses biographies quite extensively in her social studies program because she feels this literary genre offers children one of the best sources of learning about the extraordinary accomplishments of people from the past. While opening a literature-based thematic unit on *Presidents: Past and Present*, for example, Ms. Probst read Catherine Stier's book, *If I Were President* (Albert Whitman). In this simple, informative picture book, children describe what their lives would be like if they became president of the United States. Then Ms. Probst grouped together multiple copies of five books as a text set of presidential biographies. The groups finished reading their books independently, discussed them, and created charts highlighting the major accomplishments of their respective presidents. Normally, Ms. Probst stops there for, as Darigan, Tunnell, and Jacobs (2002) suggest: ". . . readers do not want to make even an informal response to every book they read. If you finish a particularly gripping novel out on the beach . . . . you don't automatically jump up and head for a closet in search of a shoe box to construct a diorama as a response to the

Ilene Cooper's **Jack: The Early Years of John F. Kennedy** (Dutton) paints a revealing portrait of a young man and his relationships with his family. Drawn from family letters, anecdotes, and quotes from his friends and family, the book focuses on Kennedy's early life, from his birth to his graduation from boarding school.

Beatrice Gormley's **George W. Bush: Our 43rd President** (Aladdin) is an informative biography that begins with Bush's childhood, and then moves to his years at Yale, training as a fighter pilot, career in business, entrance into Texas politics, and road to the White House. The author makes extensive use of letters and memoirs of Bush's parents, peers, and business partners.

TRY THIS

You need to read widely to develop your own text sets. And, when researching a particular theme, such as presidents, you must use a great deal of energy and drive to find just the right books. The American Library Association publishes an excellent resource titled *Book Links: Connecting Books, Libraries, and Classrooms.* This resource divides children's books into thematic categories and selects the best 30–40 books for each. Check this valuable resource and see if you can identify any books about presidents that you would like to add to this list.

book. More likely, . . . you [tell someone] what you've read. If you had to do a project for *every* book you read, you'd soon lose your desire to read" (p. 486). However, this topic on presidents was one of those instances ripe for a project activity. Ms. Probst considered several alternatives, but settled on having her students use what they learned about different presidents to plan and carry out an elegant dinner party with the help of parent volunteers where the presidents would be the guests.

Inside an Active Classroom

Ms. Probst informed her students that one of the most enjoyable highlights of a study of the presidents is to host a dinner party where the presidents they had read about would be the honored guests. As hosts, the students were asked to address some very important issues of protocol, or code of etiquette. Their responsibilities were divided among group members:

Invitations.   These students designed dinner invitations for the guests. The invitations included not only the typical "what," "when," and "where" information, but also informed the guests of the dress code (formal, informal, or casual), suggested time of arrival, where to park (their car or horse), and that they would be expected to deliver a few brief remarks.

The Menu.   These students planned the entire dinner with several courses. Their biggest dilemma was whether to serve food from present day or to consider the historical periods of the presidents. They eventually settled on a mixed menu with different courses representing varied historical periods, including the present.

Toast.   Because this was to be a glorious affair, these students felt a toast should be given (with sparkling grape juice, of course) to honor and celebrate the significance of the event. They wrote a toast for each presidential guest.

Message of Greeting.   These students were directed to write a "message of greeting" to the presidents that would be delivered just before dinner.

Gift.   These students were asked to think about a special gift that could be given to each president before or after dinner.

Seating.   To avoid confusion, these students felt that seating should be preassigned rather than random. Deciding how to arrange the guests to stimulate the greatest potential for good conversation was a special challenge. For instance, they argued at some length about whether two guests from the same historical era and/or political party should sit next to each other. After much deliberation, they made a diagram of the seating assignments and designed name cards to specify where each guest would sit. The students even thought of seating left-handed guests at the end of the table for comfort and convenience.

Conversation Starters.   These students had to come up with a question or two for each guest that would stand a good chance of getting a good conversation going. Ms. Probst offered a few examples, such as: "Tell me a favorite childhood memory." "When you were a child, who was your hero?" "What games did you enjoy as a child?"

Guest Speech.   It is customary for a president to offer brief remarks just before dinner or immediately after. These students were assigned to compose what the presidents would be likely to say. Sample topics included "What It's Like Living in the White House" and "How Tough the Job of President Is."

Folk Literature   Fables, myths, legends, and folktales belong to the great literature genre we refer to as *folklore*. In essence, these stories began with illiterate people and were handed down by storytellers for generations. Originating wherever people gathered—in marketplaces, during tasks such as weaving or sewing, in taverns, or around the hearth—the stories were told for listeners' entertainment and as an expression of cultural beliefs. The rich oral tradition of folktales was kept alive by generations of storytellers; the tales eventually found their place within printed literature.

Because folktales have been retold from generation to generation with every culture, they clearly reflect those cultures' beliefs, values, lifestyles, and histories. An authentic tale from China, for example, will include references to the land on which the people lived, their food, their homes, their customs, and their beliefs. One particularly entertaining and informative folktale is the Chinese pourquoi story (tells how or why something came to be) *Tikki Tikki Tembo* by Arlene Mosel (Holt). The tale tells of the family's "first and honored" son who was proudly given the distinguished, long name of Tikki-Tikki-Tembo-No-Sa-Rembo-Chari-Bari-Ruchi-Pip-Peri-Pembo. Unfortunately, as a little boy, he falls into a well and it takes so long for his brother Chang to tell someone about his plight that the elder son nearly drowns. That is why, to this day, all Chinese have short names. Young children love this story and enjoy repeating the elder son's name.

As you can see, folktales reflect a culture so plainly that it is nearly impossible to confuse a folktale from a Chinese village with a folktale from West Africa. This is a major reason folktales belong in social studies classrooms: They help children understand a culture's past through its values, beliefs, and customs.

Take, for instance, this passage from *Mufaro's Beautiful Daughters* by John Steptoe (1989), a Cinderella tale from Africa:

> Nyasha kept a small plot of land, on which she grew millet, sunflowers, yams, and vegetables. She always sang as she worked, and some said it was her singing that made her crops more bountiful than anyone else's. (p. 4 of an unnumbered text)

Elementary school children learn so many things about early African culture as they read this fascinating tale, including crops grown in gardens and the significance of such birds as the Carmine Bee-eater and the Crowned Crane. Steptoe's careful research paints a vivid picture of what life long ago was like in the region of Africa where the story originated. Children enjoy the engaging tale as they learn about the plants and animals of the rainforest and about the architectural wonders of the great wall that enclosed a magnificent city built on a plateau in southeastern Zimbabwe around 1100 A.D.

Teachers using any type of literature in their history programs must remember that they have a responsibility not only to provide the books, but also to encourage students to reflect on what they read. They can use a variety of strategies, many of which are described throughout this text—stories, poems, journals, descriptions, words, illustrations, and graphic organizers. In the accompanying vignette, Linda Klaus-Fazik models an effective strategy for creating a graphic organizer in response to the reading of a Navajo tale.

Inside an Active Classroom

To exploit the use of folk literature, Linda Klaus-Fazik, a fifth-grade teacher, read aloud the book *Nannabah's Friend* by Mary Perrine (Houghton Mifflin), a sensitive story of how a young Navajo girl bridges the gap between the security of home and the world outside. She thought this was an excellent book to use for historical study, especially since the children would immediately identify with Nannabah and her plight. When she finished reading the book, Ms. Klaus-Fazik used three separate prompts to trigger oral responses: (1) What did you notice in the story? (2) How did the story make you feel? (3) What does this story remind you of in your own life? Then, to help her students analyze Nannabah's moral fiber, Ms. Gilland worked together with her students to construct a web of Nannabah's character traits. See their character web in Figure 3–4.

FIGURE 3–4
Character Web

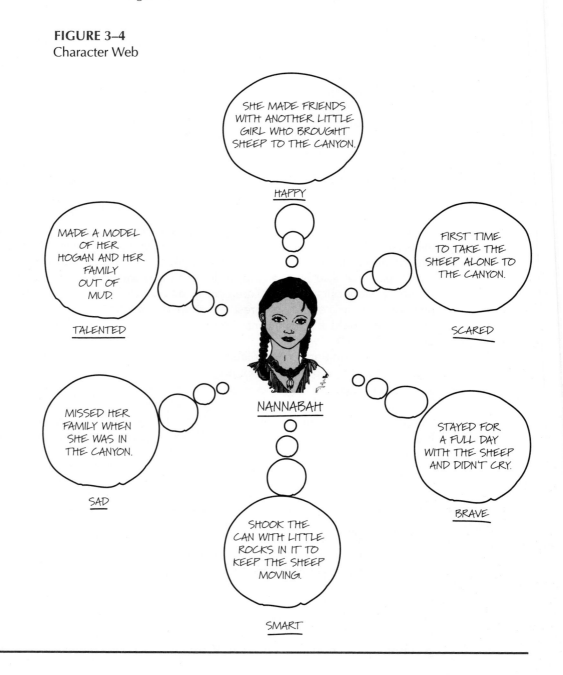

Folk literature has deep roots in all cultures. Through this genre, students broaden their understandings of those cultures, as well as sense the common bonds that have linked together cultures for centuries. Countless books have memorable impact and may serve as the substance around which you could plan multiple learning opportunities in history.

To ensure that important benefits actually emerge from the use of all three types of historical literature in your classroom, you must carefully research the story content so that you are able to place the students into an accurate time and place context. For example, I recall observing a field experience student read Elizabeth George Speare's *The Sign of the Beaver* to a group of fourth graders. She did a good job during the introductory phase, telling the students that the story took place long ago in the Maine wilderness where Matt is left by his father to tend a new cabin while he returned to Massachusetts for the rest of the family. The students located Maine and Massachusetts on a map and traced the probable route Matt's father had taken. That was good, but to further establish the story background, the field experience student went on to display a large study print illustrating Native Americans of the past (because their interactions with Matt are central to the story). The idea was very nice, but the story is an Eastern Woodlands story. The study print, however, depicted a buffalo hunting camp of the Cherokee (Plains Indians) with its cone-shaped tepees and campfire. The student complicated her error by referring to the Cherokee shelters in the study print as "wigwams." As the regular classroom teacher stepped in to help correct the error-filled introduction, I couldn't help wonder about how pre-service teachers might be convinced of the importance to confirm the accuracy of what they are teaching.

The many benefits of historical literature can be realized only if you place the story content in an accurate context. Historical fiction is based on a strong background of fact and should be used as a vehicle to enlighten, not confuse.

Some helpful resources for assessing and selecting quality sources of historical narratives follow:

- *Notable Children's Trade Books for Young People*, compiled annually since 1972 by the Children's Book Council in cooperation with the Book Review Committee of the National Council for the Social Studies (NCSS). The annotated book list is published once a year in *Social Education*. To obtain a single copy, send a check for $2.00 payable to the Children's Book Council along with a self-addressed, 6-by-9-inch envelope with 3 oz. postage to the Children's Book Council, 12 West 37th Street, New York, NY 10018. The list may be downloaded from the CBC website (*www.cbcbooks.org*).

- *Social Studies and the Young Learner*, a quarterly magazine published by NCSS, features a regular article on books appropriate for elementary social studies as well as suggestions for use. To subscribe ($15/year), contact the National Council for the Social Studies, 3501 Newark St. NW, Washington, DC 20016; (202) 966-7840.

- *An Annotated Bibliography of Historical Fiction for the Social Studies, Grades 5–12*, by Fran Silverblank, published by Kendall/Hunt for the National Council for the Social Studies.

Textbooks   While discussing the nature of appropriate historical narratives in elementary school classrooms, it is only fair to address the topic of textbook use, for much has been written over the years about the drawbacks of textbook-centered social studies instruction. Ravitch and Finn (1987), for example, criticize textbook-centered instruction because it typically requires students to "listen to the teacher explain the day's lesson, use the textbook, and take tests. Sometimes they memorize information or read stories about events and people. They seldom work with other students, use original documents . . . , or discuss the significance of what they are studying" (p. 194).

Good social studies teachers are aware of these difficulties and avoid overdependence on a single textbook, regardless how good the textbook might be. In spite of their shortcomings and misuse, the plain fact is that we need social studies textbooks. Because history is such an enormous subject and because teachers charged with teaching history in elementary schools frequently don't know as much as they should about every topic they are required to teach, many need the textbook as a broad overview of the topic to be taught.

Widespread use by social studies teachers is not hard to understand. When elementary school teachers are expected to use sophisticated instructional strategies and activities in all school subjects, including math, reading, spelling, writing, and science, the thought of having specially "packaged" help in social studies greatly reduces the pressure and anxiety of daily planning. In addition, textbooks provide extensive treatment of subject matter that is organized sequentially from one grade level to the next. Each teacher from kindergarten through grade 8 knows what was done in earlier grades and what will be expected in later grades, thereby minimizing gaps or repetition. Finally, school districts and teachers appreciate the comprehensive nature of the teacher's manuals, which come complete with goals, objectives, lesson plans, suggestions for activities, and tests.

Teachers at all levels of experience acknowledge the helpfulness of textbooks, but beginning teachers tend find them especially valuable. They usually begin their teaching careers with serious classroom management concerns and textbook-based instruction helps reduce those concerns by putting the teacher in control of all aspects of instruction. Although textbooks virtually take teachers "by the hand" and guide them through the instructional process, beginning teachers must eventually loosen their grip on the textbook and become skilled at encouraging students to work and plan together, to explore problems, and to come up with their own solutions.

The reality in today's educational climate is that textbooks are frequently the chief source of instruction, even for experienced teachers. Regardless, it is still possible to help most students like history and learn productively. This may get me into trouble with my colleagues, but I'm really not sure if it's the method of instruction that produces student growth or if it's the skill of the individual carrying out the method. For that reason, I have often said that if I had a choice, I would prefer a great textbook-oriented social studies teacher over a poor multi-resource teacher. Teachers who do well with a textbook approach consider the varied reading abilities of their students; they encourage collaboration and cooperation; they make sure that students' conceptual and experiential backgrounds are connected to the reading material; they confront students with challenging problems; and they supplement the textbook with a wide variety of activities, literature sources, and hands-on materials.

The following classroom episode illustrates how José Zabala was able to engage his children's historical thinking, even when the sole source of instruction was a social studies textbook.

Inside an Active Classroom

The purpose of Mr. Zabala's lesson was to help students understand the major factors that transformed many colonists from loyal British subjects to dissidents on the verge of revolutionary war. He began by announcing to the class that the school district budget just bottomed out and very little money was available to purchase the supplies necessary to finish out the school year. A committee of teachers had met to study the problem and decided that a good source of revenue would be to have students pay a small fee each time they put something into the wastebasket, used the restrooms, got a drink of water, or sharpened their pencils. Mr. Zabala asked the students if they thought this was a fair solution to the district's money crisis, especially since they had never before been required to pay such a "tax." He also raised the question of whether teachers had the right to impose such a tax on students. Mr. Zabala involved the students in an active debate of the options available to them (avoid paying the fee, boycotting classes, protesting the plan, complaining to the local newspaper) and the consequences of their actions.

Mr. Zabala then encouraged the students to recall that the Seven Years' War drained the treasury of Great Britain, so the British government desperately needed to raise money. Britain began to do something it had never done before—it decided to impose taxes on the colonies. The class drew parallels between the British taxation plans to their tongue-in-cheek classroom "tax." Then, to begin the day's textbook reading assignment, Mr. Zabala invited predictions about what the British might tax in the colonies and how the colonists might react to those British taxes. After the students exhausted their ideas, Mr. Zabala directed them to read a section in their textbooks to find out (1) what the British decided to tax, (2) the colonial reaction to each British tax, and (3) the British response to the colonists' reactions. After a short discussion of the reading selection, the students summarized the three British taxes described in the textbook selection: (1) the Stamp Act, (2) the Townshend Duties, and (3) the Tea Act (see Figure 3–5). Mr. Zabala

FIGURE 3–5
Graphic Organizer

directed the students to chart each on a graphic organizer. (Note how the organizer directly relates back to the stated purposes for reading.)

Textbook-based instruction can be effective when teachers connect the topic of instruction to the children's lives and supplement instruction with a wide selection of resources and activities. These special experiences pump life into the curriculum and deepen the students' understanding of history.

Young Historians Write Historical Narratives

Why should students write in social studies? Although seemingly complex, this question is easy to answer: Social studies is a curriculum area "that is as appropriate for writing as the gym is for basketball" (Murray, 1987, p. 54). The social studies curriculum offers rich and varied contexts in which students can write frequently and purposefully; an environment in which writing in different forms can be perceived as necessary and useful. In this section, we will explore how writing can be employed in dynamic social studies classrooms and, specifically, examine the many ways we can enhance learning in history through writing.

When children are exposed to a wide variety of historical narratives, they will develop an interest in using the styles of their favorite authors as a model to write their own narratives. This propensity for imitation is important because replication plays a productive role in students' learning to write in any genre. All writers, either by accident or design, begin by imitating the style and content of other writers. Take advantage of this imitative urge and encourage it; your students will soon begin to develop their unique "writing personalities."

Many authors serve as excellent models for student writing in history. The works of Jean Fritz, "a master biographer" who has written about several periods in American history, particularly the Revolutionary War, are quite exemplary. Her series on the Revolutionary War contains several stories that show historical characters as real people, helping children enrich their understandings of history in an enjoyable way.

In writing their own biographies, then, students must focus on the qualities that make a model author's books so first-rate: (1) a realistic description of the time when and place where the person lived (biographies can be written about living people or historical figures), (2) an accurate characterization of the person, (3) a careful accounting of the significant events in the person's life, and (4) the values and interests influencing the person to act as he or she did.

Conducting the research required to complete their original biographies and putting thoughts together to form a written portrait help students understand the people who have made history. One student's biographical sketch of Sacagawea is shown as an example of a short biography in Figure 3–6.

In composing their own stories, children must learn that all historical narratives, including biography, historical fiction, and folk tales, have a *setting*, which is usually

FIGURE 3–6
Biographical Sketch

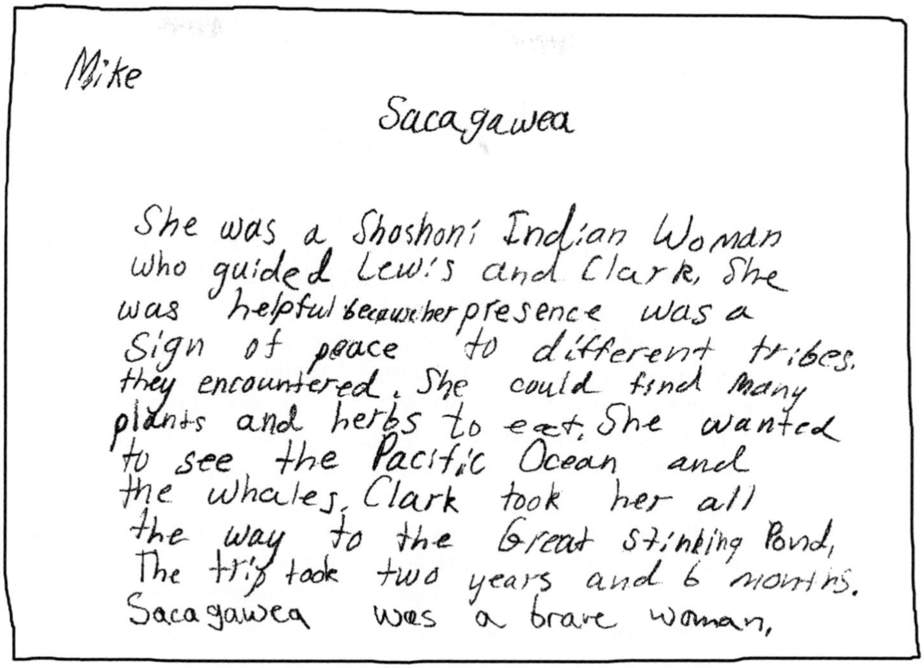

Mike

Sacagawea

She was a Shoshoni Indian Woman who guided Lewis and Clark, she was helpful because her presence was a sign of peace to different tribes, they encountered. She could find many plants and herbs to eat, She wanted to see the Pacific Ocean and the whales, Clark took her all the way to the Great Stinking Pond, The trip took two years and 6 months. Sacagawea was a brave woman,

described early in the story and helps the reader create vivid pictures of distinctive times (stories can take place in the past, present time, or the future) or places (stories can take place anywhere). They learn that the second element of historical narratives is comprised of the story *characters*. What are their physical and emotional attributes? How do they look, dress, and feel? What do the characters say? What do the characters think? Third, they learn that the story has a *plot*, or sequence of events. The plot describes the action—what the characters do and what happens to them. In most picture books, the plot is relatively simple with one main sequence of events, but in chapter books the plot becomes more complex with one or more subplots that underlie the main events.

In most cases, the stories written by elementary school children will have relatively simple plots. Their stories usually contain a single episode but, in a few instances, two or three episodes might follow one another, building on each other as the story takes form. Regardless of the number of episodes, the plot is more than a sequence of events. To engage the reader, a good plot must have a tension-building conflict, a difficulty to rise above, or an engaging problem to solve. Finding out how these complexities are resolved captures the reader and makes her or him want to keep reading to the end of the story. The plot usually has three parts: (1) a problem, conflict, or difficulty (with nature, with society, between characters, or within the character), (2) roadblocks (the character faces obstacles in an attempt to solve the complexity), and (3) the solution (a turning point in the story where the roadblocks are overcome). The solution brings a simple but satisfying ending to the story that is either anticipated by the reader or surprises the reader with an unexpected twist.

Composing historical narratives is an especially relevant form of writing in history because narratives necessitate conducting research and personalizing the data to provide an accurate account of the major events of the time. In helping students understand how to express themselves through this genre, it is always a good idea to use high-quality trade books as models.

Beginning any piece of written work is a challenge for all writers; however, starting a historical narrative can be especially difficult for children. Because many children have trouble establishing a historical frame of reference for a story's setting (both time and place), they may struggle in their attempts to establish believable characters, a distinctive time frame, and a realistic setting. As a result, it is not unusual for a child's historical narrative to begin with "Once upon a time far, far away, there was a (person) named . . . . " To help students overcome such difficulties and write successfully in the narrative form, teachers find it helpful to infuse meaningful historical content within a proper writing framework.

In the following illustrative account, Maria Stanitis used the Storypath approach as the framework of instruction to support her young historians as they worked to complete a historical narrative about the winter of 1777 when George Washington and his troops camped at Valley Forge.

Children learn much when they write their own historical narratives and make their products available for others to enjoy.

The Storypath Approach The instructional approach used by Ms. Stanitis is built on the principle that, for instruction to be meaningful, children' enthusiasm for stories should be used to teach important concepts and skills in history. In her Storypath curriculum, students contribute to the development of a story as they acquire new and deeper understandings about the topic under study.

The Storypath approach was originally developed in Scotland during the 1960s (known as Storyline there) and has been popularized in the United States during the past few years by Margit McGuire at Seattle University. You can locate additional information on the Storypath approach at Dr. McGuire's website *http://fac-staff.seattleu.edu/mmcguire/storypath.html*. Several Storypath units are available from SRA (*www.sraonline.com*). Each Storypath unit begins by helping children establish the setting and characters for their story. Then, students are confronted with a critical problem that sets in motion the story's plot. The Storypath episodes are shown in Figure 3–7.

Ms. Stanitis regularly begins any Storypath by having the students, working together in small groups, create a setting for the topic under study. In this case, the class is learning about the Revolutionary War and, more specifically, the winter George Washington and his troops spent at Valley Forge. Ms. Stanitis began the Valley Forge Storypath by telling the students they would be writing a story that takes place in 1777 in a well-known location in southeastern Pennsylvania. To prepare,

FIGURE 3–7
Episodes of a Storypath Unit

Creating the Setting

Students create the setting by completing a mural or other visual representation of the topic they will be studying.

Creating Characters

Characters are added to the mural or visual representation.

Context Building

Students are involved in activities that stimulate them to think more deeply about the people and place they have created. Important concepts are deepened and reinforced.

Critical Incidents

Characters confront a problem characteristic of those faced by people of that time and place.

Concluding Event

Students plan and organize an event that brings closure to the unit.

she asked the students to locate Valley Forge on a map depicting significant Revolutionary War battles. This first step helped orient the students to the story's setting. Ms. Stanitis then went on to help her young historians build a slightly deeper understanding of the setting. The students, in small groups, were to create a mural based on this description she read aloud to the class:

> After his defeats at Brandywine and Germantown, General George Washington led his army of about 10,000 troops to Valley Forge, a relatively out-of-the-way location along the Schuylkill River, 25 miles northwest of Philadelphia. A nearby small valley had once been the site of a blacksmith shop, so the locality became known as Valley Forge. Washington chose the bare, hilly plateau because the higher location gave him a panoramic view of the landscape, which would make the encampment easier to secure and defend. The troops arrived at Valley Forge on the 19th of December and, eight days later, the deepest snow of the season fell. The next few days brought the winter's bitterest cold. The troops were beset by periods of cold then warmer weather, which would cause the snow to thaw and then refreeze. You can imagine what a muddy mess it would be to carry out drills, or even move from one part of the camp to another.
>
> Washington's soldiers had little food and too little clothing to protect them from the cold. The Continental Congress could not provide adequate supplies to fill the soldiers' needs. There was no shelter for the men when they reached Valley Forge. Tents provided their only protection against frost and wind. Their commander-in-chief insisted that he, too, would live in a tent until his troops were able to cut down trees and construct log huts.
>
> These are General George Washington's orders to his troops about building log huts in the winter of 1777:
>
> "The soldiers were to be formed into twelve-man squads, each charged with building its own hut. These shelters were to be made of logs chinked with clay, and were to be six and a half feet high, fourteen feet wide, and sixteen feet long. They were to be aligned along company streets, with doors (made of boards, if available, otherwise of split-oak slabs) facing the street. There would be a fireplace in the rear, made of wood and 'secured' with clay."

After Ms. Stanitis read the description, the student groups met together to talk about the landscape features that would comprise their mural. Some decided that the snow-covered rolling hills of Valley Forge would amply illustrate the setting, but others insisted that that tents, log huts, camp fires, bare branched trees, heavy gray clouds, and large boulders would make the scene more complete. Others thought it would be a good idea to add the Schuylkill River in the background, the smithy's shop in a dell, and a few muddy roads. One group, setting its mural off from the rest, decided that a cutaway view of a log hut should be central to its design. In a short time, all were satisfied with their plans and went to work building their murals.

The focus of this mural construction activity was not to make an exact replica of the military camp, but to help students construct their own idea of the time and place.

Some teachers might show their students pictures of Valley Forge in 1777 or give them much more detailed information than that read by Ms. Stanitis. But, when teachers give too much, the students often tend to merely replicate what they saw, read, or heard instead of build their own unique mental picture of the landscape features. Ms. Stanitis did not underestimate what young students can do by themselves. It is important to remember that the process of designing a mural and talking about it prior to creating is a "rehearsal" process for the actual act, not an end in itself. Before many children write, they like to draw a scene and talk about it. Then they write about the scene they drew. Called *pictorializing*, this appears to be a useful preparation (or rehearsal) strategy many young writers use before putting words on paper.

After the students pulled together the landscape for their murals, Ms. Stanitis led a discussion with the framework of these prompts:

- What do you imagine life was like in this camp?
- How might it feel to live in this camp?
- How did the weather affect the living conditions?
- What might a historian say about the events at Valley Forge?

Next, the young historians brainstormed a list of words they felt adequately described the Valley Forge landscape. Using a black marker, the students wrote words such as "freezing," "snowy," "bitter," and "dangerous" on index cards (one word to a card). The cards were posted around the mural to create a sizable word bank. To better connect her students to the place they created, Ms. Stanitis asked each group to use the words and the mural to write a paragraph or two describing the scene. One group wrote this about its mural. "The Army was camped on a hill overlooking a small valley. The place was called Valley Forge. It was wintertime and very cold. They lived in tents for awhile but George Washington gave the troops orders to build log huts. Twelve men lived together in a 16×14 foot log hut. Each hut had a stone fireplace. Most of the huts were built about 2 feet down in a hole in the ground but were about 6 feet high. They had dirt floors. The huts were drafty, cold, smoky, and awfully unhealthy."

Ms. Stanitis explained that now that the setting for their story was firmly in mind, the young historians would next need to describe the characters. The groups went to work talking about the people who occupied the camp, what they looked like, and what work they would have been doing. Ms. Stanitis found that some students were interested in conducting additional research to make their characters as true to the time as possible while others were satisfied to simply capture the overall flavor of the era. Ms. Stanitis acknowledged each of these approaches and found that both were productive. She did, however, provide a wide range of resources, including picture books and appropriate websites, to help them gather necessary data.

Once the students were satisfied with their research, they painted characters on their landscape murals. The groups named their characters and completed a short biographical description for each. Danusia wrote this character sketch, for example, to describe a pitiful character she painted on her group's mural: "Thomas Gates was in miserable shape. He looked like a skeleton—pale, sick, and sad wrapped in a thin blanket. He was sitting next to a smoky fire. He didn't have a coat or a hat or shoes. Just after Christmas his feet and legs froze so bad that they turned black. A doctor had to cut them off." Few descriptions were as heartrending as Danusia's, but most were quite descriptive of the squalor and suffering the troops were forced to endure. Ms. Stanitis went on to encourage the students to think about how these single character descriptions might be connected with others to create interesting story ties.

The next Storypath episode required the students to establish a deeper understanding of the events at Valley Forge. Ms. Stanitis presented a list of suggested topics for the students to research and write a one-page report. Some possible choices were: what the troops ate, getting supplies to Valley Forge, sanitation and personal hygiene, and leaving Valley Forge. Suggesting research topics might be considered to be a bit too structured for those who believe that students write better reports if they select the topic, but Ms. Stanitis decided that specifying the topics would be a better approach for this particular unit. (She makes every effort to meet the varied needs and interests of her students with less structured research activities in forthcoming units.)

Obviously, however, social studies teachers do not simply assign students a report to write and send them on their way. They must model the process of report writing. To help them begin their reports, Ms. Stanitis led a discussion about where the students might locate information for their various topics. For example, she suggested that the Internet offers many excellent sites for this topic. She then modeled how the students could take notes from a source of information and organize the notes for the report. Ms. Stanitis introduced a graphic organizer to show how she takes information from her notes and organizes it into paragraphs with a main idea and supporting details (Figure 3–8). Just as the act of pictorializing (constructing the mural) served as a rehearsal tool during the initial phase of Storypath, Ms. Stanitis used a graphic

FIGURE 3–8
Organizing an Informational Paragraph

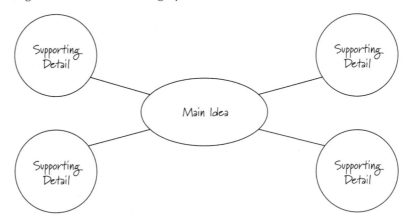

representation as a rehearsal technique to help students consider what information they wanted to use in their reports and how they should organize the information.

When the students completed their graphic organizers and written reports, they were asked to prepare a short oral presentation so that everyone would know more about the Valley Forge experience. In reporting on the morale at Valley Forge, for example, Chelsoon's group wrote the following information: "Washington was a great general, but the spirits were very low and there wasn't very much military skill at the Valley Forge camp. There was a lot of gambling and fighting. Some men even walked away from camp when they wanted to. The men were brave, but they didn't know how to march together or even how to move on the battlefield. They knew how to use their bayonets more for cooking over a fire than for fighting. All this changed when Baron von Steuben arrived in February. The men loved Baron von Steuben. He drilled the men and trained them until they were a mean fighting machine. The men had new pride and their spirits grew because of von Steuben."

Ms. Stanitis operates with a conviction that a good writer must gather a rich store-house of information about a topic before she or he can compose an informative, attention-grabbing story. "If an author is going to write about something," Ms. Stanitis avows, "she or he better know a good bit about it." Convinced that her students were now at the point where they had ample background information to compose historical narratives, Ms. Stanitis asked them to recall the three story elements: "Let's think of the three elements that make up historical stories, or narratives." A recorder wrote each on the board as the elements were suggested: (1) an engaging setting, (2) strong characters, and (3) an exciting plot. Ms. Stanitis helped the students combine the three elements into a descriptive sentence: "We include three important elements in the stories, or narratives, we write in social studies: setting, characters, and plot."

Ms. Stanitis read a short picture book to serve as a model of the three story elements: Ann Turner's *Katie's Trunk* (Macmillan, 1992). The book tells the story of Katie's Tory family who lived in fear of persecution by the rebels. When a group of rebels comes to raid Katie's home, Katie hides in a trunk. A rebel neighbor, finding her in the trunk, distracts his rebel friends instead of turning her in, thus leaving Katie untouched and unhurt. The point of the story is that there were examples of real human compassion on both sides. After a short open-ended discussion of the book, Ms. Stanitis helped her students analyze the story by using a story mountain technique suggested by Darigan, Tunnell, and Jacobs (2002). See Figure 3–9.

Ms. Stanitis helped each group pull together the essential features of setting and characters as they were shown on the mural and described in related writing activities. Then, she introduced the third story element—plot—by reading an informational sheet containing a real problem George Washington faced at Valley Forge. Keeping the setting and characters in mind, the students listened to the following problem as Ms. Stanitis read:

Washington agonized over the conditions his army was forced to put up with. All of his troops were without heavy coats, some without jackets of any kind, half without blankets, more than one third without shoes, and a few without

FIGURE 3–9
Story Mountain

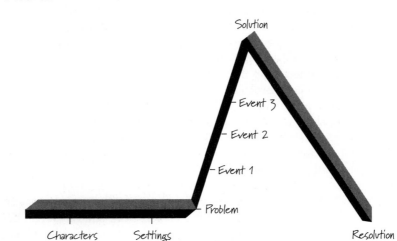

shirts. *None had enough to eat; some had gone hungry for days. Worn out and in poor health, men were deserting in great numbers, heading home to their families and farms. It was a dark moment for the Revolution and for George Washington. From his crude headquarters, he wrote to warn Congress: "unless some great . . . change suddenly takes place . . . this army must inevitably . . . starve, dissolve or disperse."*

At that instant, says Revolutionary War historian Edmund Morgan, Washington was indeed "giving Congress the facts of life: you can't fight a war without an army. He was operating at a big disadvantage."

Yet even as Washington attempted to keep his army from falling apart, he found himself challenged on another front. Prominent individuals in the freedom movement—for the most part, some members of Congress—had began to question Washington's ability to lead. Over the course of the next several months, Washington was plagued by a small but vocal faction calling for his dismissal. By doing so, they built up a very real distraction at a moment of severe crisis. So, even as he suffered with the hardships of Valley Forge, George Washington faced another severe ordeal—critics who questioned his suitability to lead.

As the student groups met to discuss Washington's problem, Ms. Stanitis once again brought out the story mountain graphic organizer to show her students that the graphic can be used not only to analyze an author's story but also as a rehearsal tool to draft their plot plans as well. "Once I have the setting and characters in mind," explained Ms. Stanitis, "I try to think of a problem that would be appropriate for the main character. Then I ask myself, 'How can I help my character solve this problem?' 'Do I need other characters to create a good ending?' 'What course of action might have helped my character rise above her or his problem?'" The students helped Ms. Stanitis fill out the story mountain by suggesting possible events that could lead to a solution for George Washington. From there, the students worked cooperatively to complete their own story mountains and, eventually, their historical narratives. Now that her students had something to say, Ms. Stanitis guided them through the rest of the writing experience with strategies experienced writers use when they compose text for a specific audience. Called the *writing process approach*, Ms. Stanitis organized her classroom as a writing workshop where children functioned as real authors. What happens during such workshops? In brief, Ms. Stanitis involved her students in the following processes:

- *Researching* as a real author must
- *Rehearsing* what they want to say and how they want to say it
- *Drafting*, or getting ideas down on paper
- *Revising and editing*, or checking to see if ideas are stated well and whether conventions (spelling, capitalization, and punctuation) are accurate
- *Publishing*, or sharing the written piece with an audience

Through this series of Storypath activities, Ms. Stanitis's young historians were learning how to gather historical information and organize it for a process writing experience. They used effective rehearsal strategies such as pictorializing and graphic organizers to help plot out cohesive, sensibly developed paragraphs.

Ms. Stanitis helps her students use a variety of rehearsal strategies throughout the school year, for there is no one right way for all writers to rehearse; the preferred form for any writer is an individual matter. It is beyond the scope of this text to go deeply into the writing process; you may find it useful to read the appropriate sections in the text used for your language arts course. But it is important at this point to describe how Ms. Stanitis brought closure to this writing experience. She knew that her young historians enjoyed publishing their own books and did so for many of the writing projects in which they were involved throughout the school year. It was apparent that publishing was valued by looking at a corner of the room where the sign "GoodBook Publishing Company" was clearly visible. After the writers completed their Valley Forge manuscripts, they took their stories to the classroom publishing company where they were polished and printed by a staff of expert workers. The class loves to be involved in these behind-the-scenes publishing departments:

- *Production department.* Puts pictures and stories together and gets them ready for printing. (Students who know how to use the word processor, or have a desire to learn, can make special contributions here.)
- *Art department.* Designs book covers; illustrates stories, if necessary.
- *Advertising department.* Creates ads (with pictures) that highlight new books.
- *Mechanical department.* Runs the printer or copier, collates the pages, staples them, and gets them ready for distribution. Many books are produced with hard covers.
- *Circulation department.* Places the books in the classroom library and delivers first print copies to the principal, other teachers, and classmates.

Primary Sources: Connecting With the Past

Several years ago, I was given my great grandfather's treasured pocket watch shortly after he had passed away. The watch was extraordinarily special to him because it was the first item of material worth he had treated himself to after selling his cow and using the money to escape his peasant's life in Ukraine to find a job on the railroad in the United States. My great grandfather had already retired from his menial railroad job by the time I was a youngster, but one of my earliest and fondest boyhood memories is admiring the intricate design on the watch's shiny gold cover and watching the delicate second hand rotate in a steady beat on the watch's flawless face. I remember watching my great grandfather's habit of slowly sliding out the watch from his faded coverall pockets as I sat with him on his front porch and listened to stories he told in broken English about his early life in Ukraine. I'm still not sure if he really needed to know the time or whether the watch was a satisfying reminder of the path he had traveled in life, but the obvious pleasure that surfaced on his mustached face is still firmly etched in my mind. Naturally, I was thrilled as a young man to have inherited the gold pocket watch because it helped me remain in touch with my great grandfather and his stories, even though he was physically no longer with me.

As I think more deeply about my great grandfather's pocket watch, I cannot help but make a connection to the study of history in our schools and how important it is to teach children through the use of primary sources. It is much as Potter (2003) states: "[Primary sources] are part of the past; they are with us today; and touching them allows us, quite literally, to touch and connect with the past" (p. 372).

Like my great grandfather's pocket watch, primary sources of historical evidence are extraordinary. They have the power to arouse interest in and imagination of the past. Remnants of the past help us to identify with and appreciate earlier times and places and to rouse memories in young and old alike. Interactive experiences with primary sources set fire to students' curiosities and help stimulate their interest in history.

We learned in the previous section that children's literature is an essential tool for nurturing an interest in and knowledge of the past. The use of these appropriate narratives helps produce a rich context for learning. Combining hands-on artifacts with narratives makes the learning experiences even more inspiring and memorable. Listening to someone demonstrate and talk about the rich Chinese tradition of kite making may be interesting, but handling an authentic Chinese kite and making a dragon kite after listening to *Dragon Kite of the Autumn Moon* by Valerie Reddix (Lothrop, Lee & Shepard Books) is truly extraordinary.

The primary sources used by historians to study the past may be classified as either written or nonwritten.

Written Evidence

Examining original written sources from the past helps students form a personal attachment to history. Anything written down can give historians clues about the people and events of the past—official documents, diaries, letters, songs, and the like.

FIGURE 3–10
Ad for a Runaway

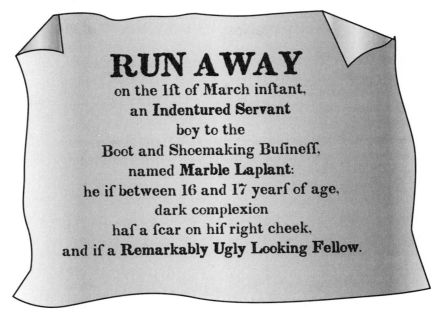

Documents Consider the advertisement for a runaway apprentice from the early 1800s in Figure 3–10. Among the advertisements in old newspapers, you will often find in these kinds of reward notices interesting clues about 19th-century life. Young boys were commonly hired out to artisans to learn a craft. They were housed and fed at the craftsperson's expense in return for training, working for free during their apprenticeship. Such advertisements usually offer historical clues, describing the clothing the runaway wore and comments on his appearance and temperament. With their "striped row trousers," "gingham roundabouts," "brown flannel jackets," "old straw hats," or "dark fustian pantaloons," these "remarkably ugly fellows" may have "lost two of their fore teeth" or "had three fingers cut off at the first joint on the right hand." These descriptions provide remarkable portraits of working-class people of 150 years ago. When children read original accounts of their escapades, they emerge as real individuals rather than as statistics or textbook portrayals. In this case, help your students analyze the evidence by asking questions:

- Why did the apprentices run away?
- What hardships did they face?
- Why did boys want to be apprentices?
- Why were apprentices mostly boys?
- How valuable was an apprentice to his master?

FIGURE 3–11
Ad From a Colonial Newspaper

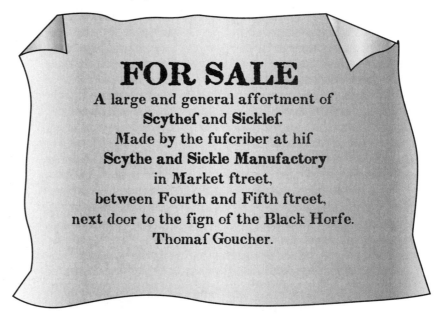

FOR SALE
A large and general affortment of
Scythef and Sicklef.
Made by the fufcriber at hif
Scythe and Sickle Manufactory
in Market ftreet,
between Fourth and Fifth ftreet,
next door to the fign of the Black Horfe.
Thomaf Goucher.

A section of the front page from Benjamin Franklin's *Pennsylvania Gazette* would give students insight into life in our country more than 200 years ago. Published in Philadelphia, our country's biggest city in 1787, a typical front page would contain ads such as the one shown in Figure 3–11.

Students can be guided to examine some interesting aspects of this evidence:

- The front pages at that time were mostly ads.
- The letters *f* and *s* looked alike.
- Advertisers referred to themselves as "subscribers."
- There were no building numbers. People were guided by signs that had pictures, not words. Many people could not read.

As a follow-up to examining the sample ad from the front page, you could have students research other occupations that could have been advertised in the *Pennsylvania Gazette* during Franklin's time—blacksmiths, milliners, tinsmiths, gunsmiths, wig makers, sail makers, shipbuilders, boot makers, and weavers. The students could then publish their own replica front page, trying to duplicate the language and other conventions consistent with the early history of our country.

Letters Letters from the past reveal interesting information about the famous as well as the infamous. For example, we have learned a lot about Benjamin Franklin through his letters. They have informed us that he was one of the most vocal opponents of selecting the bald eagle as our national symbol. It is now a well-known story that Franklin felt the turkey would have been far more representative of the newly formed United States. But, how did anyone find that out?

Through calendars and date books, it is known that Franklin was in France when Congress chose the national symbol in 1782. Angry, he wrote a letter complaining of the decision. Of the eagle, Franklin wrote, "He is a bird of bad moral character; he does not get his living honestly; you may have seen him perched on some dead tree near the river, where, too lazy to fish for himself, he watches the labour of the fishing-hawk; and when that diligent bird has at length taken a fish and is bearing it to his nest for the support of his mate and young ones, the bald eagle pursues him and takes it from him. Besides, he is a rank coward; the little kingbird, not bigger than a sparrow, attacks him boldly and drives him out of the district."

Franklin continued, "The turkey is in comparison a much more respectable bird, and withal a true original native of America. . . . He is . . . a bird of courage, and would not hesitate to attack a grenadier of the British Guards who would presume to invade his farmyard with a red coat on."

All of us have heard stories of Franklin's disapproval of selecting the bald eagle as our national symbol, but few have ever read his words. Think about how much actual written accounts, or accurate replicas of them, would enliven the investigative efforts of your young historians.

Journals and Diaries   Journals or diaries are personal, daily records of occurrences, experiences, and reflections. In the past, because there were few other options to record daily events, journals or diaries engaged countless numbers of people, both the great and the commonplace. Historians rely on their journals and diaries as one of the greatest sources of evidence to learn about the past. Just look how this diary of a 16-year-old rebel girl living in Gallatin, Tennessee, during Union occupation of the area sheds light on the struggle for survival during the Civil War.

March 3d

Snow all melted and weather fine. Gen. Payne rode out this evening to look at the stock, in his last trip he killed only one man (citizen, he always kills citizens when he cant find soldiers) swears he will kill every man in Gallatin and Hartsville if bush whacking isn't stopped shortly.

The spirit of the times can be clearly revealed by examining such compelling sources of historical knowledge. It is interesting to compare this Sourtherner's real concern for "bush whackers" with the same concern expressed by 16-year-old Jeff Bussey. Jeff, a character in Harold Keith's Civil War novel, *Rifles for Watie* (New York: Crowell) joins a group of new volunteers discussing why they joined the army.

"My family's Union. Mammy didn't want me to go to no war. But we knowed the bushwhackers was hid out in the brush, stealin' money and hosses and chokin' boys my age when they found 'em. I didn't wanta git choked. I runned away. I wanted to run away sooner."

Diaries, alone or in combination with other instructional resources, can be an exciting addition to any history program and open up a wealth of possibilities to extend children's learning on any topic.

Many good websites offer original diaries for classroom use. The DoHistory website (*www.dohistory.org/interests/i_teaching.html*), for example, not only brings a diary's words directly to your students, but also uses a special "magic lens" that changes the diary from a handwritten to a transcribed version as it is moved over the handwritten version. This is a very useful tool since many historical diaries have been written in a script that is very difficult for elementary school children to read. Children simply use the computer's mouse to move the lens around the diary page to see the "magic" transcription of the handwritten diary page. Many other unique historical documents have been scanned in and transcribed on this site, along with examples of how historians use such documents in their investigations.

Children's Simulated Historical Documents

It should be clear by now that one of my major beliefs is that literacy can be a significant part of social studies education. By using the writing process in a content subject such as history, children become more aware of what they know and feel comfortable drawing from their knowledge to express growing ideas through print. Surely, children do not learn to write only during that part of the day designated as "language arts class" but also write while involved in subjects such as social studies, which offer a rich content framework that facilitates various kinds of writing. *Prose* is the term we give to an assortment of writing forms that, in addition to historical narratives, offer students a variety of productive opportunities to express themselves through print—journal writing, letter writing, diaries, and newspapers.

It is best to set up students for success as they first begin writing in these new forms. Be sure to review the components of the writing process before you start and plan to model and demonstrate the techniques associated with each writing form. Remember, too, that imitation plays a large part in other forms of prose writing just as it does in writing historical narratives. As you share real diaries, newspapers, historical journals, and other primary sources of written historical evidence with your students, they will be most highly motivated to imitate what they see and try their hands at creating their own versions. Take advantage of this inclination to imitate the style and structure of other writers and encourage it.

Period Newspapers   Period newspapers offer a thought-provoking writing form appropriate for the study of history because they help students express the content of what they are learning as well as influence the attitudes and beliefs of others through such tactics as political cartoons or editorials.

A trip to a newspaper publisher and a careful inspection of the local newspaper can help children understand how newspapers are designed and produced. Although newspaper staffs differ among newspapers, all generally include the following positions, which many teachers have challenged their students to mimic in the classroom:

- *Publisher.*   Owner or person who represents the owner; responsible for the overall operation of the newspaper.

- *Editors.*   Responsible for several facets of newspaper production, such as deciding what goes into the newspaper, assigning reporters to cover events, determining where to position the stories, or writing their opinions of significant events (editorials).
- *Reporters.*   Cover the stories by digging up the facts and interpreting them.
- *Feature writers.*   Produce special columns such as jokes and riddles, lost and found, and recipes.
- *Copy editors.*   Read stories for mistakes and adjust length to meet space requirements.

Students will be interested in writing several types of stories for their period newspaper. Depending on the era being studied, some possibilities include:

- *Front page* story about a national/world/local event from the period
- *Editorial column* responding to the story
- *Original political cartoon* about the event
- *Sports section* with stories about popular sports or athletes of the day
- *Real estate section* with original advertisements showing what homes were like at the time
- *Help wanted section* showing the kinds of jobs people had
- *Classified section* exhibiting the kinds of things people might be selling or wanting to buy
- *Movie review* assessing a movie or illustrating a movie poster from the time
- *Fashion page* containing illustrations and descriptions of the styles of the period
- *Food guide* via columns describing the recipes and/or meals that were popular
- *Advice column* describing the types of problems people had and counseling that reflects the prevailing attitudes of the period.

After assigning the students to the news gathering, writing, and illustrating jobs, you will want to get the rest of the class involved in the behind-the-scenes departments comparable to those described earlier in the discussion of classroom book publishing companies. As an example of one group's efforts to publish a period newspaper, consider Curtis Yannie's fifth-grade class, which fashioned a newspaper set in Revolutionary War times.

Inside an *Active* Classroom

Mr. Yannie's students were involved in a study of the Revolutionary War. Their front-page stories took form beneath these blaring headlines: "British Evacuate Boston,"

"Grand Union Flag Unfurled Over Boston," "Redcoats Invade New York," "Congress Approves Declarartion of Independence," and "Washington Stuns Hessian Fighters." Feature articles detailed such items of interest as quilting, candle-making, and the steps of drying food for winter. An advertising section offered articles for sale (spinning wheels, bed warmers, teams of oxen, pewter tableware, flintlock rifles, wigs). An employment section offered such jobs as post rider, saddler, tanner, wigmaker, tavern keeper, chandler, mason, cooper, hatter, and printer. An editorial page displayed a political cartoon showing a crowd of Continental soldiers pulling down an equestrian statue of King George III as they celebrated the signing of the Declaration of Independence in Philadelphia, and an editorial solicited funds for the relief of widows and children of the patriots "murdered" at Lexington. There was a book review of Thomas Paine's *Common Sense,* and a sports section detailing the results of such popular events as stool ball, quoits, arm wrestling, and gunny sack races. When finished, the period newspaper contained several pages that were stapled together and distributed to the other fifth-grade classrooms.

Diaries   Diaries are short, private accounts of and reactions to daily events. They absorb elementary school students because they are real and personal; young historians not only see a piece of direct evidence but also come into contact with human emotions, values, and attitudes of the past. Diaries allow students to come in contact with the language and customs of the times, free of any alteration by a writer. Thereby, diaries add context and a human touch to historic events. Diaries that chronicle the events of people's lives in days gone by add great interest to the study of history. For example, in the summer of 1863, a young woman joined her uncle's family in their migration from Ohio to the Idaho Territory. Her name was Lucia Darling. During the course of the three-month journey, Lucia kept an extensive diary. The diary recorded camp life, daily activities, encounters with other wagon trains, interactions with Native Americans, and landmarks along the route.

After students read selected pages from Lucia's diary, a teacher might ask them to imitate her diary by creating a diary page for an immigrant or migrant person today. Or, it is possible to connect Lucia's diary to the act of composing historical narratives. For example, the students can create fictional members of Lucia's wagon train and go on to use Lucia's diary as a source of information to weave a story about the characters' chores and responsibilities, hardships, and other experiences.

In this manner, children could be introduced to diary writing by asking them to pretend to be a historical figure and write down personal thoughts and feelings as though they were experiencing the historical event. Imaginatively placing themselves in the shoes of real people, such as Columbus during his journey to America, can serve as a strong stimulus for diary writing. The following diary entries were written by a student pretending to be a sailor on one of Magellan's ships that was unable to complete the circumnavigation of the globe in 1522:

The storm lasted two days and two nights. I never saw waves so high or the wind blow so hard. Our ship was thrown against huge rocks and was smashed to bits. We held onto our lifeboats for longer than I could remember—every sailor was scared stiff. We finally spotted some land. . . .

Fresh water is disappearing. Our captain divided us into four groups. Each group was to go in a different direction to search for fresh water. In mid-afternoon the fourth group found a freshwater spring on the west side of the island. . . .

Writing simulated diaries is easy for children if they have had an opportunity to examine actual diary pages from the past. Oftentimes, models of journal writing can be found in good children's literature sources. Penny Coleman's *Girls: A History of Growing Up Female in America* (Scholastic) is a good example. The book is a compelling history of the lives of diverse American girls (slaves, pioneers, immigrants, rich, poor) told through their diaries, memoirs, and letters. Regardless of the source of inspiration, children can use diary writing as an effective tool to understand their world and to communicate knowledge of it.

Letters   Letter writing offers another major type of writing option for social studies classrooms. If students have had an opportunity to invent journals, then letter writing is a reasonable next step. Friendly letters and diaries are both conversational in style and express the writer's account of important events and emotions attached to them. As with all other writing forms, models of letters from the past are necessary to help youngsters analyze the conversational style and the format of the times. If writing a simulated letter to your father during colonial days, for example, the proper greeting would be *Honour'd Sir* and a proper ending would be *Your Dutiful Daughter (or Son)*. Also in keeping with authenticity, students should write with the implements commonly used at the time. A letter during colonial times would have been written with quill pen—a goose, peacock, pheasant, or wild turkey feather. Ink was made by crushing and boiling down such natural vegetation as cranberries or walnut shells. This may be difficult to do in typical elementary school classrooms; educational supply companies, though, sell small colonial writing kits containing a goose feather and dry ink for about $3.00 each. There were no envelopes during colonial times, so students should simply fold the letter and seal it. A blob of hot sealing wax was used during colonial days, but pressing a small ball of clay to seal the simulated letter would work fine.

Klaus Hubben offers a fine example of imaginative letter writing. While his fourth graders were learning about Christopher Columbus, he asked them to pretend to be Columbus writing a letter to Queen Isabella requesting support for his explorations. See Figure 3–12 for an example of an imaginative letter.

Potpourri of History Writing Opportunities   Here are some writing forms that can supplement the major suggestions presented so far in this text:

- ABC books where each letter of the alphabet tells something about a topic (for example, *The ABCs of Native American History*)

FIGURE 3–12
A Student's Letter Written From the Perspective of a Historical Figure

> Dear Queen Isabella,   Oct. 1491
>   If you'll give me
> financial help I can prove that
> this world is round. I have been
> studying sailing since the age
> of 13 years old and am a
> very experienced sailor I could
> get my crew and me out of
> any storm we run in to.
>   I can bring you back
> spices, treasures and any thing
> else I may find on this voyage.
> I have been sailing from a
> young age and should be successful
> I hope you'll consider my request.
>
>   Your Loyal subject,
>
> C. Columbus, Navigator

- Calendars where each page incorporates an illustration and information about a historical topic (for example, a calendar with each month illustrating and describing one of the "12 greatest inventions in history")
- "Big books" where each page contains a combination of drawings and brief text about a topic under study (for example, a book about the history of railroads in the United States)

- Radio, television, or movie scripts about a historical event that can be performed by the students
- How-to books where students write instructions for something related to a historical unit (for example, *How to Make a Barrel*)
- Recipe books that describe foods eaten in different eras (for example, favorite foods of America's past presidents)

The goal of all forms of historical writing is to present ideas precisely and creatively. Just think of the potential of using several writing activities during a unit on Thanksgiving, for example: Students could write letters from Plymouth colony to a relative in England describing the voyage across the Atlantic, a recipe book describing all the foods available at the first Thanksgiving dinner (with drawings), thank-you notes to Squanto for helping them learn the Indian way to plant corn, a script to reenact the first meeting of the Pilgrims with Samoset, simulated entries from Squanto's diary telling of his first contact with the Pilgrims, or reports on Thanksgiving celebrations in other nations. Through assignments like these, children gain valuable practice writing in different forms, for different purposes, and to different audiences.

Oral History

Bringing in someone to tell stories of personal experiences related to particular places or times is an idea with exciting possibilities for any classroom. Known as oral history, these stories need not be major projects; all that is needed is someone interesting to spin tales of times gone by. Take the time Jim Mosteller, 93 years old, visited my classroom and mesmerized my children with firsthand accounts of turn-of-the-century life. "When we got automobiles around here, you couldn't use them in the winter," Mr. Mosteller said. "My father had one of the first cars in town. It was one of those open cars with leather seats and brass lamps. I'll never forget one Sunday; we had eleven flat tires!"

Mr. Mosteller had the children's undivided attention when he told what a dollar would buy in 1939: one dozen eggs, a loaf of bread, a pound of butter, and a half-pound of bacon. He also told the children about a whistle-stop campaign during which Teddy Roosevelt visited town in 1912 ("I can see him to this day") and the transfer of the Liberty Bell on a flatbed car from Philadelphia to San Francisco for safekeeping during World War I.

You should use valuable sources of historical information like Mr. Mosteller both for the children's enjoyment and as a source for researching and recording details from the past. These experiences give students a clearer understanding of and appreciation for people and events of the past.

Simulated Oral History Oftentimes a teacher can arouse strong interest in an area of historical investigation by simulating the narrative of someone who has lived in the past. The teacher-as-historical figure creates mental images for the students through spoken words and gestures, reacting and responding to audience needs. Based on real events, teachers help children reach beyond the boundaries of immediate time and into the world of the past. Schreifels (1983), for example, brought life to one of her history topics by taking on the role of a famous explorer:

> The day I discovered my fifth grade class had no idea who Vasco da Gama was—and cared less to find out—was the day I vowed to come up with some way to provoke interest in historical personalities. If da Gama and the rest of the early explorers were to become more than hard words to be stumbled over in a textbook, I realized, something drastic—and dramatic—had to be done.
>
> The next morning during social studies class, I slipped into the hall, plunked an old beehive hat on my head, swept a wraparound skirt over my shoulders and reappeared as an unreasonable facsimile of Vasco da Gama, fifteenth century sea captain. I introduced myself with my best Portuguese accent and invited questions.
>
> At first there were merely giggles, until I threatened to make every student walk the plank unless I got some proper, respectful questions. The first was about how I got there (via a time machine that just happened to look like a filing cabinet). Eventually someone wanted to know just who I was.
>
> "I'm Vasco da Gama, and I'm very famous."
>
> "For what?" they all demanded.
>
> I then proceeded to regale them with stories of my sailing prowess. Ever since that time, I've found I need only lean on the filing cabinet to get everyone's undivided attention. "Is the time machine going to bring us another mysterious person?" students plead. Quite often the answer is yes. And although these time machine visitors may have fuzzy historical memories, they serve to stimulate real interest in people of the past. (p. 84)

As Schreifels advises, you need not "go overboard" to involve students personally and motivate them to learn. Some of the most effective techniques require very little extra teacher preparation time to organize.

Interviews

Conducting interviews is a superb way to introduce children to the process of collecting oral historical data.

If any interview is to be productive, it is essential that students are able to carry out the three basic interview stages that precede the writing of a story or report: *planning, interviewing,* and *reconstructing.* Impromptu interviews seldom are successful. Each of the following recommendations will not need to be employed each time the children conduct an interview; familiarity with the individual being interviewed will determine which are of most importance.

Planning   Once the students have decided to interview someone, they should call or e-mail in advance to make an appointment. They should identify themselves by their name, grade, and the name of their school. They should describe the purpose of their research in brief and general terms. If the students plan to interview several individuals in connection with their research, they should interview the most important person last, because they will be better prepared based on the knowledge gained from the earlier interviews. The students should conduct as much research as possible in advance on the person to be interviewed. Sources might include family stories, the library, public records, the Internet, and people you know who can provide background information. Questions should be written in advance and brought to the interview on an easy-to-write-on pad. The students should take notes as they ask each question because it will help in the writing phase. It is certainly helpful to bring a tape recorder, but the students should first obtain the permission from the person they are interviewing.

With good questions, student interviewers will be able to obtain quality data from their subjects. Here are four simple questioning strategies they will want to employ:

1. *Ask clear questions.* Questions should be easy to understand, short, and devoid of jargon or slang.

2. *Ask single questions.* Students should ask only one question at a time.

3. *Ask open-ended questions.* Open-ended questions allow room to respond with more information. For example, "What do you think about the growth of technology during your lifetime?" or "What is your opinion of the music young people listen to today?" will produce deeper responses than "Technology has really mushroomed during your lifetime, hasn't it?" or "Is the music young people listen to today different from the music you listened to as a young person?"

4. *Follow certain responses with well-timed probes.* The purpose of probing is to deepen or clarify the response to a question; for example, "Could you please say a little more about that?" or "Do you have any additional examples?"

Interviewing A short period of relaxed, casual conversation is advantageous prior to the actual interview. It will loosen up both the interviewee and the interviewer. The actual interview questions should be as short as possible and the respondent should be given plenty of time to answer. Students should be aware of some of the principles of *active listening*; that is, reacting to rather than simply receiving the information. Active listening obviously includes receiving and retaining the ideas of the interviewee, but it also requires the interviewers to communicate interest by responding both verbally and nonverbally through body movements, facial expressions, and short comments or expressions of feeling (such as surprise or sadness). Rephrasing an interesting comment, a mere nod of understanding or approval, a "hmmmm," to indicate interest, or just a smile or frown are examples of active listening practices.

Reconstructing As soon as it's practical after the interview, the students should find a quiet place to analyze their handwritten notes; fore, during the course of the interview, they may have jotted down things that won't mean a thing a day later. Some of their scribbling may have been so slapdash that it requires decoding; the students will be better able to decipher the scribbles soon after the interview than if they waited. To speed up the writing process, the students might use a code to pull their notes together; they could, for example, underline or put asterisks alongside quotes that seemed most appropriate.

Conducting interviews is a superb way to introduce children to the process of experiencing oral history. Most children are familiar with interviewing; they regularly see people interviewed on television. Capitalize on these experiences by videotaping a short television interview and look for what a good interviewer does.

You can provide your young historians an opportunity to practice being classroom interviewers before they actually conduct their first formal interviews. This can be done by showing the students an out-of-the-ordinary item and encouraging them to keep asking questions until they get at the story behind the object. You can play the "interviewee" role as the children assume the job of "interviewers."

For example, one day Mario Fiore walked into the classroom with a Native American dream catcher dangling from his left hand. "I have something interesting here," Mr. Fiore announced to his puzzled class. "It's going to be your job to interview me until you are able to find out as much information about it as you can. I will not tell you anything beyond the information you ask for." Twenty excited pairs of eyes took in every feature of the dream catcher: "Where did you get it? Who made it? Why does it have feathers on the side? Why is it important for Native Americans?"

A special interview had begun! Notice that the youngsters started asking closed questions and eventually moved to open types that not only gave them a deeper collection of information but also provided insight into the lives of the Native Americans. Through experiences like these, children quickly learn how different questions can give them different types of information, but, most of all, they learn that people hold information, and that it can be extracted by using a series of strategic questions.

When children are comfortable with the interviewing process, have them plan an actual interview with a person who might contribute new insights into a historical topic.

Inside an *Active* Classroom

Yvonne Perry-Segarra used Bonnie Pryor's book, *The House on Maple Street* (Morrow), to set the scene for an interview project in her classroom. In the story, the past is linked to the present as lost objects from early times are unearthed in a contemporary child's yard: for example, an Indian child loses an arrowhead and a pioneer child loses a china cup. A discussion of dramatic changes in the American family through the years followed the book reading. Students talked about several eras, but became particularly focused on how hard it must have been for people to grow up without the technology that has become so omnipresent today. "What did kids do for fun back then?" asked these youth living in an era of cell phones, satellite or cable TV, the Internet, and CDs.

Knowing that modeling a process results in greater student achievement, Ms. Perry-Segarra suggested inviting her grandfather to school to interview him about what it was like for him as a youngster. Ms. Perry-Segarra told the students that her grandfather was an antique radio buff with an extensive collection of authentic radio show CDs from the 1940s (the "Golden Age" of radio). Jointly, Ms. Perry-Segarra and her young historians developed a set of questions to ask him about radio programs and the reasons they were so popular.

Ms. Perry-Segarra's grandfather not only visited class to be interviewed, but he staged an "Old-Fashioned Radio Night." Using a replica of an old console-style radio, he recreated an atmosphere of family and friends gathered around the radio to listen to their favorite programs. He shared brief recorded excerpts from sports and news events; played the song "Sentimental Journey" by Les Brown and his orchestra from the popular music show, "Your Hit Parade," and watched with joy as the students listened to one of the popular comedy shows of the era, "The Jack Benny Program." He dressed in the popular clothing style of the 1940s, and he ended his interview by offering the students a stick of Beeman's Gum, one of the most fondly remembered munchies of the time.

The children watched, listened, commented, and asked questions as they became immersed in radio's days of glory. After her grandfather left the room, Ms. Perry-Segarra gathered the children together and invited them to share their thoughts. Sensing their interest was still high, Ms. Perry-Segarra asked the students to bring in family photos from the 1930s and 1940s, looking especially for pictures showing the family radio. The photos were examined for clothing and hair styles, furniture, and other characteristics.

Using this experience as a model interview for her students, Ms. Perry-Segarra asked her students to brainstorm a series of questions they might ask their grandparents to find out what life was like in the bygone era when they were in elementary school. Each student suggested a question by writing it on an index card. The cards were collected and examined by the class as a whole. Questions requiring simple *yes* or *no* answers were discarded while those which stood the best chance of drawing out more detailed information were kept.

After the cards were arranged in a useful questioning sequence, the students were ready to conduct their interviews. Some grandparents lived in or near the same community as the students, so face-to-face interviews were possible. Other grandparents lived far away so they had to be interviewed by phone or e-mail. Students were free either to use a tape recorder or to jot down notes to help them remember what was said during the interview, but most found that the tape recorder worked best. (They jotted down notes anyway, just in case the recorder malfunctioned.) The children listened carefully and actively to their grandparents' responses to make sure the desired information was being gathered. If it wasn't, they asked probing questions to clarify points or draw out additional information.

Next, Ms. Perry-Segarra's young historians reconstructed the information and wrote interesting narratives of their interviews. Each historical narrative was read in class, and then bound into a class book. Sample reconstructive notes from one child's interview are shown in Figure 3–13.

FIGURE 3–13
A Student's
Interview With
His Grandfather

10/6/92

Interview

My interview is with my grandfather whom I call "Grampy." Grampy was born in 1912 in Rathmel, PA. Grampy is 80 years old and is my father's father. He is the oldest member in my family. Counting him he has 8 brothers and sisters. Three of them are still alive. He now lives in Sayre, PA, alone, with his fat cat named "Mama Cat." Grampy loves to tell jokes and tells them all the time. My dad usually calls him at night and Grampy always has a joke

Question: What kind of hobbies did you have when you were 12?

Answer: He liked to go fishing and hunting. He couldn't get a hunting license untill he was 12. Most of his time he worked on the slackpile. His job was helping the family. Once and a while he went swimming. He paid $.10 for a movie. His brother would take them in his Model-T Ford. He still fishes but does not hunt.

Question: What was your first car? How much did it cost?

Answer: Grampy's first car was a 1929 Essex. It cost him $500 to get it. He was 23 years old when he got it.

Nonwritten Sources (Artifacts)

Artifacts include all the nonwritten objects—photos, paintings, coins, furniture, tools, and the like—that help historians reconstruct the story of human life. I like to use the term *accidental survivors* to describe artifacts because very few of them were intentionally preserved for the future in hopes that others would have them as evidence of life in the past. Photographs, for example, give us interesting clues about the past. A vintage classroom photograph can tell us a great deal about school life during the early part of the 20th century—what the students wore, what their hairstyles were like, what their classrooms were like, what school supplies they used, how they were taught, and even what they studied.

How do you locate primary documents and artifacts for your classroom? Gray and Owens (2003) admit there is no surefire way of locating these sources, but offer a number of suggestions on how to start. If you are looking for materials to enliven your lessons, the authors suggest you start in your own attic (or grandma's). It's amazing what you'll be able to find—immigration papers, old photos, letters, postcards, diaries, and report cards, just to name a few. One of the best ways to find documents on a person or event is through an Internet search. The National Archives Digital Classroom (*www.archives.gov/digital classroom*) and the Library of Congress American Memory Collection (*memory.loc.gov/ammem/amhome.html*) are two excellent sources.

For research on a local topic, you might want to check with the local historical society, museum, or library. Parents are an excellent resource for historical materials. Either make an announcement detailing your needs at an open house meeting or send a note home requesting specific materials for a topic under study and you will most surely receive more than you expect. Many teachers can help with school-related research. Old yearbooks, report cards, records, equipment, materials catalogs, and photographs can help young historians compare yesterday's schools with today's. Cemeteries and other gravesites can offer a unique picture of the past. If cemeteries interest you, the Association of Gravestone Studies (*www.gravestonestudies.org*) or Colonial Williamsburg's online lesson, History Comes Alive in the Graveyard, will help (*history.org/history/teaching/graveyrd2.cfm*).

Special collections of artifacts and documents related to historical topics or themes are often assembled by social studies teachers to motivate young historians and give them a firsthand look at the past. Creating a collection for a particular historical period authenticates the experience for children and helps them learn abstract historical concepts. Teachers report that these artifact collections increase students' interest, enhance their understanding, and make classroom discussions more meaningful and interesting. One teacher, for example, compiled an artifact kit for a unit on ancient Egypt. It contained a model mummy coffin, necklace with a dangling ankh, panel from a false door of a tomb, a tablet with hieroglyphs, and photographs and documents. These items motivated students to learn more about Egypt from various resources and helped them relate background information to new learning experiences throughout the unit of study.

A major part of studying history is using the tactics employed by historians. Students must examine oral and written records as well as artifacts and books for evidence to explain the past. This is the way to teach history—by allowing children to investigate as historians. Provide situations where they can examine historical materials firsthand. Bring artifacts to the classroom, invite guest speakers to demonstrate items from the past, and visit living museums and historical sites to examine original sources. Young historians should use the historian's methods of investigation to study a variety of local, regional, state, national, or international topics.

Inside an Active Classroom

To open a new topic of historical investigation, Peggy Logan displayed a large chest-type box on which was inscribed the words "Historical Treasure Chest." Together with the children, she opened it and inside they found four pieces of primary source materials—a photograph, a map, a newspaper article, and a model of a World War II B-17 bomber.

Ms. Logan helped the students gather basic information about the materials. The photograph was of an Army Air Corps eight-person crew taken during the closing days of World War II. The B-17 model was an example of the aircraft they flew. It was named "Miss Anthracite" for the coal mining heritage of the pilot's home town. The newspaper article was about Debra Pieri, a second-grade teacher who has been telling the story of the pilot, First Lieutenant Arthur "Dutchy" Sauler, to anyone who will listen—students, authors, politicians. The article detailed the heroism that Sauler demonstrated in 1945 when, as a 21-year-old pilot, his B-17 was hit by anti-aircraft fire during a mission to bomb the rail routes of retreating German forces. It seems that two of the craft's engines were destroyed by the enemy fire, but Dutchy stayed at the controls long enough to allow his crew time to bail out safely. Tragically, Sauler was the only crew member to perish. The map showed the location of these dramatic events.

The students carefully examined the artifacts and became intensely curious about each one and the story they told. There was no other information in the box, so the students decided to look to other resources to fill in the gaps. They found follow-up newspaper articles that told of exhaustive efforts by Pieri, as well as Sauler family members and friends, to have Sauler awarded the Medal of Honor. However, the Department of Defense has judged that Sauler's actions, although brave, merited only the Silver Star, our nation's third-highest decoration for valor.

"He sure was a brave guy," offered Andrew. "I think he should be given the Medal of Honor."

"Yeah," agreed Anita. "How much braver can anybody be than to save seven lives and lose his own?"

"Just think of what's going on in Iraq," added Chaim. "I know it's 60 years later, but I wonder how many heroes are saving lives every day over there. It would be great to hear their stories."

After the students talked about the heroism of Dutchy Sauler, they were invited to create a "Historical Treasure Chest" documenting an interesting story from their own family's past. They were asked to look through their personal and family's belongings for primary source materials that tell their own story-photographs, diaries, letters, childhood drawings, a ticket to a sporting event, a birth certificate, or even a receipt from a local restaurant. The students were directed to consider any four or five authentic items that could serve to give important information about an important family event or accomplishment. Then, they were to write an explanatory story explaining why they chose those particular items for their treasure chest.

Next, the students exchanged their treasure chests with another student (but not the explanatory stories), each answering in writing the question, "What does this treasure chest tell me about my classmate?" In other words, what might each student learn about a classmate by examining what he or she has put into the box? Finally, Ms. Logan's class created a class exhibit of all the treasure chests along with the explanatory stories, and discussed what the contents of the various treasure chests might suggest about their class as a whole.

Historical documents offer a strong and powerful link to the past. Whether telling the story of someone the students have never known before or of their own families, historical documents offer a fitting hands-on link to another time and another place. Unfortunately, in many classrooms, historical documents are thought of much as museum pieces—too valuable to touch so they are kept under lock and key. While documents such as these unquestionably deserve our utmost attention and respect, it is important to include the myriad of items that offer critical historical information and help students engage in meaningful learning experiences. Just have them examine the contents of a "Historical Treasure Chest" and you will see how motivated they become to learn about life in another era.

Visits to "Living Museums"

The world outside the classroom is rich in historical learning experiences. By taking trips outside of school, students experience things firsthand that are impossible in the classroom. Visiting museums and "living history" sites to observe the clothing, houses, furnishing, tools, and other artifacts enlighten and enrich understandings of any historical period.

A list of places to visit can range from A to Z, from antique shops to the zoo. Regardless, the challenge is to effectively draw out student understandings from wherever you choose to go. A fifth-grade teacher, Soojeong Kim, who was teaching a unit titled Colonial Life in America, makes the value of such trips crystal-clear. She realized that her students' failure to comprehend time and place concepts might stifle their curiosity and interest in studying colonial America, so she arranged a trip to an authentic living museum in Cooperstown, New York.

Inside an Active Classroom

The children's spirits were instantly aroused as the class walked up the path connecting the parking lot to the restored colonial village called the Farmer's Museum. Authentic in every detail, the village was an actual working farm in which people dressed in period garb and used authentic implements to perform the duties of colonial farmers. About halfway up the path, the class fixed their eyes in horror as a farmer led a huge ox hauling a cart directly toward them. None of the children had ever before seen a real ox; few know exactly what an ox was. "Let me outa here!" shrieked Frank guardedly as the snorting animal, covered with flies and oozing slobber, ambled up and stopped next to him. The farmer invited Frank to pat the ox, but Frank was too scared to try.

"I never knew an ox was so big," Lois marveled as she reached up and patted its wet nose.

Following Lois's lead, several classmates approached the ox, some patting it and others commenting on its size, smell, and drawing power for flies. Some children were satisfied to simply look at the ox, while others ran away from it when it made the slightest movement. One or two even made faces at it. They did all sorts of things. The farmer told the class about the importance of oxen to colonial life, and they were enthralled with his story. He thanked them for stopping and told them that his tired animal needed to go to the barn for a rest.

From that day on the children all knew exactly what an ox was. Pictures of oxen, stories of oxen, or a video of oxen could never hope to approach the sounds, smells, sights, and tactile sensations of the real animal.

The ox experience seemed to transform the students from audience to actors. "That was awesome," shouted Tahben in anticipation. "What else is there?"

The first building the students came to was a school, where a "school marm" taught them about the ABCs exactly as a teacher would have done in colonial times. Spirits soared as the children went to the barn, where workers involved them in the entire process of making linen from flax. Ms. Kim was as fascinated by the process as the children. She, too, had never before seen linen made from flax even though she taught the concept from textbook diagrams for years. By now, it was getting late and Ms. Kim tried to get the class to move on to the tanner, wigmaker, blacksmith, gunsmith, cooper (barrel maker), and glass blower, but the children insisted on staying at the barn for the corn husking bee and gunnysack race. At every stop, the children had an opportunity to touch, handle, and use. Ms. Kim had a tough time pulling them away from each stop so they could visit the next exhibit. It was apparent that Ms. Kim and her students were quite new to this world of the past, not old hands who have been there and done that. They were thrilled to be placed in the role of "historians," passionately and actively exploring the past.

The next day, when the students came back to their classroom, they were primed and ready to go to work. Ms. Kim involved the class in several learning activities that focused on the events at the Farmer's Museum. To conclude the day, she read aloud a book that seemed to be a perfect connection to one of the most fascinating adventures from their trip, *Ox-Cart Man,* a Caldecott Medal-winning book by Donald Hall. The story is about a father who loads up his ox-cart with the many things his family has been making and growing all year and begins a 10-day trek to market in Portsmouth during early autumn. Naturally, Ms. Kim related their field trip experiences to the story and drew out a quantity and quality of ideas rarely experienced before. It was amazing to see how much the field trip helped students understand and make sense out of the story as well as all subsequent learning activities.

The world outside the classroom is a stimulating place for young historians. Explore your community for these "hidden" resources and even you might learn new knowledge beyond the here and now.

CHRONOLOGY

Up to now, we have looked at the kinds of classroom experiences appropriate for helping elementary school children construct historical knowledge and thinking behaviors. However, we have not yet addressed one additional area of historical

Words cannot duplicate the effectiveness of watching this metalsmith at work in a Colonia-era living museum.

thinking—chronological thinking—a process that is at the heart of history. Students understand chronology when they are able to determine the dates of historical events and to sequentially arrange the events in time. In its National Standards for History, the National Center for History in the Schools (1996) made a strong case for teaching chronological thinking in our schools: "Without a strong sense of chronology—of when events occurred and in what temporal order—it is impossible for students to examine relationships among those events or to explain historical causality. Chronology provides the mental scaffolding for organizing historical thought" (p. 62).

Young historians must understand that human events take place over time, one after the other. It is important to establish this linkage to reconstruct events and tell the stories that establish relationships between important events. Young historians must learn the measures of time that all historians use—day, week, month, year, decade, and century. Using the calendar is one way to do this, but strategies for teaching calendar-related skills is a topic that goes beyond the scope of this text. We will look at event chains and timelines, however—specialized tools that allow young historians to place historical events in meaningful sequence.

Event Chains

At times, a social studies learning experience may deal with a sequence of important happenings, such as major milestones of the Westward Movement, or the significant highlights in the life of an important historical person, like the rise and fall of Alexander the Great. An event chain is useful in describing the sequence of these important events and how one event led to the other by presenting a series of frames that break up and sequence the key segments. Figure 3–14 illustrates a sample event chain.

Timelines

Timelines are representations of key historical events arranged chronologically within a particular time period, often consisiting of illustrative material accompanied by short written commentary. As children study the past, timelines help them put events into temporal perspective. However, simply furnishing your students with a commercially produced timeline and asking them to interpret it will not help develop a solid understanding of the chronology of events. Young historians will learn more from timelines if they construct them.

For the very youngest children, construct timelines on topics related to their immediate experience. Illustrate routines of the daily schedule, for example. Have the children talk about what they do in school each day and pick out an illustration (or photo) that shows it. The children can arrange the illustrations or photos in sequence according to which activity takes place first, second, and so on.

Extend their ability to sequence major daily events to something else that has great meaning in children's lives—holidays and school vacations. Cut out a symbol for each major national holiday, for example. These will vary, depending on the culture of your school and the nature of cross-cultural holidays as you learn about them.

FIGURE 3–14
Event Chain

THE REVOLUTIONARY WAR
INITIATING EVENTS

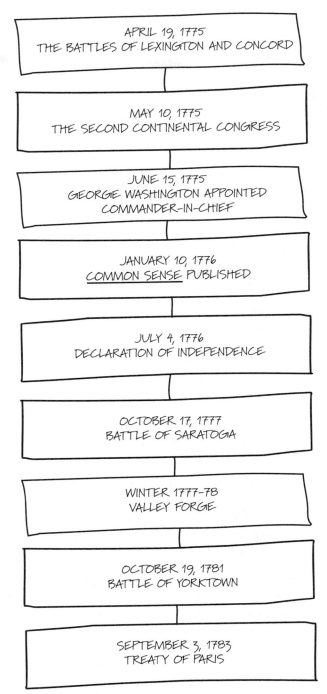

APRIL 19, 1775
THE BATTLES OF LEXINGTON AND CONCORD

MAY 10, 1775
THE SECOND CONTINENTAL CONGRESS

JUNE 15, 1775
GEORGE WASHINGTON APPOINTED
COMMANDER-IN-CHIEF

JANUARY 10, 1776
COMMON SENSE PUBLISHED

JULY 4, 1776
DECLARATION OF INDEPENDENCE

OCTOBER 17, 1777
BATTLE OF SARATOGA

WINTER 1777–78
VALLEY FORGE

OCTOBER 19, 1781
BATTLE OF YORKTOWN

SEPTEMBER 3, 1783
TREATY OF PARIS

FINAL OUTCOME

FIGURE 3–15
Sequencing Holidays

The children can use clothespins to clip the symbols in temporal sequence (see Figure 3–15). The children must decide which symbol comes first, second, and so on as they place the symbols in proper sequence.

After your students complete sequencing major events such as these, they should be ready to create their own timelines of slightly longer spans of time; perhaps a timeline highlighting the stages of a human's life span, of the children's lives, their families' histories, or a timeline of their community's history. These timelines can be as simple or as sophisticated as your students' abilities will dictate. For example, Silas Dillman read Tomie de Paola's book *Now One Foot, Now the Other* (Putnam), a touching story about a strong emotional attachment between a grandfather and child. After a short discussion, Mr. Dillman organized his students into small groups and asked each group to draw a sketch on a sheet of $8\frac{1}{2}''\times11''$ drawing paper that illustrated one of the significant life stages: "Birth," "Learn to Walk," "Learn to Talk," "Ride a Bike," "Go to Kindergarten," "Enter Fourth Grade," "Go to Middle School," "Enter High School," "Graduate from High School," and "Go to College" or "Go to Work." After they were done, Mr. Dillman took the students to the playground. Those holding the "Birth" card were the starting point for the timeline. Next, the children thought about the age at which they began to walk. Mr. Dillman instructed the children holding the "Learn to Walk" card to begin at the "Birth" point and evenly pace the number of steps it would take to get from birth to walking. He used the same process for each of the other illustrations. When the chronological sequence was complete, Mr. Dillman led the students in a discussion of the uneven distances among the various cards.

Mr. Dillman extended this strategy to demonstrate the sequential nature of historical events. His young historians were first asked to read Derek Dingle's biography of Jackie Robinson, *First in the Field: Baseball Hero Jackie Robinson* (Hyperion). Then small work groups were directed to illustrate sheets of drawing paper with the major events from Jackie's life. Then they went to the playground and walked off one step for each year between events. This strategy is especially appropriate in the upper grades, since history concepts are quite difficult for most primary children to comprehend.

You could use a similar strategy when bringing timelines back from the playground and into the classroom. If students attempt to walk off years between events as they did on the playground, they will quickly learn that taking one step for each year will cause them to bump into walls. They will soon discover that a smaller unit of measure is necessary for their classroom timelines, perhaps one or two inches to represent a year rather than one step.

When working with smaller-scale timelines in the classroom, emphasize accuracy. An imprecise scale distorts time relationships and interferes with true chronological thinking. Sequencing the major events in a famous person's life is a good way to start smaller-scale timelines. Let us consider Horacio, a student from Mr. Dillman's classroom who read the biography of Jackie Robinson. If he were to create a smaller-scale timeline of Jackie's life, he would first select and summarize the important life events and then list each in sequence. This is how Horacio initially organized his data:

A Timeline of Jackie Robinson

1919
Jack Roosevelt Robinson is born in Cairo, Georgia.

1936
Jackie attends George Washington High School in Pasadena, California. He is good at all sports—he even won the city's Ping-Pong championship.

1941
Jackie meets Rachel Isum at UCLA. He is the first athlete in UCLA history to win a letter in four sports in one year.

1942
Jackie joins the army.

1945
Jackie joins the Kansas City Monarchs of the Negro American League. On October 23 he signs a contract to play for the Montreal Royals. Montreal was the top minor league team of the Brooklyn Dodgers.

1946
Jackie marries Rachel. Jackie plays his first minor league game for Montreal. Montreal wins the "Little World Series." Jackie scored the winning run.

1947
Jackie plays in his first major league game for the Brooklyn Dodgers. He is named the National League Rookie of the Year.

1957

Jackie Robinson retires from baseball. He played ten years with the Dodgers. The Dodgers won six pennants and one World Series when Jackie played.

1962

Jackie is inducted into the Major League Baseball Hall of Fame.

1972

Jackie Robinson dies on October 24, at age 53.

Horacio was quite familiar with computer applications and enjoyed using the computer to assist in social studies projects, so he searched approved Internet sites for access to a timeline generator. He found one at *www.teach-nology.com/web_tools/materials/timelines* and used it to create a timeline as shown in Figure 3–16.

FIGURE 3–16
The Life of Jackie Robinson

The Life of Jackie Robinson	
1919	• Jackie Robinson is born
1941	• Won letters in four sports at UCLA
1945	• Jackie joins the Kansas City Monarchs
1946	• Jackie scores winning run in "Little World Series"
1947	• Jackie plays for Dodgers. Is named Rookie of the Year
1957	• Jackie retires from baseball
1962	• Jackie is inducted into the Baseball Hall of Fame
1972	• Jackie Robinson dies at age 53

Horacio encountered a slight problem as he attempted to transfer the data from his summary list to the timeline, however. He had selected 10 highlights to summarize Jackie Robinson's life, but the timeline generator allowed Horacio only eight cells. Horacio studied his ten events carefully and eliminated two from the list so he could complete the computer-generated timeline. As you can see, the timeline construction process involves much more than the perfunctory task of arranging events in sequence. Important problems must be solved and critical decisions must be made all along the way.

Inside an Active Classroom

Bernice Yocum's sixth graders used the life of Nellie Bly as the starting point for a wide variety of historical activities, including timeline construction. Bly was one of the most daring journalists in 19th-century America. Born Elizabeth Cochrane Seaman, she adopted the name Nellie Bly from a Stephen Foster song. Nellie Bly became world famous when in 1890 she went round the world by boat, train, and horse in just over 72 days, thus beating the fictional record set by Phileas Fogg in Jules Verne's *Around the World in Eighty Days*. As part of their special study project, students first listened to Ms. Yocum read Joan W. Blos's delightful book, *Nellie Bly's Monkey* (Morrow). It is a fictional biography told from the perspective of Bly's unusual pet. After that charming introduction, the students went to work learning all about Bly's life. They mostly learned from informational books and Internet sources, but used other resources such as newspapers and magazines as well. As part of the study project, students emulated Bly's craft by trying their hands at investigative reporting. They researched modern travel records. They wrote poems about Nellie Bly. They dramatized important events in Bly's life, such as the time she posed as a poor sweatshop worker to expose the cruelty and grim conditions under which women labored. And they created a "Nellie Bly Timeline" book that depicted an important event in her life story on each page. The young historians enjoyed illustrating and writing historical narratives for their handmade timeline book. Producing the timeline book was a splendid way to involve students in active learning and helped them better understand the course of Bly's life. Then, as they continued to learn more about the important events in her life, the students were able to insert additional annotations and drawings on the pages.

R. T. Cerovich tried the following timeline activity with his students: Mr. Cerovich organized the class into groups of three, asked each group to divide a sheet of drawing paper into eight squares, and to sketch on each square an invention that Mr. Cerovich had randomly passed out to each group such as false teeth, electric fan, personal computer, aspirin, ice cream cone, laser, video camera, Barbie doll, and Ferris wheel. The students created a "Prediction Timeline" by cutting out the squares and

TEXT SET 6

Theme: Timelines (one book from five different eras through the years 1620 to 1900)

Jean Fritz's **Who's That Stepping on Plymouth Rock?** (Putnam) is my choice to start the timeline. It is a humorous, highly interesting story of the most popular granite boulder in our country. Fritz, in her distinctive style, crafts an amusing tale of the history of Plymouth Rock from the time the Pilgrims first landed on it to how it became the impressive moument it is today.

James Lincoln Collier's and Christopher Collier's **My Brother Sam Is Dead** (Macmillan) is my choice for the Revolutionary War era. Collier describes the heartbreak that strikes the Meeker family when one son (Sam) joins the rebel army while the rest of the family tries to stay neutral in a Tory town. Young Tim is caught between his brother's patriotism and his father's support of the British.

Pam Conrad's **Prairie Songs** (Harper & Row) captures both the loneliness and beauty of the Westward Movement. The story takes place on the Nebraska prairie where Louisa and her shy brother Lester live quite happily with their parents. A new doctor arrives with his beautiful and delicate pregnant wife, Emmeline. Louisa idolizes Emmeline and tries to teach the New York family the ways of the prairie. As the story moves on, both families are faced

attaching them to the places on a timeline to indicate the years when they thought their inventions were made. Mr. Cerovich then had the students research their inventions, learn the story of each, and verify the year when their inventions were actually produced. Each group's contributions to the preliminary timeline were adjusted properly and all of the inventions were sequenced accurately to form a long Invention Timeline.

Timelines are a great way to place in perspective the accomplishments of a renowned historic figure or stories of important events. They help students bring chronological awareness to history and establish a rich framework upon which historical narratives can be summarized or created.

AFTERWORD

History has long been a valued part of schooling in America, and it continues to exert a major influence on what and how social studies is taught in our nation's elementary schools. Many have praised its value for producing good citizens over the years, but none has done so more eloquently than Winston Churchill, who once proclaimed, "The further backward you look, the further forward you are likely to see."

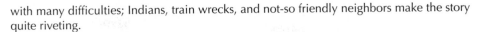

with many difficulties; Indians, train wrecks, and not-so friendly neighbors make the story quite riveting.

Patricia Lee Gauch's **Thunder at Gettysburg** (Coward) is based on 14-year-old Tillie's autobiographical account of the famous Civil War battle. The girl, who leaves her home one day to help watch some neighbor children, gets accidentally caught behind battle lines in the famous battle at Gettysburg.

Katherine Patterson's **Lyddie** (Puffin) helps students visualize the inside of a late-19th-century textile mill. Lyddie was a farm girl who goes to work in the fabric mills of Lowell, Massachusetts to earn enough money to pay off the family's debts. She finds long hours of factory work, the wretched living conditions of dormitory life, the frequency of tuberculosis, and harsh treatment of women. The book describes the grit and determination of Lyddie to succeed, as well as her personal growth.

TRY THIS

Make a large timeline of an historical era, using a large roll of craft paper. Let the students decide which dates are important enough to be placed on the line. Make the students support their choices with good reasons, and try to keep the timeline from being entirely a list of wars. Decorate the timeline by drawing or painting illustrations for each selected event. Create a text set that includes one book from each of the selected dates.

Such statements underscore the importance of developing the skills and sensitivities of historical consciousness in our schools. In a society steeped in triumphs and tragedies, knowledge of our past helps us to develop pride in our successes and discontent with our errors.

We cannot, however, expect children to become interested in the study of history when all we ask them to do is memorize facts from a textbook. Surely, content is an important part of history, but we must also be aware of the processes of history. Young historians must have regular opportunities to explore history rather than simply be exposed to it. We must lead students to perceive the nature of history itself. Those strategies will help students acquire a more balanced sense of history—it is not only something one knows but also something one does.

REFERENCES

Beatty, P. (1987). *Charley Skedaddle*. New York: Morrow.

Darigan, D. L., Tunnell, M. O., & Jacobs, J. S. (2002). *Children's literature: Engaging teachers and children in good books*. Upper Saddle River, NJ: Merrill/Prentice Hall.

Eisenberg, L. (1991). *The story of Sitting Bull, great Sioux chief*. New York: Dell.

Freedman, R. (1989). *Lincoln: A photobiography*. New York: Clarion.

Fritz, J. (1982). *Homesick: My own story*. New York: Putnam.

Gray, T., & Owens, S. (2003). From attics to graveyards: How to locate primary documents for your classroom. *Social Education, 67*, 386–388.

Milton, J. (1987). *Marching to freedom: The story of Martin Luther King, Jr.* (pp. 4–5). New York: Dell.

Murray, D. (1987). In N. Atwell, *In the middle*. Portsmouth, NH: Heinemann/Boynton Cook.

National Center for History in the Schools. (1996). *National standards for history*. Los Angeles: Author.

Potter, L. A. (2003). Connecting with the past. *Social Education, 67*, 372–377.

Ravitch, D. (1978). Tot Sociology. *American Educator, 6*, 38.

Ravitch, D., & C. Finn. (1987). *What do our 17-year-olds know? A report on the first national assessment of history and literature*. New York: Harper & Row.

Schreifels, B. (1983). Breathe life into a dead subject. *Learning*, March 1983, 84.

Young Geographers:
Investigating the People/Place Connection

WHAT DOES GEOGRAPHY LOOK LIKE?

At the beginning of November, Gloria Shin launched her third graders into one of the most enjoyable and instructive projects they had participated in during the year. She began by reading the book *Flat Stanley* by Jeff Brown (HarperCollins). In the book, Stanley Lambchop is squashed flat as a pancake by a falling bulletin board. Stanley otherwise is just fine and discovers many advantages to being flat. He can slide under doors, go down into sidewalk grates, and even be folded up small enough so that his parents can put him in a large envelope and mail him off to California to visit some friends. After reading the book, Ms. Shin kicked off the Flat Stanley project by asking her students to design, make, and send their own Flat Stanleys out into the wide, wide world.

Each young geographer began the project by designing a paper Flat Stanley and printing her or his name, return school address, and classroom e-mail address on the back. A brief statement of what the project was all about was also included for the recipients to read: "I am sending you a Flat Stanley and his journal. Please write down some of the things you do with Flat Stanley. Thank you." The students then made journals and, for 2 days, wrote about the major events in Flat Stanley's life. Their journal entries would serve as models for Flat Stanley's hosts. For example, Jerome wrote: "We took Flat Stanley to the mall. He liked seeing all the stores. Flat Stanley ate two chocolate chip cookies!" On the cover were the words "Passport to America." Inside were printed these instructions from Flat Stanley: "Dear Friend: Please finish my journal. Include places I've been and sights I've seen. A souvenir, or best yet, a photo of you and me together at a special place we visited would be nice! Sincerely, Flat Stanley. P. S. Would it be possible to send my owner a postcard from your town?"

The Flat Stanley, the journal, two little souvenirs (a class photo and an inexpensive item of local interest), and a self-addressed envelope with return postage were inserted into oversized envelopes and sent to participating classes (on a prepared list) in other parts of the United States. A send-off party, which included music and food, was a huge success. Each student shared a moment alone with his or her Flat Stanley before saying good-bye. A small spray of confetti was thrown on the box holding all the envelopes and a loud "Bon voyage!" was chorused before the students took them to the post office to be mailed.

Maps, atlases, and other reference materials became important tools for Ms. Shin's young geographers as they searched for the wonderful places their Flat Stanleys were visiting. For example, locating Fargo, a small city in eastern North Dakota, was a thrill for Hyung Sook. Margaret had received a postcard from a student in Greenville, Mississippi, and the class was eager to find out just where Greenville was located. A sticker was placed on a wall map to mark each location that had been visited by the Flat Stanleys. Students learned new names and new places as well as the physical features of different geographic regions. Some hosts sent e-mail messages to Flat Stanley's original owners, detailing his new adventures and providing information about the weather/climate, local sites of interest, population, industries, and seasonal activities.

By December 15, most of the Flat Stanleys had returned from their journeys. The journals were full of marvelous information about their exciting adventures. The envelopes were often overflowing with little souvenirs—local leaves, stickers, postcards, and photographs. Ms. Shin's social studies class spent the next week of school reading through the journals and recording the path of each Flat Stanley's travels. The class honored the Flat Stanleys who had not yet returned with a Missing in Action poster, complete with pictures of the absent Flat Stanleys and their owners.

The project ended as Ms. Shin's students wrote thank-you letters to Flat Stanley's hosts. This fabulous project helped the young geographers in Ms. Shin's room learn much about the world around them.

Gloria Shin continually strives to provide the best possible learning experiences for her students. From this quick look into her classroom, it is easy to see how Ms. Shin stirs the students' curiosity about the world and captures their imagination with a wonderfully inspiring, developmentally appropriate geography project. Ms. Shin is confident she can best help her children learn geography by offering them interesting and fun activities and by encouraging them to take on challenging questions about their world. Ms. Shin doesn't confuse geography with requiring her students to memorize where places are located. Although she understands it is important to know where places are (especially if you want to find your way back home after a movie), she knows it is even more important to understand why places are located where they are and how they got there. Ms. Shin constantly challenges her students to think about things such as how and why their school was built where it is, where the shoes they are wearing came from and how they were transported, and why palm trees are more plentiful than pine trees in their community. In Ms. Shin's approach to teaching, students are helped to think of geography both as a source of information about the world and as a way of thinking and acting. They are helped to comprehend basic geographic information—facts about location and place—as well as the more complex understandings related to human interactions with the environment. Some teachers may think it's proper to teach geography by handing out a worksheet, assigning students to locate the major cities of Mexico, conducting place location drills, or assigning country reports (that will be most assuredly copied from an encyclopedia or website). Ms. Shin is convinced that such uneventful "teaching" will not only fail to meet her district's geography standards, but will also result in yet another generation of students oblivious to the excitement that geography can offer.

WHAT IS GEOGRAPHY?

You may not have a clue about where the Republic of Tajikistan really is or whether Zzyzx is a community in the United States or an animal at the zoo, but geography is standing by ready and willing to help you find out. What is geography? I don't want to get too fussy about a definition for the discipline at this time for, as with history, every geographer gives a slightly different version of what the discipline is or should be. For the purposes of this text, geography will be formally defined as "an integrative discipline that brings together the physical and human dimensions of the world in the study of people, places, and environments. Its subject matter is the Earth's surface and the processes that shape it, the relationships between people and environments, and the connections between people and places" (Geography Education Standards Project, 1994, p. 18). In short, geography can be thought of as the science of space and place—the study of the Earth's natural environment and how it influences people.

As is also true of history, all informed citizens must know geography. There is no doubt that a strong grasp of geography equips people to make better-informed decisions about how to use our planet's resources. For example, geography helps us answer questions like "What can be done to arrest global warming?" and "Is this the best location for the recycling plant?" Geography also investigates the ways by which our land has influenced the way people live. For example, most people know that there are five Great Lakes in the United States—Huron, Ontario, Michigan, Erie, and Superior. But not everyone knows that the Great Lakes came into existence only about 10,000 years ago and that they were formed by the actions of receding glaciers. The same glacial movement formed the landscape features of the upper Midwest—hilly land and rocky soil not fit to grow wheat. These geographic features convinced our early pioneers to "substitute the cow for the plow" and become successful dairy farmers instead of wheat or corn farmers during the 1800s.

In dynamic social studies, young geographers learn how to describe places on the Earth's surface, explain how these places came to be, and appreciate the delicate bond between humans and their physical environment. They learn geography by asking the same questions professional geographers ask: Where is it? Why is it there? How did it get there? What is the relationship between the people and this place?

Each element of our definition of geography has been expanded upon to this point. Before we go on to another topic, I want to make sure we address the element stated in the first three words of the definition—that is, geography is "an integrative discipline." It is interesting to note that, of all the disciplines comprising social studies, geography is among the most open to incorporating the content and processes of other disciplines. A deep curiosity about our world motivates geographers to communicate with anybody who might help them better understand it. We only have to look at the way geography and history can work together to more clearly explain the integrative nature of the discipline. For example: "How did New Orleans' location on the Mississippi River help it become the nation's fourth-largest city in 1830?" "Why was the Erie Canal built between Albany and Buffalo during the early 1800s?" "What geographic obstacles did the railroad workers face in building the transcontinental railroad during the 1860s?" Cooperating with various disciplines is a vital dimension of comprehending the Earth as the home of people. An example from Milo Kozachek's classroom helps illustrate the integrative nature of geography.

Inside an Active Classroom

Mr. Kozachek felt that a recording of an old folk song and excerpt from a journal would be valuable attention-grabbers to draw his fifth-grade students into a study of how the Erie Canal played a central role in America's growth during the early 1800s. The canal, completed in 1825, linked Albany to Buffalo, and eventually New York City, and greatly reduced freight costs for shipping goods between the established eastern cities and the expanding western frontier. Goods that once cost $90–$100 to ship between New York and Buffalo now cost only $4 a ton. Towns along the canal, including Buffalo, Rochester, and Syracuse, boomed. Because of the Erie Canal, New York City became the largest center of trade in the United States. The success of the Erie Canal set off a burst of canal building throughout the country.

Mr. Kozachek brought to class an old recording of *The Erie Canal* (also known as *Low Bridge*) he had purchased from the Erie Canal Museum in Syracuse, New York. He asked the students to recall songs like *I've Been Working on the Railroad* that were sung by workers to make tedious tasks easier. Mr. Kozachek then played the recording of *The Erie Canal* for his students, and they listened intently. He then explained that mule drivers sang this song as they traveled along the canal. The tempo of the song was set by the slow and steady plodding of the mules as they pulled the barges back and forth along the length of the canal. Mr. Kozachek then passed out copies of Peter Spier's book, *The Erie Canal* (in which the words to the song are printed along with fascinating illustrated details of the canal system), played the recording again, and invited the students to sing along. He told the students that social scientists often use songs, diaries, and other primary resources to learn about the past. In this case, they were to act as young historians and young geographers while using the song and the book to learn how the construction and operation of the Erie Canal affected people's lives during the early 1800s.

The Erie Canal (Low Bridge)
I've got an old mule and her name is Sal
Fifteen miles on the Erie Canal
She's a good old worker and a good old pal
Fifteen miles on the Erie Canal
We've hauled some barges in our day
Filled with lumber, coal, and hay
And every inch of the way we know
From Albany to Buffalo
Low bridge, everybody down
Low bridge for we're coming to a town
And you'll always know your neighbor
And you'll always know your pal
If you've ever navigated on
The Erie Canal
We'd better get along on our way, old gal
Fifteen miles on the Erie Canal
'Cause you bet your life I'd never part with Sal
Fifteen miles on the Erie Canal
Git up there mule, here comes a lock
We'll make Rome 'bout six o'clock
One more trip and back we'll go
Right back home to Buffalo
Low bridge, everybody down
Low bridge for we're coming to a town
And you'll always know your neighbor
And you'll always know your pal
If you've ever navigated on
The Erie Canal

Mr. Kozachek next passed out a map of the Erie Canal and the students traced its route from Lake Erie to the Hudson River, making sure they located the cities mentioned in the song. He then distributed a copy of a simulated diary entry he had made up from fact after reading several firsthand accounts of travel on the Erie Canal (see Figure 4–1). It helped unlock the meaning of several passages from the song. The students were to use the words in the song along with the journal excerpt to find evidence to solve the following mysteries:

- What source of power moved the boats through the canal?
- At what ports did the boats stop?

- What did the boats carry?
- How long was the canal from beginning to end?
- How were passengers affected by the call, "Low bridge, everybody down?"

After examining two primary resources (the song and the simulated journal entry) and two secondary resources (Spier's book and the map), students were directed to think about additional data sources that might help them visualize the physical characteristics and patterns of human behavior related to the Erie Canal during that historical period. Mr. Kozachek asked them to suggest any other sources they might consult for more information about life on or near the canal.

The students recommended newspaper articles, paintings, a visit to the Erie Canal Museum in Syracuse (only about 10 miles from the school), and researching websites.

FIGURE 4–1
Simulated Diary Entry

An Excerpt from a Canal Traveler's Journal

May 5. Arrived in Schenectady at about one o'clock. As soon as the stagecoach stopped, up stepped a muscular gentleman who cried out, "Gentlemen, do you want to go to the West? We start at 2 o'clock, gentlemen. Only 3 1/2 cents a mile with superior accommodations!"

"Don't take passage in that boat," called a second fellow. "I'll take you for half the money in a fine boat." In no time there were at least a half dozen more boat captains, all anxious for our passage and at almost any price we pleased. We wanted to see the boats ourselves before we were to take passage in any, so we sallied forth to the canal and selected a superior boat of the Clinton Line. The captain agreed to take us to Utica, a distance of 89 miles, for one cent and a quarter per mile!

Climbing up to the roof of the boat, I joined several other travelers who were conversing on deck. Everyone enjoyed the fresh air and scenery until the helmsman blew his horn and bellowed, "Low bridge, everybody down!" The first few times this happened, we merely ducked to avoid the bridges overhead. However, we soon resorted to lying down to avoid several low ones. (Many bridges are no more than 8 feet, while the boat itself is a full seven.) It required great attention and care in passing the bridges, for you may get knocked down and join the company of the canal fishes! A woman next to me told of a child being knocked from the roof and the mad attempt to rescue her. Thank God she was rescued! Such things, however, do not often occur.

Our boat was one of the fastest on the canal, for horses instead of mules pull it. The captain was a bit adventurous as he regularly exceeded the four miles an hour speed limit. The day seemed to move slower than the boat, but, at last, nightfall came and I was immensely exhausted. The sleeping quarters were quite uncomfortable. Three layers of canvas cots extend from the walls. The canvas was prone to wearing thin so if the person above is a bit plump, the canvas can sag so much that the person may end up lying on top of you.

There are a number of good sites, including Erie Canal OnLine (*http://www.syracuse.com/features/eriecanal/*). The students will enjoy following 14-year-old Elizabeth as she makes her way from Amsterdam to Syracuse. After conducting additional research, the young historians created a large annotated wall map of the Erie Canal at its completion, labeling the canal locks, towns, and other waterways. Relating the project to the children's lives today, Mr. Kozachek asked his young geographers to think about the sources they used for information about the Erie Canal and how they might relate to any current form of public transportation. What types of resources might be useful to a future historian as he or she attempts to uncover information about transportation in 21st-century America?

It would be instructive for you and your classmates to carefully analyze Milo Kozachek's instructional episode to determine how many discrete disciplines were involved in this integrative experience. It's a given that history and geography were there, but how many others can you find?

WHY IS GEOGRAPHY IMPORTANT?

What's the point of teaching geography in the elementary school? There is no question that we are now living in an interconnected world and that virtually *every* aspect of life can be placed in a global perspective. For that reason, it is essential to know about people and places around the world, and geography can help us effectively face the challenges of our time. A good geography program helps students better understand their community and our nation, and their relationships to other places and cultures. Geography also gives us tools we need to help us move from place to place in the world and to make rational decisions about our environment.

How are our nation's schools preparing students to function in this changing world? Forget for a moment about such refined thinking abilities as making rational decisions about our environment; let's first address the question of the degree to which our students are comfortable with even the most basic geographic knowledge, such as finding the United States on a world map. Educators were shocked when a recent nine-nation survey conducted by the National Geographic Society (2002) found that one in five young Americans (high school and college youth) could not locate the United States on an outline map of the world!

The survey asked 56 geographic and current events questions of young people in nine countries around the world and scored the results with traditional grades. Sweden led all nations with an average score of 40 correct answers while the Americans got a D, finishing in next-to-last place with an average of 23 correct answers. Mexico ranked last with an average score of 21, just three points from a failing grade.

Not one nation received an A, which required an average score of 42 or better on the 56 questions. Here are some interesting findings from the survey:

- Thirty-four percent of the young Americans knew that an island used on the "Survivor" television series was the Marquesas Islands in the eastern South Pacific, but only 30 percent could find the states of New Jersey and Missouri on a map of the United States.

- When asked to locate 10 specific states on a map of the United States, only California and Texas could be found with any degree of regularity by a majority of those surveyed (89 percent). Just 51 percent could find New York State, 49 percent found Pennsylvania, and 44 percent located Illinois.

- On a world map, Americans could find on average only 7 of 16 countries in the survey. Only 89 percent of the Americans surveyed could find the United States on the map; 29 percent could not locate the Pacific Ocean, the world's largest body of water. Still, over 80 percent of all the youth participating in this survey said it was either "absolutely necessary" or "important" to know where places in the news are located.

- Although 81 percent of the surveyed Americans knew that the Middle East is the Earth's largest oil exporter, only 24 percent could find Saudi Arabia on the map.

- Finally, although 95 percent of the Swedes participating in the survey could correctly estimate their own country's population, only 25 percent of the participants from the United States could correctly do so. This placed the United States in last place on this item, a full 10 percent lower than the next highest finisher, Mexico.

Disturbed by such findings, educators claimed that at no time in our nation's educational history has the level of geographic literacy been so low. Although the data you just examined had to do only with recalling facts, higher-level geographic thinking is impossible without a firm command of such information. Knowledge is the essential underpinning for problem solving and discovery; it helps us think more rationally about issues like ocean dumping, droughts, voting patterns, and the revitalization of cities. Students not only need to know that Washington, D.C., is our nation's capital, but why. Knowledge stokes a young geographer's curiosity: "Why are the rainforests of Central America being cleared at such an alarming rate?" "Why is the New York State Thruway located where it is?" "How did Mumbai (Bombay) develop into such a large city?"

Succinctly, the Geography Education Standards Project (1994) advises that students need to study geography for reasons that range from the most profound to the most utilitarian:

- *The existential reason.*   Humans want to understand the intrinsic nature of their home, that pale blue dot in the vastness of space. Geography helps them understand where they are.

- *The ethical reason.*   Life is fragile; humans are fragile. Geography provides knowledge of Earth's physical and human systems and of the interdependency of living things and the physical environment. This knowledge, in turn, provides a basis for people to cooperate in the best interests of our planet.

- *The intellectual reason.* Geography focuses attention on exciting and interesting things, on fascinating people and places, and on things worth knowing because they are absorbing and because knowing about them lets humans make better-informed and, therefore, wiser decisions.

- *The practical reason.* With a strong grasp of geography, people are better equipped to solve issues at both the local and the global level. In summary, geography has the power to help students acquire knowledge of our Earth and where important places are located. It also stimulates student interest in their surroundings, develops an awareness of the variety of human and physical conditions around the world, and promotes a sense of wonder at the splendor of the physical environment. And, perhaps most importantly, geography helps students build up an informed concern about the quality of the environment, thereby advancing their sense of responsibility for the care of our Earth and its people.

What Should Young Geographers Know or Be Able to Do?

The most helpful steps to improve the teaching of geography have been efforts of the National Geographic Society, National Council for Geographic Education, and the Association of American Geographers. Offering strong leadership and direction, these professional groups have published guidelines proposing what should be taught to our nation's children. These guidelines have been widely circulated and subsequently used for curriculum development purposes in school districts throughout the United States.

The first significant contribution to the improvement of geographic education was originated in 1984 by the National Council for Geographic Education. Its Committee on Geographic Education (1984) issued a publication entitled *Guidelines for Geographic Education*, the contents of which became widely known as the "Five Themes of Geography." The themes offered a design of five big ideas around which geographic instruction should be organized: *location, place, relationships within places, movement,* and *regions.*

The Five Themes of Geography

Given the option of anywhere in the world, where would you choose to live? When faced with such an intriguing decision, I find that some people tend to make snap decisions while others will think for awhile to consider the possibilities. It's a tough decision because all locations on Earth have their advantages and disadvantages in regard to human habitation; one person's like is another's dislike. I once asked my class this question and was surprised by their different responses. One student said Salt Lake City was her "dream location" because she is an avid skier and would love

An attractive display of materials and books serve to motivate and inform young geographers as they discover the world through the Five Themes of Geography.

to ski all winter long on the powdery snow for which Utah is so famous. She loves everything about winter and had longed for years to live in such a "perfect" place. On the other hand, another student selected Santa Barbara, California, where *he* says everything is "perfect." He pointed out that days are usually mild all year long, with clear blue skies filled with bright California sunshine. Because there is no real "off-season," this student crowed that he'd be playing beach volleyball in January and enjoying temperatures in the mid-60s while the other student would be freezing on the snowy slopes of Utah.

Whatever location you've chosen as your "perfect" place to live, the key is that several factors would have played a huge part of your decision. Those factors are quite probably aligned with the five themes (see Figure 4–2) selected by the National Council for Geographic Education, the framework upon which the content of geography should be taught.

1. *Location: Position on the Earth's Surface.*   Location answers the question, "Where are we on the Earth's surface?" Location may be absolute or relative. *Absolute location* refers to a specific position on the Earth's surface by using such identifiers as latitude and longitude or a street address: "The Great Salt Lake is in Northern Utah," pinpoints the location of a place as does, "Santa Barbara is 34° North latitude and 119° West longitude." *Relative location* means

FIGURE 4–2

Five Themes of Geography

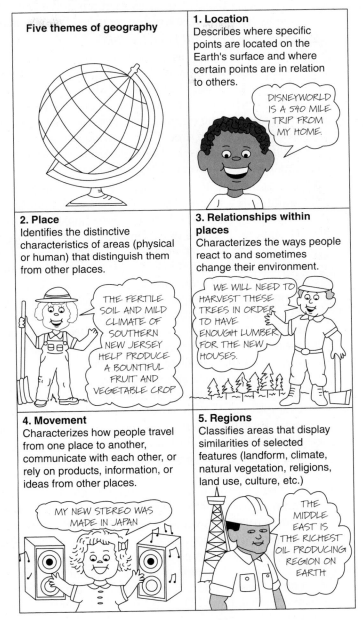

to locate a place respective to other landmarks, the direction or distance from one place to another. For example, "Salt Lake City is southeast of the Great Salt Lake," or, "Beachside Santa Barbara is the hub of a large coastal California county lying northwest of Los Angeles, just off Highway 101."

2. *Place: Physical and Human Characteristics.*   All places on Earth have unique characteristics that distinguish them from other places. *Physical characteristics* include such features as rivers, lakes, mountains, wildlife, soil, precipitation, and beaches. For example, "Wasatch Mountain snow has been called 'The Greatest Snow on Earth!'" *Human characteristics* deal with the changes that people have made to the environment. For example, Santa Barbara didn't exist until pioneers settled the area: "On a spring day in 1782 the Padre Presidente of the California Missions, Father Junípero Serra, and the Spanish Governor de Neve founded the mission of Santa Barbara."

3. *Relationships Within Places: Humans and Environments.*   The physical features of a location affect people in different ways. An explanation of those ways can be divided into three parts: how people have been changed by the environment, how the environment has been changed by people, and how people depend on the environment. How people have been changed by the environment is often called *adaptation*. Whenever people move into a location, they often make lasting changes there because of the nature of the environment. For example, if a city is located on a fertile plain, it may become the hub of a thriving agricultural center. And, if a city is located near a fault (break or crack in the Earth's surface), it may experience earthquakes. Therefore, people will explore different construction materials, shapes, and design options that affect the durability of their buildings.

How the environment has been changed by people, or *modification*, is the way people alter their surroundings to satisfy themselves. In Salt Lake City, for example, large water projects are in the works to divert water from nearly 100 miles away because the growing population is exhausting the existing water supply. And, in Santa Barbara, the Gibraltar Reservoir has been built on the Santa Yves River as a source of water for the community. Another good example is clearing the rainforests of Central America to make room for grazing cattle

Depending on the environment refers to people's reliance on their environment for something important, such as using trees as material to build new houses, oil to run vehicles and factories, or rivers to transport goods and natural resources. Geographers study all the effects—positive and negative—that arise when people establish relationships within places. Sometimes a human act, such as damming a river to prevent flooding or to provide irrigation, requires consideration of all the possible consequences. For example, dams offer many advantages. They are used to generate electricity through water power, to boost water supply systems, and to create artificial lakes for recreation. However, dams can also harm the environment. They can interfere with fish migration and damage the habitats of other wildlife by reducing water flow.

4. *Movement: Humans Interacting on the Earth.* People network with other people, places, and things almost *every* day of their lives. They travel from one place to another; they communicate with each other by phone or e-mail; and they rely upon products, information, and ideas that come from far beyond their home locations. Students should be able to recognize where resources are located, who needs them, and how they are transported over the Earth's surface. The theme of movement helps students understand how they are connected with, and dependent upon, other regions and other people in the world. For example, southwest of Salt Lake City are the Oquirrh Mountains, the site of the largest open-pit copper mine in the world. The mine produces copper that is shipped to all areas of the United States and throughout the world. Once you arrive in Santa Barbara, traveling around town is a breeze. Most of the major attractions are in a compact downtown where, if you don't feel like walking, you can grab a pedicab, Santa Barbara's answer to the rickshaw.

5. *Regions: How They Form and Change.* A basic unit of geographic study is the region, an area on the Earth's surface whose characteristics make it different from other areas. The unifying characteristics may be physical, political, or cultural, but through the concept of regions, geographers divide the world into manageable units for study. Geographers divide the world into many different regions, depending on what they are interested in studying. They may define regions according to types of land, climate, or characteristics of people. Therefore, we have land regions such as the Central Plains, Great Plains, Appalachian Highlands, or the Pacific Coast. Using a land region classification scheme, then, we are able to assign Salt Lake City to our nation's Great Basin and Santa Barbara to the Pacific Coast region. The Earth is divided into 12 climate regions, including tropical wet climates that are hot, muggy, and rainy year round and desert (arid) climates that receive little or no measurable rainfall. Some regions are defined by people speaking the same language or having the same religion. Or people regions might be based on where different ethnic groups settled after they came to this country. Geographers bicker about all sorts of regions and proclaim that a certain place should or shouldn't be included in some region. In what region is your college or university located? What are its characteristics? In how many other regions could it be a part?

Now that you have learned a little about the five themes, think about how you might be able to use them. Imagine for now that you are a television reporter. An important discovery of a lost land has been made, and you have been assigned to interview the team of geographers who discovered it. What are some questions you might ask the geographers about this new place? We can assume you are familiar with the five themes and will ask important questions from each. Here are some questions to get you started:

- Where is it?
- What does it look like?

TEXT SET 7

Theme: Favorite Books About the Prairie (Regions)

Eve Bunting's **Dandelions** (Harcourt Brace) tells the story of a pioneer family as they move west in the 1800s to make their new home in Nebraska. Mama, Papa, and their two daughters, Zoe and Rebecca, have left their home in Illinois to settle on the prairie. When Zoe and her family arrive at their claim, nothing sets it apart from the miles and miles of surrounding prairie. Zoe has never seen Papa so happy or Mama so sad and lonely. After Zoe and her sister plant a patch of dandelions on the roof of their sod house, Mama agrees that their family is hardy and will bloom just as the dandelions are sure to do.

Pam Conrad's **Prairie Visions: The Life and Times of Solomon Butcher** (HarperCollins) is a collection of photos and stories about photographer Solomon Butcher and turn-of-the-century Nebraska. Well illustrated with black-and-white photographs, most of them full page, it includes family stories, anecdotes, and biographies of the men, women, and children of Custer County.

Patricia MacLachlan's **Sarah, Plain and Tall** (HarperTrophy) tells the touching story of a widowed prairie farmer with two children, Anna and Caleb. He advertises for a wife and mother. Sarah Elizabeth Wheaton answers Jacob's ad and arrives from Maine. But she quickly becomes homesick, especially for the ocean she misses very much. The children fear she will

- How many people live there?
- What kind of climate does it have?
- What are the natural resources and how are they used?
- What kind of houses do the people live in?

That is just a start to the questions you will use during the interview, and they will yield only the barest information about the new place. Keep expanding your list so you can report in much more detail about the discovery. Keeping in mind the five themes, what are some other questions you might add?

National Geography Standards

Ten years after the release of the five themes, an alliance of four professional geography groups calling itself the Geography Education Standards Project (1994) released a set of National Geography Standards titled *Geography for Life.*

leave and, when she goes off to town alone one day, young Caleb, whose mother died a day after he was born, is fearful that she has gone for good. But she returns and explains that, though she misses her home, "The truth of it is I would miss you more."

Ann Turner's **Dakota Dugout** (Aladdin) combines poetic text with plentiful illustrations to help readers learn of life on the prairie through the eyes of a woman who actually lived with her husband in a sod house on the Dakota prairie.

Pam Conrad's **My Daniel** (HarperTrophy) takes place at a time when fossil fever hit everyone, a time when people would kill for dinosaur bones under the ground. When she's 80 years old, Julia visits her grandchildren, Ellie and Stevie, in New York City. She takes them to the Natural History Museum to show them the dinosaur she and her brother Daniel discovered on their farm in Nebraska when they were young. While there, Julia feels the presence of her dead brother and weaves together the story of the great dinosaur rush.

TRY THIS

Work together in groups of 4 or 5. Think about other geographic features that distinguish regions throughout the world: oceans, lakes, rivers, and swamps; trees and rainforests; deserts; and mountains. Each group member should find one book for that geographic region so that your group builds a text set of 4 or 5 books.

Geography for Life aimed to replace the well-respected five themes of geography with a proposal it called the "six essential elements of geography." Actually, the six essential elements consisted of items similar to the five themes; however, they were more comprehensively described and were referred to by different terminology: *the world in spatial terms*, *places and regions*, *physical systems*, *human systems*, *environment and society*, and *the uses of geography*. Although the two documents used contrasting terminology and varied in depth, they were quite consistent with one another in terms of content. The standards did not supplant the five themes of geography, which have remained a useful tool for organizing geographic instruction. The five themes and six elements are often used jointly to offer broad guidelines for state standards documents and school district curriculum guides. A publication prepared by the National Geographic Society and available from the National Council for Geographic Education, entitled *Key to the National Geography Standards*, provides a useful summary of the standards and of how the themes relate to them.

The National Geography Standards' 6 essential elements and 18 standards are listed in Figure 4–3.

FIGURE 4–3
Geography for Life: National Geography Standards

The World in Spatial Terms

Geography studies the relationships between people, places, and environments by mapping information about them into a spatial context.

The geographically informed person knows and understands:

1. How to use maps and other geographical representations, tools, and technologies to acquire, process, and report information from a spatial perspective
2. How to use mental maps to organize information about people, places, and environments in a spatial context
3. How to analyze the spatial organization of people, places, and environments on Earth's surface

Places and Regions

The identities and lives of individuals and peoples are rooted in particular places and in those human constructs called regions.

The geographically informed person knows and understands:

4. The physical and human characteristics of places
5. That people create regions to interpret Earth's complexity
6. How culture and experience influence people's perceptions of places and regions

Physical Systems

Physical processes shape Earth's surface and interact with plant and animal life to create, sustain, and modify ecosystems.

The geographically informed person knows and understands:

7. The physical processes that shape the patterns of Earth's surface
8. The characteristics and spatial distribution of ecosystems on Earth's surface

Human Systems

People are central to geography in that human activities help shape Earth's surface, human settlements and structures are part of the Earth's surface, and humans compete for control of the Earth's surface.

The geographically informed person knows and understands:

9. The characteristics, distribution, and migration of human populations on Earth's surface
10. The characteristics, distribution, and complexity of Earth's cultural mosaics
11. The patterns and networks of economic interdependence on Earth's surface
12. The processes, patterns, and functions of human settlement
13. How the forces of cooperation and conflict among people influence the division and control of Earth's surface

Environment and Society

The physical environment is modified by human activities, largely as a consequence of the ways in which human societies value and use Earth's natural resources, and human activities are also influenced by Earth's physical features and processes.

The geographically informed person knows and understands:

14. How human actions modify the physical environment
15. How physical systems affect human systems
16. The changes that occur in the meaning, use, distribution, and importance of resources

The Uses of Geography

Knowledge of geography enables people to develop an understanding of the relationships between people, places, and environments over time—that is, of Earth as it was, is, and might be.

The geographically informed person knows and understands:

17. How to apply geography to interpret the past
18. How to apply geography to interpret the present and plan for the future

Source: Geography Education Standards Project. (1994). *Geography for life: National geography standards 1994.* Washington, DC: National Geographic Research & Exploration, pp. 34–35.

Inside an Active Classroom

Because the social studies program in her school district is standards-driven, Becca Kahn, a fifth-grade teacher from Flagstaff, Arizona, has developed new ways to think about geography and its key skills. As a committed teacher, Ms. Kahn was eager to incorporate the standards into her instructional plans. She realized that implementing the standards would require adding new activities and strategies to her professional repertoire but, because adjustments take time, effort, and careful personal reflection, her principal recommended that the district's teachers implement only one or two new changes to their teaching each semester. This semester, Ms. Kahn chose to move toward transforming her curriculum to a standards-based model by selecting the second essential element, places and regions, as a focus. Her goal was to meet this standard by offering her students interesting activities and by encouraging them to think deeply about their surroundings. This was accomplished within the context of sending an "exchange package."

Ms. Kahn asked her students to collect objects in a package that could clearly describe life in Flagstaff. The package would then be sent to fifth-grade students in a friend's classroom in Elmira, New York. The students selected items such as a small chunk of volcanic cinder, a branch of ponderosa pine, a plastic fish, a cowboy hat, a pair of mittens, and a small piece of silver jewelry with turquoise stones. The students then wrote a letter that explained each item. Figure 4–4 shows one paragraph of the letter; it describes the significance of including the pair of mittens. The students from Elmira arranged a package of items and explanatory letter that characterized their city and region and sent it back to their new friends in Flagstaff.

FIGURE 4–4
Student Letter

In Flagstaff it snows a lot during wintertime. Sometimes it snows as much as 2 feet. There are many winter sports in Flagstaff. People especially like to go to the mountains to snow ski. I like to go snowboarding.
Jeffwan

The National Geographic Society's Xpeditions has a new series of web pages containing splendid resources for using the standards. A link to each standard offers related classroom activities (*www.nationalgeographic.com/xpeditions/*). It is well worth a look at Xpeditions for its useful explanations of the geography standards and suggestions for putting the standards into action.

The themes and standards are applicable to all school districts in the United States, but districts are encouraged to adjust each to local interests and needs. To illustrate how this process can work, let us examine the accompanying case study, which outlines the positive results that can easily be achieved with a little careful planning and a commitment to geography on a daily basis (O'Mahony, 2003).

Because current curriculum standards have provided a basic framework of useful content and classroom-tested instructional strategies that can be tailored to the specific curricular needs of local school districts, geography has become a much more dynamic subject than it was in the past. Geography standards stress the importance of children interacting with their own environment, so it is not uncommon to see today's students working both in and out of their classrooms, often in unusual locations, as they actively and collaboratively investigate their natural and human environments. O'Mahony (2003) provides an exciting account of how an entire school in Erie, Pennyslvania became a standards-based "geography classroom" where fun activities help teach youngsters the fundamentals of geography.

Inside an Active Classroom

Perry Elementary School in Erie, Pennsylvania, could be a typical inner-city school, just like other schools with social issues, cultural diversity, and ethnic challenges rooted in immigration and poverty.

It has the same stats as other thorny neighborhood schools. But Perry Elementary is different. Poised on the cutting edge of a growing geography reform movement in the United States, Perry integrates geography throughout the curriculum. Teachers use geography as a springboard for launching instruction in reading, literature, science, math, and history. All the while, they are emphasizing the five themes of geography.

How does Perry build schoolwide enthusiasm for geography? Here are some geofriendly examples:

- Students eat lunch in a geo-centric decor featuring the 50 states and an enormous map of the world. One wall of the cafeteria is emblazoned with lists of the "The Ten Most Populous Countries," "The Ten Largest Countries," and "The Ten Longest Rivers." Another showcases pictures of children from around the world in native dress. An electronic sign flashes the geography question of the day.

- The school's hallways flaunt murals depicting scenes from Australia, China, Japan, and other far-from-Pennsylvania lands. Flags of many nations hang from the rafters. A poster in a much-traveled stairwell proclaims, "Vexillology—the Study of Flags and Their Origin."

- Perry has forged "sister-school" relationships with schools in Japan, Canada, the People's Republic of China, the United Kingdom, and Australia.

- During morning announcements, a grade-specific geography question is posed over the public address system, with a free pizza for the class whose representative is first to arrive in the office with the correct answer (no running allowed!).

- With hats from around the world, a map-rug instead of chairs, scales to weigh yourself in stone and kilograms, a large-screen TV for viewing nature films set in international locales, and maps, maps, and more maps, the Gilbert M. Grosvenor Geography Learning Lab was designed to be an "inviting place that students couldn't wait to visit and hated to leave," according to Principal Grode.

- Even the Perry mascot embraces the schoolwide theme. Toby the Traveling Bear has been all over the world. He's visited Russia, China, Europe, Australia, and Africa. Toby once got lost in Frankfurt Airport and has climbed to the top of Mount Kenya.

Clearly, Perry's geography immersion education is working. Its students—an ethnically and socioeconomically diverse group, one-quarter of whom receive special education—consistently rank above average in state and national standardized tests. And they're geographically literate. Just ask Gil Grosvenor, a man who knows a little something about geography (he's chairman of the board and former president of the National Geographic Society). After visiting Perry Elementary School, Grosvenor offered this assessment: "I'd bet second graders there would score better on geography tests than students at Ivy League schools."

IN GENERAL, HOW SHOULD GEOGRAPHY BE TAUGHT?

By preparing students with the knowledge and sensitivities to make wise judgments about their environment, you will be developing caring citizens and powerful decision makers. That's certainly a worthy ambition for the future of our nation and the world, but one very important question begs to be answered before we can hope to achieve it: How does a society that has not learned geography well teach it to a new generation? A step in the right direction would be to make the subject more interesting and more worthwhile for our students. Professional education is the key to helping teachers master the specialized content of geography and the distinctive teaching methods that engage students in active learning. If teachers do not receive the necessary training in the content and processes of geography, they run the risk of teaching it like they might have been taught in elementary school—memorizing state capitals and the major exports of a country. As one of a new generation of teachers, you must stand ready and willing to take on the role of "expert" in the field. Becoming an expert entails more than knowing the content and processes of geography and mastering the recommended strategies for teaching them. You must help children understand that our Earth is shared by people and other living things and must be carefully maintained. You must also recognize the need for geography in a contemporary world where our continued existence hinges on the attitudes of our nation's young citizens toward our fragile planet.

Implementing an instructional program in the elementary school that places students in the role of young geographers requires an understanding of six distinct phases that underlie geographic study: (1) observing, (2) speculating, (3) investigating, (4) extending, (5) reinforcing, and (6) evaluating. These skills are often most accomplished in dynamic social studies classrooms either through *teacher-guided discovery experiences* or through *independent projects*.

Teacher-Guided Discovery

Teachers who prefer to use teacher-guided discovery strategies assume the role of facilitator, modeling and leading the way for their students. A detailed classroom example of teaching the five phases of geographic investigation follows.

Observing

The process of geographic inquiry begins with observing an actual place, such as a pond, building, or road, or a representation, such as a video, photograph, or illustration, and answering the question, "What do you see here?" The process of geographic understanding begins with what the students can clearly observe. These observations are designed to help students describe and define places, so you might begin by having students write about or draw simple maps and illustrations to record their observations. Unquestionably, the most ideal geographic learning experiences begin by engaging students in direct observations of locations within their environment and recording what they observe.

Certainly, it is impossible for teachers to take their students to every place under study. No one would expect teachers from Boise, Idaho, or Caribou, Maine, for example, to take their students to Amazonia so they could directly observe the natural beauty of the world's largest rainforest. Therefore, teachers must use multiple resources for instruction: primary documents, photos, videos, maps, globes, atlases, charts, informational books, periodicals with numerous pictures and maps, textbooks, and virtual field trips on the Internet through such sites as *The Field Trip Website* (*www.fieldtrips.org/trips.htm*). Although they are considered important instructional resources,it is important to avoid complete dependence on standard textbooks. Good social studies teachers emphasize active learning through the use of varied resources.

Ernest Frombach, for example, initiated a thematic study of Homes Around the World by inviting his fourth graders to draw models and tell stories about their own

Observational experiences lead to the construction of geographical intelligence.

homes and families. He wanted to connect the concept of homes with their own backgrounds of direct experience. After discussing the likenesses and differenes of the homes in their classroom. Mr. Frombach displayed large study prints of homes from around the world and guided the observation and discussion with these questions: "What kinds of homes do you see here? In what ways are these homes like your homes? In what ways are they different?"

Convinced that field trips are valuable observational experiences that can assist young learners to gain a better understanding of geographic concepts, Mr. Frombach provided his students with regular opportunities to observe and experience things firsthand. For this unit on Homes Around the World, some types of homes could not be observed directly (adobe homes and yurts, for example), so field observations were unimaginable. However, Mr. Frombach knew it was possible to take a trip to Hoopes Park so the children could study the oldest still-standing structure in the community, a well-preserved stone farmhouse originally built in 1738. This stone farmhouse, built by Thomas Hoopes using stone from an adjacent quarry, is important to the community and can be found nestled in a grassy plot at the center of the park that bears his name. The children enjoyed visiting this site and learned a great deal about the property's charm as they examined its original architectural details.

According to local historian Craig Moore, the house is one of just 47 known still-standing stone houses that were built by the late 18th century in their part of the county. The students stood in awe of three stone fireplaces (two more are still hidden behind plaster walls), a stone wall that separated the main house and the kitchen, original wide-plank oak floors, raised six-panel doors, and deeply recessed window sills. They also loved the simple closed staircase that led to the second floor and an original plank door with a 200-year-old wrought-iron thumb latch that opened to the basement.

"It's a real piece of history," gushed Jill, who had never been inside a house as old as this.

"There's nothing else like it," agreed Anthony.

When included as observational experiences, Mr. Frombach found that field trips benefit his geography program in these ways: (1) hands-on learning permits students to interact with real things rather than try to learn from abstract examples, (2) students develop a greater appreciation of the environment they will investigate, and (3) examples observed in the field can be related to other classroom work. To increase the potential benefits of field trips, however, there needs to be careful preparation. Before the trip, help the children think about, discuss, and record what they are likely to see. Encourage them to ask questions they will want to investigate. Talk about whom they may want to interview at the site or what would be possible to bring back to the classroom.

When the class goes to a site, the students should take field notes and make sketches of what they are most interested in or what they would like to learn more about when they return to school. When they return to the classroom, it is important to discuss the field trip: what happened, to whom they spoke, what they saw, and what they learned. Sketches or field notes become the basis for detailed illustrations or for the construction of models; field notes are used to write summary accounts of or narratives about the trip.

It is a fact of life, though, that regardless of how well you plan the trip, many unexpected surprises and benefits will be sure to crop up. For example, on the Hoopes Park trip, Ethan yanked on Jamielle's homemade necklace and sent beads rolling in every direction; midway through the visit, Carl was terrified by a goat's loud bellow and screeched, "Get me outa here! I wanna go home!" After Mr. Frombach took care of those troubles, Carrie brought up her snack. And when the class returned to school, individual letters of thanks revealed some interesting "confessions":

> Dear Sir:
>
> I am sorry about the way our class acted on our trip to your park, but I did not personally curse or anything. I hope you let us come back. Our friend who pulled down his pants is sorry!

> Dear Sir:
>
> I am sorry that our class was bad on its trip to the park. I apologize for exposing myself. I hope you let us come back. (P.S.—I am a boy.)

Speculating

Geographic investigations begin with observations, but they don't stop there. Observations lay the foundation for more complex understandings such as why things are where they are and how they got there: "Where is it located? Why is it there? What

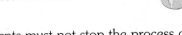

do you think has caused it to look this way?" Students must not stop the process of learning about a geographic location simply by looking at and describing it. They must speculate about possible answers to "where" and "why there" questions.

Mr. Frombach, continuing the topic of Homes Around the World, asked his young geographers to look for clues in the pictures and during the field trips so they could think about how climate, natural resources, and other physical features of locations that might have influenced the selection of building materials and the design of a home. He asked, "How have the people adapted their homes to the environment?" This process should not be pure guesswork, but rather a systematic form of deductive reasoning that calls on students to use previously acquired understandings and experiences to make reasoned inferences. These inferences, in turn, will be tested by students while they uncover supportive data.

Investigating

In this third phase of geographic inquiry, young geographers gather information about locations and about the human characteristics of those places. To answer geographic questions, students must be helped to gather information from a variety of sources in a variety of ways. In the earlier elementary grades, literature, videos, resource persons, Internet sites, or any other suitable informational sources might supply valuable information. In the middle and upper elementary grades, students can engage in these and other investigative activities such as library research and fieldwork (taking photos, distributing questionnaires, conducting interviews, collecting samples, and reading and interpreting maps).

Because of the wealth of information on each type of home, Mr. Frombach decided it would be most efficient to subdivide his class into specialized research groups such as "yurts" (Mongolia), "adobe homes" (American southwest), and "leaf huts" (Central African rainforest). Mr. Frombach visited each group and used timely prompts to direct and extend thinking. For example, while visiting the adobe group, he offered prompts like these: "What kind of homes are these? Where are they found? What are they made of? How were they made? Why are they made this way? How do these homes compare with ours? Why are adobe homes so popular in different parts of the world? Do you think that homes in these areas will always be build this way?"

Regardless of the grade level, *something* constructive must be done with the results of the students' research. Mr. Frombach felt it was important to first help each group organize its research into an informational paragraph or two. We will study what he did with the adobe group as an example.

Mr. Frombach began the process by asking the students to list on a chart all the factual data they uncovered about adobe homes around the world. When the chart was filled with many words and phrases, he asked the students to study it carefully and think about this question, "Do any of these items seem to belong together?" As the students studied the chart, they circled their selections with a black marker. Mr. Frombach then asked, "Why did you group these items together?" and invited the students to explain the common characteristics of all the items in the group. Next, Mr. Frombach asked the students to come up with a label that encompassed the characteristics of all the items in the group. Since the students had circled places around the world where adobe homes can be found, they simply called this group "Places."

Mr. Frombach then explained, "We are now going to use the information you circled to write a paragraph." Then, with the understanding that many informational paragraphs begin with the main idea, he asked, "Please say in one sentence what all these items seem to be telling us."

There was no response for what seemed like an eternity because this was a difficult question. Then Amanda suggested, "You can find adobe houses all around the world."

"Yeah," agreed Yanming, "they're all over."

"Good thinking," praised Mr. Frombach as he wrote the suggestions on the chalkboard. "This is a great way to start our paragraph. Let's examine the two ideas closely and try to combine them into one sentence to begin our paragraph."

Again, there was a constructive lull in the classroom as the children thought hard about their charge. Eventually, several suggestions were made; the children settled on, "The world is full of adobe houses." The group scribe then recorded the first sentence on a large sheet of chart paper.

"Now that we have our topic sentence," instructed Mr. Frombach, "we'll need to focus on the underlined items in order to add details to the paragraph." After deciding on the order that the supporting details should be written, the "adobe group" drafted this paragraph:

The world is full of adobe houses. The most adobe buildings can be found in the southwestern part of the United States. Especially in the desert areas of New Mexico and Arizona. These include both homes and missions. Adobe homes can be found in other Spanish-speaking countries like Mexico, Peru, and Bolivia. Surprisingly, adobe homes can be found in the arid regions of western China, in Iran, and on the island of Cyprus. Depending on the location, adobe homes can be found in all kinds of different shapes, sizes, and colors.

Next, the group studied its paragraph and reworked it under Mr. Frombach's guidance. For example, they realized that "Especially in the desert areas of New Mexico and Arizona" was an incomplete sentence so it was combined with other ideas into a complex sentence: "Most adobe buildings can be found in the southwestern part of the United States, especially in the desert areas of New Mexico and Arizona." Likewise, they edited the rest of the paragraph and wrote the final copy on chart paper. Appropriate illustrations then were added.

Later, responding to a similar instructional sequence by Mr. Frombach, the students circled in red those items dealing with the history of adobe building, in blue those items dealing with the building process, and in green those items dealing with the advantages and disadvantages of living in adobe homes. Each subsequent paragraph was added to the first chart and displayed in the group's work area to summarize what it had learned about adobe as a building material. It is obvious that the students were refining specific writing skills, such as writing an informational paragraph, as they learned about homes around the world.

Extending and Reinforcing

You may extend and reinforce the children's learning by using small-group writing activities, constructing models, making maps, studying tables and graphs, or examining all kinds of literature. Having had such a stimulating data-gathering experience, children will have much to share. For example, Mr. Frombach wanted to take the unit beyond the ordinary to where the action is. During his unit on Homes Around the World, students had learned that early Pueblo Indians, the Anasazi, built adobe homes by using the "puddling method." They built walls by placing handfuls of wet adobe on a mound, letting it dry, and adding another layer. They would add layer after layer rather than stacking bricks. The Spanish introduced adobe bricks to the Pueblo Indians, and, because of its many favorable properties, adobe remains a building material of preference today.

To help his students understand how to build with the adobe material, Mr. Frombach adapted the adobe brick-making process accurately described by Byron Augustin and Michael Bailey (2001). Before actually involving students in the activity, Mr. Frombach built wooden frames from common lumber, one frame for each team of four students (see Figure 4–5), to be filled with wet adobe to make bricks. The inside dimensions of the frame were 8×10×4″ (although the traditional size of adobe bricks is 10×16×4″). Mr. Frombach left an additional 6 inches of wood on each corner of the long sides to serve as handles for removing the frame once the adobe had set. If you would rather not make the wooden frames, locate one or two sturdy cardboard boxes whose tops or bottoms measure approximately the same as the

FIGURE 4–5
Frame for Shaping Adobe Brick

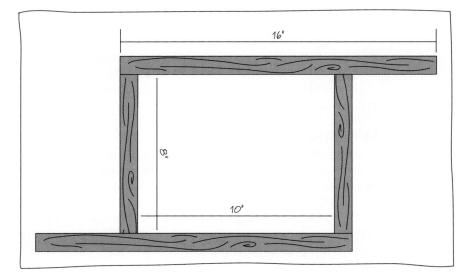

frame. Measure 4″ up from bottom with ruler and draw a line all around the box. Take a utility knife and cut along the line. The resulting shallow box will serve as an *adobera*, or adobe mold. You may wish to make miniature molds for an indoor project.

Mr. Frombach set up work stations outside on a hard asphalt surface and placed at each station a wooden frame, a sheet of wax paper that extended beyond the sides of the frame, two large plastic bags, a putty knife, a one-gallon plastic water jug, and three or four handfuls of hay. He then directed the students through the following course of action:

1. Mix earth, straw, and water using a shovel and hoe in an appropriate outdoor site. (Students need to be careful not to mix with hands and shovel or hoe at the same time.) Mix to a thick consistency or paste, adding the water slowly. This is the mud or *zoquete*.

2. Test the consistency by forming a baseball-size patty from the material. Hold it waist high, and let it drop to a hard surface. If the adobe splatters everywhere, it is too wet, and more dirt is needed. If the material breaks apart into pieces, the material is too dry, and a little more water is needed. If the patty stays together and makes a solid "thump," the material is ready to shape into an adobe brick.

3. Lightly wet the inside of the cardboard mold with a wet rag. Pour stiff mud into mold and turn over carefully. If using the wooden frame, students should spread out the sheet of wax paper and place the form on top, making sure that the wax paper extends beyond the outside edges of the form. They place the adobe mixture in the form and pack it tightly to force out all air pockets.

4. The cardboard molds can be turned several times to allow them to dry evenly. Allow the adobe to dry for three or four days in the sun before handling. Lift the cardboard mold slowly to release the adobe. Or, if using the wooden frame, remove the bricks from the forms by taking a putty knife and cutting around the interior edges of the form, loosening the brick. Then take the form by the handles and lift it from the brick.

"Congratulations, class," smiled Mr. Frombach wryly. "Only 6,000 more and we'll have enough to construct our own little house!"

Like Mr. Frombach, social studies teachers around the country have developed significant learning situations in which their children are actively and directly involved in doing something real.

Evaluating

The final phase of geographic inquiry is making personal judgments about the situation: "Have the people been wise in using the environment in such a way? Is this the most productive use of the land or its resources?" All personal opinions must be supported with sound reasons: "If not, why not? If so, why?" Since so many conditions of our world are intimately associated with the wise use of our physical environment, skills in this realm are of primary importance to children, the adult citizens of the future.

It is this physical environment–people linkage that makes geography such a valued component of today's dynamic social studies. Geographic terms and place locations are important; students need to know and use correctly the appropriate geographic terms and concepts. However, to become truly geographically literate, students must apply their basic skills and understandings to discovering relationships among people, places, and other phenomena. For example, generalizations about the influence of weather on homes or elevation of a region on agriculture are fundamental geographic relationships necessary for increasing geographic literacy.

Independent Projects

In some portions of the social studies curriculum, students are dependent on the teacher for guidance and direction. In others they can work more independently. The independent investigations carried out either by a class or by small groups of students are commonly known as *projects*. The project method does *not* mean copying information from encyclopedias and other sources of second-hand information followed by drawing illustrations to be hung on the classroom wall to impress visitors. Project work refers to a set of teaching strategies that enable teachers to engage students through in-depth studies of interesting topics. When teachers implement project work successfully, students can be highly motivated, feel actively involved in their own learning, and turn out superior work.

Independent projects do not normally encompass the complete geography program, but in combination with teacher-guided inquiry, projects will complement systematic instruction by responding to the varying needs and interests of children. Nearly all geography topics can be studied through the use of projects, but the younger the students, the more concrete, present-day, and hands-on the topic should be. Projects are a lot like good stories; they have a beginning, middle, and end, which are commonly referred to as the *opening*, the *investigating* or *producing* phase, and the *culminating activity*.

Key Events of a Project

Projects usually start with an *opening event*, which serves to stimulate initial interest in the topic. The opening event might come from primary sources such as classroom guests, field trips, real objects, special events, or illustrates processes. Or, they might be secondary sources such as books, magazines, photos, maps, and videos. Whatever the source, the idea of the opening event is to help students develop a strong attachment to the topic and to associate their past experiences to it. Therefore, you will want to encourage your students to recall any previous experiences related to the opening event. As students begin to come up with questions they would like to investigate, write them down and post the list so they can guide future data-gathering efforts. In effect, students should examine what they already know, and decide what it is they want to know. Many teachers like to use charting techniques during the opening event as a way of listing questions as they arise and organizing what the students already know (or think they know) about the topic. Webs and K-W-L charts work well; see Chapter 6 for a detailed explanation of those techniques.

During the second event, the students become engaged in *investigating* and *producing* something. Teachers help students investigate their problems by making available a variety of resources, including real objects, books, Internet sites, and other research materials. It is crucial to provide a wealth of research materials, but extremely critical for geography projects to involve students in field work or to arrange for them to speak with experts. The students will search for information to solve their problem by conducting an experiment, directly observing a phenomenon, or interviewing someone, to name a few potential investigative strategies. As the students work, their teachers will help them apply research skills such as collecting, organizing, and interpreting data. Although most of the work in any project is done by the students, they often require substantial guidance from their teacher to execute their plans and ideas.

During this second event, it is important that students conduct the research and reflect on their findings in order to create something that represents what they have learned. Some children need time to reflect on new knowledge to understand it fully in their own terms, so don't hurry students through this segment. Imaginative activity can be challenging for some children. As the students ponder what they should do, the teacher can offer them imaginative ways of personalizing their new knowledge through print, art, drama, and community action.

- Publishing-related experiences—newspaper, magazine, book, letter, poem
- Art experiences—illustration, diagram, model, collage, mural, mobile, diorama
- Drama experiences—reader's theater, play, skit, video presentation, puppets
- Community action—petition, service project, letter to newspaper

The culminating event involves communicating or sharing with others the work of the project. This process provides an excellent opportunity to review and evaluate all that has been going on during the past days or weeks. But, because projects often produce a number of interesting products and exhibits, there is usually too much to share. So, the class has to be selective in deciding what to share with other classes, the principal, or the parents. Finally, the teacher can use children's ideas and interests to make an evocative transition between the project being concluded and the next topic of study.

This summary has highlighted the general features of projects, but it is important to think of each project as being distinctive. The teacher, the children, the topic, and the location of the school all contribute to the uniqueness of each project. An example of a geography project that started out through interest generated by a fifth-grade teacher, Carmie Lazar, is described in the accompanying vignette.

Inside an *Active Classroom*

Ms. Lazar's students liked to take virtual trips on the Internet and showed a lot of enthusiasm for travel. She decided to capitalize on their passion and put them to work as intern travel agents for the classroom-based World Wide Travel Agency. To create interest, Ms. Lazar and her students received a pretend letter one day from Mr. John Doe, an imaginary client who planned to do some extensive traveling throughout the United States in the near future and wished to arrange his itinerary through the World Wide Travel Agency. The students were impressed with the potential business this new client could bring to the agency but were a little unsure if they could handle it. They wanted to help this important client, but needed to get some information about what travel agencies do. No problem here; Donyelle's mother ran the local travel agency and was more than happy to arrange a visit to her business. The students returned to the classroom teeming with posters, pamphlets, guidebooks, and brochures. These materials helped the students understand the kind of information tourists need. They learned firsthand about the business and what it takes to promote travel to the different regions of our country.

Ms. Lazar and her students agreed that it would be in their best interest to designate sections of the classroom as separate "travel agency offices," one to deal with each region of the United States. After the students were divided into small groups, each came up with its own office name and displayed a business sign. The individual offices displayed a map of the United States that included the names of selected regions of the United States: Middle Atlantic region, Great Lakes region, and so on.

Each travel agency office was ready for business, but then students realized they needed to first design an advertising package for their respective region with materials similar to those they brought back from their trip to the real travel agency. They decided it would be best to produce a guidebook, travel poster, travel brochure, magazine advertisement, and a radio/television compaign.

Before they began their task, Ms. Lazar asked the students in each travel agency office to focus their research activities on the kinds of attractions for which their region was noted: sandy beaches, scenic mountain trails, historic sites, industry, or agriculture. Some groups found information in magazines and books, others decided to watch a video, but all found a wealth of information on various Internet sites. After they finished, each group illustrated a large poster and used a few well-chosen words as a caption. For example, the group investigating America's Southwest focused on the Grand Canyon and used the caption, "A Grand Adventure!"

The brochures were eye catching, too. Patterned after commercial brochures, there were colorful illustrations and captions on the front of each. For example, a steaming loaf of bread dominated the front of the group responsible for enticing visitors to "The Central Plains: Our Nation's Breadbasket." Another brochure had a drawing of a wide-eyed, smiling potato that invited visitors to "Come on out to Idaho. There's more here than just us potatoes." The children chose six important features of the region to highlight on the inside, each feature accompanied by text and illustration. The back of each brochure included a small map of the region, directions on how to get there, and sources of further information.

The purpose of the magazine ads and radio/television campaigns (30-second spots using the classroom video camera) was similar—to draw visitors by describing the important features of the region. Students were advised that each form of advertising needed a concise message so potential customers wouldn't be bored by excessive detail.

The guidebooks were much more comprehensive. Ms. Lazar showed commercial guidebooks that students used as models to create their own. Each guidebook had these features:

- A preface that briefly promoted the attributes of the region
- An introduction that served as a slightly more comprehensive guide to the region's attractions, climate, geographical features, and chief products
- A history section that included significant dates and events as well as the important people who have lived in the region
- A calender of events highlighting fairs, celebrations, and seasonal attractions
- A places-to-see section that included the capital, information about major cities, museums, parks, zoos, recreational activities, historical sites, and businesses
- A food and shelter section with information about hotels, restaurants, and campsites, as well as their costs

To culminate the activity, Ms. Lazar requested that each travel agency office share its advertising campaign with the other offices in the World Wide Travel Agency. Parents were invited to visit the classroom to enjoy the students' work. All children learned a great deal about the various regions through participating in this enjoyable, productive project.

The project approach to geography is an appropriate teaching strategy that confronts students with geography-related problems as a focus for research activities. Project activities can involve the whole class or small groups; they can extend over several months or take as little time as a day. Regardless, children take the initiative in completing projects. The teacher sets the scene and falls into the role of a facilitator, supporting the children's efforts. Projects can be initiated from the children's spontaneous interests, or they can flow from an interesting experience provided by the teacher. The current interest in projects stems from our growing knowledge about the probing, wondering minds of the children we teach. Geography projects are a source for nurturing their natural responsiveness and interest in the world around them.

MAPS: THE TOOLS OF GEOGRAPHERS

It is impossible to teach or learn geography without using a map or even several maps simultaneously. Maps are absolutely necessary for collecting data about places on the Earth's surface. Thus, desk and wall maps, globes, and atlases are essential requirements for all dynamic social studies classrooms. The Geography Education Standards Project (1994) added: "Geography has been called 'the art of the mappable.' Making maps should be a common activity for all students. They should read (decode) maps to collect information and analyze geographic patterns and make (encode) maps to organize information. . . . For students, making [and using] maps should become as common, natural, and easy as writing a paragraph" (1994, p. 43). One of your major tasks in developing a solid geography component in your social studies program is to help children acquire the basic skills necessary to construct and interpret maps.

WHAT IS A MAP?

A map is a graphic representation of the Earth's surface (or a portion of it) drawn to scale, as seen from above. Maps use colors, symbols, and labels to represent the features of a particular location. A map provides information on the location of places, the distance between places, and pathways for travel and communication. Maps also show variations in terrain, heights of natural features, and the extent of vegetation cover. Maps can show many other things, too, but the finest maps available are worthless unless the map user knows how to read them.

When teaching maps and globes, it is logical to begin by helping children establish a basic idea of what maps are. Often, however, teachers will start by telling their students that a map is an image of the Earth much like one would see if viewing the landscape from above in an airplane, or "a bird's eye view." This might be a useful explanation for the upper elementary school grades and above, but for younger children the top-down metaphor is quite confusing. That is because, as Piaget informs us, children are quite egocentric during the early grades; that is, they see things pretty much from one point of view—their own! They just can't believe that everyone else doesn't view things the same way they do.

Piaget conducted a study, called the "mountain study," to investigate his idea of egocentricity. He devised a square board with three distinctly different plaster mountains arranged as shown in Figure 4–6. He would position children in front of the

FIGURE 4–6
Piaget's Mountain Arrangement

simple mountain range and then ask them to pick from four pictures the view that they currently see. Next, he would introduce a doll who "strolled" around the table, stopping at each of the three remaining sides of the square. The children remained seated at their original position and selected pictures showing how the doll saw the mountains at each stop. Younger children would continue picking the picture illustrating the view from where they were sitting; older children (past the age of 8 or 10) picked correctly what the doll would see from its perspective.

INTRODUCTORY MAP SKILLS EXPERIENCES

For younger children, then, to think of a map as an aerial view does not work. Instead, an awareness of a map as being a picture of some place on the Earth's surface (or part of it) may be more easily understood. Think of early map awareness as a developmental process that seems to happen together with picture awareness. Most children come to school having a variety of experiences with pictures in storybooks, television, movies, cereal boxes, and magazines. Thus, they understand that pictures represent ideas and that they may be used to express ideas or information, too. Thinking of a map as a "picture of a place" provides a better foundation for instruction than trying to get children to understand that a map is an aerial view of a place on the Earth's surface. Young children already possess knowledge of the immediate world around them (the design of their classroom, school, and playground), and that understanding should be used as the starting point for map instruction.

Because all children up to about the age of 8 are egocentric, especially those with limited opportunities at home, they must be offered instructional opportunities that work with their egocentric predispositions, not against them. Make available blocks, boxes, and other construction materials for use in a variety of informal construction activities. Children might make buildings large enough to play in—houses, stores, the airport, or their school—play in them, and endow them with meaning drawn from their own experiences. These buildings become tangible representations of real places in the environment. In essence, that's what a map is. The structure becomes for the children a concrete connection to something real; therefore, children must build and play before formal map reading can begin.

Children build, play, tear down, and build again as they enact roles in settings that have the most meaning to them. No matter how a structure gets started—whether a child comes to the classroom building area with an idea already in mind or whether an idea grows as the building materials are manipulated—the child strives to translate an idea into reality. Consequently, the structure reflects the child's knowledge of the world. Just watch a group of young children as they design and build a representation of their neighborhood. The buildings take shape and soon cars, buses, and trucks maneuver up and down the streets, engines roaring and tooting at all the pedestrians. Skillful teachers will interact with children during such play, offering verbal prompts that help develop the foundational spatial concepts requisite for later map reading demands:

Block representations of familiar environments are the most valuable premapping learning tools for young children.

"Which of these trucks will fit through the garage door?"

"How did you get those blocks to balance?"

"What kinds of signs will be needed for your road?"

"Can you make a ramp for the fire truck to get into the station?"

"How can you make the road longer?"

"How could you make this building higher?"

"How can the car get to the store if this street were closed?"

"Is the flower shop as tall as the apartment building?"

"Can you design a bridge that will help the bus get across the river?"

You can learn a lot about children by watching and listening. Then, by offering judicious prompts, you can help children think about their structures and find new relationships among established ideas.

BEGINNING MAP SKILLS INSTRUCTION

If there is a single area of controversy in geography education that stands out above all others, it may be agreeing on the most appropriate time to introduce children to formal map instruction. Although social studies textbooks and scope and sequence charts often include various map basics as early as first grade, there is considerable disagreement whether children are cognitively ready to do anything with maps before second or third grade. Despite this dissension about the best time to begin map instruction, there is widespread agreement that when instruction is developmentally suitable, children are capable of learning about maps.

The first step in creating a developmentally suitable instructional program is to become aware of the particular skills required to read and make maps:

1. Locating places
2. Recognizing and expressing relative location
3. Interpreting map symbols
4. Developing a basic idea of relative size and scale
5. Reading directions
6. Understanding that the globe is the most accurate representation of the Earth's surface

Three-Dimensional Classroom Maps

Initial formal mapping experiences should be with a location thoroughly familiar to the children. Their early premapping play structures were usually representative of places in the environment where they have had experiences, so continued attachment to a mapping location significantly influences the students' movement into more formalized study of maps. Therefore, the most appropriate way to begin is to explore the immediate environment and reproduce it with concrete building materials. This is the beginning of formal map instruction, through the manipulation of concrete materials in order to represent a place in the environment. The place to begin map skills instruction appears to be a place that is most directly observable and meaningful—the classroom.

Begin an initial classroom map-making project (it usually works best with middle-of-the-year or late-year second graders) by having available one empty, clean half-pint milk container for each student, if your school gets milk in these containers. If not, a number of small identical boxes will work. Direct the children to cut off the tops so that they have a square, open-top box. Turn the box over so it is standing on the open end and cut away parts along the sides with scissors so that the cartons appear to have legs (see Figure 4–7).

FIGURE 4–7
Milk Carton Desks

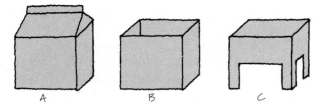

Discuss the cardboard desks with the children, focusing on how they are models of their real desks. Encourage the children to paint the desks with tempera paint, glue construction paper books or pencils on top, and put their name cards on the fronts of the desks.

When the desks are completed, ask one child to put her desk on a large sheet of cardboard, such as a removed side of a refrigerator packing box, that you have placed on a worktable or on the floor. Explain that the cardboard represents the classroom floor, but on a smaller scale. Let the student observe where her desk is located in the actual classroom and then examine the cardboard to determine where her milk carton desk should be placed. Once she places her desk correctly on the cardboard, the construction process moves quickly. A child who sits next to the first child places his desk "next to Holly's." As children take turns placing their desks on the classroom model, they are experiencing and using three basic map-reading skills:

1. Recognizing that their milk cartons stand for their real desks (interpreting map symbols)
2. Finding where their desks should be placed (locating places)
3. Determining the placement of individual desks in relationship to the other desks (recognizing and expressing relative location)

Next, ask the children to bring to school empty boxes they might have around the house, from small jewelry boxes to boxes about the size of a toaster. Divide the class into committees, each of which is responsible for constructing a classroom feature such as the piano, teacher's desk, or a learning center. Keep a careful eye on the children as they select the boxes most appropriate for their particular feature. Often, the group responsible for the teacher's desk will select the largest box, even though that box is proportionally much larger than the teacher's desk, because children think of their teacher as an extremely important person in their lives and thus deserving of the largest available box. However, you should encourage the children to look carefully at their own real desks in comparison to yours so they can eventually select a box that closer represents the true size relationship.

Sometimes children come up with quite amusing ideas as they work on making relative size decisions. For example, one teacher found that all students had completed their assigned classroom features and were ready to place them on the growing three-dimensional map, but Alice remained at the back of the room busily working on her model wastebasket. When the teacher approached Alice to see what was going on, he discovered that Alice's progress was being delayed by a strong desire to be as accurate as possible with her job. Since the classroom wastebasket was full of discarded paper, Alice was cutting dozens of tiny pieces of paper for her wastebasket and folding or crunching them in order to precisely reproduce the real thing. It took forever!

To complete their assigned features, students should decorate and paint the selected boxes so they are ready to join the student desks on the growing classroom map. This phase of map construction is critical, as it contributes to the emergence of a "bird's-eye-view" concept. This idea entails forming a mental picture of something as if it were viewed from above, much as a bird might view something as it flies over.

You can help develop this concept by encouraging the children to look at their features from directly above as they place them on their growing classroom map. That way, they will see only the tops of the desks, tables, and file cabinets and begin to understand that this is how a real map is constructed. Notice that during this phase of construction, the three previous map-reading skills are extended and reinforced, and a new skill is introduced: developing an idea of relative size and scale.

Once the model classroom has been properly arranged, you can further extend and reinforce map skills by using their map as a learning tool.

Locating Places

"Put the teacher's desk where it is located in our classroom."

"Where would you place the piano? The file cabinet?"

"Point to the box that shows the puppet stage . . . the worktable . . . the teacher's desk."

"James, can you find Michelle's desk? Put your finger on it."

"Put your finger on the aquarium. Now trace the path you would take to answer the door."

Recognizing and Expressing Relative Location

"Whose desk is closest to the coat rack?"

"Trace the shortest path from the reading corner to the door."

"Which is closer to the door, the science center or the teacher's desk?"

Interpreting Map Symbols

"Pick up the box that represents the puppet stage."

"What does the red box stand for?"

"How can we show the coat rack on our map?"

Developing an Idea of Relative Size and Scale

"Which is larger, the file cabinet or the piano?"

"Which box should be smaller, the teacher's desk or the worktable?"

"Point to the smallest (or largest) piece of classroom furniture."

Flat Maps

The three-dimensional model of the classroom can be easily transformed into a flat map by following a few simple procedures. First, have the children look at their three-dimensional map from directly above and discuss what they see. Then, dividing responsibilities, ask the students to put a piece of construction paper beneath each feature and trace around the outside of each with a crayon. As the three-dimensional features are removed and the outlines are cut out with scissors, the children should label the remaining outlines, such as "file cabinet" or "Bart's desk," and glue the outlines in their appropriate places. The three-dimensional map gradually becomes a flat map as traced outlines replace the models. For the children to understand how the flat map functions in the same way as the three-dimensional map, you should ask questions like those used for the three-dimensional map. Effective discussion is as important for this flat map phase as for the three-dimensional phase.

Model Communities

Building representations of real places should not stop with the three-dimensional classroom. In second or third grade, the process of building a model community is a thrilling and challenging project that can last all year long. It provides a way for students to learn about their community and master beginning map skills as well.

As with the model classroom, most materials for the model community consist of packaging items easily found around the house. Oatmeal boxes and toilet paper or paper towel rolls are excellent building materials for trees, cylindrically shaped buildings, silos, or structures such as large oil storage tanks. Cereal boxes, tissue boxes, candy boxes, and pasta boxes easily represent tall buildings, apartment houses, or stores. Different size milk or juice cartons make nice houses with peaked roofs. All you need to do is provide the proper work materials (construction paper, tempera paint, crayons, marking pens, and school glue), and the children will go right to work. To give the children an idea how these materials might be used, show them how you would make a model of your own house. For example, cover a milk carton

Constructing three-dimensional models help young children grasp the idea that maps are representations of real places in the environment.

with red construction paper, glue on yellow windows and green doors, paint on a blue roof, and a house begins to take shape. A cardboard cylinder painted brown and covered with columns of green adds a tree to the landscape.

I like to start the actual community model with something the children can directly observe—the school building. Walk around the outside of the school and carefully note its shape and size. Then, encourage the students to look over the boxes and decide on one that might be best to represent their school. Discuss the colors of construction paper that might be used to cover the box as well as any possibilities to highlight special features (trees, flagpole, parking lot) so it would look as much like the real school as possible. Toy cars, school buses, bicycles, and other vehicles also add to the realism.

The model community can expand outward from the school as students visit the immediate neighborhood, a shopping center, the zoo, and community services buildings. You might limit the project to the immediate school neighborhood or extend it throughout the year as the children learn about all the elements of communities or neighborhoods.

Story Maps

Good children's books offer superb opportunities for exposure to early mapping activities. Some books are perfect; chain stories that the children (or teacher) can illustrate easily are excellent selections. For example, in Eric Hill's popular "lift-the-flap" story *Spot's First Walk* (Putnam), a curious puppy meets all kinds of new animal friends as he wanders behind fences, by a chicken coop, and near a pond on his first venture away from home. As you read the story, invite the children to predict whom they might meet under each flap. When the story is finished, have the children draw pictures of the snail, fish, bees, hen, and other friends Spot met along the way. Their simple illustrations can be arranged as a floor display, creating a sequence map of Spot's travels. The children can retell the story by explaining what happened at each point as they walk along their "map." It might be fun to cut out "puppy footprints" from construction paper and have the children place them on the floor to trace Spot's footsteps (pawsteps?) as they travel from place to place. Other stories appropriate for story maps include *Katie and the Big Snow* by Virginia Lee Burton (Houghton Mifflin), *Rosie's Walk* by Pat Hutchins (Macmillan), and *Harry the Dirty Dog* by Gene Zion (Harper). A sample story map for the traditional tale *The Three Billy Goats Gruff* is shown in Figure 4–8.

Mental Maps

Geography Standard 2 states that, to be geographically informed, students must be able to understand "how to use mental maps to organize information about people, places, and environments in a spatial context." A mental map is an effective way of organizing social studies content (webs and charts, for example), but it is also a useful way of keeping in mind images of the Earth's surface. Basically, a mental map is

FIGURE 4–8
Story Map

Theme: Books for Easy Mapping

Gene Zion's **Harry the Dirty Dog** (HarperCollins) is an enjoyable story about a little white dog with black spots who likes everything but taking baths. One day when he realizes his owners are planning a bath, he decides to bury the family's scrubbing brush and run away. This is where his adventures begin. Harry meanders all through town getting so dirty that his family can't recognize him when he returns home. In a stroke of genius, Harry unearths the bath brush, begs for a bath, and the rest is history.

Virginia Lee Burton's **Katy and the Big Snow** (Houghton Mifflin) is an old-fashioned tale of Katy, a brave and untiring tractor from the city of Geoppolis, who works as a bulldozer in the summer and a snowplow in the winter. Most of the winters have snowfalls too small for Katy to plow but when the big one finally hits, the town is covered in a thick blanket of snow. The power lines are down. The mail can't get through. Everyone and everything is stopped but Katy! Suddenly, the entire community is dependent on the brave snowplow who plows out the city.

Pat Hutchins's **Rosie's Walk** (Aladdin) tells the story of Rosie the hen who leaves the chicken coop and sets out for a little walk around the barnyard. Following her every move is the fox, but she doesn't know it. Inadvertently, she leads him into one disaster after another as she foils successive attempts on her life. She returns safely to the coop, blissfully unaware of the fox's attempts to catch her.

an informally drawn representation of what a person thinks a place on the Earth looks like. For example, look at Figure 4–9, a mental map like one drawn by one of my students. This quickly sketched, simple outline has a fairly good recognizable identity. You've probably figured out that it is the United States because its sizes are roughly proportionate, the bulges and indentations are roughly where they should be, and important cities serve as helpful location markers. All of us have used mental maps throughout our lives. Did you ever draw a simple map of your bedroom as a youngster? What about sketching out a map to help someone find your house? Mental maps can be of continents, countries, cities, and oceans, or they could be the layout of your campus. Whatever the representation, people develop and refine their mental maps through personal experience and from their social studies program. The development and refinement of mental mapping is an important part of geography because they reflect students' skill in observing and thinking about the world in spatial terms. Young geographers will add detail and structure to their mental maps as they learn more about the world around them. Therefore, mental maps for young children include their schoolroom, school, bedroom, home, neighborhood, or community. As they read, observe, and experience more about the world around

Norman Bridwell's **Clifford Takes a Trip** (Scholastic) finds Clifford at home all alone as his family takes a trip that is too far for Clifford. He is left with the lady next door. Lonely for his family, Clifford sets out to find them. Determined, Clifford bravely overcomes several obstacles along the way until he reunites with Emily Elizabeth and the rest of his family.

Susan Blair's **Three Billy Goats Gruff: A Norwegian Folktale** (Scholastic) is a classic folktale about three clever billy goats who outwit a nasty troll. The goats hunger for the green grass on a hillside, but must cross a bridge that a troll lives under. The youngest billy goat "trip traps" over the bridge first and is met by the troll who threatens to gobble him up. The smart little goat convinces the troll to wait for his bigger brother who, in turn, convinces the troll to wait for the biggest brother. When the biggest brother arrives, he butts the troll off the bridge and opens up the road to the green hillside where the three billy goats graze until they get nice and fat.

TRY THIS

This text set should be considered a guide to begin a collection of stories that best meet your children's needs. You should select books that have a strong potential for follow-up activities to help develop and reinforce early mapping concepts. Using my suggestions for designing mapping activities to accompany *Spot's First Walk* as a model, select any book from this text set and design a follow-up mapping activity appropriate for children in grade 1 or grade 2.

them, students can draw mental maps of geographic features such as oceans, continents, countries, or mountain ranges.

Refining Map Skills

Because map construction projects or story experiences cannot guarantee complete mapping competency, you will need to offer various opportunities to reinforce the specific map and globe skills. With appropriate experiences spread throughout the early grades, most new skills can be developed and strengthened in a rewarding and satisfying manner.

Map Symbols

To reinforce the idea of map symbols through activities that go beyond the construction of these early maps, present the children with a few easily recognized symbols they might see every day, such as those in Figure 4–10. Ask the children what each symbol or sign means to them. What do they stand for? Emphasize that symbols represent real people, places, things, or ideas. Following the discussion, ask the

FIGURE 4–9
Mental Map of the United States

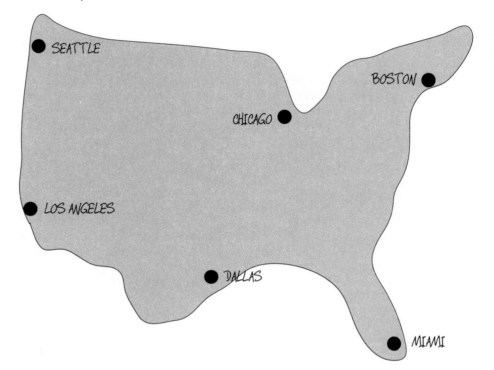

children to pair up and have each child draw a secret symbol without allowing his or her partner to see. Then have each pair try to guess what each other's picture represents. If they have difficulty getting started, offer suggestions such as road signs, punctuation marks, math symbols, and the like. Prepare a bulletin board display of their efforts after they have shared the symbols with each other.

Explain that a symbol is a sign that stands for something. Illustrate this idea by sharing a familiar object, such as a toy airplane. Ask the children to draw an airplane, say the word, and write the word on a piece of paper. Help children understand that some sounds are symbols, some pictures are symbols, and some printed words are symbols. The children should now be ready to understand that the special set of symbols groups people commonly use to communicate ideas is called a *language*. In the United States, most citizens use the English language to communicate orally and in print. In school, we learn English as our main language, but we also learn other languages, such as the language of maps.

To move from this introductory lesson on symbols, write the word *tree* on the chalkboard and hold a short discussion on trees. After the students have shared their ideas, emphasize that the written word *tree* stands for a real thing just as the spoken

FIGURE 4–10
Familiar Symbols

word and a map symbol do. Ask the children to suggest what the illustrated symbol for tree would be in the special language of maps. Follow this procedure while helping the children make up their own symbols for houses, factories, stores, libraries, lakes, roads, and mountains. Don't be overly concerned if their symbols are not the same as standard map symbols; at this point you are more concerned with the overall concept of symbolization.

Next, show your students real maps and introduce standard map symbols once the children are familiar with the concept. Remind the children that maps are symbols on paper and that the symbols on maps represent real things. Show them photographs or slides of a railroad, a bridge, and a building. Then display the corresponding map symbols. Ask the students to link the symbols to their matching pictures and add the word labels. Follow this progression (photo or picture—symbol—word label) whenever new map symbols are introduced in your classroom (see Figure 4–11).

Direction

The best method of introducing young children to the skill of finding directions on a map is through a participatory learning experience. Primary-grade children enjoy

FIGURE 4–11
Introducing Map Symbols

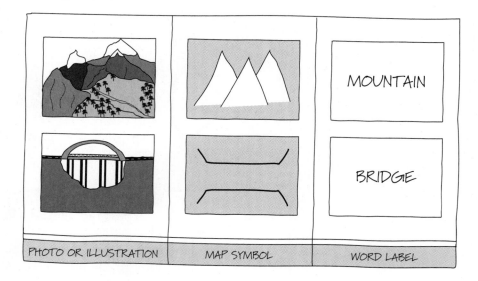

going outdoors with simple compasses to find the cardinal directions (north, south, east, and west). After they locate north on the compass, the children will soon learn that south is behind them, east is to the right, and west is to the left. If the children are outside at noon on a sunny day, they will find a new clue for determining direction—in our northern hemisphere, at noon, their shadows will point in a northerly direction. Once they determine north this way, the other directions will be easy to find. To help them remember the other directions, ask the children to search for outstanding physical landmarks. Have one child face in a northerly direction and select the first obvious feature, such as a large building. Give the child a card labeled *North* and ask her to stand facing in that northerly direction with the card in her hands. Then select a second child to stand back-to-back to the northerly child. Ask the children what direction he is facing. If no one says "south," tell them. Ask the second child to find an outstanding physical feature to the south, such as a large tree, and give him a labeled card to hold. Repeat this procedure when explaining the east and west directions.

By associating landmarks with directions, the children begin to understand that directions help us locate places in our environment. You may ask, for example, "In what direction must I walk if I want to go to that large hill?" To help reinforce these directional skills, provide a number of follow-up activities; for example, "Simon Says" can be adapted to a directional format: "Simon says, 'Take three steps west.' Simon says, 'Turn to the south.'"

After the children have had this fundamental introduction to direction, extend the understandings to their classroom map constructions. Ask them to place their direction labels on the appropriate walls on the classroom maps, but do not label the front of the room north and the back of the room south if these are not the true directions. After determining the classroom directions by using the compass or checking with the previously established reference points, teach the children to orient maps in the proper direction whenever they use them. This may involve turning chairs or sitting on the floor; however, by always turning themselves and their maps in the direction of true north, children avoid the common misconception that "north" is the direction toward the front of the room.

Scale

The idea of scale should be introduced in an informal way rather than in a mathematical sense in the primary grades. Children must realize that maps need to be small enough to be easily carried and readily used. Give the children sheets of drawing paper and tell them to draw their own version of the large classroom map. Some children will immediately reduce the size of the classroom features proportionately. Others will have greater difficulty trying to reproduce the large classroom features on their smaller papers. They often start by drawing one feature as big as it is on the large map and then wonder why they don't have room to include all the rest. Remember that children's sense of proportion, like other perception skills, are yet unrefined. Whether it's making a fire station that is too small for the fire truck or drawing a classroom map out of proportion, size relationships do not yet take on full meaning.

The Globe

Since the early primary-grade child's concept of the Earth is fairly unsophisticated, planned instruction in globe-reading skills is often not successful. Nonetheless, you should not totally omit globe-related activities from the primary classroom. With simplified 12-inch globes, children can understand that the globe is a representation of the Earth, much like their constructed maps were representations of a real place. The globe should include a minimum amount of detail and preferably should show the landmasses in no more than three colors and the bodies of water in a consistent shade of blue. Only the names of the continents, countries, largest cities, and largest bodies of water should be shown. Globes that show more detail easily confuse very young children.

With young children, globes can become valuable informal teaching tools. When reading stories, children may wish to find where their favorite characters live; you can show them the geographic location. For example, if you are reading the children a story that is set in Los Angeles, you may want to show them where Los Angeles is in relation to your community. However, even this would be a meaningless activity unless you relate it to the children's own experiences. You may say, "A globe tells you where places are. Pictures tell you what the place is like." Then, point out where Los Angeles is located and show a large picture with familiar landmarks. Children who hear about the North Pole at Christmastime may want to find out where it is located. Television stories or newspaper articles may suggest other places in which the children are interested. The teacher can use times like these to familiarize young children with characteristics of the globe and with the fact that they can use the globe to locate special places. The basic globe concepts for development in the primary grades are: (1) to understand the basic roundness of the Earth, (2) to understand the differences between land and water areas, and (3) to begin to locate the poles, major cities, and the United States. Teaching suggestions follow:

- *Have the children distinguish large land areas from bodies of water.* Primary-grade children can learn that the Earth is mostly made up of water and seven large land areas known as continents. They should know that our country is called the United States of America and that it is located on the continent of North America. North America is made up of several countries: north of the United States is Canada, and south is Mexico. The Atlantic Ocean is east of the United States, and the Pacific Ocean is west. The United States is made up of 50 states; most touch each other. Two states that don't are Alaska and Hawaii. By the end of the primary grades, children should locate their home state on a map of the United States (see Figure 4–12).

FIGURE 4–12
Early Grade Globe Concepts

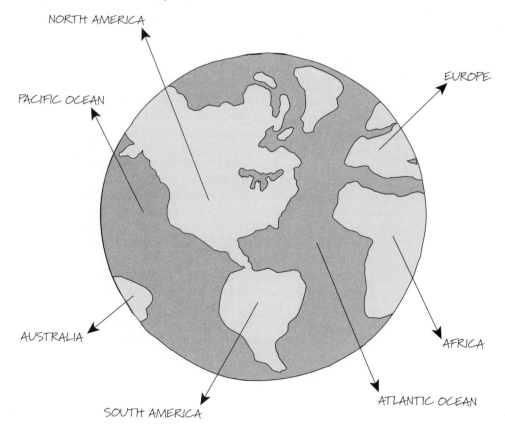

- *Talk about how it would feel to be an astronaut and be able to look at the Earth from a satellite.* Have the children describe how the landmasses and bodies of water would look. Show a satellite photo and map of the Earth.
- *When studying about families around the world, tape small pictures of people in traditional dress to their corresponding countries on a large papier-mâché globe constructed by the children.* Discussion of the need for different types of clothing can lead to an awareness of warm and cold regions of the Earth.

MAP INSTRUCTION IN THE MIDDLE AND UPPER GRADES

The identical six map and globe skills introduced and reinforced during the early grades are again the ones used in the later grades but in more highly sophisticated contexts and for different purposes. Children in the early grades were developing concepts of what a map is and learning the basics of how to read maps by constructing their own maps and being helped to acquire the six basic skills through related teacher-initiated questions and prompts. They see maps in their textbooks that (1) are simple in nature, usually depicting familiar places such as a zoo, park, or neighborhood or imaginary places such as Candy Land or Space Land; (2) contain mostly pictorial or semi-pictorial symbols; (3) often represent an environment such as a neighborhood or community that can be directly experienced by all the children; and (4) gradually expand outward to show, with minimal detail, the continents, the United States, or the route a letter would take if mailed from their hometown to Mexico City, for example.

In later grades, children put these skills to use by employing maps to gather information and to solve problems. In short, the map reading is transformed from learning to read maps to reading maps to learn. An example from Bynam Faw's classroom illustrates how a map construction activity similar to that described for younger children can be used to develop more highly refined concepts and skills.

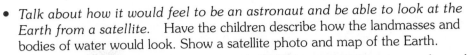

Inside an Active Classroom

Bynam Faw's fifth-grade social studies curriculum focuses on the major regions of the United States, with major emphasis on integrating the disciplines of geography and history. The current region under study is the Great Plains. Students have been enthralled with stories of how settlers pushed west into the Great Plains during the 1860s and settled in what are now Kansas, Nebraska, South Dakota, and North Dakota. They learned that wheat grew well in the rich soil of the Great Plains and became the most important crop of the region. However, they also found out that early farmers faced many challenges that often ruined or damaged their crops—storms, dry spells, insects, blizzards, and floods. Nevertheless, the pioneers were relentless and worked hard to build successful farms throughout the region.

One of the major resources for the study of this region was the collection of Little House books by Laura Ingalls Wilder. Most recently, the class had been reading *Little House on the Prairie* (Harper and Row), a story filled with adventures about the pioneering Ingalls family moving to the wild Kansas country. Today, Mr. Faw planned to help his students explore the kinds of buildings the Ingalls family could have found in a small prairie town: "Imagine that you are going with the Ingalls family on a trip from their farm to a small prairie town. What do you expect to find there?" After a brief discussion, Mr. Faw divided the students randomly into teams of two and assigned each team to a center dealing with a major building: one-room school, church, hotel, general store, livery stable, blacksmith shop, jail, lumberyard, barbershop, cooper (barrel maker), and saloon. The students were advised that they would become "experts" on these places by examining a website Mr. Faw had accessed for each group (*hoover.archives.gov/LIW/pioneertown/activities_pioneertown.html*).

After the students completed their research, they were directed to write a short descriptive paragraph on index cards detailing what they uncovered. The one-room school team, for example, wrote this narrative:

> *Schools in early prairie towns were one-room school houses. There you could find students ages 6 to 16 and eight grades in one room. There was one teacher for all of them, and older students often helped the younger ones.*

The index cards were displayed on a large chart to summarize the kinds of buildings that would be found in small prairie towns of the 1860s. Next, students were instructed to use any of a number of cardboard boxes that Mr. Faw gathered beforehand, along with construction paper, paint, crayons, and other art materials, to construct a model of their buildings. First, Mr. Faw reviewed with the students the materials that the pioneers used to construct these buildings and advised them that they were free to use the computer, encyclopedia, textbook, or any library references to gather any additional information. The students went right to work and, after the buildings were constructed, they were arranged on a tabletop display (with the index card information chart behind them). The groups were eager to function as tour guides, telling other classroom "sightseers" about their pioneer town when they came to visit throughout that day.

Place Location and Direction

As children move through the elementary grades, they continuously use directions and examine a map to find places. The major difference, however, is the level of sophistication of the map itself. Comparing this process to reading a book, you might say that children are taught to read stories in first grade but only at a level appropriate for that stage of development. Later, as the children's skills mature, they are introduced to newer, more difficult stories. Likewise, the maps that early primary-grade children read gradually evolve into more specialized maps, many of which require them to understand grids, a concept that combines knowledge of place location and direction. Middle- and upper-elementary-grade children move toward functionally employing maps with grids, such as road maps, to acquire information for a specific purpose. Erma Moonflower used a road map to help her fourth-grade students reinforce their symbol, place location, and direction skills and at the same time learn about the ever-expanding highway system in the United States.

Inside an *Active* Classroom

First, Ms. Moonflower and her students reviewed the concept of how various signs and symbols communicate information on road maps, helping travelers get to their destination without trouble. However, as is the case with all maps, the students were aware that they need to know what the symbols mean if they are to be of assistance. For this lesson, Ms. Moonflower asked the students to work in pairs and distributed a road map of the United States showing two major types of roads: interstate highways and United States highways.

Today, the students were going to learn some interesting facts about interstate highways. First, Ms. Moonflower displayed a sample highway sign for each of the two major highways (see Figure 4–13).

Ms. Moonflower asked the students to examine their road maps and decide which of the two sample signs represented an interstate highway. After a discussion during which they called on past experiences and word knowledge skills, the students decided that the first sample sign represented interstate highways because they recalled seeing such signs as they traveled with their families, because their road maps showed these signs were on the roads that connected two or more states, and because "interstate" means traveling between two or more states.

Ms. Moonflower then asked her students to carefully examine the map of the interstate highway system to see if they could see any pattern by which the highways were numbered. Quickly, Richard detected that interstate highways going east and west had even numbers while those going north and south had odd numbers. Ms. Moonflower

FIGURE 4–13
Interstate and U.S. Highway Signs

INTERSTATE

U.S.

passed out a yellow highlighter marker to each group and asked the students to trace each north-south highway with yellow. After each group did so, Ms. Moonflower asked the students to identify the states through which the highways passed. She then challenged them to see if they could find a definite pattern with only the highlighted north-south interstate highways. It took a little time, but the students eventually discovered that the higher the number, the farther east the highway: for example, I-95 runs north and south along the east coast while I-5 does the same in the west.

Next, Ms. Moonflower passed out a pink highlighter to each group and asked the students to highlight the east-west interstate highways. In like manner, she directed the students to identify the states through which each passed and challenged them to uncover a numbering pattern. They found that the highest even-numbered interstate highways were in the north, and they gradually got smaller as one traveled south. For example, I-94 in Michigan was northernmost on their maps while I-4 in Florida was southernmost.

Ms. Moonflower then assigned one interstate highway to each group and asked them to use a marking pen to trace their highways on a large political map of the United States. They then made properly shaped interstate highway signs to label their routes. As they accomplished the task, several groups noticed that some interstate highways had 3-digit numbers. They wondered why their research informed them that these were branches off or loops within the primary routes.

To culminate the lesson, Ms. Moonflower passed out to each group a smaller political map of the United States and asked each to recommend a route for a new interstate highway, number it according to the pattern discovered previously, and justify why the highway would be beneficial to the people of our nation.

Latitude and Longitude

In the upper elementary grades, children extend their knowledge of grids as place location devices to the system of latitude and longitude. This system consists of east-west lines called *parallels of latitude* and north-south lines called *meridians of longitude* (see Figure 4–14).

The parallels of latitude, imaginary lines encircling the Earth, measure distances in degrees north and south of the equator (designated as zero degrees latitude). The parallels grow smaller in circumference as they approach both poles. The meridians of longitude, also imaginary lines encircling the Earth, converge at the poles and measure distances in degrees east and west of the prime meridian (designated as zero degrees longitude).

The importance of grids as a means of locating places can be illustrated with a large, unmarked ball. Lead a discussion comparing the similarities of the large ball and the Earth as represented by the classroom globe. Glue a small plastic ship to the ball and ask the children to describe its exact location, imagining themselves shipwrecked and needing to radio their location to be rescued (the ship marks their wreck). They will discover that this is nearly impossible, since there is no point of reference from which to describe an exact location. For example, if the children say the

FIGURE 4–14
The Earth's Grid System

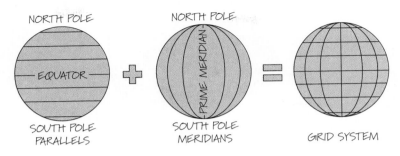

ship is located on the front side of the ball, you can turn the ball and the statement will be incorrect. If they say the ship is on the top of the ball, turn it back again to the original position. Gradually, the students will experience the frustration of locating places on a globe without agreed-on reference points. After some deliberation, they will most likely suggest the addition of parallel east-west lines and instruct the rescue squad to search an area "three lines down from the middle line."

On closer examination of this arrangement, and after prodding from the teacher, the children will discover that the rescuers need to travel all around the world along the "third line down from the middle line" to find them unless given even more precise locations by devising meridians, or north-south lines. The rescue squad then only needs to find where the two points meet. Eventually, the children can be led to locate many well-known places in the world using latitude and longitude. Determining precise locations by using actual degrees of latitude and longitude may be beyond the capabilities of most fourth- and fifth-grade children. Guide them, however, in using latitude and longitude for locating general areas, such as the low latitudes (23½° north and south of the equator), the middle latitudes (between 23½° and 66½° north and south of the equator), and the high latitudes (between 66½° north and the North Pole, and 66½° south and the South Pole). Children can generalize about the climatic similarities within these areas. In which latitudes are most cities located? Where is the weather warm (or cold) throughout most of the year? Show them how to find places east or west or north or south of their location by using meridians. After careful observation, they may find many surprising facts. For example, Rome, Italy, is nearer the North Pole than New York; Detroit is north of Windsor, Ontario; Reno, Nevada, is farther west than Los Angeles; the Gulf of California does not touch California at any point; and the Pacific Ocean is east of the Atlantic Ocean at Panama. All early grid instruction should be general and avoid as much as possible the use of degrees in place location.

Relative Location

Simply locating places on maps does not give students a true understanding of geography. Children must understand the influence of place location on people's lives and how one physical feature may influence another. Recognizing and expressing relative

FIGURE 4–15
Rainfall and Vegetation Maps of Africa

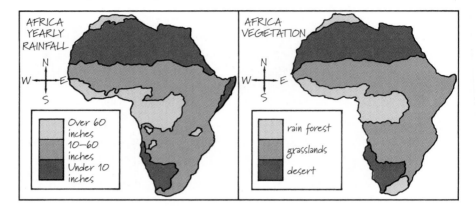

location is a sophisticated map skill because it involves not only locating places but also understanding interrelationships among geographical features, such as the influence of rainfall on the vegetation of a region. For example, upon examining a rainfall map of Africa, shown in Figure 4–15, children should be able to determine the type of vegetation that might grow in each region and how this influences the ways people live.

In the early primary grades, children develop concepts of relative location by explaining why different places in the classroom are located where they are ("Why do you think the science center is located next to the sink?"). The concept is expanded in the intermediate grades as children develop the ability to interpret the influence of physical factors, such as mountains, deserts, valleys, and oceans, on human life. The effects of these geographic features should be discussed, along with humans' attempts to change conditions for their own benefit, as Mariamma Varkey does in the accompanying example.

Inside an Active Classroom

Mariamma Varkey found that a simulation activity was a good way to help her students understand how people adapt physical conditions of a location to meet their wants and needs. First, Ms. Varkey distributed a map of Newtown, a hypothetical community. It has a busy downtown section through which a new highway must be constructed. Ms. Varkey assigned each student a building through which the highway must pass. Mark was assigned the bakery, Lifeng the florist shop, Gustav the hospital; others were given a place of worship, historic house, apartment building, department store, pizza parlor, movie theater, YMCA, auto dealership, supermarket, and so on. Ms. Varkey displayed a large wall map of the downtown area and asked the students to write their names next to their assigned locations. She informed them that the highway had to be completed with minimal delay, so the entire business community needed to meet to decide where to put the highway. Ms. Varkey decided that tunnels or bridges were acceptable, but she didn't suggest them before the students had a chance to think of those ideas by themselves. Similarly, Ms. Varkey's students took part in simulations where decisions about other interactions between humans and nature needed to be made, such as the effect of a large shopping mall on an undeveloped rural area, the effect of a toxic chemical plant on local streams and lakes, and the effect of a huge dam on what had been pristine farmland.

Often, teachers have their students construct special-purpose maps that highlight the people–place connection of geography. Product maps are good examples. See Figure 4–16 for a sample.

FIGURE 4–16
Product Map of South America

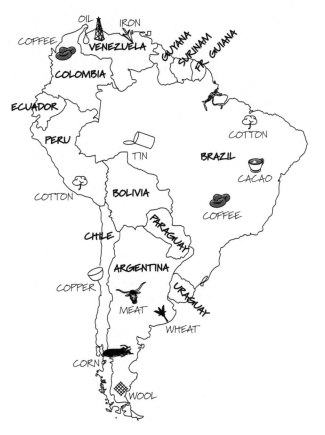

Map Symbols

Maps and globes use symbols to represent a region's characteristics. In the primary grades, pictorial or semi-pictorial symbols are recommended; as a rule, the younger the child, the less abstract the symbols should be. However, as with younger children, always present a picture along with the pictorial symbol. Emphasize the importance of looking at the legend before using a map. Bruno Tonge expanded his students' understanding of map symbols by offering them the following experience.

Inside an Active Classroom

To start, Bruno Tonge played a CD of Woody Guthrie's song *This Land is Your Land*. The folk song describes many of the landforms found in the United States "from California to the New York island." Mr. Tonge made a transparency of the lyrics so the students could follow the words as they listened. After the song finished, Mr. Tonge asked the students to discuss the images that formed in their minds. Then he read the beautifully illustrated picture book version of the song, *This Land is Your Land* by Woody Guthrie (Little, Brown). The book is based on the song, which Guthrie originally recorded in 1949. Interestingly, the book contains some of Guthrie's original lyrics that were omitted in the popular version of the song.

Next, Mr. Tonge invited the class to join him on a simulated airplane trip across the United States from the west coast to the east coast. "Hello, this is your captain speaking," announced Mr. Tonge. "Please fasten your seatbelts and prepare for take-off." After turning up his player full blast, Mr. Barnes played a sound effect CD of an airliner taking off. As the sound diminished and the captain announced the plane had reached cruising altitude, the students were advised they could unfasten their seatbelts. During the imaginary flight, Mr. Tonge called the students' attention to the many landforms that spread out beneath them: "Notice that the brown and yellow Mojave Desert is disappearing behind us. If you look carefully out of your window, you will see the green-forested peaks of an enormous range of mountains stretching out below. Of course, these mountains have a much cooler and wetter climate than the desert."

As Mr. Tonge's imaginary flight continued eastward, his monologue continued to include descriptions of the major landforms: Great Plains, Central Plains, Mississippi River, Appalachian Highlands, and the Atlantic Coastal Plain. Each time a new feature was introduced, Mr. Barnes showed large pictures of the landform as well as a map of the major landforms that cover the United States.

After the plane "landed," the students reviewed the map and discussed the colors and symbols located on the legend. The students were then organized into groups, each responsible for researching more information about what they would observe and experience if they were able to visit the landforms they were introduced to on their transcontinental flight—deserts, mountains, rivers, plains, and highlands.

Lastly, Mr. Tonge decided to reinforce the idea that maps and globes use color or shading as a symbol to show elevation of land from sea level; his students should understand that color is a special kind of symbol. Therefore, Mr. Tonge mounted a large sheet of paper to the wall on which he drew a blank map of the United States. Each research group used crayons to color the landforms according to the way they are conventionally represented on maps.

Scale

To portray geographic features of the Earth on a globe or flat map, you must use the concept of scale to ensure accurate size and space relationships among the features. This is accomplished by reducing the size of every real feature in an equal percentage. Introduce children to the concept of scale by comparing a class picture to the actual size of class members. Lead them to realize that the picture represents a real group of children, but in a much smaller way.

Perhaps the most appropriate formal map scale to use at the elementary school level is the graphic scale. Place a scale of miles at the bottom of the child's map. Children can place a cardboard marker between any two points (Los Angeles and San Francisco) on their maps, place a dot for each city, and then lay the edge of the marker along the scale. The segments of the scale on Figure 4–17 are of equal length and represent miles on the map. Comparing the marks on their cardboard marker to the scale, children will see that the distance between Los Angeles and San Francisco is approximately 350 miles.

Understanding the Globe

Recall the basic globe-reading skills we discussed for the early grades: informal instruction aimed mainly at helping the children realize that the globe is a model that

FIGURE 4–17
Using a Graphic Scale

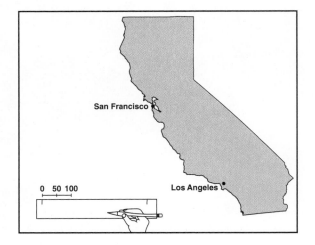

represents the Earth. Their major formal map-reading experiences up to this time dealt with flat maps on which they located cities and other places of interest. They learned how to tell direction and how to compute the distance between one place and another. Now they must learn that a globe is the only accurate map of the Earth, and is an even better tool for studying locations, directions, or distances than a flat map. To emphasize this, you may want to show a satellite photograph of the Earth and compare it to a classroom globe. It is fairly easy to find satellite photographs; one option is to request them through the United States Weather Service. NASA has an extremely useful searchable directory of images and animations of the Earth on its website (*http://visibleearth.nasa.gov*).

After you compare satellite photographs to a classroom globe, illustrate just why the globe is more accurate than flat maps. Using a large, thin rubber ball or a globe made from papier mâché, cut the ball in half and draw an outline of North America (or any random shape) on the ball. Have the children apply hand pressure to flatten the ball and discuss the resulting distortions. Then use scissors to cut through the ball along lines that represent longitude lines. Have the children try to flatten the ball again. Although the ball flattens more easily, the drawn outline still becomes distorted. Help the children discover that this is a major problem faced by mapmakers (cartographers) when they attempt to make flat maps of places on the Earth (see Figure 4–18).

Globes help to show shapes of areas exactly as they would appear on the Earth's surface. Unfortunately, maps are not able to do this. Representing a curved surface precisely on a flat map has confounded cartographers for years. A classroom globe

Globes present interesting and challenging tools for children to figure out how to read.

FIGURE 4–18
The Globe as a Flattened Ball

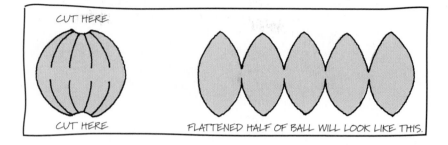

shows shapes and areas more accurately than maps. Therefore, globes and maps should be used reciprocally while developing the skills outlined in this chapter.

As the children explore the globe, they should understand that the Earth can be divided into hemispheres (hemi- is a prefix meaning "half of"; thus, "half of a sphere"). If we live in the United States, we live in the northern half of the globe, or the Northern Hemisphere. At the same time, we live in the western half of the globe, or the Western Hemisphere. The equator and the prime meridian split the Earth in half in each direction to form the hemispheres. Other significant lines that encircle the Earth and run parallel to the equator are the parallels of latitude, discussed previously. Two important latitudes are the Tropic of Cancer and the Tropic of Capricorn. The region between these two lines, including the equator, is called the tropics. The Tropic of Cancer is north of the equator; the Tropic of Capricorn is south of the equator.

Map Selection for the Classroom

It is important to provide a wide variety of maps for the young geographers in your classroom, both as sources of information and as models for their own map construction:

- *Political maps* show the boundaries of countries, states, cities, and other political entities that were created by people as opposed to naturally occurring boundaries such as rivers or mountain ranges.

- *Physical maps* highlight the physical features of a place, such as rivers, lakes, and mountains.

- *Topographic maps* are representations of three-dimensional surfaces on flat pieces of paper. They typically use shading to show landscape features and elevation.

- *Raised relief maps,* a version of topographic maps, use raised surfaces rather than shading so you can actually "feel" the mountains.

- *Weather maps* are perhaps the type of map most frequently seen by most people. Weather maps show the temperature, precipitation, sunshine, storms, and other weather-related features of a region.

- *Special-purpose maps* are maps that depict special subjects or features of an area: the world's language families, average annual rainfall in the state, natural resources, goods produced in various parts of the state, party line voting state by state in a national election, or the soil types of the Northeast.

- *Historical maps* show events and patterns that occurred in the past. They may show the routes of the explorers to North America, for example, or how something such as a nation's borders have changed over the years.

- *Road maps* help us figure out a good route between two places. If you want to travel from Boston to Atlanta, a good road map will tell you how far and in which direction you must travel.

Inside an Active Classroom

Irina Carlson helped her students understand that space and place analysis is the cornerstone of geography and that maps are the principal tools in performing that analysis. She asked her students to name all the different maps they have seen or used, which she listed on the chalkboard. Ms. Carlson then grouped her students into teams of four and directed each team to look through its textbooks for 5 minutes in an effort to find as many different kinds of maps as they could. The groups each made a list of the different maps and identified the page numbers on which they were found. They compared their new list to the one developed at the beginning of the lesson. The students were surprised to find that there were so many different kinds of maps in their textbook.

Next, Ms. Carlson asked the students to discuss why there are so many different kinds of maps. They concluded that it is impossible to display everything about a place on a single piece of paper. Therefore, for a map to communicate information clearly, it must be restricted in the number of things it shows.

Ms. Carlson then showed a large, clear aerial photograph of Pittsburgh and its environs. The students were asked to discuss what they observed, focusing specifically on the variety of geographic features—highways, mountains, rivers, bridges, center city, residential areas, shopping malls, buildings, and so on. Each group was then randomly assigned a different type of map, including political, physical, topographic, raised relief, weather, historical, road, and thematic map of choice. The groups used the large photograph as well as any needed reference materials to produce a specialized map of Pittsburgh, their home community.

Students must be helped to understand that they can learn many things about a region from different types of maps. In addition, they can communicate to others what they know about a place by constructing many kinds of maps of their own. If elementary school students are going to acquire geographic competency, they must acquire the necessary tools and techniques to think geographically. Geographic information is compiled, organized, and stored in many ways but, to think geographically, maps are central to understanding and analysis.

AFTERWORD

A lot has changed in the field of geography education. Geography is once again recognized as a core curriculum subject in our elementary schools. New professional standards for teaching geography have joined the five themes as guidelines for what American children should learn in kindergarten through grade 12. Many state departments of education and local school districts now use these standards and themes as guidelines for instruction and for curriculum development. However, the most dramatic changes affecting geography education are changes in the world itself. Many countries do not have the same names they once had, borders have changed, and some countries have dissolved while others have blossomed into existence. Advanced communication makes it possible to become instantaneously connected to people all over the world. The global economy has become increasingly competitive, and precious natural resources are becoming scarcer. The environment becomes more fragile with each passing day.

How can geography help us successfully face these challenges? Studying geography helps develop the skills and understandings that enable us to become geographically informed. That is, geography's tools and techniques help us to better understand where things are and how and why they got there. Geography helps us better understand our relationships to other cultures and environments. Such vision and understanding forms the basis for making reasoned political decisions on all levels, from global trade to the best location for a new community high school.

From creating community maps to deciphering road maps, this chapter offered simple, enjoyable suggestions to teach young geographers the fundamentals of geography. As the power and beauty of geography are unlocked in dynamic social studies classrooms, children can much more clearly see, understand, and appreciate the web of relationships among the people and places on Earth.

REFERENCES

Augustin, B., & Bailey, M. (2001). Adobe bricks: Building blocks of the Southwest. *Middle Level Learning, 12,* 4–9.

Committee on Geographic Education. (1984). *Guidelines for geographic education: Elementary and secondary schools.* Washington, DC: Association of American Geographers.

Geography Education Standards Project. (1994). *Geography for life: National geography standards 1994.* Washington, DC: National Geographic Research & Exploration.

National Geographic–Roper 2002 global geographic literacy survey. Retrieved from http://www.nationalgeographic.com/education/teacher_community/pdf/NGS-Roper-GeoLitReport2002.pdf

O'Mahony, K. (2003, March). Transforming geography in our schools. New horizons for learning. Retrieved from http://www.newhorizons.org/trans/omahony.htm

Young Political Scientists:
Future Citizens in Action

WHAT DOES CIVICS LOOK LIKE?

Helena Moonka's students are gathered around a work table at the back of the classroom. Anna Mae carefully measures one turtle while Bradley weighs another on an electronic scale. They and their classmates are finding out that learning can be useful . . . and fun. Ms. Moonka's classroom became one of the first classrooms around the country to become involved in a long-term project to save Vietnam Pond turtles threatened with extinction. These Southeastern Asian turtles have vanished from their home habitat in a tiny area of Central Vietnam. Their natural habitat either was destroyed by the chemical Agent Orange used during the Vietnam War or has been converted to rice fields. Because there is no protection program in their homeland, the Asian Turtle Consortium has tapped several schools in the United States to help address the plight of this species. The schools will work to breed a new generation of Vietnam Pond turtles in the United States and send them back to conservation sites in Vietnam.

Ms. Moonka's class received 10 turtles in October and has been faithfully feeding, weighing, and measuring them since then; they have kept careful records of the turtles' development. The turtles were about 1½ years old when they arrived, and the five largest will be sent back to Vietnam at the end of the school year. "It's a big responsibility," commented Marisol. "I was really excited when I found out the importance of this project. When I was little, I always wondered what I could do to help animals in danger of extinction. Now I know I can make a difference."

Buoyed by their involvement in the turtle project, Ms. Moonka's students were energized to tackle new opportunities for community volunteerism with boundless enthusiasm and energy. They adopted a local park and pledged to keep it clean, packed breakfasts for the homeless as part of a Martin Luther King Day community service project, collected funds for the March of Dimes, made placemats and took them to a local nursing home to decorate meal trays on Valentine's Day, and raised $200 for a classmate's family whose house was destroyed by a tragic fire. Through their incredible thirst for involvement, Ms. Moonka's young political scientists took their first ambitious steps into the realm of real-life learning called *service learning.* Service learning encourages active assistance through student projects that meet the needs of groups within the community. Service learning helps students become engaged in community matters as conscientious citizens and helps give students the assurance that they are useful to the general public and can make a difference in their communities. Although service learning cuts across all curricular areas, it is a big part of the discipline known as *civics,* sometimes called *political science* or *government* in high school or college.

What Is Civics?

Civics is the study of our political and legal systems, about our rights and responsibilities as citizens, and about how our government works. Specialists who study governments and the obligations of citizenship are called *political scientists.* In this chapter, elementary school students will be referred to as *young political scientists* because, in dynamic social studies classrooms, they participate in citizenship education activities throughout the year, applying their civic knowledge to the solution of real problems—just like professional political scientists. Their role in the classroom is based on the belief that education in a democracy must be what Alexis de Tocqueville called "an apprenticeship in liberty."

The unquestioned central goal of public education over the years has been to prepare students for effective citizenship. The National Council for the Social Studies (2001) has defined an effective citizen as one "who has the knowledge, skills, and attitudes required to assume the 'office of citizen' in our democratic republic" (p. 319). To ready themselves to occupy this esteemed office, first conceptualized by Thomas Jefferson, NCSS (2001) advises that students participate in well-planned and organized citizenship education programs in which activities

> expand civic knowledge, develop participation skills, and support the belief that, in a democracy, the actions of a person makes a difference. Throughout the curriculum and at every grade level, students should have opportunities to apply their civic knowledge, skills, and values as they work to solve real problems in their school, the community, our nation, and the world. (p. 319)

WHY IS CIVICS IMPORTANT?

In 1782, few believed that a unified nation could be created out of a collection of "free and independent states" spread out over a vast expanse of land. Each state had incredibly diverse economic interests, was fearful of an overly strong federal government, and remained fiercely loyal to established regional, ethnic, and religious ties. The newly independent states often fought each other over land and money, and, to add fuel to an already blazing fire, there was no national political organization with the power to settle their disputes. Over the next 5 years, the situation escalated to such a level that many people agreed the new union of states could not survive without a strong federal government. Therefore, in the hot summer of 1787, 55 delegates from 12 of the 13 states gathered in Philadelphia for "the Grand Convention," which was charged with the daunting task of creating a strong federal government while protecting the rights of the individual states. The delegates, known as the *framers,* took 4 months to draw up the plan—the United States Constitution, a document that spelled out the government of a new nation. It was from this unsettled start that the seeds of one of the grandest political experiments of all time sprouted its roots—a republican nation with a representative democracy.

By the late 1700s, after the Constitution was ratified, many of the early disputes among the states began to fade and a new feeling of patriotism emerged. It was especially fitting that education was considered an important factor that would guide the country and its people into the future. Central to the framers' conception of a successful democratic representative government was an informed public citizenry capable of exercising their rights and responsibilities in an informed and meaningful manner. And this potential, according to Thomas Jefferson, grew from civic education. Civic education would provide the knowledge and courage to "enable every man to judge for himself what will secure or endanger his freedom." If citizens did not know the Bill of Rights, for example, how could they weigh individual freedoms against the needs and welfare of the common community?

From the beginning of our nation's history, civic education has been, and continues to be, central to public education and essential to the survival of American democracy: "'Government of the people, by the people, and for the people,' in Lincoln's phrase, means that the people have the right to control their government. But this right is meaningless unless they have the knowledge and skills to exercise that control and possess the traits of character required to do so responsibly" (The Center for Civic Education, 1994, p. 2). Therefore, dynamic social studies is based on a conviction that civic education is fundamental to the preservation of our constitutional democracy and, therefore, the primary component of all education in the United States.

WHAT SHOULD YOUNG POLITICAL SCIENTISTS KNOW OR BE ABLE TO DO?

The goal of civic education is the development of informed, responsible citizens committed to the principles of American constitutional democracy. Their effective and responsible participation grows from the acquisition of a body of knowledge and a set of applicable participatory skills. Toward this goal, the Center for Civic Education (1994) established a set of standards specifying what students should know and be able to do in civics. The K-4 standards are summarized in Figure 5–1. The standards are not intended to be used as a basis for a national curriculum in civics, but simply to offer a guide to teachers so they know what they should teach their students and as a framework for curriculum developers on which they might build high-quality civics programs.

Because her school district has implemented a standards-driven social studies curriculum with a strong emphasis on civics, Claire Boyer, a second-grade teacher at Media Elementary School, was responsible for using the civics standards as a guide for planning classroom instruction. She always enjoyed taking the study of local government beyond the textbook to where the action was, so she turned her students loose on a civics adventure that was firmly grounded on the recommended standards. Specifically, Ms. Boyer hoped to have her students actively engaged in understanding how the well-being of communities is established and maintained as well as simulating civic life in the community. Guiding her efforts were the following standards.

I.A.   What is government?

I.C.   Why is government necessary?

I.D.   What are some of the most important things governments do?

I.E.   What are the purposes of rules and laws?

III.D. What are the major responsibilities of local governments?

Inside an Active Classroom

For her special standards-driven civics project, Ms. Boyer challenged her young political scientists to build a town for themselves and run it. To start the project, Ms. Boyer invited her students to pretend to be adult citizens in their community of Media 30 years in the future. To draw them into the future, she read them a "letter from the Environmental Protection Agency" dated 30 years from now demanding that all families move from Media as soon as possible due to severe and irreversible pollution problems. The families, traveling together in search of a new place to settle, were led to a large, empty room in the school basement made available just for their project. To keep track of the victims of this unfortunate plight, the "citizens" were required to fill out *Official Community Census Forms*. After they completed the census, the citizens of this new town, named "New Media" by vote, built homes for themselves

FIGURE 5–1
Civics Content Standards

I. What Is Government and What Should It Do?

A. What is government?

B. Where do people in government get the authority to make, apply, and enforce rules and laws and manage disputes about them?

C. Why is government necessary?

D. What are some of the most important things governments do?

E. What are the purposes of rules and laws?

F. How can you evaluate rules and laws?

G. What are the differences between limited and unlimited governments?

H. Why is it important to limit the power of government?

II. What Are the Basic Values and Principles of American Democracy?

A. What are the most important values and principles of American democracy?

B. What are some important beliefs Americans have about themselves and their government?

C. Why is it important for Americans to share certain values, principles, and beliefs?

D. What are the benefits of diversity in the United States?

E. How should conflicts about diversity be prevented and managed?

F. How can people work together to promote the values and principles of American democracy?

III. How Does the Government Established by the Constitution Embody the Purposes, Values, and Principles of American Democracy?

A. What is the United States Constitution and why is it important?

B. What does the national government do and how does it protect individual rights and promote the common good?

C. What are the major responsibilities of state governments?

D. What are the major responsibilities of local governments?

E. Who represents you in the legislative and executive branches of your local, state, and national governments?

IV. What Is the Relationship of the United States to Other Nations and to World Affairs?

A. How is the world divided into nations?

B. How do nations interact with one another?

V. What Are the Roles of the Citizen in American Democracy?

A. What does it mean to be a citizen of the United States?

B. How does a person become a citizen?

C. What are important rights in the United States?

D. What are important responsibilities of Americans?

E. What dispositions or traits of character are important to the preservation and improvement of American democracy?

F. How can Americans participate in their government?

G. What is the importance of political leadership and public service?

H. How should Americans select leaders?

from large packing boxes put aside from a shipment of new furniture the school received that summer. The citizens painted and pasted until they were satisfied the boxes looked like "real houses" and brought a sense of reality to the empty room. Streets were laid out and named: a street sign bearing the name "Dunlap Street" was a tribute to Mr. Richard Dunlap, the principal of Media Elementary School, but no one was quite sure of the inspiration for Grape Road or Ice Road. A town newspaper was launched to chronicle the daily progress of New Media's citizens and to keep its populace informed. "Pollution Sends Townspeople to New Land" blared the headlines on January 7, the first day of the project. A subsequent story read, "Townspeople Paint the Town," in reference to the construction of new homes.

The day after the families completed their homes, they held a town meeting to discuss potential community problems, with Ms. Boyer presiding for the first meeting only. As is often the case with youngsters this age, they could foresee no problems in particular. However, Ms. Boyer was quick to suggest some—fires, crime, and problems that might arise if she could not lead future town meetings. Discussion led to the establishment of police and fire departments and an election for mayor. The children quickly set up minimum qualifications for voter registration and went about soliciting candidates for the mayoral position. Seven candidates immediately announced their intent to run, but three dropped out of the race the following day—they were too busy. Campaigning and debating began as students forged their platforms: Alex promised low taxes, and Curtis vowed gun control. Candidates then planned campaign strategies, showing that political make-believe mirrors political reality. There was, to be specific, the "great cookie caper," involving Alex and her closest opponent, Curtis. On the last day of campaigning, Alex distributed "Vote for Alex" pamphlets decorated with paper hands grasping real chocolate chip cookies. Curtis's followers quickly cried "Bribery!" and complained that Alex was trying to buy votes. The matter went to the election board, which found that "No influence was obtained through the distribution of the cookies."

Following her landslide 14–2 victory, Alex immediately appointed Curtis as chief of police and presented him with his first book of tickets. Using his tickets to control the breaking of laws such as speeding (running in the halls) and loitering (daydreaming), Curtis eventually learned the powers of his position. Through it all, Alex made new friends, was subject to the pressures of old ones, and generally learned that a position of authority has its rewards as well as its pitfalls. "I learned I'm never gonna be the real mayor," she reflected. "Even just pretending to be the mayor is a tough job."

Alex and her council members provided crucial leadership as the town began to grow through its hectic early days. Other classrooms acquired a sense of civic responsibility and offered to contribute to the growth of New Media. The first graders, studying the topic "Needs of People," contributed a food store complete with everything to satisfy a shopper's needs (Bob's California watermelon: $20 a pound). The third grade, studying "What Towns Need," built an electric power station, stringing yarn lines from one cardboard tube light pole to another all around town. The fourth grade, not involved in a relevant social studies topic at the time, demonstrated the interrelatedness of the physical and social sciences. They wired up streetlights by connecting batteries to light bulbs, thus applying their knowledge of energy to making lives better for people. The fifth grade, anxious to contribute with the rest, made a cardboard trash truck (complete with oatmeal-box "trash cans" for the customers) and a bus from cardboard boxes. Finally, the kindergarten class spruced up the entire town with pink, white, and red paper flowers.

The entire village of New Media grew through the remainder of the school year as the children added new features to show what they were studying. The students served as perfect hosts as visitors from area elementary schools came to Media Elementary School to witness the expansion of New Media.

In this exemplary classroom experience, Ms. Boyer set in motion a well-chosen project intended not only to address the targeted standards, but also an important educational aim recommended by the NCSS (2001) in its position statement, *Creating Effective Citizens:* "Students are provided with opportunities to participate in simulations . . . and other activities that encourage the application of civic knowledge, skills, and values" (p. 319). Simulations and activities that directly involve the students in experiencing and making decisions provide a rich context for standards-driven civics instruction.

IN GENERAL, HOW SHOULD CIVICS BE TAUGHT?

As we have learned, our nation's public schools bear a significant and historic duty to enhance the acquisition of civic knowledge and civic responsibility in our nation's youth. Schools fulfill this duty through both informal and formal experiences that begin during the earliest years of schooling and extend through the upper grades. Informal experiences include all the strategies teachers use to establish a cohesive, supportive, democratic classroom community characterized by warm, friendly interactions among all members. The informal curriculum is centered on the governance of the school community and the relationships among those within it. Adults who govern in accordance with constitutional principles and who display traits of character worth emulating are needed to manage the classrooms and schools of our democratic nation.

Informal Civics Instruction

Informal civics instruction refers to the classroom management techniques teachers employ to create a spirit of democratic community. Democratic teachers strive to create a strong, cohesive team feeling among the members of the class, fostering an attitude of "we're all in this together." Citizenship education happens when teachers accept students as partners in developing a mini-democratic society.

Elementary school classrooms are matchless settings for helping students undergo early and meaningful experiences in responsible citizenship. These experiences begin on the first day of school, for at no other time during the school year does anticipation and hope soar so high. Returning from a summer's respite, children are excited about returning for a fresh, new start. Sadly, one of the first things many teachers do with these eager young scholars is to invalidate their enthusiasm by informing them right away who's the boss: "Read them the 'riot act' as soon as they step inside the door. Jump on them for every little thing; don't let anything go by. If you do, it only gets worse!"

They go on to recommend, "Don't smile until Thanksgiving! You've got to be like the Gestapo or they'll run all over you."

Not surprisingly, democratic teachers roundly reject this approach. "That's ridiculous advice," they counter. "Children should see their teacher as a positive influence, not as someone to keep clear of. Teachers need to smile, not scowl. If you don't smile until Thanksgiving, neither will the children!" All too often the only memories the students go home with from a "don't smile" teacher's classroom on the first day of school is how mean the teacher seemed. They will remember nothing else of consequence.

At the beginning of the school year, teachers need to establish trusting relationships with their students, making them feel that the teacher is on their side and that they are accepted. Students who sense they are accepted are ready to take on the challenges of a new school year.

Establishing Rules

Establishing rules with children is an important part of the first days of school. When children have a voice in the rule-making process, they develop a sense of ownership and pride that sets the tone for the rest of the school year. Teachers find that children work best when they have a hand in making the rules and are more inclined to remember the rules, respect the rules, follow the rules, and take a role in group problem solving should classmates have trouble following the rules. Most importantly, the process of collaboratively defining classroom rules builds skills in and respect for democratic processes.

Beginning teachers readily accept the idea of collaboration, but often are uncertain about how to carry out the process of jointly determining rules early in the year. The process is often overwhelming to those who sense a need for establishing classroom control during this beginning phase of their professional careers. There is nothing wrong with starting off your first year of teaching with a set of your own rules and consequences. However, once you acquire greater confidence in your management skills, you will want to give your students a sense of control, too. The following scenario offers an example of the rule-making process as carried out by an experienced teacher in a fourth-grade classroom. The script can be easily followed in its entirety or adapted for different grade levels or individual situations.

Inside an Active Classroom

Darin Yamauchi prefers to tap the rich storehouse of children's literature whenever he initiates a new topic of instruction in his classroom. At the start of the school year, he enjoys using Marie Winn's book *Shiver, Gobble, and Snore* (Simon & Schuster), a particularly suitable story for helping students grasp the importance of rules. It focuses on a funny king who made silly rules. In his kingdom lived three unhappy subjects: Shiver, who was always cold; Gobble, who was always hungry; and Snore (guess what he liked to do). Many of the king's rules severely limited the cravings of these one-of-a-kind characters, so they decided to move away to a place where there would be no rules. Alas, the three friends discovered that disputes could not be resolved in their new land—because they had no rules! They finally decided that to live peacefully, they must make rules. After reading the story, Mr. Yamauchi guided his children through a discussion: "What are rules? Who made the rules in the kingdom? Did the rules make sense or were they foolish? Did all the people want to obey the rules? Why or why not? What did they decide to do? What else could they have done? What have you learned about rules?" The purpose of these questions is to encourage children to realize that rules are necessary to protect people's rights and to keep them safe from others' unacceptable behavior.

Following the general story conversation, Mr. Yamauchi divided his class into small discussion groups. Based on the story, he directed each group to suggest guidelines for making good rules. Here are some of their recommendations:

- The rule should be clear enough so everyone understands what it means.
- The rule must be fair, so everyone can do what is expected.
- The rule must have consequences; everyone must know the outcome of not following the rule.
- Rules should be posted in the classroom for everyone to read.

The next day, Mr. Yamauchi led a discussion about rules: "Tell me some rules, or laws, that citizens of our community are required to follow. Why are these rules important? Who made these rules?" He then made a connection to their classroom community: "Are rules important for our classroom? Why are rules important? Who should make these rules?" The discussion ended with agreement that rule setting should be a shared process.

The process of shared rule setting starts with a direct question: "What are some important rules that can help us live together harmoniously in our classroom community?"

"You mean like no chewin' gum?" Danylo mumbled through a wad of gum pocketed inside one cheek.

"Like no pushing and hitting?" wondered Lisa.

"Yes," answered Mr. Yamauchi. "Any of these would be fine."

For this phase of the process, Mr. Yamauchi divided his class into small groups and suggested that the groups brainstorm possible classroom rules. They deliberated for about a half hour. Mr. Yamauchi then randomly selected one group to write its first two recommendations on the chalkboard as the other groups crossed off similar items from their lists so they wouldn't be repeated. The groups, in turn, repeated this process until a whole-class list was collected on the board. This list was long and, combined with accompanying discussion, the process took a great deal of time as groups brought up specific incidents to go along with each suggested rule. Mr. Yamauchi ended up with a list of more than 40 rules, most of which were stated in negative terms: "Don't fight," "No talking out loud unless you raise your hand," "Don't take things without permission." Groups tended to make a negatively stated rule for every inconsequential situation they imagined ("No looking out the window during class").

Next, Mr. Yamauchi and the students reviewed their list. He asked the question, "Do any of these rules look like they might go together?" He offered the students an example from their list: "Here's what I mean—'Don't talk out of turn,' for example, might be combined with 'Raise your hand when you want to talk.'" The students used colored chalk to underline those they wanted to group together. Mr. Yamauchi now hoped the students would defend their categories, so he asked, "Why did you group these rules together?" The question helped students see how one general rule can supplant several small ones. To further develop this idea, Mr. Yamauchi challenged the students to create one big rule that might take the place of all the little rules in each category. Four general rules remained.

Next, Mr. Yamauchi objected that rules beginning with "no" often seem harsh to him, so he asked the students to rephrase any negatively stated rules as positive ones. The final task involved making a permanent chart listing the classroom rules, having each child sign it, and displaying it prominently in the classroom. Here is the list Mr. Yamauchi's students constructed:

- Be polite and kind to others.
- Respect the property of others.
- Follow all classroom procedures (they listed several, such as ways of using the pencil sharpener, using the restrooms, getting a drink of water, participating in fire drills, returning assignments, talking among students, and so on).
- Try to solve disagreements ourselves. If we can't, we will ask the teacher for help.

Although the example from Mr. Yamauchi's class involved fourth graders, the process can be quite easily adjusted for younger children. Rozella Worobetz, a teacher in the same building as Mr. Yamauchi, shortened the process of rule making with her second graders. Ms. Worobetz felt that, for younger children, the teacher should display four important rules at the beginning of the school year rather than have them develop a list themselves: Be on time, be prepared for class, respect other people, and respect other people's property. Once students are familiar with those four rules, they help with suggesting guidelines for each. Their responsibility is to suggest specific behaviors associated with each rule.

Using either approach, teachers retain the right to add rules or veto suggestions. As in our federal system of checks and balances, teachers must use their professional judgment to protect the rights and responsibilities of the group as a whole.

Class Meetings

Have you had a disagreement with your roommate recently? What about a member of a work group who neglects to do her part? We all have had experiences that make us realize just how stressful and complicated human relations can be. If they are that

Challenging children to think about classroom rules is a basic way to stimulate their construction of knowledge about democratic processes.

difficult for adults, think about how complicated relationships can be for young children who are egocentric and impulsive by nature. Oftentimes these youngsters are thrust together with potentially incompatible classmates and find themselves in situations where they have little, if any, control. Just imagine the anxiety and stress these children face—assignments that are too difficult, children picking on each other, too much homework, wondering how they fit in; the list is monumental. McClurg (1998) recommends that, "At the year's beginning the teacher's first job is to reduce anxiety and reassure each child that his or her needs and point of view will be recognized and valued in this new place. That is the role and purpose of a regular, formalized [classroom] meeting" (p. 30). The purpose of classroom meetings is to find constructive solutions to student problems. They offer the reassurance that everybody will work together to live a democratic life in the classroom.

The younger the children are, the more difficult it is for them to think of things from another's perspective, so it takes great effort on the part of the teacher to get classroom meetings to run smoothly. A teacher's role will vary according to grade level, but to make meetings function constructively, a few guidelines must be followed. Class meetings are best carried out in an environment where children can share freely and where they realize that what each has to contribute is worthwhile. Meeting in a circle, semicircle, or oval provides the greatest attention and maximum participation, as children can see one another when they talk and listen. A democratic group leader, the teacher first serving as a capable model, helps the children to grasp the difficult procedure of discussion:

- Clearly present the topic of discussion. Make sure everyone understands what the problem is. Problems are usually of two major types: (1) those dealing with schoolwork and (2) those arising from difficulties among students.
- State the rules of good discussion—signal when you want to speak, listen carefully to others, and be respectful of everyone's opinions (no put downs, complaining, or fault-finding).
- Use active listening strategies (e.g., paraphrase a student's comments or ask clarifying questions).
- Summarize what has been said. All ideas should be quickly repeated: "Let's go back and recall what was said."

Classroom Symbols

One of the factors contributing to the bonding together of states into a new nation was the introduction of patriotic symbols. Children have a spirit for bonding together as a classroom community at the beginning of a new school year, too, and teachers can take advantage of their excitement by planning activities that have to do with building class spirit. Study either national or state symbols and ask the children to develop a list of symbols they would like for their classroom community: flag, song, motto, great seal, flower, animal, tree, cheer, colors, and so on. All suggestions should be welcomed and the class should vote to determine the preferences in each category.

For those that can be designed and illustrated, the students should do so and display them proudly throughout the year. Others should be used when appropriate: the classroom song may be sung on Monday mornings or Friday afternoons, the class cheer can be used to reward special academic accomplishments, and the great seal may be used on classroom stationery.

Sometimes, students even like to select a classroom name that they will be known by throughout the year—two that I remember well are "Ms. Beam's Dreams" and "The Nova Superstars." It is surprising how much community spirit can be generated by involving children in choosing these special symbols.

Classroom Holidays

We all agree that national holidays such as Independence Day or President's Day help build a feeling of national pride and patriotism. The same can be said for classroom spirit; special classroom "holidays" help enhance a sense of group identity. Special days might include *hat day* when everyone wears a favorite hat to school; *color day* when students wear their school colors; or *retro-day* when students come to school dressed as students did in the 1970s or 1980s. It is fun to immerse the class totally into the day it is celebrating by gearing your curriculum to the theme, reading appropriate books, displaying suitable pictures, and playing fitting music.

Games

Several games in which students must cooperate to reach a goal can be used to help the group function as supportive classroom members and enhance classroom cohesiveness.

Genevieve Bourbonnais uses group-cohesiveness activities in her fifth-grade classroom because she feels that they help her students understand and appreciate the role of interpersonal cooperation in forming a productive learning community. One of her favorites is a game called Pipe Line.

Inside an Active Classroom

Ms. Bourbonnais starts the game of Pipe Line by giving each student a sheet of 9"×12" construction paper and two large paper clips. She directs them to roll their sheet of construction paper into a 12-inch tube having a 1-inch overlap. The students then use a paper clip to fasten down each end. See Figure 5–2.

Next, Ms. Bourbonnais separates the group into two teams and has them face each other in two parallel lines. She directs each team to hold their paper tubes end-to-end to make a long pipe. She then crushes two sheets of tablet paper into balls small enough to fit into the tubes and places one in an end tube of each team. She then gives the order, "Go!"

The students must pass the paper balls from one tube to the next. If a ball falls, the last student to have it in his or her tube picks it up and starts it going again. Passes can be made only from tube to tube in sequence. When the paper ball reaches the end of the line, the teams reverse the direction. The first team to get the ball back to the beginning point is the winner.

FIGURE 5–2
Cooperative Game Cylinder

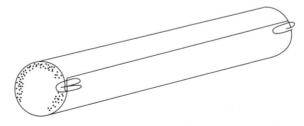

Although the children learn a great deal from cooperative games like these, follow-up discussions help solidify the targeted behaviors. First and foremost, always let students know that you value their cooperative efforts. Then talk with them about the behaviors that contributed to each group's success (or lack of it). You might want to offer constructive feedback: "While I was watching, I saw that Gary was a bit unsure about

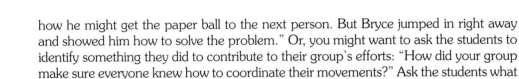

how he might get the paper ball to the next person. But Bryce jumped in right away and showed him how to solve the problem." Or, you might want to ask the students to identify something they did to contribute to their group's efforts: "How did your group make sure everyone knew how to coordinate their movements?" Ask the students what they might be able to do better in a similar situation the next time they try it.

Don't expect your students to become a cohesive, caring community after only a week or two of these activities. A close community takes time to forge—don't rush or become impatient. Use a variety of informal group activities throughout the year, and your students will soon exemplify and demonstrate core democratic values and skills.

Formal Civics Instruction

As children become involved in meaningful democratic classroom life and are given significant opportunities to participate in classroom governance, they will develop a greater insight and appreciation for civic life in the community, nation, and world. The Center for Civic Education, in its influential National Standards for Civics and Government (1994), maintains that such knowledge is communicated to students through formal instruction that provides students with

> a basic understanding of civic life, politics, and government. It should help them under-
> stand the workings of their own and other political systems as well as the relationship of
> American politics and government to world affairs. Formal instruction provides a basis for
> understanding the rights and responsibilities as citizens in American constitutional democ-
> racy and a framework for competent and responsible participation. (p. 1)

Effective civic education, then, has a content base, but not superficial coverage of facts—for example, "The federal system of government divides power among the executive, legislative, and judiciary branches"—without regard for what the facts mean. Students often find such instruction trivial and uninteresting because their teachers fail to establish the relevance of civic knowledge to their lives. Therefore, as young political scientists, students must know not only the facts of civics, but also how to ask questions and answer them. Young political scientists must know what political scientists do. Some civics experiences commonly found in elementary school classrooms follow.

The Constitution of the United States

Normally a part of the fifth-grade social studies program, the children learn that the Constitution is the cornerstone of our government, the basic and supreme law of the United States. In 4,543 words, the Constitution outlines the structure of the United States government and the rights of all American citizens. The Constitution is known as a "living document" because it is flexible enough to be changed (amended) when necessary. The Constitution is divided into three parts:

- Preamble—this explains the purpose of the document.
- Articles—these describe the structure of the government (legislative, executive, and judicial branches) as well as the process for amending the document. There are seven articles.

- Amendments—the changes made to the Constitution. The first 10 are called the Bill of Rights; 27 amendments have been approved since 1791.

Karla Griffin realized that the wording of the original United States Constitution places difficult reading demands on most fifth graders, so she chose to familiarize her students with the Constitution by first showing them a replica of the original document and explaining its importance as the basic and supreme law of our nation. Then she asked the students to quickly skim the three main parts.

Inside an Active Classroom

After each part was skimmed, Ms. Griffin asked the students to give a short explanation of what it was about. Then, to deepen their understanding of the Constitution, Ms. Griffin passed out copies of *Shh! We're Writing the Constitution* by Jean Fritz (Putnam). In an engaging style, Fritz transports the reader back to the Constitutional Convention in Philadelphia to tell the story of the birth of our Constitution. Following both of these experiences, Ms. Griffin directed her students to plan and present a skit about the Constitutional Convention. Some students were assigned to role-play specific delegates to the Constitutional Convention, such as Benjamin Franklin and James Madison, while others were to portray imaginary television news reporters. The reporters were to interview the delegates about their positions on the real issues. Ms. Griffin recorded the interviews on videotape so everyone could later view the entire dramatic scene.

Following this introduction to the Constitution, Ms. Griffin planned an extended sequence of activities centered about an easy-to-read version of the Constitution. The students read the Preamble and Bill of Rights and summarized each in their own words. Ms. Griffin did not become impatient with their error-filled efforts, for she realized even college students and adults have difficulty interpreting and summarizing the Constitution. Isn't helping us decipher the Constitution one of the main reasons why we have the U.S. Supreme Court? She did, however, try to capture what was important in those parts.

One day, for example, a news article told of how a dozen dogs were terribly mistreated by their owner. A photo accompanying the story displayed several of the incredibly undernourished, scrawny, sickly dogs. The students spent some time discussing the ways these dogs in particular, and animals in general, are sometimes badly treated. "It's like they need a Constitution!" blurted Charlie.

"Not a bad idea," chimed in Jaung.

Seizing the opportunity, Ms. Griffin divided the students into three groups. Each group was to use the simplified United States Constitution as a model and work together to write a Preamble and Bill of Rights for an "Animal Constitution." When they finished, the groups compared their Preambles and Bills of Rights, eventually merging them into a single document designed to protect the rights of all animals.

Teachers serious about helping students understand the Constitution look for any opportunity to relate its principles to their lives. Rather than limiting instruction to the memorization of First Amendment rights, for example, Yvonne Jordan encouraged her students to compile a "First Amendment Diary" to personalize what they learned about the rights guaranteed under the First Amendment.

Inside an Active Classroom

First, Ms. Jordan's students read that when the Constitution was ratified in 1789, some states refused to go along with it because they felt the Constitution, as written, failed to protect the rights of the people. The delegates agreed that a Bill of Rights was needed and that it should be added to the Constitution as amendments. Otherwise, they fearred that the entire Constitution would need to be re-reatified. The Bill of Rights was made up of 10 amendments. The First Amendment specifies that:

> *Congress shall make no law respecting an establishment of religion or prohibiting the free exercise thereof; or abridging the freedom of speech, or of the press; or the right of the people peaceably to assemble, and to petition the government for a redress of grievances.*

FIGURE 5–3
First Amendment Diary

	RELIGION	SPEECH	PRESS	ASSEMBLY
READ THE MORNING NEWSPAPER			✓	
WENT TO A BASKETBALL GAME WITH MY FRIENDS				✓
READ AN ARTICLE IN SPORTS ILLUSTRATED			✓	
PHONE MY FRIEND TO MAKE PLANS TO GO TO THE MALL		✓		✓
SEARCHED THE INTERNET FOR HELP WITH MY HOMEWORK		✓	✓	
WENT TO CHURCH WITH MY FAMILY	✓			
ATTENDED SUNDAY SCHOOL CLASS	✓			

So that the students operated from a common understanding of the First Amendment, Ms. Jordan helped the class rewrite the Bill of Rights in their own words:

People are free to practice any religion they want. The government cannot stop citizens from saying or writing what they want. The people have the right to gather together to discuss problems they have with the government and to inform the government of their problems.

The students then recalled the freedoms guaranteed by the First Amendment: freedom of religion, freedom of speech, freedom of the press, and freedom of assembly. Each of these freedoms was listed horizontally along the top of a grid titled, "First Amendment Diary." Along the left side of the grid, students were asked to list the protected activities they were engaged in over a weekend. They were to place a check in a grid indicating which of the guaranteed rights protected them as they engaged in those activities. Tyler's diary is illustrated in Figure 5–3.

On Monday, Ms. Jordan helped her young political scientists compile a class list of all the entries, and led a discussion of the data with questions like these:

- How many times did you rely on your First Amendment rights?
- How might your weekend have changed without the First Amendment rights?
- Which rights were exercised most? Least?

Through this activity, Ms. Jordan demonstrated that civic knowledge is indeed important and that it must have relevance to students' lives. Civic education is something more than studying flowcharts of "How a Bill Becomes a Law" or reading a textbook chapter on the "Separation of Powers." Students more clearly understand civics by participating in the processes they are studying.

As children experience the dynamics of a democratic classroom and learn about the United States Constitution, they should become involved in activities that help them apply their understandings to the classroom community, in general. In any democratic society, including the classroom, everyone is bound by the rules and laws fairly established by its members. To help clarify this idea, one teacher extended a discussion of the Constitution by encouraging the students to create their own classroom constitution (see Figure 5–4).

National Symbols

Among the events that helped forge a sense of national identity and spirit following the Revolutionary War was the introduction of special national symbols: the eagle as the symbol for America, the Great Seal of the United States, the Star-Spangled Banner as our national anthem, and the American Flag. These helped define America as a new nation and became representative of a new history and culture. National symbols evoke a sense of unity and patriotism. Think back to the tragic terrorist attack on the United States on September 11, 2001, for example. Many Americans

FIGURE 5–4
Classroom Constitution

Grade 6 Constitution

We the students of Grade 6, Room 14, in order to form a more perfect class, do establish this *Constitution of the Sixth Grade.*

Article I. Officials

1. There will be two branches of our government: the executive branch and the legislative branch.
2. The executive branch is made up of the President, Vice President, Secretary, and Treasurer.
3. The legislative branch is made up of all the rest of the members of the class.
4. Two candidates each for the offices of President, Vice President, Secretary, and Treasurer shall be nominated the Friday before the third Monday of each month.
5. Election of officers shall take place the third Monday of every month by secret ballot.
6. A student may hold a term of office only once.

Article II. Qualifications of Officers

1. Everyone automatically becomes a member of the legislative branch when entering Room 14 as a student.
2. Students must have these qualifications to be an officer:
   a. must be a member of Room 14 for at least two weeks.
   b. must be honest and trustworthy.

Article III. Duties of Executive Branch

1. *President*
   a. The President shall run all class meetings.
   b. The President shall take charge of the class in the teacher's absence.
   c. The President shall help the substitute (show him or her where things are).
   d. The President shall appoint class helpers.
2. *Vice President*
   a. The Vice President shall help the President when necessary.
   b. In the absence of the President, the Vice President shall take over.
3. *Secretary*
   a. The Secretary shall take notes at all class meetings.
   b. The Secretary shall take care of all class mail (letters, thank you notes, and so on).
4. *Treasurer*
   a. The Treasurer shall take care of all class funds.

Article IV. Duties of Legislative Branch

1. To approve, by majority vote, class helper assignments.
2. To approve, by majority vote, any decision for which the class is responsible.
3. To volunteer for class helper assignments:
   a. clean chalkboard
   b. feed fish
   c. water plants
   d. pass out papers
   e. take lunch count
   f. serve as class librarian
   g. greet room visitors
   h. keep art materials orderly
   i. check attendance
   j. run errands
4. To approve, by two-thirds vote, any amendment to this constitution.

Article V. Presidential Vacancy

The Vice President shall take over if the President's office is vacant, followed by the Secretary, and then the Treasurer.

Article VI. Class Meetings

Meetings shall be held each Friday from 2:30–3:00 p.m.

Article VII. Amendments

1. An amendment may be proposed by any member of the class.
2. An amendment must be approved by two-thirds vote of the legislative branch.

Amendments

Amendment 1.
An elected official shall temporarily give up any classroom helper jobs held during his or her term of office. (Approved: February 10)

Building a respect for our nation's special symbols helps promote a sense of patriotism and pride.

turned to the American flag as a symbol of strength and unity and hoped that such patriotism would not end with the events of September 11. An understanding of and respect for national symbols have undergone renewed importance in dynamic social studies classrooms.

Inside an *Active* Classroom

Students in Isabel Tarango's fifth-grade classroom gathered around a yellow rug they called their "Conversation Station." The Conversation Station was a meeting place where the class would come together to talk about special ideas. Ms. Tarango designed this unique sharing center because she believes classroom communication can be most effectively facilitated when children can see one another in a well-designed location.

On this day, Ms. Tarango wanted the class to meet in the Conversation Station to introduce a new topic of study, "Major Flags Throughout American History." Before beginning any new topic of extended study, Ms. Tarango likes to make sure her students connect their previous knowledge and experiences to the new information, so she unfurled a large, contemporary flag of the United States and discussed the colors, stars, and stripes.

Since the major emphasis in this study was going to be research and writing (finding out and informing), Ms. Tarango felt her students required a model of expository writing, since children tend to write better original pieces after looking firsthand at patterns they find in books. Therefore, she brought to class the book *Flag Day* by Dorothy Les Tina and illustrated by Ed Emberley (Crowell). She read the first six pages of the book—a short history of flags. Ms. Tarango helped her students summarize and analyze the information by completing a story map.

Realizing that the study of major flags in American history was too broad for one written report, Ms. Tarango broke it down into small, manageable segments for small-group investigation: British Union Jack, Grand Union Flag, Betsy Ross's Flag, Star-Spangled Banner, Flag of 1818, Flag of 1912, and Today's Flag. The plan was for small groups to investigate each flag, write a short report, share the reports orally, and compile them as separate chapters of a class book, "Flags Throughout American History."

The next stage of the research project involved developing a list of questions students needed to ask about their specific flag. Ms. Tarango's class decided that each small group should answer the same questions as modeled in the book, *Flag Day:* What colors were used? What symbols were used? When was it adopted? Why was it changed? The questions provided a starting point for further research and served as a focus for students' writing.

Next, the students searched through a variety of reference materials, including the Internet sites (*www.foundingfathers.info/American-flag/*). Ms. Tarango monitored this portion of the research process carefully, for she feels that children must learn to choose relevant information and avoid word-for-word copying from a book, encyclopedia, or other source of information. "Nothing can be more deadly," snarls Ms. Tarango, "than to allow a child to stand in front of a classroom and read a report that was copied word-for-word. You'll hear frequent pauses, the child will speak in a monotone, and he or she will struggle to pronounce unfamiliar words."

To help them organize their reports, Ms. Tarango gave the students a number of index cards. She explained that these would be referred to as *information cards* because each would be divided into two major sections: a large circle at the top of the card represented the dot of the letter "i," and the bottom rectangular section represented the stem. The students then printed the main idea (usually the first sentence of a paragraph) on the top section (the dot of the *i*); in the bottom section they listed all the supporting details (see Figure 5–5). This visual aid helped the children summarize the information effectively and guided them as they wrote their reports.

For the sharing stage of flag research, Ms. Tarango used a tactic she called the "TV News Magazine." In a TV News Magazine format, an "investigative reporter" from each research group sets up an area of the classroom where he or she shares the group's written piece with an audience of four or five classmates (or children from other classrooms). Several investigative reporters function simultaneously and repeat their presentations as their classmates revolve through the areas. Ms. Tarango's investigative reporters donned simple costumes and used commonplace props to help the audience get a feel for the historical era. For example, the investigative reporter

FIGURE 5–5
An "i" Card

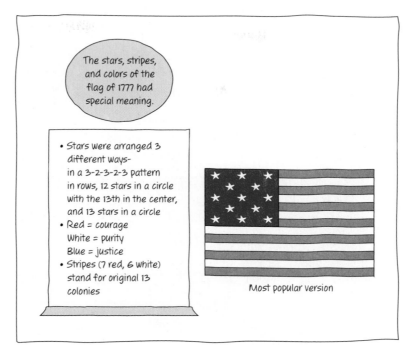

The stars, stripes, and colors of the flag of 1777 had special meaning.

• Stars were arranged 3 different ways-
  in a 3-2-3-2-3 pattern in rows, 12 stars in a circle with the 13th in the center, and 13 stars in a circle
• Red = courage
  White = purity
  Blue = justice
• Stripes (7 red, 6 white) stand for original 13 colonies

Most popular version

presenting the Grand Union Flag wore a pair of glasses pulled down over his nose like Benjamin Franklin, and the reporter who told of the Betsy Ross Flag placed a feather alongside a copy of the Declaration of Independence.

As part of its presentation, each group displayed a drawing of its selected flag and read a short report describing the flag's historical significance. Figure 5–6 is an example of the report that was read aloud by the first group for our Colonists' earliest flag, the Grand Union Flag.

After researching several other national symbols in like manner (Uncle Sam, the eagle, the Star-Spangled Banner), Ms. Tarango helped the students connect their new understandings to their own lives. Comparing life in their classroom with our nation, Ms. Tarango divided the class once more into small study groups. This time, she assigned a different symbol to each group: song, flower, flag, animal, motto, and great seal. Each group was challenged to create an original symbol for the classroom. The symbols were displayed proudly in the classroom all year and contributed immeasurably to a feeling of classroom spirit and pride.

FIGURE 5–6
Student Flag Report

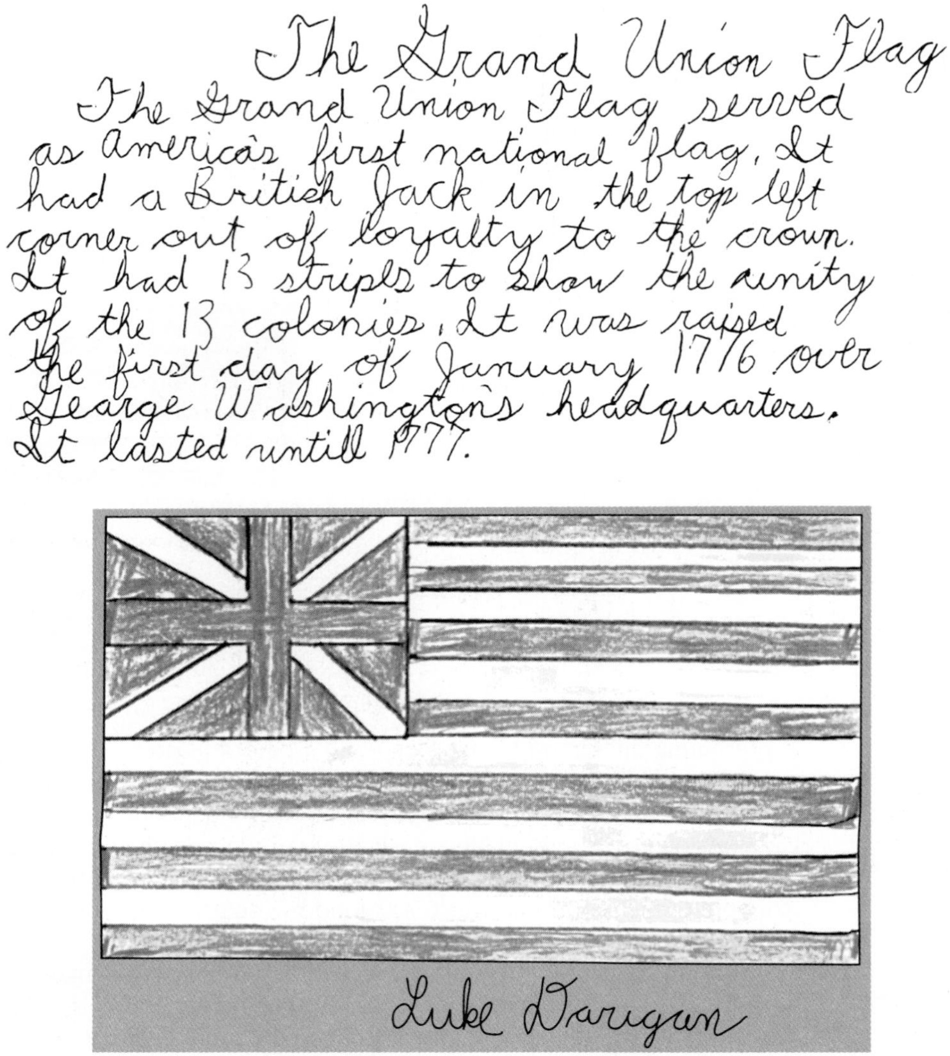

> The Grand Union Flag
>
> The Grand Union Flag served as America's first national flag. It had a British Jack in the top left corner out of loyalty to the crown. It had 13 stripes to show the unity of the 13 colonies. It was raised the first day of January 1776 over George Washington's headquarters. It lasted untill 1777.

Luke Darigan

Elections and Voting

One of the best ways to educate young people about what it means to be a citizen in a democratic society is to get them involved in major citizenship responsibilities such as voting. Voting offers an excellent opportunity to learn civic responsibility and shared decision making in a meaningful and motivating context. By participating in

Theme: The American Flag

John Herman's and Robin Roraback's **Red, White and Blue: The Story of the American Flag** (Grosset & Dunlap) describes how the American flag originated and how it evolved over the years from the Revolutionary War, to the westward movement, to a walk on the moon. Children should get a real feel for its importance as the symbol of our country.

Wendy Cheyette Lewison's and Barbara Duke's **F Is for Flag** (Grosset & Dunlap) is another book that tells the story of the flag that is a symbol of the United States of America. It explains how a flag can mean many things—a symbol of unity, a sign of welcome, and a reminder that everyone in our country is part of one big family.

Alexandra Wallner's **Betsy Ross** (Holiday House) is an easy-to-read rendition of the life and contributions of Betsy Ross, with illustrations and information that should grab children's attention. It is well known that there is controversy surrounding Ross's role as maker of our nation's first flag, but children will enjoy Wallner's account of Ross's suggestion to General Washington to use a star with five points rather than six. Directions are given for Ross' technique of making a perfect 5-pointed star with one snip of the scissors.

Pam Munoz Ryan's **The Flag We Love** (Charlesbridge) is a poetical description of the American flag. Each double-page spread features a rhymed verse and strong, patriotic illustration. Each verse is explained by a box containing interesting historical tidbits. The book is not a history of the flag, but shows how the flag has been important as a symbol of strength and unity in such moving scenes as being draped on Lincoln's coffin, flying over the Vietnam War Memorial, and reflecting off the visor of an astronaut walking on the moon.

Peter Spier's **The Star Spangled Banner** (Dragonfly) brings the words of the national anthem to life. Containing a reproduction of Francis Scott Key's original manuscript, the book highlights the War of 1812 and the battle that inspired Key's words. The illustrations flow along with the lyrics to create an image of heroism and sacrifice: soldiers feeding their horses, schools and businesses, Arlington Cemetery, the Statue of Liberty, cities and rural farms, synagogues and churches, and a Friends Meeting House all celebrate the uniqueness and diversity of our nation.

TRY THIS

The flag is but one symbol of our nation; there are many others. Put together a text set of books telling the story of other important symbols of the United States.

the entire voting line of action (determining voting issues, suggesting possible choices, casting and tallying votes, and confirming the outcome of the vote) children directly experience how a democracy works.

Initial voting experiences should involve issues of interest for the entire class. It is no secret that unless people are interested in a voting issue, they will not be motivated to participate in the voting process and will likely come away from the experience with a feeling that voting is not important to them. Therefore, initial votes should be taken on issues that mean something special such as determining the group's favorite storybook character, foods to serve at a classroom party, which animal makes the best pet, and who will win the Super Bowl.

Children should be encouraged to thoroughly discuss the issue before they take a vote, making arguments in support of the position they are willing to defend and trying to persuade their classmates to vote in their favor. It should be emphasized that opposing points of view should be presented with empathy and respect. The children must realize that it is normal for people to hold different opinions about things and that these differences should not break down friendly relationships.

The vote itself should be carried out carefully. Try to remember that young children do not understand the voting process as an adult does, so some of the procedures we take for granted may be confusing to them. Consider, for example, the practice of having the children raise their hands and then counting the results. Oftentimes young children will raise their hands as soon as a teacher says, "Raise your hands if . . . " whether they want to vote that way or not. Others will lower their hands before their votes are counted, and some may raise their hands more than once (even though they're directed not to). Instead of raising hands, it might be best to:

- *Poll children.* You can list the children's names on a chart and ask each child how he or she votes. The children can then cast votes by placing a tally mark next to their names. The class can then count the votes for each option.

- *Construct name graphs.* Have the children print their names on three 3″×5″ index cards. Ask each child how he or she votes and then place the index card in a line or a stack corresponding to the option. Again, the entire class will be involved in counting the votes.

- *Use secret ballots.* If children become too forceful while trying to influence others to vote their way, it might be best to give each child one piece of paper, ask her or him to indicate a choice, and drop it into a box. Again, the entire class should carry out the vote count.

Voting opportunities also should be a part of the older child's classroom, for it exemplifies one of the duties and responsibilities of citizenship in a democratic society and demonstrates why voting matters. In the upper grades, however, it is common to extend the students' understandings of the voting process as it applies to the election of officials at the local, state, and national level. Gordon Palmer, for example, focused on the question, "So how does one get to be president of the United States?"

Inside an Active Classroom

"Pat Apatosaurus in 2004!" "We back Rex!" Sound like strange election slogans to you? Not if you were visiting Gordon Palmer's fourth-grade classroom.

Mr. Palmer kicked off the election activities for the 2004 presidential election by assigning students to search through an easy-to-read version of the United States Constitution for the three requirements a candidate for the presidency must meet: (1) at least 35 years old, (2) a natural born citizen of the United States, and (3) a resident of the United States for 14 years. "But how does one actually get to be president of the United States?" challenged Mr. Palmer. Finding that his children were fairly uninformed about the process, Mr. Palmer put to advantage his students' interest in dinosaurs to help them learn the election process.

To begin, Mr. Palmer reviewed with the children that dinosaurs can be classified in many ways, but the two most popular categories seem to be meat eaters (carnivores) and plant eaters (herbivores). By randomly picking slips of paper from a box, students were then assigned to the carnivore or herbivore "party." Each party met and selected a party name: the herbivores decided to call their party the Herbocrats while the carnivores favored the Carnublicans. Mr. Palmer explained that each party would meet to select a candidate for "dinosaur president." However, in order to vote, each student must register.

Mr. Palmer distributed 5"×8" index cards to the students and asked them to print their names and addresses on the cards. The students then signed their cards. The Herbocrats and Carnublicans designed symbols for their parties and drew them on their registration cards. To be properly registered, the students went to a prearranged area in the classroom where an instructional aide checked their signatures on the class list, stamped their cards, and crossed their names off the list. They were told to put the cards in a safe place, as they would need to be presented as verification of registration when it came time to vote.

Each party was allowed to select three potential candidates for dinosaur president. This was compared to the primaries during the actual presidential election process. During the primaries, party members vote for the candidate that will represent their party in the upcoming general election. Therefore, the Herbocrats selected Stegosaurus, Triceratops, and Apatosaurus. The Carnublicans went with Tyrannosaurus Rex, Deinonychus, and Raptor. The party members were divided on the issue of which dinosaur would represent them best, so each party mounted a primary campaign, including buttons, stickers, and hats to wear at a rally. Of course, countless speeches, posters, and mock TV commercials extolled the virtues of each potential dinosaur candidate.

While the primary campaign was running its course, Mr. Palmer and his students made a voting booth from a large packing crate the custodians had rescued from the trash pile. They placed an appropriate "United States Polling Place" label at the top and decorated it with various patterns of red, white, and blue. It was important that the students have a place to vote in privacy.

At last, it was time to complete the first step of the election process, with each party selecting its candidate. Each party held its election, with officials making sure to check the registration cards and that each registered voter picked up only one ballot. After the election committee tabulated the results, Tyrannosaurus Rex emerged victorious from the Carnublican Party while the Herbocrats selected Apatosaurus. It was then time to focus on the national convention, step two in the election process.

During the national convention, the party finalizes its selection for one presidential nominee and each presidential candidate chooses a dinosaur running mate.

After each dinosaur party selected one presidential candidate, step three—the general election process—began. Candidates campaigned in the other fifth grade classrooms in an attempt to win the support of voters. In November, students voted for one dinosaur candidate. Each party published an election newsletter containing background information about the candidates. They made campaign buttons, bumper stickers, and posters. As in the primaries, they wrote campaign songs and slogans. Most importantly, each party was directed to write a platform that presented its candidate's view on all issues of importance. The highlight of the whole experience was a spirited "dinosaur debate" with all the protocol observed during regular presidential television debates.

On voting day, students in Mr. Palmer's class lined up at their packing box voting booth to elect the first dinosaur president. They clutched their registration cards and voted for their choice, again by secret ballot. The votes were counted and the winner was announced later that afternoon. Tyrannosaurus Rex won in a landslide. The students felt that since this was the fiercest meat-eating land animal that ever lived, it would be most suitable to rule the land of the reptiles. Of course, a huge victory celebration took place that afternoon (arranged and hosted by aides and parents). Everyone had a great time. In addition, the voting booth stayed in the classroom and was used for all other important classroom votes that school year.

Mr. Palmer surely realized that when a person casts a vote in the general election, he or she is not voting directly for a candidate. Instead, that person is actually casting a vote for a group of people known as *electors*. The electors are part of the Electoral College and are supposed to vote for their state's popularly elected candidate. However, the Electoral College system can confuse many adult voters, so Mr. Palmer chose not to include it in his election simulation. Should you try the simulation in the future, it would be interesting to find a way to make the Electoral College a part of the process.

Children should learn that one of the most important ways they can participate in their government is to exercise their right to vote. By voting, people have a voice in their government.

Civic Responsibility

Today's civics education takes on a much different character than it did in the past. The ultimate goal of civics education has shifted from imparting knowledge to producing citizens who are both knowledgeable and committed to the principle of civic responsibility. A commitment to civic responsibility—voting, letter-writing to public officials, volunteering one's service in various public capacities, and a wide range of other activities—begins in the elementary school classroom and manifests itself in the dispositions of adult citizens who participate fully in our democratic society.

Civic responsibility also engages students in community service projects, therefore advancing the principles of citizenship and good character. It is a powerful approach to civics education that empowers children with an understanding that they can make a difference in their community. Fulfilling civic responsibilities also enhances student self-esteem as children learn that their actions can truly make a difference.

Sharon Kletzien, a colleague at West Chester University, has developed a model community service program that has received national acclaim. Called Kids Around Town, the program's goal is to promote among elementary school children an understanding of how active citizenship participation can influence local public policy issues. The Kids Around Town model includes seven interdisciplinary steps: knowing the local government, choosing a local issue to explore, researching the issue, analyzing the issue, solving the problem, taking action, and assessing the project. The children select an issue that affects them locally, such as cleaning up litter in a community park, abandoned housing, juvenile crime, land-use issues, litter, or bicycle safety. The issue then serves as a springboard for study and action. The students plan strategies and actions to tackle the issue.

Cooperative learning is particularly recommended for investigating community issues by the program developers because cooperative learning helps create a classroom community that is a microcosm of a democratic society. A specific cooperative structure recommended by Kids Around Town is called "Academic Controversies" (Johnson & Johnson, 1999). Useful for discussions of all controversial issues, the basic form for structuring Academic Controversies follows:

1. The students choose a topic on which two well-documented positions (pro and con) can be prepared. The students must understand their positions completely and know where to find information to build a rationale underlying their pro or con position.

2. Students are assigned to groups of four. Each group is randomly divided into two pro and con teams.

3. Each pair is assigned its tasks: (a) knowing its position, (b) locating information relevant to its position, and (c) preparing a series of persuasive arguments to defend its position.

4. Each team presents its side of the issue to the other team forcefully and persuasively.

5. Teams reverse perspectives by presenting the opposing position as forcefully as they can.

6. Teams drop their advocacy and attempt to reach a group decision by consensus.

7. The class develops a plan of action to implement its final position.

The concern for encouraging public service and involvement is mushrooming today and, with growing public support, many schools have been quick to adopt community service programs. In a sense, they concur with the sentiments of one astute 11-year-old who observed, "We have freedom in this country but it stinks. Drugs . . . alcohol . . . crime . . . war. There's no good news anymore. We need someone to come in and clean out America!" Education for democratic citizenship means we must practice what we preach in our social studies classrooms. Telling students about the worth of civic participation is one thing; involving them in community service is better. When students roll up their sleeves and get involved, they understand what we really mean by citizenship responsibilities. Students are likely to become highly engaged in community service projects when they see that their actions can make a difference in real life.

Inside an Active Classroom

Mirka Warczka's sixth graders became extremely upset about a newspaper article describing the accidental unearthing of a mass grave as a construction crew was excavating a site for a new office complex. The article described the backbreaking efforts of a university professor to research the story and find out about these remains. He found that they were the remains of 57 Irish immigrants who died of cholera while building a railroad in the late summer of 1853. Their job was to clear and straighten out a portion of hilly land for a set of train tracks. The men had been working here only 6 weeks before they died. They were unceremoniously dumped in a mass grave that was located at the busy crossroad where the office complex was to stand.

"I can't believe it," blurted Charles. "Those men meant nothing to the company that hired them."

"Yeah," agreed Katrice. "They were all but erased from any human record."

"I wish there was something we could do to give them proper recognition," offered Diane.

"Maybe there is," suggested Mr. Warczka. "Let's think about it."

The students researched the situation a bit further and found that a group of interested people had planned a dedication ceremony to honor the workers in about a month. The group's goal was to unearth as many remains as might exist and provide the men with a proper burial at the site. They had planned to plant an oak tree at the site to commemorate the occasion.

The students wanted to attend the ceremony and received permission to do so as a class project. Mr. Warczka suggested the students contact the state historical commission to see if they could help add to the ceremony. Because of the students' initiative, the commission contributed a historical marker that now stands next to the strong oak.

"I can't believe we're here," whispered Katrice at the dedication ceremony.

"Yeah," agreed Wesley. "I wonder how many other immigrants were treated this badly."

Civic Dispositions and Virtues

Up to this point, we have limited our discussion of civics education to helping students develop rich understandings of governmental practices and public policy as well as aiding them to make connections between what they learn in school and their lives as citizens in a democracy. But the vision of contemporary civics education transcends even these two noble goals. An essential part of civics education deals with making a commitment to civic dispositions and virtues—the core values necessary to nurture and strengthen the ideals of American democracy. In its Curriculum Standards for Social Studies, NCSS (1994) described this realm of instruction as going beyond the content of civics to the formation of dispositions required of effective citizenship. Standard X (Civic Ideals & Practices) states: "Social studies programs should include experiences that provide for the study of the ideals, principles, and practices of citizenship in a democratic republic" (p. 30).

In the elementary grades, students are introduced to civic dispositions and virtues throughout the day as they experience life in democratic classrooms. The dispositions and values of our nation are exemplified by the sense of community created in a democratic classroom: Everyone operates for the common good of all. How do teachers address the responsibility of teaching civic virtues in ways other than establishing a democratic classroom environment?

In addition to those informal experiences, the Center for Civic Education (1994) established this standard as a guideline for formal instruction in civics: "Students should be able to explain the importance of the fundamental values and principles of American democracy" (p. 22). To achieve this standard, the Center advised that students should be able to explain the importance for themselves, their school, their community, and their nation each of the following fundamental values of American democracy:

- individual rights to life, liberty, property, and the pursuit of happiness
- the public or common good
- justice
- equality of opportunity
- diversity
- truth
- patriotism (p. 22)

There has been a resurgence of concern during the past decade that patriotic values like these have fallen out of favor. However, Ryan (1993) comments that this realm of civics education has reemerged as a popular trend "because people are banging on the schoolhouse door. The invitation is coming from the outside. Parents and policymakers are disturbed by a total inability of our culture to pass on its values" (p. 1). Lickona (1993) sees the motivating force as a "growing national sense of moral crisis and what people speak of as a steady moral decline" (p. 1). Society is now turning back to the schools and demanding that certain widely held core values or virtues underlying American democratic society should be at the heart of the school curriculum, the purpose of which is to systematically develop the character of our students.

Literature as a Source for Learning About Character

Stephanie Koszalka, a fifth-grade teacher, read these and similar comments about patriotic values and was tremendously influenced by the well-reasoned commentaries of such respected scholars. She immediately searched for classroom strategies that might help her develop the civic character of her students. Ms. Koszalka discovered that one

Reading quality children's books—together or all alone in a quiet spot—is one of the best ways to incorporate character education into the social studies curriculum.

of the most frequently suggested strategies is to involve children personally in stories of the lives of people who have demonstrated heroic democratic values. Ms. Koszalka was already aware of the power of superbly written biographies and their enduring themes of sacrifice and responsibility, power and oppression, failure and achievement. And she knew that these stories vicariously engage students in the lives of others, help them see the world through others' eyes, and make them aware of human potential. Her major stumbling block was finding a theme that would grab the children's imagination and draw them into the stories of people who made a difference.

Ms. Koszalka's quandary was resolved as she watched the opening of the 2002 Winter Olympics on television. She looked on in admiration and respect as New York City police officer Daniel Rodriguez sang *God Bless America* with determined patriotism. She reflected that if the shocking events of September 11, 2001, had not transpired, there would in all probability be an entertainment figure standing in Officer Rodriguez's place. However, September 11 refocused our nation's collective image on heroes and their importance in our lives. Heroes help us aspire to similar goodness. Their character traits and important contributions serve as distinctive models of good citizenship.

Theme: Heroes

Judith Heide Gilliland's **Steamboat: The Story of Captain Blanche Leathers** (DK) tells the story of Blanche Leathers who was determined to become a steamboat captain when she grew up, an unheard-of occupation for women at the time. But she persevered and fulfilled her dream in 1894, becoming known as the "Angel of the Mississippi."

Robert Coles's **The Story of Ruby Bridges** (Scholastic) recounts the hatred and prejudice directed toward the first African-American child to attend an all-white elementary school in New Orleans. With courage and dignity, Ruby overcomes tremendous obstacles and becomes an important part of history for all Americans.

Chris L. Demarest's **Lindbergh** (Crown Children's Books) is a captivating narrative of an amazing feat. On May 20–21, 1927, Charles Lindbergh made the first solo, nonstop New York to Paris flight in the *Spirit of St. Louis.* After the 3,610-mile, 34-hour flight across the Atlantic, Lindbergh became an international hero and the most famous man in the world.

David A. Adler's **Lou Gehrig: The Luckiest Man** (Harcourt) is a powerful biography of a remarkable athlete who will always be remembered for his strength, modesty, and dignity. During his 14 glorious years as a New York Yankee, Lou played in 2,130 consecutive games, a record that stood for decades. Lou considered himself a lucky man even though he was diagnosed with a rare and fatal disease on his 36th birthday.

John B. Severance's **Gandhi: Great Soul** (Clarion) is a spellbinding portrait of Gandhi's childhood, education, stay in London and South Africa, and his fight for India's freedom. Mahatma, in Sanskrit, means "Great Soul," a nickname Gandhi earned for dedicating his life to helping India free itself from British rule. Gandhi was a model for using patient, peaceful resistance.

TRY THIS

Let us imagine that you and a class partner have been awarded a $100 grant by your college or university to pull together another five-book text set on the theme of "Heroes." By taking advantage of this special five book offer, you will be able to select from a variety of enjoyable, educational books to suit the specific learning needs and interests of young historians. You may visit *www.amazon.com* to select any five titles from its list, but must keep the total cost below $100. This price includes all shipping and handling charges. Provide a sketch of the books you selected, patterned after the descriptions here.

"That's it—heroes. That's exactly the theme I was looking for!" thought Ms. Koszalka. She then pulled together a series of dynamic learning experiences, including a text set of five different titles on the theme of "Heroes" and carried out the instructional procedure described in the following feature, "Inside an Active Classroom."

Inside an Active Classroom

Ms. Koszalka kicked off "Hero Week" in her classroom by inviting real-life local heroes to visit: a retired teacher who was also a Holocaust survivor, a former pilot who flew bombing raids over Germany during World War II, an ex-Negro League baseball player, and a former member of a nonviolent civil rights group who once was jailed for 21 days for her activities.

Then, convinced of the power of good books to exemplify wisdom, courage, and inner character, Ms. Koszalka pulled together five copies of five different books about people who made a difference—male and female, various cultures, the famous and not-so-famous, adults and children.

Ms. Koszalka introduced these books to her students during a short mini-lesson. The mini-lesson began with Ms. Koszalka's oral reading of Barbara Cooney's picture book *Eleanor* (Viking). The book tells of how Eleanor Roosevelt overcame difficult childhood experiences to develop into the great person she turned out to be. When she finished reading, the children talked at great length about how different experiences during Eleanor's childhood helped her grow into a brave and loyal adult.

After the discussion, it was time for the students to go to work and select their own hero books from the text set Ms. Koszalka had pulled together. Ms. Koszalka gave a short sketch of each book and then turned the students loose. Her simple directions were that they were to look at the different books, but not select the first one they grabbed. They were just to sample the different offerings to see which ones they might like to read (she called this a "gallery tour"). As the students examined the books, Ms. Koszalka circulated throughout the area, informally talking with them and making a few timely suggestions for students who needed extra guidance.

After they completed their "gallery tour," Ms. Koszalka passed out slips of paper and asked the students to write their names at the top. They were then to list their first through third choices for books. Then, after school that day, Ms. Koszalka spread out all the slips and began assigning books according to choice. Because Ms. Koszalka had so many books to select from, most children were to get their first choice. However, there were some adjustments that needed to be made, and some children ended up with their second or third choices.

The next day, the children got their books, sat together in groups having the same book, and began reading about their heroes. When they were finished, Ms. Koszalka introduced a list of five traits, called the "five themes of citizenship" that seemed to capture the major attributes of heroic people: *honesty, responsibility, compassion, respect,* and *courage*. She talked about these traits with the class, then asked the students to think carefully to determine which of the five themes best described their heroes. She then exhibited hand-printed signs on which she labeled the five themes; she subsequently tacked them to the classroom walls at even intervals around the room. The students were directed to go to the area designated by the theme they selected for their heroes. It was interesting to see that students reading the same biography tended to split away from their partners to position themselves at different areas. For example, one member of the Ruby Bridges group went to *responsibility* while three others went to *courage*. Knowing that open discussions often disintegrate into idle chatter, Ms. Koszalka directed their conversations with a printed conversation guide: (1) briefly summarize the actions or values that made your person a hero, (2) explain why you selected this theme to associate with your hero, and (3) make a connection between what you've read and your own lives. Of course, Ms. Koszalka modeled these responsibilities by providing examples of what she would say based on the book she had read aloud to the class, *Eleanor.*

To bring together the entire literature-based experience, Ms. Koszalka organized the construction of a paper bag timeline. Ms. Koszalka modeled the process by showing the students a completed bag she had constructed for Eleanor Roosevelt. Each text set group was then given a strong paper bag and asked to print the name of its hero in bold letters at the top. The groups were to use this bag to show what they learned about their heroes through writing, drawing, and collage. The students were first given an outline of a coat-of-arms with four blank segments. They were directed to draw an appropriate picture or symbol (or print a word) in the segments that best answered the following questions:

1. What is your greatest personal accomplishment?
2. If you could compare yourself to an animal, what would it be?
3. What is one lesson others can learn from you?
4. What is one word you would most like people to use to describe you?

These coats-of-arms were taped to the front of the bags. The students labeled the bags with dates underneath the hero's name to show when their hero lived and printed two questions at the bottom of the bag. The students were to use questions that could be answered by looking at the coats-of-arms on the front of their bags.

One group completed Figure 5–7 for Ruby Bridges, who, in 1960 at age 6, was the first African American student to enter William Frantz Elementary School in New Orleans. The students explained that they drew a school in the first section because it showed that Ruby helped integrate the elementary school by passing through a mob of racist protestors shouting insults and threats. They selected a sheep as an animal to represent Ruby in section two because they felt Ruby had a wonderful smile and remained calm and peaceful throughout this unusual challenge. In the third section, the students explained that they chose to depict an African American child holding hands with a white child because Ruby Bridges would want to teach others that white people and black people should respect and love each other. Finally, the students wrote the word "courage" in the last section because they felt Ruby bravely faced a difficult situation with strong character. The story of Ruby Bridges showed that even small children can be heroes for each other.

When all the bags were finished on the outside, the students were asked to consider three important events from their heroes' lives and explain their significance.

FIGURE 5–7
Coat of Arms for Ruby Bridges

Then, they were to find an artifact, make a model, or draw an illustration as a representation of each event. The items were then packed into the paper bags. One item placed in the Ruby Bridges bag was a small student-drawn sign reading "Whites Only" that signified the signs the angry white people carried in protest as they gathered outside the Frantz Elementary School. A small model of an old bi-plane helped another group represent the part of Charles A. Lindbergh's life when he earned a living as a stunt show pilot.

After each group decided on its three artifacts and placed them into the bags, the young political scientists arranged their bags in chronological order. Then each group prepared a short story that told about the events represented by their artifacts. Their project was presented to their classmates. Afterward, everyone had a chance to explore the fun questions, coats-of-arms, and artifacts.

Ms. Koszalka brought her biographical study of heroes to a close by asking the students to consider three questions. The third especially challenged students' creativity.

1. If you could bring any real-life hero from the past to the present, which would you choose?
2. What five questions would you ask the person?
3. What kind of hero will our country need in the year 2050?

Good citizenship requires a clear understanding of core citizenship dispositions and virtues and a willingness to partake in responsible action directed toward the welfare of one's community. Criticizing the failure of U.S. citizens to become effectively and personally involved in preserving their nation's well-being, Parker (1989) describes the American spirit as being stuck in a state of "me-ism." Parker cites de Tocqueville's (1969) 150-year-old description of individualism to clarify: "Individualism is a calm and considered feeling which disposes each citizen to isolate himself from the mass of his fellows and withdraw into the circle of family and friends; with this little society formed to his taste, he gladly leaves the greater society to look after itself" (p. 506).

Parker contends that the demise of effective citizenship today can be directly linked to individualism. Where can such an attitude lead? According to Parker (1989), "No one knows to what it may lead. Political chaos, economic collapse, urban warfare, a quiet lapse into tyranny, or something less dramatic—anything is possible" (p. 353). Newmann (1989) agrees with this outlook and warns that "[It] threatens the very survival of the human species and the planet" (p. 357).

Critical Thinking

Early in our nation's history, reading aloud passages from the Bible carried out what we now consider character development and civic education. Even into the 1800s, instructional materials maintained a strong religious character, as we see in this selection from *The Boston Primer* (Hersh, 1980):

> Let children who would fear the LORD,
> Hear what their Teachers say,
> With rev'rence meet their Parents' word,
> And with Delight obey. (p. 16)

Passages like this were read over and over again until the children memorized them. Therefore, good civic education was described as one's ability to distinguish good from evil. Certainly, learning good from evil remains an important goal for everyone, but there is universal agreement that contemporary education must ensure that children not only know something but that they can learn from it, reason with it, analyze it, and solve problems with it; students must be helped to think deeply and critically about what they are experiencing and reading.

What is critical thinking? That's a tough question to answer, for critical thinking is such a complex mental process that psychologists have not yet been able to agree on what it is. Although there are many conflicting opinions, Ennis (1985) offers an explanation that is particularly appropriate for dynamic civics instruction: "reasonable reflective thinking that is focused on deciding what to believe or do" (p. 54). Critical thinking is reasonable and reflective when students make earnest efforts to evaluate information and analyze arguments in terms of their accuracy and worth. More important than a definition of critical thinking itself, however, is the idea that there is a better instructional road to take in social studies education than rote memorization. The NCSS Curriculum Standards for Social Studies (NCSS, 1994) support this vision by addressing citizenship in the context of civic responsibility. The Standards advise that social studies should help students develop the knowledge, intellectual skills, and attitudes necessary to confront, discuss, and consider action on such issues as national security vs. individual freedom or obeying the law vs. the right to dissent:

> Social studies educators have an obligation to help students explore a variety of positions in a thorough, fair-minded manner. As each position is studied and discussed to determine the strongest points in favor of it, the strongest points in opposition to it, and the consequences that would follow from selecting it, students become better able to improve the ways in which they deal with persistent issues and dilemmas and participate with others in making decisions about them. (p. 10)

The NCSS Task Force on Early Childhood/Elementary Social Studies (1989) takes a similarly strong position on the role of critical thinking and civic responsibility in social studies:

> For children to develop citizenship skills appropriate to a democracy, they must be capable of thinking critically about complex societal problems and global problems. . . . Continually accelerating technology has created and will continue to create rapid changes in society. Children need to be equipped with the skills to cope with change. (p. 16)

How do elementary school teachers help build critical thinking skills in dynamic social studies programs? Perhaps because there is so much disagreement about what critical thinking is and because it encompasses such a variety of sophisticated thinking skills, suggestions for classroom use are sketchy at best. However, if we want our students to be critical thinkers, then the answer lies in thinking about content in ways that evoke strong feelings. Content is crucial if thinking is to progress higher into the cognitive domain. Children must know the topic in depth, question and challenge the ideas that confuse or disturb them, and, with thinking at its peak, construct personal decisions and opinions. Critical thinking, then, cannot happen in a vacuum. Therefore, you teach first for understanding. If students don't understand, they have nothing on which to reason and reflect.

Reflecting on Meaningful Content

Critical thinking is most commonly associated with the act of reading—taking in the content and thinking about whether certain assumptions expressed by the writer are biased or valid. Young children get most of their social studies content from a variety of sources, but words in print seem to predominate: textbooks, children's literature, newspaper items, or information books such as encyclopedias. These resources often contain problems, issues, or ideas that become the lifeblood of meaningful classroom discussions. Whether these discussions involve "meaty" contemporary issues or controversial historical events, they lead students to consider carefully reasons for acts and try to examine issues from all sides. Consider this example from Imelda Zavala's first-grade classroom.

Inside an Active Classroom

Today, Ms. Zavala read *The Little Red Hen* by Paul Galdone (Seabury Press) to her eager group of first-grade "political scientists." She knew that the book was useful for many instructional purposes, not the least of which was to offer her students an opportunity for critical thinking. Therefore, after she finished reading, Ms. Zavala led a group discussion about the story's ending and the hen's decision not to share her bread with the animals that refused to help her. Did the Little Red Hen do the right thing? Ms. Zavala encouraged the class to think about why the animals refused to help and whether they might have had good reasons. The children discussed what they thought about the hen's decision and considered other choices she could have made. Finally, Ms. Zavala displayed a chart divided into three columns: (1) the child's name, (2) a "yes" column, and (3) a "no" column. Ms. Zavala explained the chart to the children and asked them to predict whether there would be more yes or no votes in response to the question, "Did the Little Red Hen do the right thing?" The children were invited to write their names and mark their votes answering the question (see Figure 5–8). Afterward, the class discussed the results.

An exemplary upper-grade script evolves as Maura Biko's fifth graders return to their classroom after recess. The soft, plaintive strains of "Negro spirituals" fill the room. Ms. Biko aims to help her students understand that slaves created these songs not only to express their deep longing for freedom, but also as coded messages that passed on secret information for escape, such as where to find escape routes and hideaways: "Steal Away to Jesus," "Go Down, Moses," "The Drinking Gourd," and "Swing Low, Sweet Chariot." But, for now, the spirituals helped create the climate for the lesson.

FIGURE 5–8
Little Red Hen Graph

DID THE LITTLE RED HEN DO THE
RIGHT THING?

NAME	YES	NO
Connie	X	
Robert		X
MarthA		X
Jud		X
Darrin	X	
Anita	X	
Amram	X	

Inside an Active Classroom

Ms. Biko assembled the class in an area of the room favorable for good listening and read aloud the book, *The Story of Harriet Tubman: Conductor of the Underground Railroad* by Kate McMullan (Dell Yearling), a fascinating story of one of America's most famous abolitionists. At the story's end, Ms. Biko initiated a "grand discussion" by asking the students to share their feelings about Harriet Tubman: "How would you describe Harriet Tubman? What evidence from the story supports your feelings?" The students offered several ideas, most of which revolved around the ideas of "fairness," "toughness," "intelligence," and "courage." Their evidence included Harriet Tubman's hard work in the fields, being whipped by owners, learning to read without her owner's knowledge, being injured while helping a slave escape, going on many Underground Railroad journeys, learning to use special tactics to escape (such as navigating by the North Star), and helping slaves whose owners refused to free them after the Civil War. During this reflective discussion, one student served as a scribe, recording the specifics on a large data-retrieval chart strategically placed near the story reading area.

Sensing that her students had begun to exhaust their ideas, Ms. Biko added a new dimension to the grand discussion. "So far," she said, "we have been talking about the many accomplishments that made Harriet Tubman a special person. You said that each accomplishment was important, but now I want to confront you with a very tough challenge: "Which accomplishment do you consider to be her *most important* contribution of all?" After much serious debate, small groups of students agreed that it was her efforts to hide and carry slaves to freedom with the Underground Railroad.

Ms. Biko then shared a few thoughts about the dangers of running away from slavery and aiding fugitives. She explained how the spirituals the children had listened to as they entered the room actually contained lyrics to aid the slaves as they made their way to the North. She then read this dilemma faced by Sie, a slave from Maryland in 1825, when his extremely troubled master came to his cabin with an unusual request:

One night in the month of January . . . he came into my cabin and waked me up . . . . For awhile he said nothing and sat . . . warming himself at the fire. "Sick, massa?" said I. "Can't I help you in any way, massa?" I spoke tenderly for my heart was full of compassion at his wretched appearance. At last . . . he cried, "Oh, Sie! I'm ruined, ruined, ruined. . . . They've got a judgment against me, and in less than two weeks every [slave] I've got will be . . . sold." I sat silent . . . . "And now, Sie," he continued, "there's only one way I

FIGURE 5–9
Pro and Con Visual Organizer

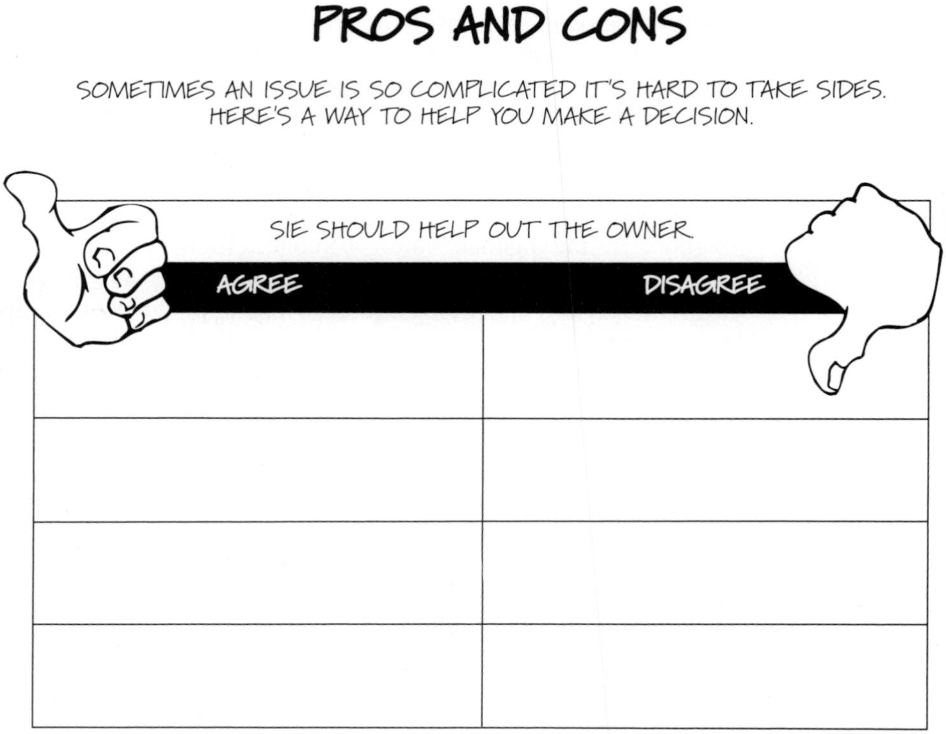

PROS AND CONS

SOMETIMES AN ISSUE IS SO COMPLICATED IT'S HARD TO TAKE SIDES.
HERE'S A WAY TO HELP YOU MAKE A DECISION.

SIE SHOULD HELP OUT THE OWNER.

AGREE	DISAGREE

can save anything. You can do it; won't you, won't you?" In his distress he rose and actually threw his arms around me . . . "I want you to run away, Sie, to . . . Kentucky, and take all the servants along with you." . . . My master proposed to follow me in a few months and establish himself in Kentucky. (Henson, 1935, pp. 162–167)

After discussing the situation to make sure the students understood what it was all about, Ms. Biko said, "Isn't it interesting that after being Sie's master for over 30 years, the plantation owner became so dependent on him? Should Sie help out the owner?"

Ms. Biko divided the children into discussion groups and asked them to decide what Sie should do. She provided a visual aid for them to organize their different viewpoints (see Figure 5–9). Each group was to consider the owner's request and discuss whether or not to help him. Every time they listed a reason to help, they had to follow it with a reason to not help; the students must always have an equal number of items in both columns. When the groups finished their lists, they told whether they would help and supported their decision with reasons why.

Throughout this lesson, Ms. Biko employed sophisticated instructional strategies designed to move her students beyond the realm of content itself and into higher-order thinking processes. She did this by sharing rich, thought-provoking content. Thought-provoking content sets in motion adventures in critical thinking, for it provides the essential substance of productive discussions dealing with feelings and civic ideals.

Graphic Organizers

As you saw with Maura Biko, teachers often use graphic organizers to help students systematize their thinking. For example, let us suppose that you are going to be teaching the concept that a stable food supply was a necessity of early settled civilizations. The concept centers on the idea that as early hunter-gatherers learned to domesticate wild animals and to sow seeds, they gradually left behind their nomadic existence and settled down to become farmers and herders. Eventually, as farming methods improved, people periodically found themselves with food surpluses. Unexpected bounty led to trade. A village with an overabundance of grain, for example, exchanged it for tools, pottery, cloth, or other goods from nearby villages. An overabundance of anything is called a *surplus,* and early civilizations had to learn how to face important decisions regarding surpluses. It wasn't always the best move to trade them for other goods; perhaps it might be best to store the surplus for leaner times.

After helping students develop these understandings, teachers can help lay the foundation for higher-order thinking. How do they do that? Colleen Nemchick shows that one way it can be effectively accomplished is by using graphic organizers to help students make important decisions. Here is how she did it.

Inside an Active Classroom

Ms. Nemchick had her students play the role of citizens of an ancient village living on the land between the Tigris and Euphrates Rivers. Their village is flourishing. Unlike others whose farmland has been scorched by the sun, theirs has an irrigation system that helps produce an abundance of grain. While other villages face a devastating famine, theirs has a bountiful supply. Once the context is established, Ms. Nemchick holds a discussion: "How do you feel about having surplus food while your neighbors are starving? Is it fair that one village should have so much while the others face famine? Do wealthy civilizations have a responsibility to help those that have less?

What should a village do with its surplus grain?

Ms. Nemchick then divided the class into three-student groups and assigned each group a number from one to three. The groups were assigned to examine the positive and negative consequences of one of these possible courses of action: all the ones considered a "store the grain" alternative, the twos considered a "sell the grain" alternative, and the threes considered a "give it away" alternative. Completing a graphic organizer helped each group consider the positive and negative consequences of their alternative. The "store the grain" group's completed organizer is shown in Figure 5–10. After completing their graphic organizers, each group shared and defended its conclusions.

FIGURE 5–10
Decision-Making Graphic Organizer

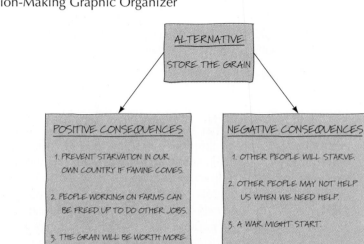

The possibilities for using graphic organizers are endless. One of my favorites is the decision tree.

Climbing a Decision Tree   Richard Remy and his associates (no date) at the Mershon Center of Ohio State University developed an interesting graphic organizer called the *decision tree*. To begin climbing the decision tree, ask how many students notice that they make decisions every day, such as what to spend their allowance on or what to wear to school. Explain that decisions are not always as easy as those; in fact, many decisions require deep thought and careful planning. All decisions require careful examination of possible alternatives. Select a decision such as what to wear to school that day. What alternatives (options) were available? In addition to identifying alternatives, decisions also involve studying the consequences (possible results) of each alternative. What are the possible advantages and disadvantages of choosing either alternative? Next, inform the students that they are going to use their ability to use alternatives and consequences in an imaginative situation by helping Sir Lottalance decide what to do about Dingbat the Dimwitted, a fierce dragon causing the villagers severe problems. Tell the students to put themselves in the place of the knight, Sir Lottalance, as they listen to the following story:

> One day very long ago, the village's bravest knight, Sir Lottalance, was riding along on his horse, minding his own business, when he came across some very sad townspeople. They were sad because the nasty dragon, Dingbat the Dimwitted, had lumbered out of his dark cave and carried off the beautiful princess from the king's castle. The brokenhearted king had offered a huge

There are so many valuable thoughts that freely flow from our children's minds when they are asked to go beyond the content of social studies.

reward for anyone who could destroy the dragon and save his daughter's life. But the first knight to try was barbecued by Dingbat's blazing breath. The second knight to try ran away in panic at the sight of the hulking creature, tripped over his own sword, and became the dragon's shish kabob. Sir Lottalance could hear the princess beating her fists angrily against the dragon and calling him all the nastiest names you ever heard. He could hear Dingbat's empty tummy rumbling as the dragon waited for another tasty meal of fried knight. Sir Lottalance was the fastest, strongest, and bravest knight in the kingdom. What could he do?

Now point to a bulletin board display showing Dingbat, Lottalance, and a large construction-paper decision tree bedecked with the sign "Occasion for Decision" (as in Figure 5–11). The "Alternative" and "Consequences" areas on the tree are initially blank. For the children to climb the tree, they will have to think of Sir Lottalance's alternatives. Ask them for alternatives. When they have described fighting or fleeing, write the responses on the alternative branches of the tree and congratulate the children for starting their climb up the decision tree.

Help the students climb higher into the branches of the tree by looking at the consequences of Sir Lottalance's decision. Ask, "What would be a good (or positive) consequence of getting out of there fast? What would be a bad (or negative) consequence of getting out of there fast?"

FIGURE 5–11
The Decision Tree

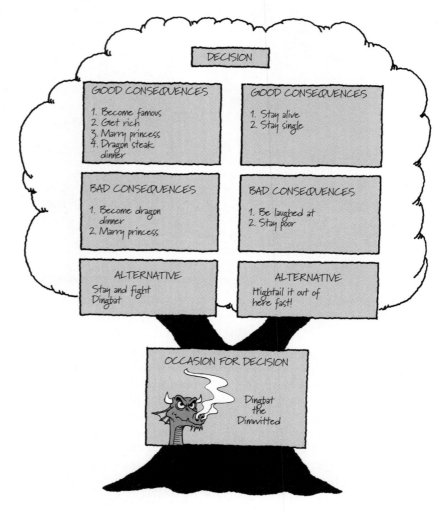

When the students have suggested ideas corresponding to "stay alive" and "be called Lottalance the Sissy," add them to the blank areas above the "getting out of here fast" alternative. Again, reinforce your students for doing a good job of climbing and remind them they still have an alternative branch to explore. Ask, "What would be some bad (or negative) consequences of fighting Dingbat the Dimwitted? What would be some good (or positive) consequences of fighting Dingbat the Dimwitted?"

Again, list each contribution as it is offered. Examine the whole tree and look for the students' sense of accomplishment. Then, weighing the consequences, ask the class to vote, deciding whether they should run away or fight. Finally, place their decision high in the top of the decision tree.

To summarize, the decision-tree strategy involves the following steps:

1. Decide what question to examine and label it at the base of the tree.
2. Abbreviate the decision in the "Occasion for Decision" sign.
3. Encourage children to think up alternatives and write them in the boxes on the branches of the decision tree.
4. Discuss positive and negative consequences of each alternative, one at a time.
5. Write in the consequences, ask the children to weigh each, and write in their goal.
6. Congratulate the children as successful decision makers.

Initial experiences with the decision tree should center on relatively uncomplicated problems, such as where to go on a field trip or what to do with friends on a free afternoon. As the children become more comfortable, increasingly complex issues could be considered, such as great historical decisions, voting for political candidates, or drug prevention.

Inside an Active Classroom

Myles Spencer, for example, used the decision tree as a graphic organizer as his fifth-grade students read about one of the most significant decisions made in the history of the United States. Rosa Parks made it in Montgomery, Alabama. Mr. Spencer asked the students to think about what they would do if they were faced with Rosa Parks's decision. Then he supplied them with an account of the incident in which Rosa Parks's decision was made.

> *Rosa Parks' feet hurt, for good cause. Her job as a seamstress in the Montgomery Fair kept her on the run. All that day of December 1, 1955, she had pinned up hems, raised waistlines, and carried dresses back and forth. When the closing time buzzer sounded, she hurried out of the store. Then she boarded a Cleveland Avenue bus, dropped her dime in the box—and hesitated. Where should she sit?*
>
> *By law and custom, the front rows of seats were reserved for white people. [Black people] sat in the back. Halfway up the aisle there was a no man's land where [African Americans] might sit until the space was needed for white passengers. There were no signs announcing these rules. In Montgomery, the capital city of Alabama, everybody simply knew them.*
>
> *But this bus was half empty, and Mrs. Parks sank into the first seat behind the "white" section. Her feet began to feel as if they were almost ready to stop hurting. It was a feeling that made it impossible for her to think about anything else. She scarcely noticed that the bus was getting fuller from one*

stop to the next. Soon all the seats were taken. A few minutes later people were standing in the aisle. White people.

The bus driver, with one eye on his rearview mirror, called, "All right, you niggers [sic], move back!"

The woman next to Mrs. Parks and two men across the aisle rose and silently made their way to the back of the bus. Mrs. Parks sat still. A white man stood beside her, waiting, but she didn't budge.

The bus driver left his wheel and strode up the aisle. "Get up!" he ordered. Rosa Parks took a deep breath. (Sterling, 1968, pp. 1–2)

The first thing Mr. Spencer did following the reading was to hold a general discussion of the story: "How do you think Rosa Parks felt at this point of the story?"

Next, Mr. Spencer split the children into groups and asked them to think about what Rosa Parks should do: "How do you think the story will end?" They were to list her alternatives and the consequences of each alternative on the decision tree. As they worked, Mr. Spencer moved from group to group and offered prompts to guide the children's thinking: "Why do you think some cities had rules establishing separate facilities for blacks and whites? Did Rosa Parks have a right to break those rules? Were the rules fair? What could happen if she did not give up her seat to the white person?" When they finished deliberating, each group shared its decision tree with the class.

The children will naturally be curious about the real outcome of this event, and their questions will flow spontaneously: "What did Rosa Parks really do? What happened to her?" The questions will indicate a perfect starting point for an inquiry session on civil rights issues. You may wish to offer the information yourself, or encourage the children to search for the answers in material you have collected for them. (For your information, Rosa Parks refused to give up her seat and was arrested. Her arrest touched off a bus boycott in Montgomery led by Martin Luther King, Jr., and was one of the major events in launching the campaign for civil rights in the South.) In 1980, Mrs. Parks received the Martin Luther King, Jr., Peace Award for the inspiration she provided to resolve racial differences through nonviolent means.

Separating Fact From Opinion

Critical thinkers must be aware of the existence of both fact and opinion when they read social studies materials. Facts can be defined as statements that are generally accepted as true and can be validated by evidence, such as, "In January 1863, President Lincoln signed the Emancipation Proclamation." Opinions communicate what people feel or believe about something; opinions cannot be proven. For example, the statement, "Harriet Tubman was the most remarkable woman in the history of our country," is, as stated, an opinion. It is true that Harriet Tubman played a major role in the history of our country, but the idea that she was "the most remarkable woman in the history of our country" is an opinion. It cannot be proven as being either true or false; it simply tells how the person felt about her accomplishments.

You must help your students distinguish fact from opinion as they weigh statements for objectivity. Don't, however, create an impression that facts are "good" while opinions are "bad." Learning about people's opinions helps us understand why they act as they do. For example, in 1846, Dred Scott's strong opinions about his status as a slave made him willing to sue his owner for his freedom. Eleven years later, the Supreme Court issued its own opinion: Dred Scott was still a slave because, in the words of Justice Roger Taney, blacks were beings "of an inferior order" and "had no rights which white men were bound to respect." Anti-slavery Northerners reacted to this decision violently. Frederick Douglass called the decision "a most scandalous and devilish perversion of the Constitution." People throughout the country held strong opinions about slavery, and the longer the problem went unsolved the stronger the opinions on either side grew. By 1861, feelings had grown to a boiling point and seven southern states seceded from the Union. The Civil War had begun.

It is important for students to see that two people, or two groups of people, faced with the same set of facts often develop very different opinions. In this case, the strong contrasting opinions of Northerners and Southerners ignited the Civil War.

Help students distinguish facts from opinions in social studies materials. Every fact should be backed up with evidence while clue words should signal an opinion. Students should realize that evaluative clue words often signal statements of opinion, such as *best, worst, brave, excellent, immoral, tightwad,* and *admirable.* Other than good books, several print sources are ideal for helping students distinguish fact from opinion-political cartoons and editorials.

Political Cartoons and Editorials Political cartoons and editorials use words and illustrations in an attempt to sway one's opinion about a particular issue. Sometimes the message of a cartoon is just plain fun—an illustrated joke. Other times, however, cartoons carry serious messages intended to influence a reader's opinion about an important issue, even though they use humor or sarcasm to make their point.

Most political cartoons deal with one central idea and are fairly uncomplicated. Cartoonists use few words to express ideas because the illustrations communicate most of the message. In addition, cartoonists will exaggerate certain physical characteristics of people to make them instantly recognizable. George Washington's hair or Abe Lincoln's lanky, tall frame, beard, and stovepipe hat are examples of the kind of distinguishing traits cartoonists select to highlight the central cartoon figure. Cartoonists also use standard, readily recognized symbols (e.g., Uncle Sam, dollar signs, the Republican elephant and the Democratic donkey, and the hawk and the dove) to quickly communicate an idea or feeling.

While selecting political cartoons for your classroom, choose those that convey the simplest of ideas in as uncomplicated a fashion as possible. Be sure the students have background knowledge about the topic or they will fail to understand the intent of the cartoon. Help the children identify the standard symbols and central characters, recognize the activity in which the characters are engaged, analyze the car-

FIGURE 5–12
Political Cartoon

Source: *Daily Local News*, West Chester, PA (14 March 1993). Reprinted with permission of Rick Cole.

toonist's point of view, determine the cartoonist's bias or purpose, and decide whether they agree or disagree with the cartoonist. Figure 5–12 is a political cartoon. You could ask children the following questions about this particular cartoon to help them understand the purposes of political cartoons in general:

1. This cartoon contains illustrations of people you may know. What do you see here? Are these real people? Can you recognize any of the people in the cartoon?
2. Who are the people in the dark clothing? Who are the others?
3. What is happening? Why are they looking at each other that way? How do they appear to feel about what is going on?
4. Have you ever had anything like this happen to you?
5. What issue do you think the cartoonist is trying to highlight? What point is he making about the issue?
6. How would you react to this situation if you were a tourist? How would you feel if you were someone in the Amish family?

Newspaper editorials serve the same function as political cartoons, but editorials use words rather than illustrations to express a specific feeling or attitude. Like political cartoons, editorials should be discussed carefully. Help the students interpret the main issue, and then help them distinguish fact from opinion by highlighting the facts in one color and the opinions in another. They should see that editorials contain a combination of both. You might ask the children reexamine the facts and write an editorial countering the opinions expressed by the original writer.

As students begin to understand the nature of editorials and cartoons as persuasive media, they develop strong interests in creating their own. John Kerrigan, for example, took exception to his principal's decision to remove the hallway door to the boy's restroom as a move to curb vandalism. To express his disapproval, John wrote a critical editorial. After he read it aloud to the class, his friend Chris drew an accompanying political cartoon. Figure 5–13 displays their joint effort.

AFTERWORD

The primary reason for educating our youth has been, and continues to be, the development of good citizens—proud citizens who make up a rich nation, a nation not made out of one people, but out of a mixture we call American. Americans have come from everywhere and for every reason—some in chains as slaves, others to search for gold, to find land, to flee famine, or to escape religious or political discrimination. Even today, America continues to be a sanctuary for the oppressed and a haven for the ambitious. Forefathers of consummate wisdom created a new kind of government for America—of the people, by the people, and for the people. To maintain this prized inheritance, all elementary school teachers must stand up and accept their responsibility to protect, nurture, and renew our healthy democratic society. They can do this by supporting and enacting the influential declaration of the NCSS (1993): "The primary purpose of social studies is to help young people develop the ability to make informed and reasoned decisions for the public good as citizens of a culturally diverse, democratic society in an interdependent world" (p. 3).

Classrooms for young citizens should have a distinctly democratic flavor. Children should know what our country is now and envision the best our country can be. As a teacher of young children, you will be an important nurturer of maximum civic growth. You will help make society. You must have a vision of good citizenship, much the same kind of vision as Michelangelo had when he peered intently at a monumental slab of Carrara marble and saw within it the Pieta, waiting to be liberated. Will you work with the fervor of Michelangelo to release responsible democratic citizens? Should society expect anything less?

FIGURE 5–13
Children's Version of an Editorial and Political Cartoon

"Are bathrooms private anymore

Mr. Towson has a great scence of humor, his last joke was the funnyest of of all. You better sit down for this Ready? Okay – He took... you sure your ready for this... Well, he took the bathroom door off See! I told you should sit down. Now you propally think all the resoribillaty has gone to his head. Well for once I think he's absolutely almost right. Heres his side. Somoone took three rolls of tolite paper in the toilet and flush it. It flooded the bathroom and the boys locker room. But taking the bathroom door off is to much. I mean you ever try and go in the bathroom with about 50 girls standing in front. But, there is a good part, the vandalism has gone down.
Now Mr. Towson has something to worry about that is weather the school board impeaches him and if the health board calls the school a health hazrd.

Har! A littel town with a littel school has there own Watergate. I can see the head of lends now "First Princepal to be Impeached." I thought Mr. Towson is a nice guy (sometimes). But the health hazard is yet a nother thing. But don't worry Mr. Towson will figure out some and we hop bathrooms are still private

                                                    Chris

OH The Bathroom, first open Door on the right

got any toilet paper

REFERENCES

The Boston Primer. (1808/1980). In R. H. Hersh (Ed.), *Models of moral education.* New York: Longman.

The Center for Civic Education. (1994). *National standards for civics and government.* Calabasas, CA: Author.

Darigan, D. L., Tunnell, M. O., & Jacobs, J. S. (2002). *Children's literature: Engaging teachers and children in good books.* Upper Saddle River, NJ: Merrill/Prentice Hall.

de Tocqueville, A. (1969). *Democracy in America* (G. Lawrence, Trans.; J. P. Mayer, Ed.). New York: Doubleday. (Original work published 1835–1839)

Ennis, R. H. (1985). Goals for a critical thinking curriculum. In A. Costa (Ed.), *Developing minds: A resource book for teaching thinking.* Alexandria, VA: Association for Supervision and Curriculum Development.

Henson, J. (1935). A slave's dilemma. In B. Brawley (Ed.), *Early negro American writers* (pp. 162–167). Chapel Hill: University of North Carolina Press.

Johnson, D. W., & Johnson, R. T. (1999). *Learning together and alone.* Boston: Allyn & Bacon.

Kletzien, S. B., & Rappoport, A. L. (1994). *Kids around town.* Harrisburg, PA: League of Women Voters of Pennsylvania.

Lickona, T. (1993). In M. Massey, Interest in character education seen growing. *Update, 35,* 1.

McClurg, L. G. (1998). Building an ethical community in the classrooms: Community meeting. *Young Children, 53,* 30–35.

National Council for the Social Studies. (1993, January/February). *The social studies professional.* Washington, DC: Author.

National Council for the Social Studies. (1994). *Curriculum standards for social studies: Expectations of excellence.* (Bulletin 89). Washington, DC: Author.

National Council for the Social Studies. (2001). Creating effective citizens: A position statement of National Council for the Social Studies. *Social Education, 65,* 319.

National Council for the Social Studies Task Force on Early Childhood/Elementary Social Studies. (1989). Social studies for early childhood and elementary school children preparing for the 21st century. *Social Education, 53,* 16.

Newmann, F. M. (1989). Reflective civic participation. *Social Education, 53,* 255–258.

Parker, W. C. (1989). Participatory citizenship: Civics in the strong sense. *Social Education, 53,* 353.

Remy, R. C. (no date). *Skills in making political decisions.* Columbus, OH: Mershon Center, The Ohio State University.

Ryan, K. (1993). In M. Massey, Interest in character education seen growing. *Update, 35,* 1.

Sterling, D. (1968). *Tear down the walls!* New York: Doubleday.

Vanderhoof, B., Miller, E., Clegg, L. B., & Patterson, H. J. (1992). Real or fake?: The phony document as a teaching strategy. *Social Education, 56,* 169–171.

The Learning Cycle:
Teacher Scaffolded Social Constructivism

WHAT DOES SOCIAL CONSTRUCTIVISM LOOK LIKE?

On a clear, crisp day just before Halloween, students from Soosan Rahimi's sixth-grade class learned there's more to cemeteries than cold gravestones and chilling ghost stories. The scene is Oaklands Cemetery, a venerable setting where young imaginations don't require much outside prompting to take wing at this time of year. Ms. Rahimi has been escorting her students on field trips to Oaklands Cemetery for the past three autumns, always around Halloween; her students' motivation to explore the graveyard, for some mysterious reason, seems to peak during this spooky season.

To prepare her students for what they would experience on this year's trip, Ms. Rahimi showed them what she begins most social studies lessons with—items she calls "interest-grabbers." In this instance, Ms. Rahimi's interest-grabber was a bronze metal star with an American flag attached—the kind that decorates the graves of soldiers who died in battle. The star had the letters GAR (Grand Army of the Republic) on it. Along with the star and flag, Ms. Rahimi showed the students a crayon rubbing of a grave marker she had made from a local cemetery. The worn, very simple stone had only the name of the deceased: "J. R. McTavish, Co. B. 9th Pa. Inf." Nothing else was written. The students were encouraged to examine the flag and grave marker. Initially, they didn't know that these items were from the Civil War era, but Richard finally spoke up: "Grand Army of the Republic! That was they called the Union Army during the Civil War. I bet this is a soldier who died in the Civil War."

"Yeah!" added Molly. "Look at the grave rubbing. It says the soldier was from the 9th Pa. Inf. He must have been a Union soldier from Pennsylvania."

261

Persistent and eager observations eventually led them to the conclusion that the items on display had something to do with the Civil War. Ms. Rahimi operates with a conviction that connecting pre-trip, personalized experiences like these to the cemetery visit helps students more effectively attain valuable understandings and sensitivities.

Following the introductory experience, Ms. Rahimi presented a series of questions or tasks that her young social scientists would use to guide their actual cemetery investigation of Civil War era grave sites, always leaving open the opportunity for the students to add their own. Here is their joint list:

- Record the average age at death for any ten men and women who died during each of the following periods: 1800–1849, 1850–1899, 1900–1949, 1950–present. During which period did they live longest? Shortest? Think of some reasons why this happened.

- Look at the gravestones of soldiers who died during the Civil War. Record the longest, shortest, most interesting, most religious, and most informative.

- How did the epitaphs on the gravestones of the Civil War era express such sentiments as regret, gallantry, and love?

- How did the grave markers bring to mind the Civil War battles that forged our nation or immortalize our great leaders as well as our more ordinary soldiers?

- Examine the writing on the gravestones of soldiers who died during the Civil War. Do any of the words or letters seem peculiar to you? List the ones that do.

- How are the gravestones of the Civil War era like those of the present? How are they different? What changes can you predict for gravestones in the future?

- Make a list of the most popular names on the gravestones from the Civil War era. Are they fashionable names today? Why?

When the class arrived at the cemetery, they were greeted by Fred Hubbert, a caretaker who led them on a general walking tour past obelisks, shrines, sarcophagi, and ornate gravestones. Some were barely legible, worn away by the wind and rain. Others were cut deep enough into slabs of granite that even hundreds of years couldn't take them away. Mr. Hubbert explained how several of these people had helped shape their community's history. "That big old shrine over there belongs to Cyrus Hadfield. When he returned from fighting in the Civil War, he opened a carriage factory on Front Street. It became one of the country's largest carriage manufacturers. Hadfield Street is named in honor of Cyrus Hadfield." As they walked, Mr. Hubbert pointed out more of the cemetery's interesting features: At one rather plain gravestone, Mr. Hubbert explained: "Jonathan Taylor was the village physician in the mid-1800s. He stopped riding his bicycle after he turned 90. He said the streets were getting too busy."

As they continued their tour, Mr. Hubbert pointed out other interesting features. "Several grave markers in that section have lambs on them," pointed out their knowledgeable guide. "Lambs were a familiar figure on the graves of young children at the time." The students discovered that some grave markers simply recorded the basic information about an individual: "In memory of Elijah Fahnestock. He was born September 15 AD 1801 and died on February 18 AD 1859." Others immortalized people with glowing epitaths: "Honorably recognized for his gallant and meritorious conduct in the War with Mexico 1849." A few included denials of death itself: "She is not gone. She is just gone away."

The cemetery stroll revealed a wealth of information for those persistent enough to try to read between the lines. For instance, one simple grave marker was etched, "Sibyl—A little refugee from N.C. who died in 1865." That marker brought out a series of questions. "What's a refugee?" they asked Mr. Hubbert. After he explained that a refugee is someone who seeks protection from something harmful, the students continued: "What kind of refugee would come to Pennsylvania from North Carolina in 1865? What kind of harm would this person face in North Carolina?"

Mr. Hubbert explained that Sibyl was a slave who was brought to southeastern Pennsylvania and granted her freedom by the Hastings family—members of the Society of Friends, a religious group strongly opposed to slavery. "You can see that she was buried along with several Hastings family members. This evidence shows that whites and blacks were buried together before it was commonly thought."

"As you see, many of the earliest monuments in Oaklands Cemetery date back to the Civil War," explained Mr. Hubbert. A bronze statue of a Union soldier sitting on his horse guarded the cemetery's fenced-in Civil War section. The students counted 24 soldiers buried there. "Here's a Union soldier who was only 14 years old when he got killed," Kendra said sadly. "That's not much older than us."

"We used to plant tulips at the base of the statue guarding this section of the cemetery, but the deer and squirrels ate them all," explains Mr. Hubbert. "We're looking into something safer that could be planted."

After this interesting introduction by Mr. Hubbert, each young historian was assigned a partner, and the dyads were sent off to different sections of the cemetery to carry out their study. The students carefully filled out their observation sheets with responses to the questions and tasks they talked about back in the classroom and made dozens of gravestone rubbings by placing large sheets of newsprint against the gravestones and carefully rubbing crayons over the paper. Everything on the gravestone (names, dates, epitaphs) transferred to the paper and provided excellent research material that could be taken back to the classroom.

Returning to the classroom, Ms. Rahimi's young social scientists pulled together and analyzed their data. Perhaps the most heartwarming outcome of the entire experience happened when several students expressed concern about the tulip bulbs that were eaten by wildlife. "I wish there was something we could do," lamented Bryce.

"Perhaps there is," suggested Ms. Rahimi. "We can check with a nursery to see if they can recommend something that the animals won't bother."

The class checked with a local nursery that day and was informed that deer, squirrels, and other wildlife love to eat tulips, but that they abhor daffodil bulbs. The students mounted a fund-raising drive, earning enough money to buy 300 daffodil bulbs. Each member of the class planted 15 bulbs that year, and as a result the base of the Civil War monument is now awash with a flood of bright yellow flowers each spring.

Ms. Rahimi doesn't bother to quiz her children on these cemetery adventures. "That's one story I'm sure they'll remember," she proclaims proudly.

In this classroom example, Soosan Rahimi used a variety of instructional strategies associated with *constructivism,* an educational approach frequently linked with the works of two leading authorities, Jean Piaget and Lev Vygotsky. Ms. Rahimi feels strongly about basing her classroom practices on time-honored authoritative support like this because she is convinced that social studies teachers cannot be effective unless their practices stand on a firm foundation of established pedagogical principles. This point of view has been supported by Piaget (1948/73) himself who wrote that a teacher ". . . should know not only his own science, but also be well versed in the details of the development of the child's . . . mind" (pp. 16–17). Piaget liked to emphasize this point by drawing an analogy between medicine and education, noting that just as a physician cannot treat a patient without deep knowledge of the body, the art of education cannot be practiced without profound knowledge of the child's mind.

Dynamic constructivist teachers such as Ms. Rahimi reject the "toss-and-catch" approach to education where a teacher lets fly with the knowledge and waits for the students to grab hold of it and cram it into their memory cache. They also reject the premise that young children are basically "ignorant adults" and that the major purpose of education is to flood their empty or semi-empty minds with a reservoir of information. Instead, they embrace the principle that children's minds are different from adult minds. Children's minds develop through a series of stages that become progressively more complex as they move from infancy into adulthood. Intelligence develops in different ways throughout these stages, each stage having a particular set of characteristics that make only certain types of thinking possible. Throughout these stages, children develop intelligence not by being told about things, but by constructing their own understandings. Brooks and Brooks (1993) elaborate:

> Constructivism stands in contrast to the more deeply rooted ways of teaching that have long typified American classrooms. Traditionally, learning has been thought to be a "mimetic" activity, a process that involves students repeating, or miming, newly presented information. . . . Constructivist teaching practices, on the other hand, help learners to internalize and reshape, or transform, new information. (p. 15)

WHAT IS CONSTRUCTIVISM?

When we address the topic of constructivism, therefore, we do not refer primarily to "what" children know, but to "how" they acquire and organize knowledge in their minds, the process by which they think and reason. We have discovered a great deal about how this happens from the work of Jean Piaget (1952), whose major contributions to our understanding of children's thinking now spans 60 years. During those years, he and his followers observed children and systematically detailed the manner by which they progressed through periods of intellectual growth from birth to adolescence. During distinct developmental periods, Piaget explained, children acquire specialized mental structures we often label *mental maps* or *concepts,* but which he called *schemata* (the singular is *schema*). Think of schemata as categories used to classify similar people, events, or ideas. When we talk about a particular schema or concept like "Puritan Society," for example, we refer to a group of people who are similar to one another. Its characteristics are so unique that "Puritan society" can be easily distinguished from "Anasazi society." Members of each category share a set of defining attributes that help us group them together. Without this ability to construct schemata, our minds would be challenged with a confusing array of unrelated gobbledygook—nothing would seem to go together.

As children grow and develop, schemata gradually become more complex and more differentiated in order to manage the information amassed from multifaceted life experiences. This is accomplished through a process Piaget calls *adaptation*. To understand the process of adaptation as it relates to mental functioning in social studies classrooms, we need to examine three essential components: assimilation, accommodation, and equilibrium. *Assimilation* is the mental process that takes place when individuals attempt to integrate new life experiences into an existing schema—in other words, trying to link a new experience to something they already know. If a meaningful connection is made *equilibrium* is sustained and the child is said to remain comfortably in a state of cognitive comfort, or "balance." However, when a child experiences something that cannot be matched to an existing schema, her or his mental state turns into an "unbalanced" status. This unbalanced status is referred to as *disequilibrium*. What happens when a child experiences disequilibrium? Fundamentally, students may opt for either of two paths: (1) they attempt to construct a new schema into which the novel element can be located, or (2) they are driven to modify an existing schema in such a way that the new element can fit into it.

Whenever a new schema has been constructed, or an existing schema modified, we say *accommodation* has taken place. Therefore, when learners encounter experiences inconsistent with what they already know, their cognitive harmony is disturbed and they strive to bring it back in balance; that is, they will attempt to alter, or *accommodate,* the existing schemata to fit in the new information.

When students adapt their schemata through the processes of assimilation and accommodation, we say that they have constructed their own understanding of the world. Students enter your classroom with knowledge and beliefs formed by their own unique experiences and, as they encounter something new, strive to group it with their previous understandings and experiences—maybe changing what they believe, maybe dumping the new information as extraneous, or maybe solving a captivating problem. Individuals make choices about what new ideas to accept and how to fit them into their established views of the world. The following paragraph describing one day in 1620 when an Indian walked into the Pilgrim settlement at Plymouth may help illustrate this point (Penner, 1991):

. . . of course the Pilgrims couldn't understand the Indian's language.

But this Indian spoke English! Before the Pilgrims could shoot, he said in a loud voice, "Hello, Englishmen!" The Englishmen were astonished.

His name was Samoset. He acted like a friend. But was he one?

The Pilgrims gave Samoset some food to eat. They gave him a place to sleep. They watched him carefully.

The next day he returned to the forest. But soon he came again, and this time he brought with him another Indian named Squanto. He [too] could speak English well. (pp. 26–27)

To attach meaning to this paragraph, a student must already know something about the adventure of the Pilgrims when they came to America on the *Mayflower*. The Pilgrims wanted to pray in their own way; they decided to leave England and find a new home. They decided to sail across the Atlantic Ocean to America, but they were afraid of what they would find there. On September 6, 1620, the *Mayflower* raised anchor, and the Pilgrims sailed for 66 days across the Atlantic. America was a wild place; wolves howled fiercely during the dark nights. The Pilgrims encountered an out-of-the-ordinary, new civilization. The Pilgrims were afraid of an Indian attack, but the Indians approached them in a friendly manner.

However, if the students had little or none of this knowledge, the paragraph would be beyond their understanding and they would probably either lose interest in the topic or became terribly confused. Let us say, though, that the students had this basic knowledge of the Pilgrims and Indians of 1620 and that the content of the paragraph was easily *assimilated* into their existing schemata. Nothing in the selection presented a conflict with what they already knew about the topic. In that case, there would be no cognitive uneasiness and the students would comfortably move on through the rest of the reading selection. However, if the paragraph contained something that conflicted with what the students already knew, they would sense a problem and become energized to restructure, or *accommodate,* their understandings so the new knowledge can somehow fit in. When the challenge of the unknown lies close enough to what students already know, they become motivated to resolve the mental conflict by striving to build new meaning from the experience. What about you? As you read the paragraph, which of the descriptions best fit your reaction to the material: Were you comfortable with all the information or did the paragraph contain something that conflicted with what you already knew about the arrival of the Mayflower?

When I gave this selection to a group of fourth graders, they asked this question at once: "How did the Indians learn to speak English before the Pilgrims came to Plymouth?" Mental conflict was created and the students were genuinely eager to reshuffle their schemata of the Pilgrims and Indians at Plymouth. Did *you* know that Samoset and Squanto spoke English? How did they learn to do that if this was their first contact with outsiders? Are you in the least bit interested in finding out how they did it? If so, you are experiencing a constructivist moment—truly determined to uncover real meaning about your world rather than simply receiving or storing knowledge. (FYI: Squanto had actually been to England twice prior to 1620. Earlier English explorers had brought him back to England, and he learned to speak English well.)

Constructivist learning is a strategic problem-solving process by which learners are intrinsically driven to construct meaning from a new learning challenge. The meaning a learner constructs does not come solely from the learning situation itself; it comes from her or his own experiences that are triggered or activated by the challenge of the new learning situation. Teachers facilitate the process of constructivist learning by creating opportunities for cognitive conflict, situations where learners are challenged to incorporate new information into existing schemata or to build new schemata. This linkage helps learners make better sense of new information. Students who can begin early in life to think of things as connected, revising their views with every succeeding year, have begun a pattern of lifelong learning.

Constructivists agree that learning takes place in this general way, but disagree on whether the process of construction occurs distinctly within each individual learner (*cognitive constructivism*) or whether it occurs as a result of people working together to make sense out of their world (*social constructivism*). To clarify these viewpoints, the social constructivist point of view will be discussed in this chapter and the next, while the cognitive constructivist point of view will be the focus of Chapter 8.

WHAT IS SOCIAL CONSTRUCTIVISM?

A major element of constructivist teaching is to make available absorbing materials and intriguing situations that appeal to the child's spontaneous and real activity. To some constructivist devotees, however, this does not mean teachers should leave children alone with a supply of learning materials and expect them to learn on their own. Instead, some form of systematized intervention within an atmosphere of mutual help and understanding is needed to provide the conditions for effective learning. In general, the construction of new ideas is interactive and collaborative. Some methods, such as cooperative learning, stress the value of interactions among the students themselves, while others, such as classroom talk, place emphasis on interactions between teacher and students. Some call attention to the value of combining both. Therefore, with social constructivism, teachers are concerned not only with selecting the materials best suited for promoting exploration and thinking, but also with cementing positive adult-student and student-student relationships, with a specific focus on efforts that lead to initiative, experimentation, and collaboration.

Throughout the example at the beginning of this chapter, for example, Soosan Rahimi offered a type of assistance that bolstered children's learning efforts by putting forward challenging projects; making available uninterrupted time to work; offering ample opportunities for cooperative and collaborative learning; arranging for an on-site experience where meaningful research could be carried out; and using a variety of questions, probes, prompts, reminders, and encouragement until students gained the confidence to do more and more on their own. In the most general sense, Ms. Rahimi based her social studies program on the belief that anything that is learned must be actively taught and that students construct ideas most effectively through social exchanges.

Educators like Ms. Rahimi have made use of Lev Vygotsky's ideas to gain theoretical support for their social constructivist classroom practices. Basic to Vygotsky's thinking is the idea that humans are fundamentally different from animals because they make and use tools. Tools make work less difficult and help people solve problems. Tools can be classified as *physical tools* (implements such as hammers, spears, or wheels that were invented to help master the environment) or *mental tools* (complex cognitive processes used to solve all kinds of problems). Because physical tools and mental tools are both critical for human survival, cultures have insisted that they be passed on from generation to generation. That is, skills, understandings, and beliefs critical to the survival of the culture must be taught to others by those who are more knowledgeable or skilled. Passing on valued skills and knowledge is where language enters Vygotsky's thinking. According to Vygotsky, learning about one's culture is most appreciably influenced by children's verbal interactions with more capable members of the culture. Whether it's learning that a red light signals one to stop at an intersection or that certain freedoms are protected by the Constitution of the United States, language is the primary tool that makes it possible for an individual to gain the knowledge essential to grow as an informed citizen. For Vygotsky, language and learning are indisputably entwined. Concepts and skills grow as children communicate with more capable members of the culture—family, friends, teachers, classmates, casual acquaintances, and all human beings. These people serve as guides and teachers, providing the opportunities for the child to grow intellectually.

Zones of Development

Since the essence of social constructivism involves recurrent classroom interactions between teacher and students or among the students themselves (learning with an "expert's" assistance), we must address the issue of what kinds of interactions are considered most productive. According to Vygotsky, children at any age have a specific range, or zone, within which they can learn. One zone consists of the learning tasks that students can complete successfully with no help. Vygotsky calls this the *zone of actual development (ZAD)*. When the teacher assigns a task and the children can accomplish it independently, the task is said to lie within their *ZAD*; they have already learned the information or mastered the skills associated with the task at hand. For example, if a teacher asks her students to identify the coordinates for five major cities on the globe and they can all carry out the task, we say the activity was within their zone of actual development.

At the other extreme are the learning tasks that students cannot complete successfully even with someone's help. No amount of outside assistance, for example, can hope to result in much learning from a group of low-achieving first graders faced with the challenge of considering the consequences of increasing diversity on the economic, social, and cultural fabric of the United States. Such unreasonable expectations are sure to generate feelings of hopelessness and disappointment for the students and the teacher.

Somewhere in between these two extremes lies the most productive zone for learning. In this cognitive region students come close to completing learning tasks successfully, but they are unable to do so without the help of a teacher or more advanced peer. This cognitive region is known as the *zone of proximal development (ZPD)*. The *ZPD* can be thought of as a construction zone where just the right amount of assisted support helps the student master a targeted skill and/or comprehend the planned content.

Scaffolding

To implement assisted learning within the ZPD, teachers must learn how to offer just the right amount of help for students as they attempt to bridge the gap between what they already know (or can do) and the intended learning outcome. This kind of adult assistance is called *scaffolding*. Adults or more competent/knowledgeable peers might provide this assistance to enable students to execute tasks within their *ZPD*. A flotation device for a child who cannot swim is a simple example of scaffolding. It is facilitative, supportive, but transitory, providing the novice with the support he or she needs only during the early stages of learning how to swim. Without an aid of this sort, the complex task of coordinating all the elements necessary to stay afloat would be practically impossible for many youngsters. The scaffold (flotation device) offers just the right amount of support until the "little guppies" are able to toss away their flotation devices and swim away on their own.

Although teachers take on several roles in a social constructivist classroom, their major responsibility is to stimulate and guide.

An educational scaffold, much like a flotation device, provides temporary support as students work to bridge the gap between what they already know or can do and the intended instructional outcome. Wood, Bruner, and Ross (1976), who were the first to use the term *scaffolding* in an educational context, defined it as "a process that enables a child or novice to solve a problem, carry out a task, or achieve a goal which would be beyond his unassisted efforts" (p. 90). As children demonstrate increasing awareness of a problem situation, the adult gradually relinquishes the leadership role and eventually turns over full responsibility of the learning experience to the child. Scaffolding allows teachers to provide the cueing, questioning, coaching, and support needed to allow students to complete a task before they can complete it independently. It is based on a problem-solving approach to learning consistent with the Curriculum Standards for Social Studies (NCSS, 1994):

> Knowledge is constructed by learners as they attempt to fit new information, experiences, feelings, and relationships into their existing or emerging intellectual . . . constructs. . . . If we want our students to be better thinkers and better decision-makers, they must have contact with those accustomed to thinking with precision . . . and clarity. (p. 7)

WHAT IS THE TEACHER'S ROLE IN A SOCIAL CONSTRUCTIVIST CLASSROOM?

The primary role of teachers in social constructivist classrooms is to promote learning, and they have at their disposal a number of general strategies to help achieve that goal. You have read about many of these strategies throughout Chapters 3, 4, and 5. Now, in Chapters 6 and 7 we will inspect the theoretically based instructional models recommended to teachers responsible for student learning in social constructivist classrooms. Social constructivist teachers in dynamic social studies classrooms view students as active travelers on a journey to understanding. They enthusiastically assume the role of "tour guide" on this journey, bringing in as much of the world as they can to school, creating a climate in which children are actively involved in their learning, and escorting the students as they strive to accomplish more difficult tasks or progress toward increasingly complex understandings. Although several models of instruction are based on social constructivist theory, the one selected for dynamic social studies classrooms has been designed with the idea of making instruction most manageable for the beginning teacher. The instructional model is based on the idea that learning occurs in a social context; therefore, the classroom must be thought of as a community of learners who build knowledge together. For knowledge to be constructed, some form of positive social interaction must be present on either or both of two dimensions: (1) *the teacher/student partnership* and (2) *the student/student partnership.*

The learning cycle, an approach to instruction that relies on dynamic teacher/student partnerships will be described in this chapter. Cooperative learning, an approach that makes the most of supportive student/student partnerships will be described in Chapter 7.

How Does the Learning Cycle Contribute to Social Constructivism?

A commonly suggested teaching approach designed to facilitate learning through a teacher's supportive assistance is called the *learning cycle*. The learning cycle is a student-centered teaching approach intended to create conceptual change through interactions within the social environment. It takes into account the students' developmental levels and helps them use their earlier experiences to construct new thought processes and develop more refined skills. In general, the learning cycle consists of three major elements, or phases, each requiring distinctive student and teacher actions and interactions: (1) exploration, (2) concept/skill development, and (3) concept/skill application. See Figure 6–1.

A learning cycle begins with the exploration phase during which the students become actively involved in trying out or experimenting with a new social studies idea or skill. Next, during the *concept/skill development phase,* the teacher assists the students as they attempt to construct their own meaning from the learning experiences. Finally, during the *concept/skill application phase,* the students transfer and apply freshly learned understandings or skills to new circumstances.

The Exploration Phase

The learning cycle begins with a high-quality exploration phase that connects with the students' previous experiences and provides a common background that helps students relate to the new experience. This initial phase has three vital purposes: (1) activating the students' prior knowledge, (2) drawing the students into the lesson, and (3) focusing the students' attention on the instructional task by establishing a clear purpose for

FIGURE 6–1
The Learning Cycle

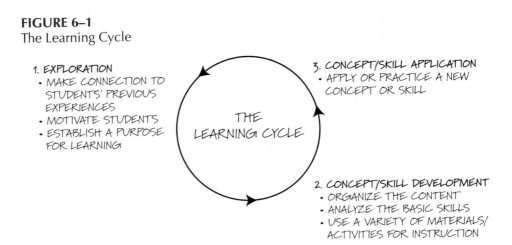

learning. In planning this phase of the learning cycle, the teacher must address questions such as: What prior knowledge do my students have of the concept targeted for instruction? Is the material too difficult or too easy? What activities can I use to encourage them to connect to their previously established understandings? How might I motivate the students and focus their attention on the material? How can I relate the learning material to the students' lives? Teachers can miss the mark in any individual lesson if they fail to pay attention to these matters.

Activating Prior Knowledge

A good learning cycle is launched when students are helped to establish a connection between what they already know or can do to the new information or skill to be learned. David Ausubel (1961) offers historically respected support of the importance of this viewpoint, stating, "If I had to reduce educational psychology to just one principle, I would say this: The most important single factor influencing learning is what the learner already knows" (p. 16). Ausubel used the term *advance organizer* to refer to the prompts employed by teachers as they assist students to retrieve past knowledge in order to connect it to the new material. In addition to Ausubel's, other terms are commonly used to describe this process. You may have heard Madeline Hunter's (1982) time-honored expression, *anticipatory set,* or Vygotsky's *external mediator* (Bodrova & Leong, 1996). Since our social constructivist strategy is primarily grounded in the works of Vygotsky, we will use the term *external mediator* in this text. Consider the external mediator to be an initial prompt, task, or activity that provides a general overview of the new material and connects the new content to the students' prior experiences (or to what they have already learned).

Teachers use a variety of external mediators with the learning cycle, but the most conventional are (1) class discussions that include thought-provoking questions, (2) provocative objects or events, and (3) graphic outlines of the material to be covered.

Class Discussions   Perhaps the most extensively used advance organizer is making an introductory statement about the material to be learned, or asking a key question, followed by a general discussion that connects the students' existing knowledge to the new material. To understand how this can be accomplished, let's visit a social studies classroom where a teacher is introducing a lesson on different types of pumps used in the oil industry.

Inside an Active Classroom

Mercer Pember's sixth graders had been involved in the study of the oil industry and are about to learn about the different ways oil is pumped from the ground. Mr. Pember begins the day's lesson by making a short introductory statement connecting what has previously gone on to the new material to be covered: "Yesterday, we discovered where some of the Earth's major oil fields are located. Today we will find out how the oil is drawn out from under the ground in those fields." Instead of providing a general description of the kind of oil pump they were going to read about, Mr. Pember asked the students to think about anything they might associate with grasshoppers. Immediately, students began to talk about the familiar insect they all knew as denizens of the lush fields in and about their rural community. Some talked about its thin, powerful back legs and how far grasshoppers are able to leap; others mentioned the antennae, the oddly shaped head, the long, thin body, and the wings. Most volunteered something, whether they merely watched the grasshoppers jump in the barren fields or used them for something rather practical—fishing bait! Mr. Pember displayed a large illustration of the insect and asked the students if this bug was the subject of their discussion. The students agreed that it was and went on to talk more about its unique characteristics. Next, Mr. Pember asked a question that raised a few eyebrows: "Here's a question I want you to think deeply about. . . . How do you suppose grasshoppers might be used in the oil industry?" The students glanced silently at one another and in due course giggled in disbelief.

"Are you serious, Mr. Pember?" they asked suspiciously.

"Of course I'm serious," countered Mr. Pember. "I know it's hard to believe, but grasshoppers actually are used in the oil industry. Turn to a partner and talk about how you think that could be."

After a few minutes, Mr. Pember invited the students to list their predictions on the chalkboard:

- "The oil workers put them in small cages and walk around a field that might have oil in it. The grasshoppers have a special sense that causes them to jump around real fast if oil is underground."

- "The brown 'tobacco' that they spit on your hand when you hold them can be collected and used to lubricate the machinery until the well begins to produce oil."

- "You'll find that more grasshoppers live in fields where there is oil underground."

After writing each prediction on the chalkboard, Mr. Pember made a direct connection to the forthcoming learning experience: "Your ideas are very interesting. Please search through the resources in the classroom research center to determine which, if any, of your thoughts explain how grasshoppers are *actually* used in the oil industry." The children quickly gathered at the center, using various books and the classroom computers to search for data to test their claims. Shortly, they returned to the discussion area and bellowed incredulously: "You tricked us, Mr. Pember! The oil industry doesn't use the grasshopper insects, they use grasshopper pumps!"

The students discovered that oil industry "grasshoppers" were large low-pressure pumps shaped somewhat like the actual insect. Mr. Pember displayed a large illustration of a grasshopper pump, as well as a model pump, next to the insect illustration and invited the students to discuss the similarities and differences. Although the oil "grasshoppers" weren't of the insect variety, signs of learning were obvious as the students continued to talk about the oil industry grasshoppers during a lively and informative discussion.

Mercer Pember pursued this line of instruction because he knew it was important for students to connect their prior knowledge of grasshoppers to this new topic before they were asked to learn more about it. This approach creates the type of mental "conflict" that energizes students to want to learn. Compare Mr. Pember's approach with another teacher who began his class discussion with the statement, "Yesterday, we read about where the major oil fields are located throughout the world. Today we're going to keep on learning about the oil industry." Then, "How many of you have ever seen a grasshopper? Today we're going to learn about how oil is pumped from the ground with a special pump called a grasshopper. Read pages 78 to 81 to find out how this special pump works."

Notice that the second teacher's background development was loosely related to the main concept of the book, but the mystery and intrigue associated with Mr. Pember's problem-based approach was missing. Mr. Pember's strategy ended up to be much more productive because it created a puzzle in the children's minds and challenged them to think. Disequilibrium brought the students' existing knowledge to the forefront, offered the teacher some insight into the students' current level of cognitive functioning, and furnished a base from which to construct new concepts.

The discussion-type external mediator is not intended to become an extended dialogue. Consider it only a quick connection to what the children already know, not something that takes so much time that it ends up being a separate lesson in itself. Five useful types of comments and questions can be used for connecting one's background knowledge to the new learning task. I have written examples of questions or comments for each category that might be used in preparation for a lesson on the Wampanoag Indians. It would be helpful to try making up your own introductory experience (á la Mr. Pember) that would enliven each discussion starter. Try to be as creative as Mr. Pember.

1. *Existing knowledge.* "Tell me what you now know about the Wampanoag Indians."

2. *Thought association.* "When you hear the names Massasoit and Hobbamock, what do you think of?"

3. *Rapid recognition.* Display key terms and ask the students to tell what they already know about them: wigwams, longhouses, deer stew, breeches, loincloths, and petticoats.

4. *Quick lesson review.* Ask questions that help connect the new learning experience to information that was learned in previous lessons: "Yesterday, we learned about a native people called the Wampanoags. Who were the Wampanoags? Describe daily life in a Wampanoag village."

5. *Open discussion.*   Sometimes an open-ended question will offer the best connection to past experiences: "We are going to read about the Wampanoag Indians. What do you know about the Wampanoags?"

Drawing Students into the Lesson   Ideally, whatever children do in our social studies classrooms would grow from an inner drive to do it—to meet all coursework with complete interest, focus, and concentration. Although this is a best possible scenario in the social studies classroom, it is seldom realized. A child, like all of us, often needs to be drawn into experiences, and social studies is no exception. Teachers must provide motivational activities to arouse enthusiasm, a desire to discover what the social studies activity has to offer. These motivational activities should involve many kinds of hands-on experiences. Mr. Pember, for example, used a brainteaser to motivate his students to read about the grasshoppers. But if he did that every time he wanted to offer an external organizer, the students would quickly tire of the routine. Therefore, for another lesson, he might select a hands-on experience to pique his students' interests: Knowing they would be much more interested in viewing a video about coal mining in Appalachia if a few lumps of coal, a bandanna, and a miner's helmet were placed in a prop box, he would encourage his students to examine the items and share what they brought to mind. Likewise, children would be spellbound as they handled a real Akua-ba doll from Ghana while you tell the story of how it is tucked into a skirt at the waist and carried by girls who hope to have children in the future. And what child wouldn't enjoy twirling a cowboy lariat prior to studying America's Old West? Real items inspire fascination for any social studies topic.

This is not meant to imply that teachers should never talk, only to stress that they enhance learning by presenting students an opportunity to interact with something real. Think about all the possibilities for bringing in *realia,* or real things, to introduce new ideas during any unit of study:

- Clothing (Indian sari, Japanese happi coat, fringed deerskin shirt of the Iroquois)
- Money (ruble, yen, mark, peso)
- Documents (wills, letters, newspapers, court records)
- Household items (colonial butter churn, Asian wok, African calabash)
- Musical instruments (Mexican guiro, Japanese den den, Zulu marimba)
- Tools (stethoscope, mortar and pestle, fishing net)
- Food (Pueblo Feast Day cookies, Mexican wedding cakes, Nigerian peanut soup)
- Toys (Chinese kites, Colonial "buzz saw," Jewish dreidel)

Oftentimes, teachers make collections of objects related to a theme and store them in boxes so they are kept well organized from year to year. These "prop boxes" can represent countries, cultures, community helpers, or most any other social studies topic. In selecting items for cultural boxes, be sure that you incorporate "present-day" samples whenever you include traditional items such as kimonos, kilts, or sombreros. If you want to put together a box containing only serapes, sombreros, and other traditional Mexican attire, for example, you will give an unfair picture of what people dress like in Mexico today unless you also include examples or photos of contemporary clothing.

To make a prop box, get a large, sturdy container that can be easily decorated (preferably by your students). Place real objects inside. Some can be bought, others might be donated by businesses, and parents are always willing to contribute items (if they're returned in the condition you received them).

Inside an Active Classroom

Orpha Diller, a student in one of my social studies methods classes, was assigned by her fourth-grade field experience teacher to plan and teach a one-week mini-unit of her choice. After considering several topics, Orpha eventually picked "Cultures and Traditions of Kenya" as the topic for her unit. Convinced that the best way to learn about a culture is to examine ordinary objects used in daily life, Orpha obtained from fellow students, parents, relatives, friends, and local ethnic stores objects that would help her students learn more about Kenya and its people.

On the opening day of the unit, Orpha hauled in an antique-like trunk that she called "Grandma's Trunk." She told the students that her family is very close and everyone felt duty-bound to help her get this important unit ready for her first significant teaching project. She went on to explain that the trunk was a gift from her grandmother who was so very proud that Orpha was about to become a teacher. It was a special trunk, her grandmother explained, because whenever Orpha needed something special to use in her classroom, all she had to do was wish real hard, say the magic word (the children decided it should be "Diller-icious!"), open up the trunk, and look inside.

In anticipation, the students and Orpha chanted the magic word together, Orpha slowly opened up grandma's trunk, and, feigning great surprise at finding each, Orpha removed the following objects one by one: *shanga* (beaded jewelry), *batik fabric*, a *skafu* (head scarf), a *mkeka* (straw mat), a *kikapu* (straw basket), *pesa* (Kenya shilling—money), *stempu* (stamps), and *kinu na mchi* (mortar and pestle). Orpha introduced the objects singly, inviting the students to examine each as she talked about them and fielded comments and questions from her students. Orpha arranged the objects on a table display and added large index cards labeling the objects. The items served as models as the students made their own masks, baskets, and beaded jewelry throughout the unit.

Another teacher, a frustrated thespian, used drama to motivate her students to learn about the globe.

Inside an Active Classroom

Entering the fifth-grade classroom appearing every bit a space alien in her metallic-type fabric shirt and pants, Betty Hunter introduced herself as Reter Nomis, a citizen of Zaxton, a planet 25 light years from Earth. "We Zaxtons have been tracking you Earthlings for some 300 years now. We have had a very difficult time understanding your language, but even more difficulty learning about you. In the six Earth years I've been observing your planet, I've had a chance only to learn a few things." She continued, "My studies of geography have informed me about such primitive things as trees, dirt, and running water. These are things I've only read about or seen in pictures on my viewing screen. Such things are a pleasure to see because our planet became so polluted that Zaxton is now depleted of them." Then, peering at the classroom globe, Ms. Hunter continued, "Because of what happened to Zaxton, my favorite kinds of lessons about Earth are lessons about geography. What can you Earthlings teach me about this planet you inhabit?" Ms. Hunter then went on to a unit that she called *Geography 101, Life on Planet Earth*.

Real experiences can serve as valuable external mediators as they raise questions in the students' minds and help draw them into the learning task. When we make early learning experiences positive and pleasurable, we stand a good chance of producing students who will be enthusiastic about, and willing to become actively involved in, learning throughout their lives.

Graphic Organizers   In addition to arousing attachment to the new content through carefully planned discussion strategies and motivational techniques, teachers often find it helpful to use attention-grabbing graphic organizers such as diagrams, charts, drawings, and other visual displays. Graphic displays of information help students consciously connect their past experiences to the targeted skills or concepts under study. In the Vygotskian framework, teachers must use these "tools of the mind" as a scaffolding device until their students eventually develop into self-regulated learners.

Bubble Trees   One example of a graphic display that helps direct student attention to what is important in the coming material is called a *bubble tree*. Bubble trees work best when relevant information can be categorized beneath a key understanding. The top of the structure identifies the core understanding; in Figure 6–2, this is "The fall of Rome." Content related to the key understanding should fall neatly into major idea categories: "barbarians" and "other causes." The tree begins, therefore, as a top bubble containing the key understanding and branches labeled as major content categories. Finally, students go through the main instructional activity and use the bubble tree to help organize the facts they uncover within each of the major content categories, eventually constructing a complex structure of branching information.

FIGURE 6–2
Bubble Tree

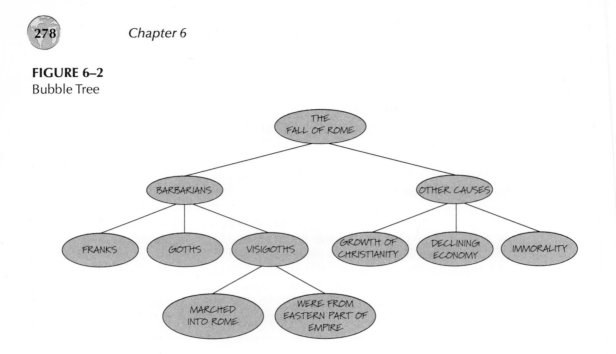

Bubble trees can be used in a variety of ways in a dynamic social studies class-room: (1) completed by the teacher before a lesson, they can present an overview, or advance organizer, for the students; (2) presented only as blank bubbles, they can tap students' prior knowledge before the lesson—as the lesson progresses, students add to, modify, and refine their suggestions; and (3) after a lesson, they can be used by students to review and organize content.

Prediction Charts Another example of a graphic outline is the *prediction chart*. Prediction charts contain a statement or series of statements related to the topic un-der study. Although one statement can be used, typically three to five statements are found on most prediction charts. Students are asked to individually respond to each statement by indicating their agreement or disagreement. Then a group discussion helps the students clarify their thoughts by eliciting reasons for each prediction.

A sample *prediction chart* is shown in Figure 6–3. Keep in mind that the pur-pose of the chart is to draw out students' honest predictions, not "correct" answers. Therefore, you must be nonjudgmental, accepting students' thoughts even if they conflict with your own. Students are quick to correct their prediction charts once they find new information in their reading. For example, their image of plantation own-ers living in huge, palace-type homes quickly reversed as they learned that some own-ers lived like that, but most lived on medium- and small-sized farms.

K-W-L Charts A final example of a highly useful graphic outline is the *K-W-L chart*. Each letter represents a different activity that guides learners prior to, dur-ing, and after the learning experience. *K* represents what the students already know about the topic. Before the learning experience actually takes place, students

FIGURE 6–3
Prediction Chart

	SLAVES	SMALL FARMERS	PLANTATION OWNERS
HOMES	ONE-ROOM CABINS WITH DIRT FLOORS. OFTEN, MORE THAN ONE FAMILY LIVED TOGETHER.	LOG CABINS USUALLY BUILT IN THE MOUNTAINS OR FOOTHILLS.	HUGE HOUSES WITH MANY ROOMS. YOU COULD COMPARE IT TO A PALACE.
WORK			
CROPS			
LIVING CONDITIONS			

discuss and brainstorm all the ideas they can associate with the topic and record their ideas on a chart, as shown in Figure 6–4. The teacher might elicit suggestions with a question such as, "Before we read this material on oceans, let's take a few moments to jot down some of the things we already know about oceans." You may need to model one or two suggestions so that students begin to see what you mean. *W* represents what the students want to know. As the students reflect on what they already know about the topic, they form questions related to gaps in their understanding. Again, the teacher might need to model a personal question and write it down on the chart to give the children an idea of what they are expected to do. *L* represents what students learned about the topic. After participating in the learning experience, students record what they discovered. They check their questions to see if each has been answered; if not, you may want to suggest other sources of information.

To illustrate, the following sequence of activities was used by Beatice Anderson to help her third graders understand how beach sand is created.

FIGURE 6–4
K-W-L Chart

K = What We Know	W = What We Want to Find Out	L = What We Learned
waves salt water large bodies of water sandy beaches vacation spots sea shells Atlantic Ocean Pacific Ocean	Where does sand come from? Why do some beaches have rocks instead of sand? What animals live in the oceans? What are the names of the oceans? How many are there? Which ones border the United States?	

1. Begin by calling the children's attention to a study print of a typical seaside land-scape. Discuss what the children *see* and encourage them to talk about the times they have visited the beach. Encourage them to consider the vastness of the beach. Ask, "Who would care to guess how many grains of sand are on the beach?"

2. Hold up a large plastic jar filled with sand. Ask, "How many grains of sand are in this jar?" Add, "We may never know the answers to these questions, but we do know one thing—how sand is made."

3. Help students generate a list of all they know about how beach sand is made on a K-W-L chart. Write everything they know (or think they know) in the *K* column.

4. Have the students list what they want to know about the topic under the *W* column.

5. Read the book *Oceans* by Seymour Simon (Morrow). Invite the students to add questions to the *W* column if they wish.

6. Direct the students to record in the *L* column all they learned about how sand is made. In addition, any erroneous information listed in the first column should be corrected.

7. To bring closure, ask students to make an entry in their social studies journals summarizing what they have learned about beach sand.

The K-W-L strategy is a favored social studies activity because it helps students actively associate their previous knowledge and experiences while establishing personalized purposes for becoming involved in a new learning experience. This procedure effectively bridges direct instruction and more independent learning in social studies.

Establishing a Clear Purpose

"Why does my teacher want me to do this?" "What am I supposed to get out of it?" Students have asked questions like these in classrooms all around the country when given ambiguous reasons for taking part in a learning experience: "Read pages 43 to 45 in your textbook. Be prepared to answer my questions when you're done." Students who are on the receiving end of such insipid instructions often ask themselves questions like these: "Why?" "What's in it for me?" They do not sense a clear purpose for the assignment and often consider textbook reading (or any other learning experience) impractical, unnecessary, or completely frustrating; they are confused by a lack of direction, so they do not push themselves into the learning experience with any degree of interest or importance. However, students who are informed about the reasons why they are to take on a learning experience are more likely to leap into the learning material actively, knowing what is expected at the end—to find out something they are vitally interested in knowing, to follow certain directions, to get a central idea, even to stimulate some personal thinking on a subject of deep interest. These are the students who will eagerly uncover new insights or knowledge, make discoveries, solve a challenging problem, experience an emotion, or simply look astonished.

As you consider this purpose-setting phase of the learning cycle, it must be emphasized that this responsibility does not stand alone; it must be linked to all that has

Constructivist teachers must be skilled not only in selecting the most useful graphic organizer for a particular topic, but also in stimulating the children's thinking and reasoning.

gone on previously. The purpose generally comes last during the introductory sequence, serving as the launching pad that propels the students into the main learning experience. Therefore, after showing her children a ship's bell, having them to handle it and ring it, and drawing out predictions about what it might be used for on a ship, a teacher directs her primary-grade students to watch a video "to find out why bells ring every half-hour on a ship." After showing a large picture print of a mushroom cloud and holding a short class discussion of the horror of the atomic bomb, upper-grade students are directed to read the picture storybook *Hiroshima No Pika (The Flash of Hiroshima)* by Toshi Maruki. To introduce the book that vividly portrays in words and pictures the horror of an atomic attack in hope that it will never happen again, the teacher says, "Read the book to learn about the pain and suffering one family experiences when the flash interrupts their breakfast of sweet potatoes on August 6, 1945, at exactly 8:15 A.M." These purpose statements focus students' attention on what to look for as they proceed through the learning activity, directing them to a particular aspect or several aspects of importance. Sometimes these will simply be oral statements while, at other times, they could be written on a chalkboard, chart, or handout so students can periodically refer to them.

With just the right amount of scaffolding experiences, students will eventually learn to set their own purposes for learning. For example, they examine the photos in their textbook prior to reading and mull over, "I wonder why banana farmers cut the stalks while the fruit is still green." They then read to find out. Students also set their own purpose when they check the heading in a newspaper, "India Arming Pakistan Border," and turn it into a question, "Are these two countries close to war?"

The Development Phase

The *development phase* builds on the exploration phase by putting forward the main experience that will develop the concept or skill more fully. During this second phase of the learning cycle, the teacher's role switches from that of "setting the table" to that of "partaking in the meal," doing whatever it will take to assist the students in their quest to learn. During the second, or concept/skill development, phase of a learning cycle, the teacher uses a variety of learning activities to make the topic or skill meaningful to students.

It is important to address a number of key questions to carry out this second part of the learning cycle: What basic concepts or skills are to be taught? What learning materials should be used to explain and clarify ideas for the students? How can teachers assist children to construct key concepts and skills? What strategies could be used to make sure the students understand the concept or master the skill? Each question is complicated and writing the responses for each lesson can be a book in itself! This shows that teaching is hard work and that good teachers spend massive amounts of time preparing lessons that help students take in, process, and organize information. These behind-the-scenes responsibilities play a key role in determining what will actually go on in the classroom during this important phase of the learning cycle.

Basic Content

To use the learning cycle well, teachers must be tuned in to subject matter. They must have a profound background of information, for each concept targeted for instruction has its own body of subordinate facts; each has a precise set of data. Teachers must be in command of this knowledge and use it to help students process and organize the information. If teachers don't know the content, how can they hope to assist students in their efforts to construct new, accurate understandings of the world? To appreciate how important it is for a teacher to fully understand the content, let us imagine that you are teaching about the native people of the past who lived in Far North and were commonly referred to as *Eskimos*. Furthermore, let us assume that you have already helped the students learn about the food of the Eskimos from the past. The cold waters of the Arctic provided Eskimos with seals, salmon, whales, and other sea life. On land, there were caribou and geese in the summer, and during the winter the Eskimos hunted bear, fox, and hare. Their favorite foods were seal and caribou meat, walrus liver, and the skin of whales. The purpose of today's lesson is to help students understand the kind of homes the Eskimos lived in long ago. Focus for a minute on the first image of an Eskimo home that comes to your mind. If you are like most people, you have most likely fashioned a mental picture of an igloo, a dome-shaped snow house sitting on a frigid, treeless, barren blanket of snow and ice. A more detailed picture might include spear-wielding whale hunters nearby, dressed in heavy fur clothing and standing near a sled ready to be pulled by a team of huskies. If you are like most people, this conventional, time-honored image would most likely guide your instruction, perhaps to the point of concluding the study of Eskimo igloos with the construction of tabletop models from sugar cubes or marshmallows. With such keen, clear-cut insight into Eskimos and their igloos, there wouldn't be any need to dig up much additional information, would there? You bet there would! If you had been methodical enough to do an information search, you would have found that the people from the Far North who we've been calling Eskimos do not use the word *Eskimo* when speaking of themselves. They are offended by that expression, primarily because it was an unpleasant word that anthropologists borrowed from American Indians. It means *eaters of raw meat*. Instead, the people of the Far North prefer to use a name that simply means *the people*. In Canada, that name is *Inuit*. In Alaska it could be either *Inupiat* or *Yupik*. The name *Yuit* is used in Mongolia.

Furthermore, focusing solely on the dome-shaped snow houses you pictured as the primary shelter of the people of the Far North would have been both illogical and culturally insensitive. In the past, the people of the Far North lived in various types of shelters. Tents made of skin (seal or caribou) provided shelter during the summer months while in winter, most built semi-subterranean sod houses. Some permanent shelters were built from logs. Yes, a dome-shaped snow house consisting of blocks cut from snow and built upward in a spiral shape was built by some groups, but only as temporary shelter while traveling or hunting. Many people mistakenly think exclusively of these dome-shaped snow structures as the Eskimo's primary igloos; actually, the people of the Far North call any place for living by that name, including the dormitory room, house, or apartment you are sitting in right now. In point of fact, *iglu* is the Inuit word for *house*, and Inuit now live in modern houses, or split-level,

TEXT SET 11

Theme: The Inuit

The cover of Mary Wallace's **The Inuksuk Book** (Maple Tree Press) displays an image of a traditional Inuit stone structure, the inuksuk, silhouetted against an Arctic sky. The inuksuk is a popular Inuit symbol, yet, for many, its purpose is a mystery. Mary Wallace, in consultation with Inuit elders and other experts, gives an introduction in fascinating text and illustrations to the many forms of the inuksuk structure and its unique place in Inuit and culture.

Brittany Marceau-Chenkie's story of Naya, **The Inuit Cinderella** (Raven Rock), was written when the author was 10 years old. Set in the High Arctic, it tells the tale of a young girl who chooses to live the traditional Inuit life with grandfather rather than move to town with the rest of her family.

James A. Houston's **Tikta'liktak** (Harcourt Brace) tells the tale of a young Inuit hunter who drifts our to sea on an ice floe and never expects to see home again. He eventually reaches a remote and desolate island where he is convinced he will starve to death. The rest of this thrilling story tells of Tikta'liktak's survival in this beautiful but rugged land.

Lydia Dabcovich's **The Polar Bear Son: An Inuit Tale** (Clarion) tells of a woman who lived all alone in a little hut at the edge of an Inuit village. She had to depend on her neighbors for

colonial, condo, or apartment *iglus,* just like the ones in which you and I live. And, like you and me, they live in towns and villages, work at contemporary jobs, wear fashionable clothing, and eat food purchased in stores. Instead of kayaks and dogsleds, they use motorboats and snowmobiles.

What would children have learned about the Inuit if they were offered what we thought we knew about this fascinating culture? In this case, the result certainly would be unjust, stereotypical, and incorrect, abusing all the major responsibilities of a contemporary multicultural society. In any lesson, we must uncover and verify considerable information so that students acquire a genuine concept of the culture, period of time, or phenomenon being studied. Consider how one experienced teacher highlights the need for a spirit of continuous learning:

> The biggest surprise of teaching, for me, was that I didn't know my subject matter. That was the one thing I had been most confident about. I had almost an "A" average in my major and felt really on top of my field. When I began teaching and had to explain concepts, I found that I had only a very superficial understanding of them. I knew stuff in kind of a rote way and when I had to explain it to someone else I kind of just fell on my face. I learned more about my subject in my first four months of teaching than I did in my four years of college. (Ryan, Burkholder, & Phillips, 1983, p. 177)

As a teacher in a dynamic social constructivist classroom, this means that you must have much information at your fingertips and access to resources that supple-

everything. She adopts an orphan polar bear cub whose superior hunting ability provides food for her as it grows up. When the men of the village grow jealous of the bear's ability and decide to kill it, she sends it away. For years afterward, she walks far out on the ice and meets the bear, who brings her salmon and seal.

Arctic Adventure: Inuit Life in the 1800s (Soundprints), written by Dana Meachen Rau and illustrated by Peg Magovern, is an interesting time travel story in which a young boy learns some interesting things about the Inuit. While visiting the exhibit on native cultures at the National Museum of Natural History, Tomas travels back in time and becomes an Inuit boy living in the Arctic during the 1800s.

TRY THIS

Explore your understanding of the Inuit more deeply. Suggest all dimensions of culture that comes to mind. Then read one of the books listed in this Text Set. Consider which of the items you listed might be the most important dimension in defining the Inuit culture. Which item do you, as a future teacher, think you should focus on when you are teaching about the Inuit? Compare your choices with those of your classmates.

ment your knowledge. The computer and a wide variety of print sources are the places to start. Check with your school or public librarian for references on a concept you wish to pursue. Constantly search for information to bolster what you already know. You should find yourself saying "I'll look it up" many times a day. Books and the computer will provide most of the needed information, but you will also want additional resources. Consult specialists both in person and by telephone, visit museums and other sites, view films or filmstrips, listen to audiotapes, and seek other opportunities to broaden your background. You will need to spend a great deal of time uncovering and organizing information—and love doing it.

Concept Analysis In addition to knowing the content, teachers in social constructivist classrooms must understand how to organize it so that the content has the most meaning for their students. The most common way to organize the content is to classify it into concept categories. Do you recall what is meant by concept categories? Concepts can be thought of as a class of ideas that share one or more similar characteristics. It helps to think of concepts much as mental "file folders" into which we sort out and store the information we gather from our experiences throughout life.

Because concept development takes place over a lifetime, we say that it is a dynamic process; that is, our mental "file folders" keep growing and changing as we accumulate experiences and find new things to put in, alter, or take out throughout our lifetimes. For example, my mental file folder labeled *mound* contained very few items early in life. First, I inserted images of a small pile of earth because my parents constantly referred to the "mound of dirt" in the far reaches of our back yard where we loved to play. Next, as a Little League pitcher, I learned that the slightly elevated pitcher's area in the center of a baseball diamond that I stood on was called a mound. So, my mental file folder grew a bit as I accumulated experiences throughout my early years of life. When I got older, I added to the growing *mound* mental file folder: I learned that any raised mass, such as a pile of hay could be referred to as a mound and even that a large artificial pile of earth or stones marking a burial site can be called a *mound*. I'm sure most of you have similar data in your *mound concept* file folders, and will use that folder throughout your lifetime to classify any new information you feel will be important enough to store there. Think about the following information as a possible addition: In A.D. 1200, the Mississippians, an American Indian culture living along the banks of the river that now bears their name, built the town of Cahokia around a huge, steep platform called a *mound*. Because it was so huge (1,000 feet long by 700 feet wide), historians estimate that the mound would have taken the Mississippians more than 200 years to complete. The mound was so colossal, in fact, that it would dwarf even the Great Pyramids of Egypt. What do you think? Will you expand your mound mental folder with that information? What factors do you feel would cause some to say, "Yes, I will!" or "Sorry, try again!"

Concepts are designated by a label, a word that helps us catalog incoming information conveniently. In the learning cycle model, learning depends a great deal on the teacher's ability to identify the defining features of the concept being taught. Many concepts, such as *mound, latitude, coin, flag, iceberg, fjord, merchant,* or *shelter*, have well-defined characteristics and are relatively easy to analyze and teach. They are called *concrete concepts* because they are easily recognized by their physical appearance. Others, such as *democracy, peace, freedom, justice, equal opportunity, liberty,* and *war* have characteristics that are much less concrete and, therefore, are much more difficult to analyze and teach. These terms, called *abstract concepts*, are much more difficult to conceptualize because we cannot visibly observe their physical characteristics. That is why you will find concepts like *family* or *home* or *firefighter* taught at the first-grade level while *democracy* or *freedom* rarely find their way into the instructional program in a formal sense before the upper-elementary school grades or even middle school.

Concept analysis is the process of breaking down a concept by identifying its defining features. To better understand how this relates directly to dynamic social studies, take a minute and think about a concept many fifth graders learn about in their social studies classes—Buddhism. For sake of illustration, let us assume that Buddhism is the concept we are responsible to teach. Now that the concept label has been denoted, we must next put forward a brief definition of it: for example, "*Buddhism*: the teaching ascribed to Siddhartha Gautama holding that one can enter into nirvana by mental and moral self-purification." Definitions are easily found in dictionaries, encyclopedias, textbooks, and other reference materials. The concept label and definition are important, but the process of concept analysis is not complete until we break down its defining characteristics, or subordinate details that help us distinguish Buddhism from Christianity, Hinduism, Judaism, Confucianism, Islam, or any other religion. Think about Buddhism for a moment. What particulars come to your mind? Are you picturing a sculpture of the Buddha? Maybe you see an image of a Buddhist monk. Perhaps words like *Siddhartha Gautama, the Buddha, India, religion, Four Noble Truths,* or *dharma* pop into your head. We store information in our minds in a number of different ways; images and words are two of the most common. The images and symbols you associate with Buddhism are a result of your past experiences with Buddhism. The forms they take are determined by the way you sort, order, connect, and make sense of the details of those past experiences.

Factstorming   The first step in expanding the concept, then, is a process of finding the relevant details associated with a concept, a process commonly called *factstorming.* Virtually any concept can be factstormed; all that is required is to create a graphic representation of what you already know about the concept. First, label your selected concept at the top of a large sheet of paper and draw a circle around it. Then, by asking probing questions (for example, "What are the teachings of Buddhism?"), list all the relevant details you can recall. Write them on the paper, draw a circle around each, and draw lines to connect them to the central concept. Repeat the process with each relevant detail. The chart is only the beginning. As we learned with the Eskimo illustration, most teachers do not know enough at this initial stage of the planning process to identify all the necessary content. They begin by brainstorming "starters," or ideas to launch the planning process. You will need to exhaustively add to and refine the starter information, for the defining features of a concept must be complete and accurate if instruction is to succeed. An analysis of the defining characteristics of the concept of Buddhism as it was researched and organized by one teacher to serve as the content source for a mixed group of fifth and sixth graders is depicted in Figure 6–5.

Notice how the most general category (Buddhism) is at the top of the teacher's paper. Under this concept label the teacher diagrammed relevant details. Taken together, these comprise the defining features that will be used to teach about Buddhism. If the teacher were to offer a narrative explanation of the hierarchy, it would include statements such as those that follow:

- Buddhism is one of the world's great religions.
- Buddhism was started in India somewhere between 563 and 483 B.C.
- Siddhartha Gautama established Buddhism.
- Siddhartha was called "the Buddha," or "enlightened one."
- Buddhist laws and teachings are called the *dharma.*
- The Four Noble Truths explain the Buddha's beliefs about suffering.
- The Buddha preached "The Middle Way"—moderation.
- Buddhists believe that the Eightfold Path leads to enlightenment. The deeds a person performs during his or her lifetime are called *karma.*
- Buddhists believe in a process called *reincarnation.*
- The good or bad karma travels with a person to the next life.

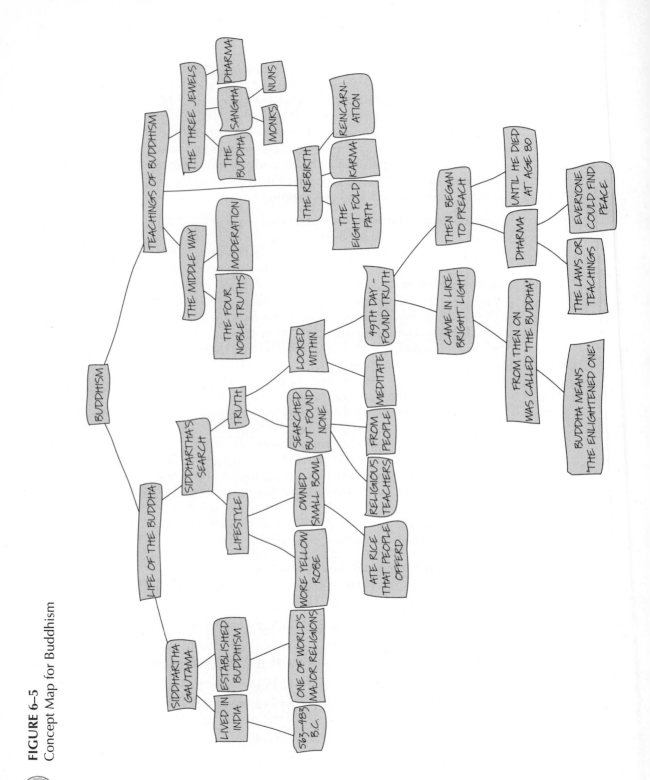

FIGURE 6–5
Concept Map for Buddhism

- The Buddhist tradition is made up of three parts, called the *Three Jewels:* (1) the Buddha, (2) the dharma, and (3) the sangha (religious community, including nuns and monks).

Although they have been abused by overly excessive rote, drill, or practice exercises, facts are highly essential ingredients of concept development. They help learners distinguish continents from countries, glaciers from icebergs, and Buddhism from Hinduism. Concepts grow from facts; facts are what give concepts their defining features. Facts serve as building blocks, furnishing the details necessary to develop concepts. Concepts do not materialize magically out of the thin air; students gradually construct them as knowledge accumulates through varied learning experiences. Without a system of organizing the wealth of information about our world, though, each fact becomes isolated and students have few options other than to memorize it—and to complain that "social studies is boring!"

A word of caution about the defining characteristics of concepts must be given here: Although facts provide the defining features that make a concept what it is, they must be selected carefully. For example, details of George Washington's $60-a-set dentures (made from ivory, wild animal teeth, or lead covered with gold), as interesting as they may be, would contribute little to enriching the concept of our presidency. However, they could provide interesting content to help construct an understanding of health care during colonial times. Concepts are superb organizational devices, but they can be constructed accurately only when learners gather meaningful information through sound, developmentally appropriate activities. Concept learning is a process of learning what key features (defining characteristics) are essential components of a concept and what other features (irrelevant characteristics) are nonessential. Learning to differentiate defining features from irrelevant features takes time and experience; this process only takes longer and becomes more difficult to master when teachers present students with unclear examples.

Basic Skills (Task Analysis)

In addition to building concepts, another major goal of social studies instruction is helping children acquire specific skills such as constructing and interpreting charts and graphs, using the computer, composing a meaningful written report, making a timeline, reading a map, creating a model, outlining information from reference books, planning an interview, making a mural, learning the steps of an ethnic dance, reading maps, comprehending textbook material, or testing hypotheses. Skills are mental or physical operations having a specific set of actions that are developed through practice. Those who support the social constructivist philosophy claim that students cannot learn skills without a teacher's help; these necessary skills are best taught and reinforced as separate lessons with clear assistance from the teacher followed by numerous opportunities for practice. This process begins by carefully breaking down the skill into a number of separate components, each of which provides the foundation for the next. The process through which the component parts of the skill are identified and sequenced is referred to as *task analysis*. In learning to read maps, for example, understanding what a map is would certainly come before a lesson requiring students to locate their state capital. In other words, instruction is sequenced so that more complex processes grow from less complex ones.

Many social constructivist teachers believe that social studies skills can be best acquired through the process of *modeling*—that is, observing someone more highly skilled and attempting to copy her or his behaviors. These teachers emphasize, for example, that it is no coincidence that better readers come from homes where parents read frequently. If children see their parents reading the morning newspaper or a book, they will be inspired to follow their lead. Nadya Luca models a set of skills that have functional value in the social studies curriculum in the following scenario.

Inside an Active Classroom

Nadya Luca felt it was important to model certain reading skills from their social studies text so that her fourth-grade students could best develop subject area literacy. The question, "What must my students be able to do in order to learn effectively from their social studies text?" served as the basis for analyzing the specific skills that would be necessary for developing subject area literacy. Look carefully at the following list Ms. Luca assembled. It served as the basis for subsequent instruction in her classroom. Students must be able to:

1. identify what they already know about the topic
2. raise questions about what they do not know
3. predict what the text will be about
4. predict what information will be found in the passage
5. relate new information to previous knowledge
6. focus their attention on the reading task

First, Ms. Luca wanted her fourth graders to relate their personal experiences to the textbook topic, so she began the social studies lesson by displaying a photograph of a small rural community and the rich, lush farmland that surrounded it. She used the photograph as a springboard for discussion of the ways people interact with and adapt to their environment, focusing especially on the need to protect natural resources: "How do people and animals rely on the fertile topsoil? How do they rely on trees. Water?" Ms. Luca and the class discussed wasteful practices such as overwatering lawns and using paper unwisely. She then asked the class how they might protect the Earth's topsoil, trees, and water supply. Following this short discussion, Ms. Luca directed her students to turn to a specific page in their social studies text. She pointed to and read aloud the chapter title, "Saving Our Land." Ms. Luca explained that when she sees a new chapter title, she always thinks for a moment about what it might mean. "It seems to me that the chapter could be about ways of protecting our natural resources like water and topsoil and trees," she suggested. "What do you suppose gave me that idea?" After they discussed Ms. Luca's idea for a short while, she asked the class to talk with a partner and produce original ideas about the chapter title. Then, as the pairs shared their original ideas, Ms. Luca wrote their suggestions on the chalkboard. Next, she asked the students to look at the text photos and the first major heading, "The Need to Protect Our Land." She said to the class, "I find that examining the illustrations and headings before I read raises questions in my mind about what might be ahead. For example, one question I had about the photo at the top of the page is, 'Why is conserving topsoil so important?' What are some other questions I might have asked myself about the heading and the photos?" Ms. Luca went through the next section, "Conservation Efforts," the same way and continued with the succeeding sections, writing each set of comments and questions on the chalkboard.

Although modeling is recognized as a highly effective and efficient method of helping students learn a specific skill or behavior, it must be emphasized that not just any model will do. Students have a greater tendency to accept their teachers as high-quality models if they perceive them as competent and capable professionals. I'm sure, for example, that you would have much more faith in a golf pro teaching you the nuances of golf than in a friend whose experiences were limited to miniature golf. Likewise, children learning how to use the Internet as a research tool are more likely to place their faith in a teacher who exhibits technological savvy rather than in one who calls in sick with a computer virus.

In addition to a quality model, students are more likely to become engaged in certain tasks when they are convinced they can succeed—that is, when they have a high degree of *self-efficacy*. For example, you may have a high degree of self-efficacy for teaching social studies to elementary school children. In other words, you are quite capable of taking the information from this course and using it to carry out effectual classroom practices. On the other hand, your self-efficacy for filling the cracks on Mount Rushmore might be slightly less advanced. Likewise, not all of your students will experience an equal degree of self-efficacy for everything you want them to learn. Some will have high efficacy for learning the Blackfoot Buffalo Dance while others are more comfortable dancing the polka. Students tend to select tasks they think they will do well and avoid those where they think they might fall short. They tend to apply greater effort to the tasks they feel they can accomplish and less effort to those at which they feel mediocre or substandard. It is important to provide just the right amount of assistance to students. More assistance than the student needs sends the implied message, "I don't really think you can *ever* do this on your own." Not enough assistance has a high probability of resulting in failure and weakened self-confidence. Verbal encouragement with little or no further assistance such as, "If at first you don't succeed, try and try again!" or "I know you can do it—don't give up" is questionable in providing a boost in self-efficacy. The key is to find the point at which your students can succeed at a task with your assistance (ZPD). At this point, they will have greater confidence in their ability to succeed and apply greater effort and determination to the task.

Materials for Instruction

Selecting learning materials and activities must be consistent with the ways children learn. For example, Jerome Bruner (1966) identified three levels of learning children move through as they encounter new information—enactive, iconic, and symbolic (see Figure 6–6). The *enactive level* includes objects, people, places, trips, visitors, and real-life classroom experiences. Within this level children represent and understand the world with authentic materials and individual actions on those objects. For example, suppose your goal for today is to help students learn about the emergence of cotton as an important cash crop in the Southeast during the late 1700s. Your enactive level possibilities include bringing in cotton bolls for the children to handle as they examine the soft fibers, observe the tiny seeds, and touch the prickly shell. By handling the real item, the students can appreciate the agony slaves experienced as they were forced to spend immeasurable hours picking out the little seeds from within the boll to free the attached fibers.

The *iconic level* offers representations of real objects when the actual objects or places themselves cannot be directly experienced. For example, there is no way your students could watch slaves picking cotton in the hot fields and emptying their sacks until they built up a huge heap of cotton. You cannot have your students observe the next 8 to 10 hours when the slaves would clean the fiber out of the cotton bolls. Moment-

FIGURE 6–6
Bruner's Three Modes of Knowing

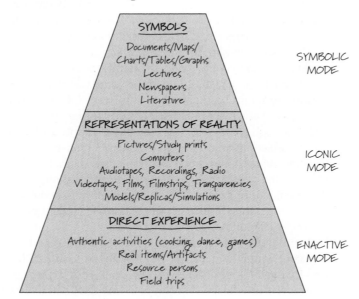

in-time limitations make this impossible. A well-produced video documentary or possibly a set of study prints with clear explanations would then be a useful substitute for the real experience. Representations of reality help children construct concepts when real things are not available. Although pictures and models are not always as motivating as the real thing, these learning resources are much more effective than trying to connect new learning to words alone. Good pictures, especially large poster-size photographs and prints, will deepen children's concepts of people and places. Dynamic social studies teachers build substantial picture files by searching hard for just the right pictures to furnish experiences that students can connect to new ideas. A good social studies classroom also contains models that mirror displays found in our best museums—not a hands-off place where students simply stand and gawk, but one that invites handling and touching. And, of course, the Internet and other computer applications have made possible new and rich learning opportunities.

The *symbolic level* involves using abstract ideas, symbols, language, and logic to represent the world. For example, good information books and other sources of children's literature can enliven and deepen the children's knowledge of how cotton is grown and processed and how the Southeast became an important cotton growing region.

Understanding Bruner's three levels of learning is important for planning and organizing the development phase of the learning cycle. They help you recognize the need for balance among the activities you choose, so that there is not too much symbolism (workbooks, practice sheets, talking, reading) and too little realia—or vice versa—in your program. As a rule of thumb, you should remember that all students thrive on a balance of solid learning experiences, but younger students need direct contact and real experiences (a visit to an orchard) and visual representations (a videotape of apple-growing procedures). Older students still require concrete experiences but are increasingly able to gain knowledge from abstract sources (listening to a well-planned lecture).

Assisting Students as They Construct Key Concepts

According to social constructivists, the act of constructing concepts cannot happen merely by exposing children to learning materials and expecting them to draw out the important understandings all by themselves. Piaget (1964) writes, "Experience is . . . necessary for intellectual development . . . but I fear that we may fall into the illusion that being submitted to an experience . . . is sufficient. . . . But more than this is required . . . " (p. 4). Piaget stressed the something "more" is crucial role of the teacher. Teachers must be effective organizers who select rich materials and create intriguing situations that arouse interest in learning, and they must be thought-provoking guides who encourage students to use language to organize their thinking. Under their leadership, social constructivist classrooms become communities of learners working together to organize knowledge and construct learning, and this goal cannot be accomplished unless there is talk. That is because language is basic to the learning process and serves as the primary tool of intellectual growth.

If teachers expect the *concept development phase* of the *learning cycle* to play a major role in knowledge construction, they must encourage students to use language—to think and talk about what they have been trying to accomplish. These language-based strategies not only help students organize and explain what they have been learning, but they also give teachers an idea of where students need supportive assistance or additional experience. Three familiar language-based strategies that help teachers build scaffolds for the construction of new knowledge include *general instructional conversations, small-group instructional conversations,* and *graphic organizers.* Using either or both of these language-based strategies completes the crucial *development phase of the learning cycle.*

Instructional Conversations   Scaffolding as a process of assisting students to construct knowledge occurs most effectively in classrooms where students come together to talk, listen, and learn from one another. Conversation is the system by which they share knowledge with one another and the primary method for developing higher-order thinking. One particular form of classroom conversation, called *in structional conversations,* has received a great deal of attention for its potential value in social constructivist classrooms (Gallimore and Tharp, 1990). *Instructional conversations* are *instructional* because they help assist learning; they are *conversations* because they involve substantive talk about concepts that were introduced and developed throughout the earlier phases of the *learning cycle.*

Instructional conversations, talk between teacher and students or among students, take place in a classroom environment where students can converse freely, presenting their ideas and opinions in whole-class or small-group situations. Teachers set off instructional conversations with well-planned questions and prompts that provoke students to think and reason about the content. Then, as the students respond, teachers listen and react to their ideas in a supportive, considerate manner.

If instructional conversations are to be productive, we must force from our minds any thoughts of traditional classroom dialogue where teachers use questions as tools of "interrogation" rather than as prompts to help students search for meaning. "Interrogations" can best be described as peppering students with closed-ended questions that require them to simply retrieve from memory any piece of specific information that was a part of the learning experience. For example, a question such as, "On what date did Congress vote to accept the Declaration of Independence?" is considered to be closed-ended because there is only one possible answer. And, once a student responds, all further dialogue stops—discussion is closed. Monotonously, closed-ended question after closed-ended question flows in a steady stream until all the facts are recited. Through this type of fruitless interface, students learn very early in their schooling that their role in classroom discussions is to send back what the teacher wants to hear rather than talk about what is truly important to them. One study reported on the wasteful nature of restrictive, traditional classroom interrogations: "When students . . . respond, typically they provide only simple information recall statements. This pattern of teacher/student interaction not only limits a student's opportunity to create and manipulate language, but also limits the student's ability to engage in more complex learning." (Ramirez, Yuen, & Ramey, 1991, p. 8)

Instructional conversations are an alternative to restrictive, traditional teacher-centered classroom interrogations. The teacher is viewed more as a guide than as an interrogator, using language to help students think about a learning experience. Although teachers may use closed-ended questions during instructional conversations, the purpose for asking these questions is to ensure that students have adequate prior knowledge about a topic to wisely discuss it rather than as an end in themselves. Conversely, open-ended questions like, "What culture other than your own do you admire most and why?" lead to more complex thinking. They challenge students to go beyond the content by engaging higher-order thought processes such as critical and analytical thinking. Students are usually more involved in class discussions when open-ended question are asked because those kinds of questions are much more thought provoking. Check your ability to distinguish open-ended from closed-ended questions by categorizing each of the following examples as one or the other:

1. What was the name of the ship that brought the Pilgrims to Plymouth Colony in 1621?
2. The Pilgrims at Plymouth Colony had very strong religious beliefs. How do you think these beliefs affected their ability to survive the hardships of the first winter?
3. When spring came, many Indians visited the Pilgrims. What questions do you suppose the Indians wanted to ask the Pilgrims? What questions do you suppose the Pilgrims wanted to ask the Indians?
4. What was the name of the Indian tribe that visited the Pilgrims at Plymouth Colony that first spring?
5. Squanto showed the Pilgrims how to plant corn. What did he teach them to use as fertilizer?

I trust you selected questions 2 and 3 as open-ended or divergent questions. Those two questions are considered to be open-ended because they are thought-provoking and intended to pull out more than a single factual response. Discussion usually is extended because students will enjoy the challenge of using the content to support their own beliefs and to question the beliefs of their classmates. Questions 1, 4, and 5 are closed-ended questions because they converage on a single, correct response. Unfortunately, when one student gives the correct response, discussion swiftly comes to a halt because there is nothing more one can think or talk about.

Using Instructional Conversations—Patterning and Framing Questions   Asking good questions, as important as the process is, represents only one critical concern in leading instructional conversations. Teachers must also be skilled at sequencing or *patterning* the questions so that students can be systematically guided toward intended learning outcomes. Questions should never be randomly selected; it is important that they have a focus because discussions happen for different reasons. Perhaps you want your students to organize and elaborate on what they've learned. Maybe you would like them to critique a controversial issue. Whatever the reason for

Learning to lead and sustain thought provoking class discussion is a key part of direct instruction.

designing a questioning plan, the purpose must be kept foremost in mind so that you are able to maintain focus throughout the instructional conversation. So, as you begin to think about the kinds of questions to ask during this phase of *learning cycle,* ask yourself these questions: "What do I want my students to gain from this discussion?" "How will the questions contribute to the overall purpose of the lesson?" Your replies will assist you to design worthwhile questions and help guide your students to deeper understanding of the targeted concept or skill.

To illustrate, let us examine the questioning patterns of two teachers, both of whom shared the same instructional purpose: to help the students understand how the migration of white settlers changed the lives of the Plains Indians. Paul Resuta decided to launch his instructional conversation by asking an open-ended question intended to draw out personal feelings: "The Plains Indians had deep respect for nature and the land. Do you think the settlers shared this point of view?" The students enthusiastically offered several different viewpoints, and Mr. Resuta challenged them to support each of their beliefs with suitable information: "What evidence do you have to support your position?" So, even though Mr. Resuta began the instructional conversation with an open-ended question, students were required to use relevant information to back up their arguments.

Grace Chacho, by contrast, preferred to set her instructional conversation in motion with a question that called for her students to summarize the content: "In what ways did the settlers upset the Plains Indians' way of life?" As the students volunteered a number of responses, Ms. Chacho transcribed each fact on an information summary chart. At the point when her students were unable to add further information, Ms. Chacho suggested, "Let's examine what you've come up with. What does this information tell you about how the Plains Indians and the settlers felt about the land? Do you think Americans of today have attitudes similar to the settlers at that time?"

Mr. Resuta asked an open-ended question to start the instructional conversation and then challenged the students to support their views with relevant details. Ms. Chacho did just the opposite; she started by asking the students to recall details with closed-ended questions and then encouraged them to draw their own conclusions from the data. Which approach is best for elementary school social studies instruction? Both are acceptable; each sequence was driven by a logical purpose, was patterned to address that purpose, and helped students cite evidence to support critical thinking. Rather than worrying about whether your sequence begins with an open- or closed-ended question, it is more important to become skilled at applying John Dewey's (1933) yet helpful "art of questioning," as proposed over 60 years ago:

- Questions should not elicit fact upon fact, but should be asked in such a way as to delve deeply into the subject; that is, to develop an overall concept of the selection.
- Questions should emphasize personal interpretations rather than literal and direct responses.
- Questions should not be asked randomly so that each is an end in itself, but should be planned so that one leads into the next throughout a continuous discussion.
- Teachers should periodically review important points so that old, previously discussed material can be placed into perspective with that which is presently being studied.
- Teachers should bring closure to the experience by guiding students to summarize the main points. This is a way of helping students understand what was important, or what should be remembered from the discussion.

Interrogations, employed simply to quiz the students about facts associated with a learning experience, gives the illusion of teaching to the uninitiated. First-rate teachers, however, know that questions must be planned so that one leads to the other throughout a logical sequence, deliberately provoking deeper thought or creating new understandings. If teachers are able to effectively guide instructional conversations, students will discover that questions can serve as a useful tool of the mind that help organize their thinking now and throughout their lifetimes.

In addition to patterning questions, it is equally important to know how to *frame* questions; that is, to provide students enough time to think of a response and to transform their thoughts into a comment that they could share with their classmates. The fundamental system for framing questions is: (1) ask the question, (2) pause for 3 to 5 seconds (wait time I), (3) call on a student to respond, and (4) pause again for 3 to 5 seconds to give the student some time to think about and share a response (wait time II). There are a number of positive outcomes when teachers give students plenty of time to think. First, a larger number of students willingly volunteer responses. Second, their responses tend to be longer, more complex, and more precise. Third, a pause provides the teacher with time to study their students' body language. With experience, you will be able to pick up their satisfaction, delight, concern, or boredom. Fourth, teachers who pause after asking questions become more patient while waiting for answers and the students become more comfortable while sharing their thoughts. In all, then, when teachers allow at least 3 seconds to pass after asking a question, we find that students will make longer responses, offer more complex answers, interact more with each other, and gain more confidence in their ability to contribute to instructional conversations.

Small-Group Instructional Conversations   One of the best ways to incorporate language-based instruction into the *learning cycle* is to offer opportunities for cooperative and collaborative learning through small-group instructional conversations. Small-group instructional conversations have become increasingly popular in social studies classrooms because, of all school subjects, social studies seems to be most fitting for group discussions. Students meet to talk about a field trip they had just taken, to respond to a biography their teacher just read to them, to plan a mural project, to compare the actions of two historical figures, to explore the ramifications of harvesting the world's rainforests, or to summarize information presented in a video.

Typically, small-group instructional conversations are sparked by a meaningful question or problem offered by the teacher or another student. The subsequent talk allows for the exchange of observations, explanations, clarifying comments, and differing points of view. Although students do most of the talking in small-group instructional conversations, teachers nonetheless have vital responsibilities. To begin, they must make sure students have a sound background of information necessary to intelligently discuss the topic. They must model good dialogic behaviors and work to create a climate of mutual respect in the classroom. And, social studies teachers must communicate expectancies like these to guide small-group instructional conversations:

- Everyone should take part in the conversation.
- Think before you speak.
- Speak honestly and openly about your thoughts and feelings.
- Listen carefully and politely to what others are saying, even if you disagree.
- Feel free to extend and expand another student's ideas.
- Ask clarifying questions if you do not understand something.
- Criticize ideas, not other students.

After the ground rules are well established and understood by all, teachers find it useful to use strategies like these to initiate good small-group instructional conversations:

- Select a topic with multiple perspectives.
  Example: *"Who should take care of the elderly when they are no longer able to care for themselves?"*
- Clarify the time frame.
  Example: *"We'll meet together for 15 minutes and then come back together as a whole class."*
- Explain the procedures in manageable steps.

Example: "*Each group will be made up of four students. Each group of four will subdivide into two pairs. Each pair of students will discuss the issue and present its position to the other two students. The group of four will hold an open discussion on the issue, making sure each student has an opportunity to voice her or his viewpoint. The group of four will then attempt to reach consensus on the issue in a way that incorporates everyone's reasoning and explanations.*"

- After the small groups have talked about the topic for the specified time, or if they have thoroughly explored the topic before the time expires, the class can be brought back together and each group can share its results. The teacher should write key points on the board, and the final conclusion can then be examined by the entire class for common themes.

Example: "*What did you learn from the conversation?*" "*What did you find you had in common with other members of the group?*" and "*Are there any ways in which the conversation could be improved?*"

Small-group instructional conversations seem to be more effective when they are structured in ways similar to those illustrated in the strategy outlined above. Additional examples of useful small-group conversation arrangements can be found in Chapter 7, *Cooperative Learning.*

To summarize, it is possible to provide language-based instructional scaffolding by involving students in general instructional conversations based on Dewey's "art of questioning" or by engaging them in small-group instructional conversations. These opportunities for constructive classroom talk provide the scaffolding needed to move a student from dependent to independent learner. Another widespread language-based scaffolding technique involves the use of *graphic organizers*. Graphic organizers provide students framework for processing information, whether recognizing relationships, outlining processes, or identifying needed information.

Graphic Organizers   Most of us learned to outline information when we were in school, so when we hear or read the term "graphic organizer" the idea of an outline or summary paragraph often pops into our heads. If you find this happening, clear your mind and think instead of replacing outlines or summary paragraphs with visual representations called *graphic organizers*. Graphic organizers are sketches or illustrations that help students represent key ideas and organize information. Often, graphic organizers are called *concept maps* because they help teachers and students pictorially "map out" their ideas. Graphic organizers help students detect helpful patterns and relationships within the content. They are able to see how ideas are connected and how information can be stored in an orderly fashion.

Graphic organizers, like instructional conversations, are considered to be language-based scaffolding experiences because students need not only draw and write in order to complete an organizer, they must also talk, listen, and think. Let's consider some of the most well-known varieties of graphic organizers. There are four basic patterns, with endless variations, that appear to have the greatest utility in social studies classrooms: *conceptual, sequential, cyclical,* and *hierarchical.*

Conceptual Graphic Organizers   *Conceptual graphic organizers* (also known as *concept maps*) are simple diagrams that spotlight a central topic or concept and show the relationship between the supporting details and the spotlighted topic or concept. A favorite concept map of social studies teachers is the *semantic web*. Semantic webs are graphic organizers that look much like a spider's web when complete—hence their name. Semantic webs are comprised of three basic elements—core concept, web strands, and strand supports.

   The *core concept,* or concept of central importance to the learning experience, serves as the focus of the web. An example of a core concept associated with the study of the New England Colonies might be "Daily Life." Place the core concept in the center of a growing matrix (see Figure 6–7) and initiate an instructional conver-

FIGURE 6–7
Web: Daily Life in Colonial America

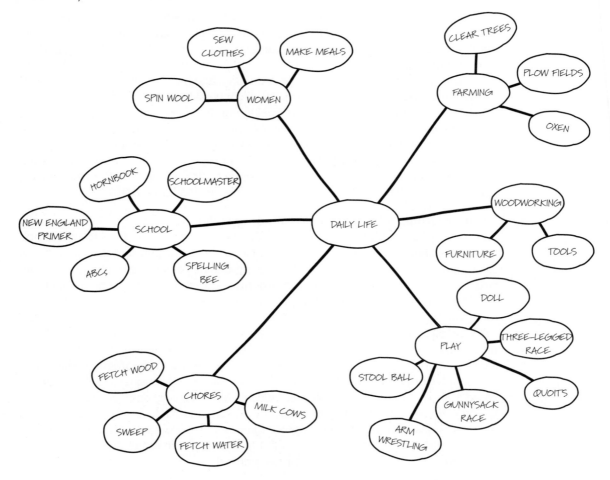

sation with a prompt like this: "As you think about the video, try to recall the different kinds of activities that made up daily life of the New England colonists."

The students then brainstorm details about the daily activities of early New England colonists. Their ideas are listed randomly on the chalkboard or a chart; the teacher probes and extends the students' suggestions as she or he finds it reasonable to do so. When the students have no more information to offer, the teacher asks them to organize the details into meaningful categories such as jobs, school, food, furniture, entertainment, religion, games, or any other label they suggest. The students' suggestions are placed at various points around the core to represent different categories of information. These points are referred to as *web strands.*

The details used by the students to support each web strand are called *strand supports.* The strand supports surround each web strand, organizing the important information. The students continue to classify and categorize ideas until a graphic representation similar to Figure 6–7 emerges. The map construction phase involves active scaffolding encounters as students must talk together in order to create and interpret the classification and categorization systems.

Sequential Graphic Organizers   The name of this graphic organizer is self explanatory; it arranges processes or events in steps or chronological order. Sequential graphic organizers are usually formed as a straight line; timelines, as discussed in Chapter 3, are good examples. Figure 6–8 shows a sequential graphic organizer similar to one drawn by a group of fifth graders to illustrate the steps its community follows to treat its water so it is safe to drink.

Cyclical Graphic Organizers   This variety of graphic organizer helps students visualize a series of connected events that occur in sequence but produce a repeated result. The months and seasons of a year, for example, demonstrate a cyclical process, as do the water cycle and the metamorphosis of a caterpillar. One cyclical process taught in most dynamic social studies classrooms is the practice of recycling. Help your students understand this process by first writing the word "recycling" on the

FIGURE 6–8
Sequential Graphic Organizer

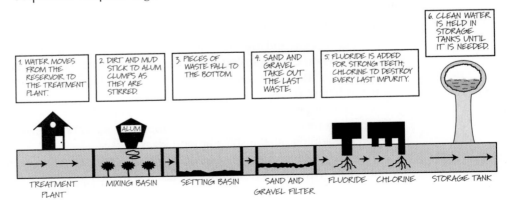

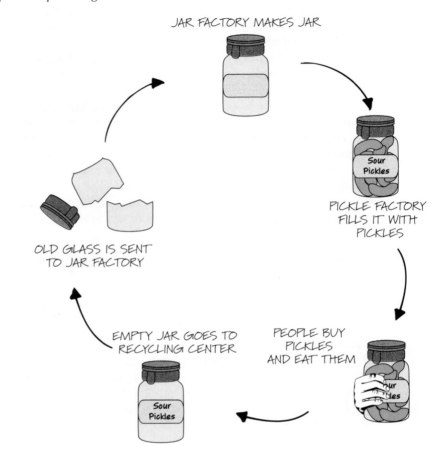

Chapter 6

FIGURE 6–9
Cycle Graphic Organizer

JAR FACTORY MAKES JAR

PICKLE FACTORY
FILLS IT WITH
PICKLES

OLD GLASS IS SENT
TO JAR FACTORY

Sour
Pickles

EMPTY JAR GOES TO
RECYCLING CENTER

PEOPLE BUY
PICKLES
AND EAT THEM

Sour
Pickles

chalkboard. Then have the students complete a cyclic graphic organizer as they learn about recycling. See Figure 6–9 for a sample.

Hierarchical Graphic Organizers   This organizational pattern centers on a main concept or process and the subcategories under it. For example, students in one fifth-grade classroom were learning about the three branches of the U.S. Government—the legislative, executive, and judicial. Their hierarchical diagram of the branches is shown in Figure 6–10.

Graphic organizers are elemental to knowledge construction. Clearly, you should offer opportunities to develop and use graphic organizers whenever you assist children in developing relationships among ideas.

Kathy Nguyen's example of using a graphic organizer can be useful as you plan to introduce them to your students. Please see the following case study.

FIGURE 6–10
Hierarchical Graphic Organizer

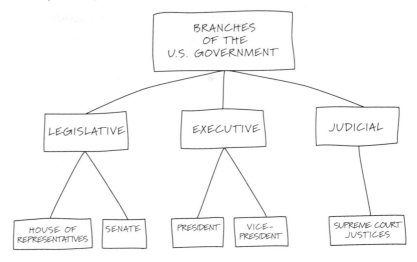

Inside an Active Classroom

After Ms. Nguyen's students finished reading *The Tongue-Cut Sparrow*, a Japanese folktale, she held a general discussion of the story and offered the following directions: "Your job today is going to be to organize the events of the story on a sheet of drawing paper. This is called a story map. A story map is a drawing that shows your personal version of the story. There are many ways you might make your story map. Some people like to draw pictures. Others prefer to use words or special charts and diagrams. Here are some samples."

Ms. Nguyen displayed story maps of simple, familiar stories the children should know, such as *Little Red Riding Hood* and *Three Billy Goats Gruff*. She shared the samples for only a short time, because she wanted students to refresh their understanding of what maps look like without developing the idea that their maps should look like the samples. She continued, "A story map can look any way you want it to look. Now, take some time to plan your own map with ideas you remembered from the story. But, please don't look back at the story right now."

After the students completed their story maps, Ms. Nguyen invited them to hold them up to share with each other. As the maps were shared, she used prompts to encourage the students to think more deeply about story characters, events, and story plot. For example, "Why did you decide to put an arrow pointing from the old man to the small chest?"

In general, there are two major ways teachers use graphic organizers in social constructivist classrooms:

- *Before instruction*—When introducing a new topic, teachers may use a graphic organizer to make visually clear the important concepts and ideas that will be covered. Teachers can also use a graphic organizer to get a good idea of the background knowledge the students have about the topic. K-W-L charts, as described earlier in this chapter, are good examples.
- *After instruction*—students construct individual or group organizers to organize knowledge and construct key concepts.

When introducing students to any graphic organizer, be sure to describe its purpose, model its use, and provide students with opportunities for guided practice. Then, when students become comfortable with the organizer, independent practice is suitable. In the end, you should encourage and assist students to create their own organizers. Figure 6–11 shows a variation of a sequential graphic organizer Jean Linton contrived when she and her fourth-grade classmates were given the assignment to write about a special talent or skill which might cause others to call them an "expert." Instead of using a single sheet of paper to build her sequential graphic organizer, Jean recalled the story of a unique hula she had created, jotted the major elements of the experience on a number of index cards, and arranged the index cards in order. Using the cards as "organizational handles," Jean then expanded on each and wrote her story. Figure 6–11 illustrates the steps of Jean's writing project. You can readily see how the graphic organizer helped Jean write a clear, descriptive account of the steps involved in creating her original hula.

Traditionally, graphic organizers like the ones described in this section have been drawn as large wall charts or illustrated in a student's notebook. Revisions were difficult; they could be made mainly by crossing out, erasing, or redrawing the graphic organizer. Now, with computer products such as *Kidspiration* and *Microsoft Word*, graphic organizers are no longer restricted by space and editing limitations. What's more, a number of websites also offer teachers and students a variety of graphic organizer generators. You might be interesting in checking the possibilities found at *www.teachnology.com/web_tools/graphic_org/*.

The Concept/Skill Application Phase

Concept/skill application is the final phase of the learning cycle. During this phase, students have the opportunity to apply and practice a new skill or concept through special projects or independent activities. Because application experiences often tend to focus on creativity and choice, they may include such things as group murals, story writing, construction projects, drama, puppetry, and music. In all of these activities, students will be asked to use what they have learned while constructing deeper meaning. The key to success in this phase of the learning cycle reflects that for all of social studies teaching—variety. Vary your activities to keep interest and motivation high. Because social studies topics differ in their complexity, some strategies will be

FIGURE 6–11
Using Cards to Organize a Sequential Graphic Organizer

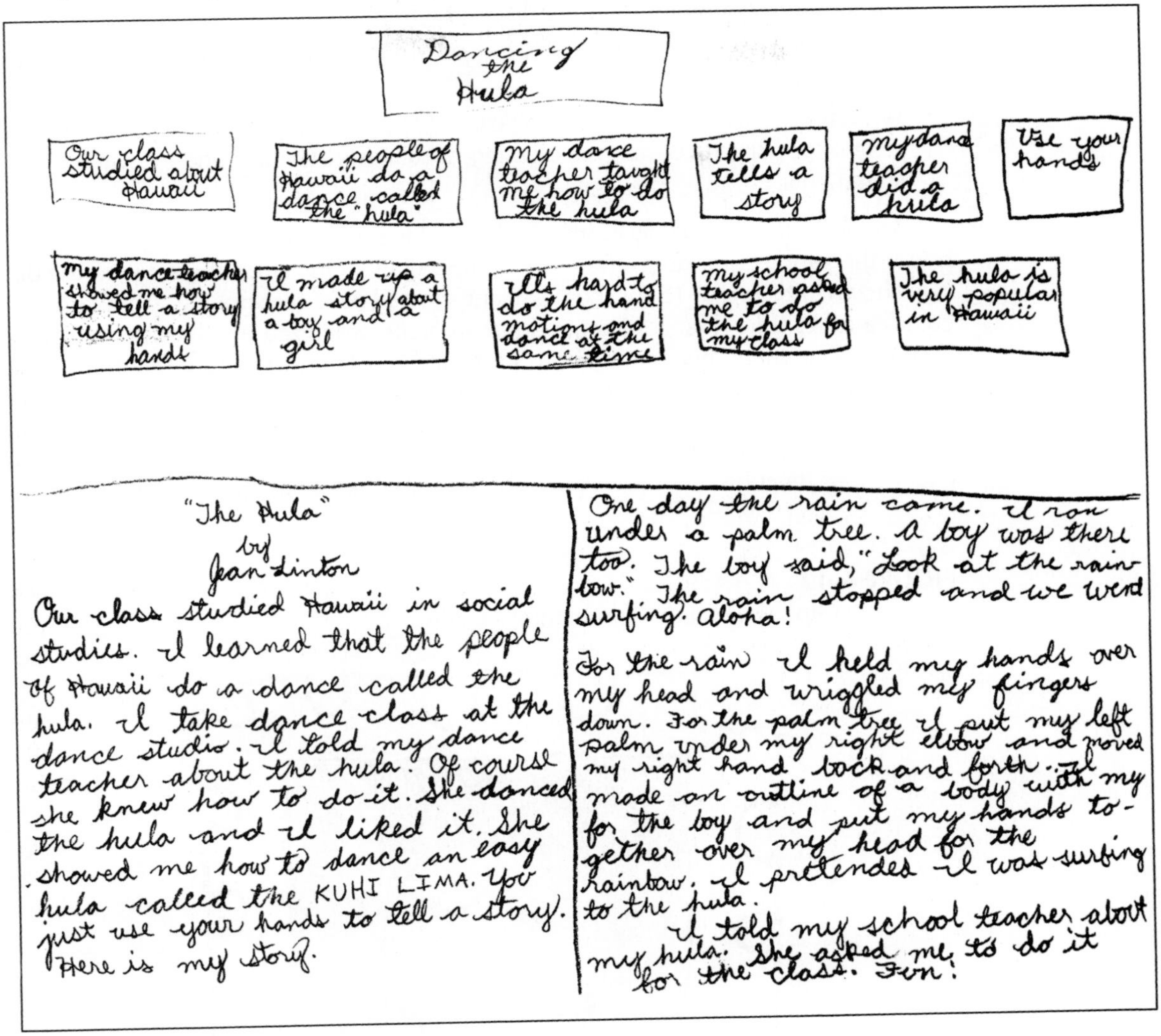

more useful than others for enriching, reinforcing, or extending the targeted concepts or skills. Some examples of concept/skills application strategies follow.

- Dramatize the firing of the "shot heard around the world."
- Bake and enjoy Harry S. Truman's favorite food, brownies.
- Give first-person accounts of famous historical events as if the students were the actual characters.

- Select geographic locations about which students would like to "cheer." Then design paper pennants with colors and illustrations that have some meaning to the location.
- Choose a favorite scene from a historical era to recreate in a three-dimensional model, or diorama.
- Write a historical period news magazine. Students write their articles in the style of popular news magazines using headlines, drawings, and eyewitness statements.

To illustrate, Bonnie Sullivan asked her students to design postage stamps to honor the various presidents they had been studying. One student submitted the design shown in Figure 6–12 for the president she had been researching, Abraham Lincoln. Another time, Ms. Sullivan and her students organized an "Inventor's Hall of Fame" to culminate their study of inventors and inventions. Figure 6–13 shows one of the plaques on display at the Hall of Fame.

By reading professional journals and organizing an idea file, you will begin to accumulate ideas for functional application experiences. Remember, though, that these experiences must be an integral part of the total direct instruction lesson, not extra

FIGURE 6–12
Postage Stamp Design as a Culminating Activity

"busy work" or a cutesy "icing on the cake" activity tacked on at the end. This final activity uses the concepts constructed by the students to discover potential relevance or usefulness. The following example shows how Gary Nicewinter used a creative application of written reports to culminate a class study of breads commonly associated with different cultures.

Written reports have wide acceptance as a culminating activity at all grade levels in social studies programs around the country. However, you cannot expect students to compose good written reports simply by announcing, "Write a report on Sitting Bull for next Tuesday," or handing out a list of topics related to the Civil War and assigning students to pick one and write a report about it. Assigning such tasks only frustrates many students and encourages them to copy every bit of information from a written resource or Internet site. Report writing itself isn't the problem, however. The real problem with social studies reports lies in our methods of assigning them. We need to show students how to investigate questions and communicate their findings, how to go beyond plagiarism to genuine communication. That's

FIGURE 6–13
"Hall of Fame" Plaque as a Culminating Activity

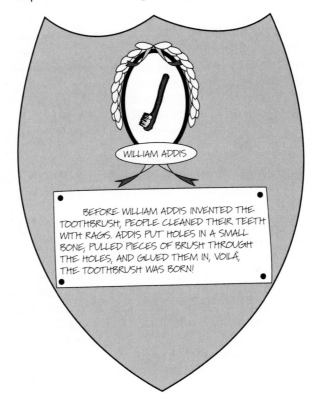

where scaffolding comes in. Good teachers know that all writing must be supported by models to imitate, so they offer their students quality children's literature as they develop into more mature writers. No matter what point they want to demonstrate about writing, there are good books to help make it clear. Good models produce good results. Gary Nicewinter understood this point, so he included a good book as he organized a learning sequence that culminated in a report-writing experience.

Inside an Active Classroom

When Mr. Nicewinter began his unit on bread, he showed his students an assortment of real bread, as well as pictures of bread and plastic models of bread: bagels, pita, baguette, paska, challah, tortillas, rye bread, cornbread, croissants, fry bread, injera, and chapatti, to name a few. Mr. Nicewinter did this not only to provide his students with a direct experience, but also to generate enthusiasm and interest, to prime the pump for the flurry of activity that naturally followed.

Mr. Nicewinter invited the children to taste the real breads and, as a class activity, had the children mark the country of origin of each on a large map. Mr. Nicewinter added another hands-on experience by giving the children small balls of prepared bread dough (available in supermarkets) and asked them to place the dough balls on sheets of aluminum foil labeled with their names. Before they put their dough into the oven, the children were encouraged to shape the balls any way they wished. The bread was baked according to directions, and the children discussed their sensory experiences as well as the physical changes they observed from start to finish. Everyone responded to this activity with enthusiasm and interest; a wealth of questions and comments followed the activity.

To begin the actual writing phase, Mr. Nicewinter formed committees around common topics of interest, which, after much discussion, were narrowed down to four: bread bakers and bakeries, bread from around the world, what bread is eaten with (condiments), and homemade bread. The children wrote on a piece of paper the two topics they would most like to pursue. Mr. Nicewinter then formed interest committees that would meet the next day.

The next day, Mr. Nicewinter assigned to each committee the task of writing its own information booklet on its chosen topic. He specified the form the writing would take, but the children would eventually determine the content. To familiarize the children with the form that their booklets were to take, Mr. Nicewinter brought to class a model of informational writing, *Bread, Bread, Bread* by Ann Morris (Lothrop, Lee, & Shepard). The book contains dazzling photographs and short descriptions of various breads being made around the world. As the class and Mr. Nicewinter surveyed the book together, they paid particular attention to the way the photographs and text were presented on each page. Mr. Nicewinter and the students agreed that their information pages would include a drawing and a sentence or two with some information about the drawing, just like the literature model.

The children worked on their bread books for about 3 days during social studies period. Most of the committees decided that their books should be about five pages long (one page for each child), but a few committees wrote more. To help the committees find information about bread, Mr. Nicewinter located suitable trade books and inserted bookmarks at the proper places. He could find no useful Internet sites for his young researchers. At the end of the first day, Mr. Nicewinter and the children sat in a circle with their papers and the books they had used to uncover information. They shared what they had done and how things had gone for them. Most had gotten as far as locating something they wanted to write about and starting their illustration. The second day was spent completing the illustrations and the associated text.

On the third day, Mr. Nicewinter talked to the children about book titles and discussed how the covers of several of the books the children had been reading contained illustrations that represented the main idea of the text. The children illustrated the covers of their own books, added titles, listed their names as authors, put the pages in order, and stapled them together. The committees shared their books with one another, and the final copies were ceremoniously added to the classroom library.

The "Bread From Around the World" committee compiled this book, along with appropriate illustrations, which they proudly titled *The Bread Book:*

Page 1: Navajos eat fry bread almost every day. It is fried in shortening, not baked.

Page 2: People from France eat baguettes. They are long loaves of bread with a thin golden crust.

Page 3: Paska is a traditional round Easter bread decorated with fancy dough. It is very special bread from Ukraine.

Page 4: Mexican people like to eat a flat bread called tortilla. Tortillas can be made from flour or corn. Some tortillas are spiced and flavored.

Page 5: Chapatti is bread from India. It is flat and round like a pancake. It is made without yeast.

The main thing about report writing is that, like all other culminating events, reports help bring about a sensible conclusion to a well-planned sequence of instructional events.

AFTERWORD

Children learn through a combination of physical and mental activity. They "mess about" and naturally want to get into or try out everything. They may come to elementary school knowing a little bit about a lot of things, but one quality they all share is a thirst for experiences that will help them find out more. When these enthusiastic, energetic youngsters come to school, they expect to learn about all that interests them in much the same way, through activity and involvement. They are not greatly interested in memorizing information or in confining activities such as completing ditto sheets or workbook pages. They want to try things out.

Helping elementary school students construct meaningful concepts is one of the foremost challenges confronting social studies teachers. A major part of this challenge is to help learners attach their backgrounds to the learning experience and to organize new information into appropriate schemata. As Piaget and Vygotsky emphasize, meaningful learning takes place only when learners are able to bridge the gap between the unknown and the known. To that end, this chapter has described the learning cycle as a system of instruction through which the teachers are able to effectively direct their students through the process of concept construction.

Developing a teaching plan is a complex professional responsibility involving a great deal of knowledge, hard work, and skill. As a new teacher, you may wonder whether the results are worth the effort. In effect, you may say, "Why bother? After all, the textbook and teacher's manual were written by experts in the field who really know social studies." To an extent, you are correct. Manuals can be helpful, especially for student or beginning teachers. As guides, though, they must be viewed as suggestions, not as prescriptions. You will probably want to start your career by using the teacher's guide closely, but as you gain experience, you will adapt it to the changing needs of the different groups of children you teach each year. The constructivist approach described in this chapter allows you the flexibility to constantly change your teaching approach within a framework of sound planning.

REFERENCES

Ausubel, D. P. (1961). In defense of verbal learning. *Educational Theory, 2,* 16.

Bodrova, E., & Leong, D. J. (1996). *Tools of the mind: A Vygotskian approach to early childhood education.* Upper Saddle River, NJ: Merrill/Prentice Hall.

Boyer, E. L. (1982). Seeing the connectedness of things. *Educational Leadership, 39,* 384.

Brooks, J. G., & Brooks, M. G. (1993). *In search of understanding: The case for constructivist classrooms.* Alexandria, VA: Association for Supervision and Curriculum Development.

Bruner, J. S., Olver, R. R., & Greenfield, P. M. (1966). *Studies in cognitive growth.* New York: Wiley.

Dewey, J. (1933). *How we think.* Boston: D. C. Heath.

Gallimore, R., & Tharp, R. (1990). Teaching mind in society: Teaching, schooling, and literate discourse. In L. C. Moll (Ed.), *Vygotsky and education.* Cambridge: Cambridge University Press.

Hunter, M. (1982). *Mastery teaching.* El Segundo, CA: TIP Publications.

Ormrod, J. E. (2000). *Educational psychology: Developing learners.* Upper Saddle River, NJ: Merrill.

Piaget, J. (1948/1973). *To understand is to invent.* New York: Grossman.

Piaget, J. (1952). *The origins of intelligence in children*. New York: International Universities Press.

Piaget, J. (1964). Three lectures. In R. E. Ripple & U. N. Rockcastle (Eds.), *Piaget rediscovered*. Ithaca, NY: Cornell University Press.

Piaget, J. (1971). *Understanding causality*. New York: Norton.

Ramirez, J., Yuen, S., & Ramey, D. (1991). *Executive summary: Longitudinal study of structured English immersion strategy, early-exit, late-exit transitional bilingual education programs for language minority children*. San Mateo, CA: Aguirre International.

Remy, R. C. (1990). The need for science/technology/society in the social studies. *Social Education, 54,* 204.

Ryan, K., Burkholder, S., & Phillips, D. H. (1983). *The workbook*. Upper Saddle River, NJ: Merrill/Prentice Hall.

Wood, D., Bruner, J. S., & Ross, G. (1976). The role of tutoring in problem-solving. *Journal of Child Psychology and Psychiatry, 17,* 89–100.

Cooperative Learning:
Student-Assisted Social Constructivism

WHAT DOES COOPERATIVE LEARNING LOOK LIKE?

After motivating his students by relating the topic of "Natural Landscapes in the United States" to their lives, Ashish Pasricha divided the class into groups of four, assigned heterogeneously by ability level. He called these base groups *Study Buddies*. To start the lesson, each Study Buddies team member drew a slip of paper out of a box. Written on the slips was any of four elements of the natural landscape found in the United States—forests, prairies, mountains, and deserts. Each Study Buddies member who drew a slip of paper with *forests* on it left her or his base group and joined with students from other Study Buddies base groups to form a specialized research team to focus solely on the study of forests. Mr. Pasricha directed this specialized research team to a private work area called the *Forest Investigation Station*. At the same time, the students who selected the other natural landscape features regrouped themselves into specialized research teams and came together at their private investigation stations to work on the topics of prairies, mountains, or deserts. Therefore, each Study Buddies group sent out one member to each of four specialized investigation stations so they could become an "expert" on one of the four landscape features found in the United States.

Displayed at each investigation station was a large sheet of chart paper with the title of each focused investigation written clearly at the top: *Forests, Prairies, Mountains,* and *Deserts.* This established the beginning stage of a conventional instructional procedure known as K-W-L. The widely used K-W-L procedure helps activate students' prior knowledge by first asking them to think about what they already

Know about the topic or problem; next, students (collaborating in small groups or as a whole class) reflect on **W**hat additional information they need to know to understand the topic more fully or to solve the problem; and finally, the students collect, organize, and record applicable information to show what they have **L**earned. Mr. Pasricha started the K-W-L procedure rolling in his classroom by asking the students at each investigation station to talk about what they already knew about their particular landscape element and to jot down their thoughts in the K column on their charts: "What does the geographic term (forest, prairie, mountain, or desert) tell us? What scene comes into your mind as you think about your landscape feature?"

Mr. Pasricha circulated among the groups and used probing questions to keep ideas flowing, to help students think through relationships within the data, and to challenge several of their contributions, especially those that were misguided: "Where did you learn that?" "Are you able to prove that?" "Can you be sure about that?" Despite his efforts, a few imprecise responses dotted the charts. Mr. Pasricha was not overly concerned and did not point out the inaccuracies, for he knew that his students would clear up their errors as they researched their topics more fully. In addition to his well-timed probes and prompts, Mr. Pasricha encouraged students to talk among themselves and to ask questions of one another as a way of thinking through the details. In Mr. Pasricha's classroom, peer talk is not discouraged; it is considered a powerful tool for learning.

After each group completed and shared its K lists, Mr. Pasricha held up an informational book on each landscape element and reminded the students that informational books provide material we often need or want either to verify what we already know or to expand our knowledge base. Mr. Pasricha is convinced that the surest way to excite students about informational books is to read aloud, so he shared a short paragraph from each book. As he read, Mr. Pasricha shared pictures, used his voice expressively to indicate interest in certain facts, and maintained eye contact with the students as much as possible. He encouraged each group to listen for words and sentences that held the most promise for their research efforts: "As I read this short paragraph, think about what makes it a good resource for your group." Next, Mr. Pasricha asked his students to mull over how the books might be helpful in addressing questions they have developed about their landscape elements—things they already knew and wished to confirm as well as things that puzzled them. The students wrote their questions in a second column on the chart, labeled *What We Need to Learn*. For example, the prairie group started with these questions: "Where did the name *prairie* come from?" "Other than the Midwest, where can prairies be found in the United States?" and "Is wheat the only crop that can be grown on prairies?"

Mr. Pasricha had prepared each group with abundant resources to help them address the last part of the K-W-L process—finding related information and organizing the data for some useful purpose. Using their own questions as a guide, Mr. Pasricha's students went right to work locating relevant information from their textbooks, informational books, videos, Internet sites, and other resources available to them at their specialized research centers. Each group uncovered a number of interesting facts about its landscape element and filled the L column with new and fascinating data. For example, the *prairie* group discovered that the French arrived in Illinois and Indiana before the English. When they saw the endless sea of grass as high as a person's head teeming with flowers, they had a word for it: *prairie,* their name for a meadow. They also went back to the K column to see if any of their prior knowledge was inaccurate and rewrote inaccurate statements to correct them. Finally, Mr. Pasricha asked the students to revisit the W column to see if there were any questions they were unable to answer. Thinking together, the students talked about how they might find these answers or where they might look to get the answers.

Mr. Pasricha fully understands that social studies research should not end simply with students compiling a storehouse of facts. At some point, students must use strategies for thinking through the content and doing something meaningful with it. Productive contexts for applying social studies content are numerous and include story or report writing, composing lyrics for a song, taking part in a debate, expressing oneself in an art medium such as an illustration or a mural, and initiating and carrying out a community action project. Keeping this principle in mind, Mr. Pasricha directed the specialized research teams to study their charted data, identify relationships, and propose a tentative plan for reporting the data back to their base groups. The students worked cooperatively and drafted paragraphs based on the information from their charts, revising and editing what they had drafted.

Finally, each specialized research group returned from their investigation station to their Study Buddies groups to share what they had learned. The students discussed their assigned landscape features, presented a summary of the information uncovered at their investigation stations, and talked about how they might represent all the information on a diorama.

To help the students make their dioramas, Mr. Pasricha had precut construction paper in 12-inch squares, a different color for each of the landscape elements. To make the dioramas, students folded each corner to the opposite corner and then cut along one fold to the center as indicated in Figure 7–1A. The free flaps were then overlapped and glued; the name of the landscape element was written at the bottom (see Figure 7–1B). Next, students made three-dimensional scenery for the diorama (see Figure 7–1C). Finally, all four dioramas were stapled or glued together to form a panorama of the landscape elements commonly found in the United States (see Figure 7–1D). After completing the dioramas, Mr. Pasricha invited the students from another class to visit while his students used their dioramas to share what they had learned.

FIGURE 7–1
Landscape Feature Project

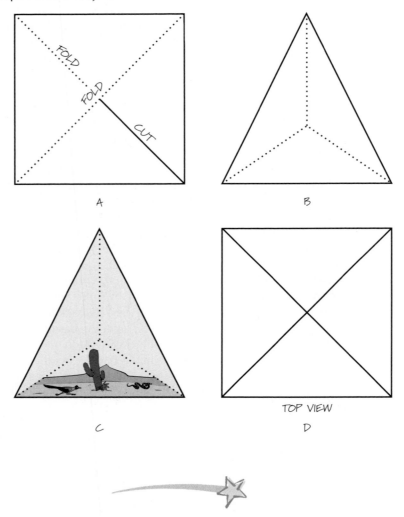

In Chapter 6, we took a close look at the learning cycle, an instructional model that spells out the teacher's responsibility for scaffolding students' learning experiences in dynamic social studies classrooms. In this chapter, by contrast, Mr. Pasricha introduces us to a second major model intended to bring about learning in the social constructivist classroom—*cooperative learning*. Mr. Pasricha chose cooperative learning as his primary instructional strategy because he believes it to be a highly promising method by which social studies teachers can concurrently achieve both academic and social objectives. Cooperative learning, sometimes called *collaborative*

TEXT SET 12

Theme: Deserts

Jean Craighead George's **One Day in the Desert** (HarperTrophy) explains how the animal and human inhabitants of the Sonoran Desert of Arizona, including a mountain lion, roadrunner, coyote, tortoise, kangaroo rat, ringtailed cat, swift fox, elf owl, and members of the Papago Indian tribe adapt to and survive the desert's merciless heat during a record-breaking July day. A terrible thunderstorm causes a flash flood—some animals will survive and some will not. This is a wonderful story about the fragile connection between all living things and the unpredictable ways of nature.

Joanna Cole's and Bruce Degen's **The Magic School Bus Gets All Dried Up: A Book About Deserts** (Scholastic) invites us to accompany Ms. Frizzle and board the Magic School Bus as it takes the entire class on a hot, but informative trip to the desert.

Gail Gibbons' **Deserts** (Holiday House) is a fact-filled book about characteristics of deserts around the world. She describes the animals, natural resources, and the flora and fauna that thrive in this harsh environment.

Kristin Joy Pratt-Serafini's **Saguaro Moon: A Desert Journal** (Dawn) informs us about the Sonoran Desert of Arizona through the journal entries of a girl named Megan, who recently moved to Arizona. The book contains beautiful full-page watercolors in the bright colors of the desert.

Robin Bernard's **Deserts: Interactive Geography Kit** (Scholastic) explores the deserts of the world through this incredible geography kit. Children will find interesting information, an array of hands-on activities, map reading, folktales, reader's theater script, art activities, book links, and two big colorful posters.

TRY THIS

Become a teacher-researcher-author. Using the books in this text set as a model, try writing an illustrated storybook about one of the remaining natural landscape features found in the United States—forests, prairies, or mountains.

learning, occurs whenever students interact in pairs or larger groups to share knowledge and experiences. In Mr. Pasricha's social studies classroom, all students work together toward a common goal, interacting with peers within learning communities to complete short- and long-term projects. Mr. Pasricha is convinced that his students learn more and learn better when they are working together to solve problems or construct concepts.

WHAT IS COOPERATIVE LEARNING?

Cooperative learning is an instructional model in which small teams, each with students of different levels of ability, use a variety of learning activities to improve their understanding of any social studies topic. Each member of a cooperative learning team is responsible for learning what is taught and for helping teammates learn, thus creating an environment for social constructivism. Because students work together to achieve common success, cooperative learning is often characterized by the old saying, "All for one and one for all." Cooperative learning specialists refer to this kind of teamwork as *positive interdependence*. Think of positive interdependence as the type of joint effort we find on a basketball court when one player passes the ball to another who in turn slam dunks the ball through the hoop. The actions of both team members were independent of each other (they both did completely different things), but the points could not have been scored for the team without the actions of both. This spirit is what is characterized as positive interdependence in cooperative learning, too—two or more students work together on a learning task, coordinating their efforts to achieve team success.

Cooperative learning, then, can truly be considered a prime vehicle of social constructivism. By *social* we mean that participants are active and contributing members of a group that achieves success through their cooperative efforts. As *constructivists,* we mean that the groups are involved in the systematic pursuit of knowledge and in efforts to apply their knowledge in meaningful situations.

HOW DOES COOPERATIVE LEARNING WORK?

Cooperative learning involves a great deal more than simply placing your students into groups and telling them to work together as a team. Cooperative learning is part of classroom management, a process that involves gaining and maintaining the mutual assistance and support of students in learning activities. To use it effectively, you need to teach your students to work effectively in groups. The outcome can be an incredibly dynamic learning environment that can be productive and enjoyable for everyone.

Working in groups, however, is often a real challenge for students and teachers. Sometimes it goes smoothly, but it can also turn out to be a disaster. The key to increasing the smooth and productive times is to examine the major factors that can influence group functioning. Some of the major factors responsible for influencing the values and behaviors prerequisite to cohesive, supportive cooperative groups in the classroom are:

- following directions
- keeping focused on the task
- completing responsibilities on time

- asking for help when you need it
- listening attentively to others
- contributing ideas when you have them
- considering the ideas and feelings of others
- offering encouragement to others
- making sure everyone has a chance to participate

Selma Wasserman (1989) recalls her frustrations with moving sixth-grade children into responsible cooperative groups when many had not had the opportunity to acquire these skills:

> The first weeks of so-called "cooperative" group work was anything but. All manner of uncooperative behavior emerged. . . . They couldn't focus on the tasks; they didn't care about each other; they didn't understand "what they were supposed to do." In the absence of clear and specific teacher direction (i.e., "Do this now and do it THIS way!"), they fell apart. (p. 204)

Wasserman described her biggest disappointment in watching her students become unruly: "My biggest disappointment was not that the children were unable to function in . . . sophisticated, mature and self-disciplined ways. . . . The killing blow was that the children wanted, asked, begged for a return to 'the way we did it in Grade 5'" (p. 203).

At that point Wasserman realized she needed to help the children learn the skills required to function as thoughtful, responsible, cooperative learners. She needed to provide experiences for students to gain practice in those skills. This was not an easy task either, for as she admits, "It may be a lot easier to teach children to read and spell than it is to teach them to behave cooperatively . . . with each other" (p. 204).

To engage students in cooperative learning, then, you must help them gain an understanding of themselves as group members and of what it takes to function effectively in a group. You do this by making interpersonal work skills an important learning goal.

This is good news—cooperative learning skills can be taught and learned just like any other skill. In addition, like any other skill, you must exercise great patience and offer meaningful opportunities to help children learn. It may be October or November before you can recognize any major shift in the way your students approach group work, but you must follow the children's lead, never moving so fast that students are overwhelmed by your efforts.

When you target a special social skill to work on, it may be most productive to begin with game-type tasks, especially those where team members must cooperate to reach a common goal. A game I have found to be particularly useful is *Puzzle Squares,* a description of which follows. Fortunately, many books and professional magazines contain suggestions for similar cooperative games.

As you locate and offer additional activities designed to help students acquire important social skills through pleasurable cooperative games, you will need to keep several important suggestions in mind:

1. *Define the skill clearly and specifically.*   Be sure students understand their responsibilities as distinctly as possible. For example, "When I say, 'talk in quiet voices,' I mean that you will need to use your 'foot voices.'" You can then show your students a 12-inch ruler to demostrate how far a "foot voice" should carry.

2. *Ask students to characterize the skill.*   A version of the *T-chart* can effectively demonstrate what is meant by skill characterization (see Figure 7–3). To construct a T-chart, draw a horizontal bar and write the skill above it in question form. Draw a vertical line down from the middle of the bar. On one side, list student responses to the question, "What would this skill look like?" On the other side, list their responses to the question, "What would this skill sound like?" You then model the skill until all students have a clear idea of how its correct performance looks and sounds.

3. *Practice and reinforce the skill.*   You cannot teach students to work cooperatively with a single lesson or experience. Growth occurs over time with meaningful practice and effective reinforcement. One teacher's effort to help her students acquire the skill of "encouraging others to contribute" is described in the following example from Barbara Wertz's classroom.

Classroom Activity

PUZZLE SQUARES

Materials

1. Cut out five heavy tagboard squares, each about 5 inches square.
2. Cut each square into three segments using the patterns in Figure 7–2.
3. Scramble the 15 pieces and put them into a large manila envelope.
4. Repeat the procedure for each set of five children in your classroom.

Goal

Each child in a group must use the puzzle pieces to complete a 5-inch square consisting of only three pieces.

FIGURE 7–2
Puzzle Squares

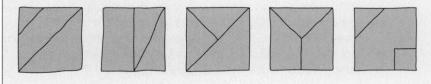

Procedure

1. Place children into groups of five and have them select a group leader.
2. Give each group leader one of the envelopes containing 15 puzzle pieces.
3. On signal, the group leader opens the envelope and randomly passes three puzzle pieces to each group member.
4. Direct the students to examine their puzzle pieces and try to make a square from them. Signal the students to begin. Most groups will complete this task within 20 minutes; therefore, allow the proper amount of working time. If the students discover their segments will not form a perfect square, they may exchange pieces with other members of their group, but only with these rules:

   a. No talking. The game must be played in complete silence.
   b. No eye signals, hand signals, or gestures. Communication of any kind is discouraged.
   c. No taking another puzzle piece from another player, unless he or she first offers it to you.

   When the time is up and several puzzles have been completed, discuss questions such as, "How did you feel when you first started working with the group? Did you find it difficult to cooperate with others as you kept working? What were some of the problems that your group experienced? How could they be resolved? What feelings did you have toward the other members of your group? What made you feel that way?"

FIGURE 7–3
T-Chart

Skill: Getting into your group quickly and quietly	
Looks Like	**Sounds Like**
• wait for a signal to go	• silence
• gather all materials	• quiet
• stand up and push chair in smoothly	• peacefulness
• walk slowly and softly to your group area	• stillness
	• noiseless movements
• wait for all members to arrive before you start your work	• hushed voices

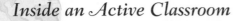

Inside an Active Classroom

Barbara Wertz formed eight three-member cooperative groups, each of which was given a short task to complete. Ms. Wertz handed out five teddy bear counters to each student. The students were directed to place a counter in a container at the center of their table each time they spoke while working on the group's task. When a student had "spent" all her or his counters, she or he could speak no longer.

When each team member's counters were "spent," each member of the group received another set of five teddy bear counters and everybody was ready to start again. A few students became quite flustered when their five counters were spent and a strong need to talk came up! But, they playfully placed their hands over their mouths and followed the rules of the activity until they received a new set of teddy bears.

This type of game usually works well with elementary school students and needs to be used only once or twice to get the message across (although first graders can become strongly attached to teddy bear counters and are sometimes reluctant to give them up). Can you imagine this method being used for a student or faculty meeting on campus? Five teddy bear counters are handed to each student or professor when they come in. When they speak . . .

If we are to prepare students for cooperative learning in the social studies classroom, we must first provide them with frequent and meaningful opportunities to function as group members. Rather than lecturing students about appropriate group behaviors, they must practice the skills that will enable them to fulfill their roles in cooperative learning groups.

WHAT ARE THE MAIN FEATURES OF COOPERATIVE LEARNING?

Although most pre- and in-service teachers are aware that cooperative learning is quite different than competitive learning, managing the procedures required to implement the model are much less known. For that reason, even expert teachers often cringe at the suggestion of managing cooperative group efforts. Consequently, you can imagine the anxiety most novices connect to the prospect of using cooperative learning strategies in their social studies classrooms. However, successful management of cooperative learning is not as difficult as it may initially appear. Cooperative group management simply involves thinking of and planning for the major procedures that teachers must follow to have a successful learning experience: (1) determining group composition, (2) selecting a cooperative learning strategy, and (3) choosing a reward system.

Determining Group Composition

From personal experiences in elementary school and in college classrooms, I have found that it is best for teachers to wait until at least October or November before plunging students into cooperative group work if they have never before experienced it. This period gives teachers a chance to get to know their students and to help forge a community classroom spirit. After about 6–8 weeks of teacher-directed social studies lessons interspersed with activities designed to instill group values and responsibilities, students will more eagerly and ably receive the idea of cooperative group work. A commonly faulty first-time approach to using cooperative learning by novice and experienced teachers alike, though, is to begin by allowing their students work in groups of their own picking. Of course, the students will undoubtedly choose to work with their friends, and the groups will not be productive. Teachers soon learn that assigning team members must be more deliberately planned and that a major guiding principle must be to avoid having close friends in the same group.

There is no magic recipe to help all teachers arrive at the ideal number of students for a cooperative learning group. You will need to experiment to see what works best for you. From my own experience, I have found that the larger the group, the more skilled the members must be for the group to function well. Therefore, the best advice is to think small. Initial cooperative learning groups for primary-grade children or older children with little prior group-work experience should be formed of pairs, or *dyads*. Primary-grade students work best in pairs because young children

Sometimes cooperative groups can be as small as two members; oftentimes dyads are the most effective beginning cooperative groups.

more easily reach agreement with only one other person. By grade 3 or 4, as the children become more skilled at working together, you might assign them heterogeneously to three-member teams. Students through middle school can function as quartets, but they need much success working in dyads and trios before they can work in groups of four. Freiberg and Driscoll (1992) have examined the common group sizes found in elementary school social studies classrooms and detail some of the benefits of each:

> *Two-person group.* This size promotes a relationship and generally ensures participation. This is a good way to begin with inexperienced "groupies" (students who have not been grouped before). In a pair, students gain experience and skill before working in a complex group arrangement.

> *Three-person group.* This arrangement allows for a changing two-person majority. Participation is very likely because no one wants to be the odd person out. Roles in this size group can be those of speaker, listener, and observer, and learners can experience all three roles in a brief period of time. This size group is appropriate for creating descriptions, organizing data, drawing conclusions, and summarizing ideas.

> *Four-person group.* A four-person group will likely have different perspectives. This size is small enough that each member will have a chance to express himself or herself and can be comfortable doing so. Often this size groups [sic] emerges as two pairs when opinions are expressed. A group of four people requires basic communication and cooperation skills, but offers ideal practice for learning group process. (p. 277)

Determining group size will mean carefully studying your students and the maturity they have developed through informal and formal group experiences. A common mistake many teachers make is to have students work in larger groups before they have the necessary skills.

In addition to group size, the actual "coming together" of cooperative learning groups begins with the careful assignment of students to teams. For most tasks, you should use heterogeneous grouping, or placing high, middle, and low achievers within the same learning group. A useful technique is to arrange your students according to ability level and assign numbers according to how many teams you want. Figure 7–4 illustrates one teacher's heterogeneous breakdown of students into four-member teams. Darcee is the top-ranked student in this classroom while Donald is the lowest, so they are both members of Team 1. Warren and Robin are next at both extremes, so they are together in Team 2. In like manner, the rest of the class is divided into teams.

Notice that even though the teacher carefully divided the teams on the basis of ability, minor adjustments needed to be made as each group's composition was examined more closely: "Are all the talkative (or quiet) children in one group? Have I put together children who act up? Did I balance gender, race, and ethnic factors? In order to complete the group's goal, must I add someone with a special skill (e.g., to draw an illustration)?"

To assure success, then, teachers must organize their two-, three-, and four-member groups so that students are mixed as heterogeneously as possible, both with an eye on academic abilities and on ethnic backgrounds, race, and gender. In all cases, teachers should never create groups based on friendship or cliques. When

FIGURE 7–4
Establishing Heterogeneous Groups

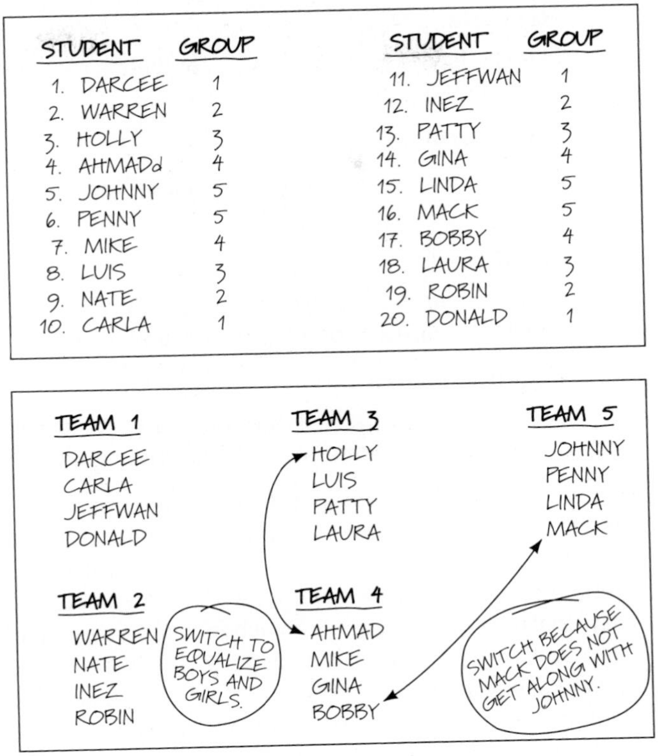

STUDENT	GROUP		STUDENT	GROUP
1. DARCEE	1		11. JEFFWAN	1
2. WARREN	2		12. INEZ	2
3. HOLLY	3		13. PATTY	3
4. AHMADd	4		14. GINA	4
5. JOHNNY	5		15. LINDA	5
6. PENNY	5		16. MACK	5
7. MIKE	4		17. BOBBY	4
8. LUIS	3		18. LAURA	3
9. NATE	2		19. ROBIN	2
10. CARLA	1		20. DONALD	1

TEAM 1
DARCEE
CARLA
JEFFWAN
DONALD

TEAM 3
HOLLY
LUIS
PATTY
LAURA

TEAM 5
JOHNNY
PENNY
LINDA
MACK

TEAM 2
WARREN
NATE
INEZ
ROBIN

SWITCH TO EQUALIZE BOYS AND GIRLS.

TEAM 4
AHMAD
MIKE
GINA
BOBBY

SWITCH BECAUSE MACK DOES NOT GET ALONG WITH JOHNNY.

groups are notably heterogeneous, students are more inclined to work together productively and will achieve success in ways and at levels that are not often found in other instructional strategies. They also tend to become more tolerant of diverse points of view and to reflect more deeply on others' thoughts and feelings.

When groups are first established, it is a good idea to give students a chance to assign individual responsibilities and to choose a group name. Students take pleasure in selecting group names because it is "cool" and because it gives them an opportunity to control an initial decision-making facet of group operation.

Different tasks call for different roles. You will need to shift team roles as the demands of unique group tasks change from assignment to assignment. Some frequently used cooperative group roles include the following:

Group Captain

Reads the task aloud to the group. Check to make sure everyone is listening. Makes the task as clear as possible. Coordinates the group's efforts; provides leadership.

Materials Manager

Gathers, distributes, and collects all research books and other supplies.

Recorder

Fills out forms and writes down and edits the group's report. Shares the group's result with the class.

Illustrator

Draws any pictures, graphs, charts, or figures that help communicate the group's findings.

Monitor

Keeps the group focused on the task. Makes sure each member of the group can explain the answer of information and tell why it was selected.

Coach

Sees that everyone has an equal chance to participate; offers praise and encouragement to team members as they work.

How long should cooperative learning groups stay together? Cooperative learning groups vary in duration, depending on the task to be accomplished. Some groups are together only a short time—until they complete a special project, study new material, or solve a problem. Others change throughout the day (dyads, for example), especially those formed quickly when teachers ask questions that have numerous possible answers (for example, listing the possible reasons why Judaism has been able to survive and prosper over the years). Others, called *base groups,* stay together for an entire year or semester, providing a means by which students can provide a sense of support and belonging to each other.

Selecting a Cooperative Learning Strategy

Teachers interested in using cooperative learning in their dynamic social studies classrooms can choose from among a wide variety of approaches. The following are examples of specific, tried-and-true strategies you might find useful.

Think-Pair-Share Discussions

This is one of the simplest cooperative learning techniques. The teacher stops at natural break points during a lesson and poses a problem. The students are given a short time to *think* about the problem by themselves. The teacher then tells the students to *pair* up: "Turn to your partner and . . . " (think about what makes the San Joaquin Valley a good place for farming, predict where the Mississippi River begins, or tell why the Cheyenne held Medicine Dances, for example). The teacher gives the students a minute or two to talk together and discuss their ideas. The teacher may ask a few groups to *share* their ideas with the whole class, but all groups are not required to share each time.

Think-Pair-Square

Like Think-Pair-Share, the teacher poses a problem and then the students *think* about it and *share* their thoughts with a partner. Instead of then sharing with the entire class, however, two dyads join together and *share* together as a foursome, or a *square*.

Numbered Heads Together

Numbered Heads Together entails a simple four-step course of action:

1. The teacher divides the class into groups of four and assigns a number to each student: 1, 2, 3, or 4.
2. The teacher asks a question related to a topic under study. For example, while studying Medieval England, one teacher asked, "What were some of the responsibilities of the women inside a castle?"
3. The teacher tells the students to "put your heads together" and work until she gives them a signal to stop.
4. The teacher calls a number (1, 2, 3, or 4). The students with that number raise their hands, become the groups' representatives, and can be called on by the teacher to respond.

Kagan (1989) reports that positive interaction and individual accountability are both included in the Numbered Heads Together technique since the high achievers share answers because they know their number might not be called, and they want their team to do well. The lower achievers also listen carefully because they know their number might be called. Therefore, students work together and help one another find answers, and all students learn what is being studied.

Jigsaw

Jigsaw is a cooperative learning technique developed by Elliot Aronson and his colleagues (1978). The process starts when the teacher assigns students heterogeneously to groups of four, called their *home group*. Each home group works on content material the teacher has broken down into sections. Each home group member is responsible for one of the sections.

Members of the different home groups who are responsible for the same sections leave their home groups and meet in *expert groups* to study and discuss their specialized sections. These students then return to their original home groups and take turns sharing with their teammates about their respective sections.

To better understand the Jigsaw technique, let's see how it is used in Jack Emerson's social studies classroom. Mr. Emerson and his fifth graders use Jigsaw frequently in social studies. To introduce the activity, Mr. Emerson divided his students into home groups of four members each. The home groups followed this procedure for a lesson on Helen Keller:

Inside an Active Classroom

1. The class started out with five home groups, each consisting of four members.

2. Mr. Emerson gave each home group member a sheet of writing paper with a different-colored adhesive dot (red, yellow, blue, green) at the top. The dots signified membership in different expert groups.

3. Students left their home groups and went to a section of the room designated by sheets of colored construction paper that matched their dots, and joined the other members of their expert groups. Mr. Emerson had four expert groups, each focused on a different aspect of the life of Helen Keller: Helen's childhood, Helen's early accomplishments, Helen's adult life, and Helen's influence on history.

4. While in their expert groups the students studied the contents of several resources and selected important information, becoming "experts" on that part of Helen Keller's life. Finally, they summarized the information on their writing paper so it could be used to teach the members of their home groups about what they learned. The experts then returned to their home groups, so there was an expert on every section in each home group.

5. Every expert shared information on his or her part of Helen Keller's life with other members of the home group. Because students were able to learn about other parts of Helen Keller's life only by listening carefully to their teammates, they were motivated to attend to one another's work.

6. Each home group planned a special presentation to share its collective learning about Helen Keller.

Pick Your Spot

Pick Your Spot is a useful cooperative learning technique that helps students to think about and share their preferences or choices on a variety of issues or topics in social studies. Developed by Ellis and Whalen (1990), the strategy is comprised of the following four steps:

1. Ask the students a question from which they are to select an answer from among alternatives. For example: "What is the one national symbol that best reminds us that we are a nation of free people?" or "Which former president would be most able to lead our country from its troubles today—George Washington, Abraham Lincoln, Franklin D. Roosevelt, or John F. Kennedy?"

2. Identify "spots" in the room that offer alternatives. Word or picture cards attached to the wall can identify alternatives for the national symbols such as "The American Flag," "The Bald Eagle," "The Liberty Bell," "The Statue of Liberty," or "The Star Spangled Banner." Ask students to quickly pick a spot and quietly congregate there.

Constructivist teachers must be skillful not only in selecting the most useful graphic organizer for a particular topic, but also in stimulating the children's thinking and reasoning.

3. Tell students at each spot to discuss their choice to see how many good reasons they can generate for their position. Have a large sheet of chart paper available so students can record their responses.

4. After allowing sufficient time to build a strong case, call on one student from each group to share the group's results with the rest of the class. After each group has reported, ask if any students would like to convert and pick a new spot. It they do, ask which argument persuaded them. Including questions or challenges from other groups can expand this step.

Student Teams—Achievement Divisions (STAD)

Robert Slavin (1995) developed STAD, one of the most popular of all cooperative learning approaches used in social studies classrooms today. The STAD process starts immediately after the students have either uncovered or been presented important social studies content. Then, the class is divided into teams of mixed ability, gender, and ethnicity. Four-member teams are ideal, but five can also work effectively. The teacher calculates a base score, or individual learning expectation (ILE), for each team member. This score is computed by averaging the student's grades or test scores from previous work. The ILE represents the student's average level of performance.

FIGURE 7–5
Awarding Individual Points

QUIZ RESULT	POINTS EARNED
PERFECT SCORE	3 POINTS
10 OR MORE POINTS ABOVE ILE SCORE	3 POINTS
5–9 POINTS ABOVE ILE SCORE	2 POINTS
1–4 POINTS ABOVE ILE SCORE	1 POINT
BELOW ILE SCORE	0 POINTS

The teacher then distributes study sheets that help students focus on the important social studies content. The study sheets can include questions, outlines, charts, hierarchies, and the like. Students work together in their teams to prepare for quizzes that are taken individually, just as in traditional classrooms. Based on quiz scores, each team member can earn from zero to three points for the group. Figure 7–5 shows how to award points by comparing the student's current test score to his or her ILE score. As you can see, every student has an equal chance to earn the maximum number of points for the team, and every student, not just the most able, has reason to work hard. Slavin feels that students should be judged on their own abilities, and not compared to others.

Each week the team earning the greatest number of points is declared the winner. All team accomplishments can be recognized in a newsletter; with a certificate, a group photo on a "wall of fame," or a button to wear around school; or with special privileges. The teams should be changed every few weeks so all class members have a chance to work with each other. Likewise, ILE scores should be recomputed every 2 weeks by averaging grades on recent tests with the old base score.

These are among the most popular of all techniques of cooperative learning. As you search the professional literature, you will discover variations of these and many new ones. Like Gerald Livingston in the following example, you might also someday create a cooperative learning technique you can call all your own. Mr. Livingston's cooperative learning technique involves writing in social studies.

Inside an Active Classroom

1. Bring in a number of objects related to a topic or theme of instruction. For example, after reading about the traditions of Hanukkah during a thematic unit on winter holidays, Mr. Livingston brought in six objects: a menorah, a dreidel, latkes, an oil lamp, a replica Torah scroll, and a model Jewish temple. One object was displayed on each of six tables spread throughout the room. Taped to the wall near each table were two large sheets of chart paper.

2. Divide the class into cooperative learning groups of four students each. Mr. Livingston explained that the objects were to be used for a writing activity that

would take place in stages, each lasting for about 5 minutes. One group would start out at each of the tables, brainstorming words associated with the object on the table and writing them down on one of the sheets of chart paper.

3. Rotate each group to the next table. Each group will now have an object different than the one it had brainstormed. The menorah group, for example, moves to the oil lamp table, the oil lamp table moves to the Torah table, and so on. The groups must write a short story about their new object on the second sheet of chart paper, using the brainstormed words of the previous group.

4. Rotate again to the next table. This time, each group revises the story written by the previous group—adding to, deleting, or revising ideas.

5. Rotate once again. Now each group edits the work of the previous groups, checking for such mechanics as spelling, punctuation, and grammar.

6. On this fourth rotation, instruct students to examine the edited piece and compose a final copy on a clean sheet of chart paper, leaving room for an illustration.

7. Rotate still one more time, assigning each group the responsibility to create an illustration for the final written piece.

8. On the last rotation, make sure each group is back at its original position, examining the story written for its object and sharing its reactions. The separate pages could be read aloud and then bound together as a chapter in a class-generated book on winter holidays.

Choosing a Reward System

With cooperative learning, students develop a strong attachment to each other and take tremendous satisfaction in celebrating their accomplishments with a common incentive or reward. These enticements often take the form of such rewards as stickers, bonus points, and snacks or recognition ("super team," "great team," or "good team"). Under these conditions they are driven toward productivity by reinforcing one another's behavior. All group members must receive a reward for the accomplishment; everyone is rewarded or no one is rewarded. For example, every group member gets 10 minutes extra recess time when group members correctly match all United States capital cities with their states. The rewards should be both enticing and inexpensive. Ways of rewarding groups include the following:

- Bonus points added to all members' scores when a team achieves an academic task

- Nonacademic rewards such as free homework passes, stickers, erasers or pencils, or extra recess time

- Social rewards such as smiles or verbal praise

Noticing special accomplishments becomes sufficient reward in most cases ("You improved your previous best test score by five points!").

Teachers in cooperative classrooms spend a great deal of time observing learning groups to assess the students' academic progress as well as their use of interpersonal and group work skills.

What Are the Benefits of Cooperative Learning?

Is cooperative learning worth the time and hard work to establish in your dynamic social studies classroom? Or, is cooperative learning a fad that will come and go like so many others in recent years? In short, research seems to indicate that the benefits of cooperative learning activities, done well, help students improve their learning and experience joy and satisfaction in assisting one another. Watching students take to cooperative learning is something like watching survivors on a lifeboat. They quickly realize that they'll either sink or swim together. They learn to be patient, less critical, and more compassionate. If they see a teammate in need, they go to his or her aid. Cooperative learning seems to be here to stay because evidence indicates it does what people say it will do. Teachers can use it with confidence in a variety of ways because the benefits of the approach are considerable.

There are no shortcuts to learning how to use cooperative learning in your social studies classroom; gaining expertise requires years of effort and long-term commitment to self-improvement. Seek help from colleagues, attend professional workshops, exchange ideas, and read widely.

AFTERWORD

Cooperative learning may be broadly defined as any classroom learning situation in which students work together in structured groups toward a joint or common goal. Of all the student-centered instructional options available for social constructivist classrooms, teachers seem to prefer this form of teaching to any other. Cooperative learning and social constructivism form an ideal partnership primarily because cooperative learning calls for students to work together to achieve goals which they could not attain individually. Instead of working as a student in competition with other students in the classroom, children are assigned the task of building a learning community where all students contribute in important and meaningful ways. In classrooms where cooperative learning is practiced, students pursue learning in groups of varying size: negotiating, initiating, planning, and evaluating together.

Cooperative classrooms do not emerge spontaneously. They are the product of teacher-led transitions from whole-class instruction to the establishment of learning teams. Once students learn to assume active roles in group efforts and begin to take responsibility for their own learning, cooperative classrooms become places where students are likely to achieve higher levels of academic success. But cooperative group work goes beyond improving academic learning. Cooperative learning helps form the foundation on which strong democratic communities can be built and maintained. It enhances self-esteem and builds the kinds of life-long interpersonal and communication skills considered necessary to function as productive members of society.

A variety of formal cooperative learning models are suitable for elementary school social studies classrooms, such as Think-Pair-Share, Numbered Heads Together, Jigsaw, Pick Your Spot, and STAD. Regardless of the specific approach, however, cooperative learning seems to have three essential features: students work as teams, teams are heterogeneously formed, and reward systems are group-oriented.

Managing a cooperative learning classroom changes the social constructivist teacher's role from that of directing whole class learning through the learning cycle to that of managing small group learning teams. Gone for the most part is the planning and presentation of three-part lessons; in its place teachers become primarily concerned with helping students grow into a community of learners.

REFERENCES

Aronson, E., Blaney, N. T., Stephan, C., Sikes, J., & Snapp, M. (1978). *The jigsaw classroom*. Beverly Hills, CA: Sage.

Ellis, S. S., & Whalen, S. F. (1990). *Cooperative learning: Getting started*. New York: Scholastic.

Freiberg, H. J., & Driscoll, A. (1992). *Universal teaching strategies*. Boston: Allyn & Bacon.

Kagan, S. (1989). The structural approach to cooperative learning. *Educational Leadership, 47,* 12–15.

Slavin, R. E. (1984). Students motivating students to excel: Incentives, cooperative tasks and student achievement. *The Elementary School Journal, 85,* 53–62.

Slavin, R. E. (1995). *Cooperative learning* (2nd ed.). Boston: Allyn & Bacon.

Wasserman, S. (1989). Children working in groups? It doesn't work! *Childhood Education, 5,* 204.

Inquiry and Problem Solving:
Cognitive Constructivism in Action

WHAT DOES COGNITIVE CONSTRUCTIVISM LOOK LIKE?

Students in Sheila Kirtland's fifth-grade social studies class have been investigating various customs of people around the world. One day, as they were watching a video on diverse cultural traditions, the students became particularly interested in the historically popular Islamic greeting of keeping the palm of one's hand open and touching the breast, forehead, and lips, signifying endearment in heart, thoughts, and words. Traditional greetings of various cultures around the world became the rage in Ms. Kirtland's class as the students engaged in a spontaneous and productive discussion of the many interesting ways people greet one another: "The people of Japan bow politely when greeting someone." "The French and other continentals 'kiss' one another on both cheeks." "Boy Scouts in America shake left-handed—the hand nearest the heart—with the three middle fingers extended to the other person's wrist." The highest degree of curiosity in the topic surfaced, however, after some students demonstrated the handshaking styles of present-day athletes. The main question was, "Who started all of this?"

Ms. Kirtland encouraged her students to pursue their interest by helping them locate and explore various resources that might assist them with an answer. Some searched the World Wide Web, using *Yahooligans* (*www.yahooligans.com*) as a starting point. Others looked through books and magazines. A few students thought they might uncover information by interviewing parents, teachers, and other adults. Their research uncovered some fascinating information, such as discovering that the practice of grasping and shaking hands goes back to earliest civilizations when the right hand normally held a weapon. If empty, however, the extended right hand became a gesture of welcome and peace. They also learned that although the handshake has been by far the most popular greeting throughout the United States, it is viewed as senseless and inconvenient in other parts of the world. Many countries believe it is the most potent means of spreading disease and, for sanitary reasons, prefer the bow as practiced by the people of Asia. The students uncovered that, in terms of handshaking, as far back as the 16th century the Ashanti of Africa had a handshake and an expression of greeting: "Five must lie within five." The Dutch of old ended business negotiations with a ritualistic hand slapping, high and low, which served as a basis for the expression "striking a bargain."

As far as identifying the source of the modern "shaking" variations practiced by present-day athletes, Ms. Kirtland's students discovered that, although they are rooted in African American culture, the evidence was inconclusive as to who actually started the practices: Basketball player, Magic Johnson, claimed to have originated the "high five" at Michigan State in 1980, but long jumper Ralph Boston argued that the "slap five" began among African-American track athletes on the international track circuit prior to 1968. Some insist that revolutionary handshakes started as far back as the 1940s when African American musicians greeted each other with a special shake accompanied by the jive phrase, "Gimme a little skin, man." Regardless of their origin, Ms. Kirtland's students became convinced that the new handshakes were not just a passing trend.

"They're not just a fad," argues Kareem. "I've high-fived a million times! No contest."

"People will keep inventing handshakes until the end of time," added Lillian in support. "The possibilities are endless."

"I agree," volunteered Nicole, "but by the time you learn all the handshakes, the season is over!"

Ms. Kirtland supported her students throughout this exciting fact-finding investigation because she is convinced that the most worthwhile learning in social studies occurs when children work at what *they* want to know. Her viewpoint is based on a belief that elementary school students are naturally inclined to dive headlong into whatever excites their interests and that social studies teachers should be a little more flexible, a little more spontaneous, and a little more willing to help them explore their world. In this teaching episode, for example, Ms. Kirtland recognized that her students' interest in handshaking was exceptionally strong so it was important to risk a temporary departure from the regular curriculum so they could find a solution to their absorbing problem. Such a strong inner drive to unlock for themselves the mysteries of their world is well illustrated through the comments I once overheard a second grader make after his teacher asked what it would be like to know everything.

"Awful," the little boy responded.

"Awful?" inquired the teacher in disbelief. "Why do you think knowing everything would be awful?"

"'Cause then there'd be nothin' to wonder 'bout!" answered the youngster.

In the vein of this astute second grader, teachers in dynamic social studies classrooms inspire their students to look at their social world with a sense of awe and wonder. "If teachers are reluctant to take risks, how will they ever inspire risk taking in their students?" Ms. Kirtland asks. "It is the job of social studies teachers to arouse, not suppress, the natural curiosity their students carry to school. The students are often their own best teachers." In that single persuasive statement, Ms. Kirtland summed up the beliefs of those who contend that social studies education should be "student-run." These educators draw a majority of their support from cognitive constructivists who propose that knowledge is best constructed through self-initiated inquiry and individual problem-centered investigations. The assistance of adults and more knowledgeable peers is considered important, but not essential.

Cognitive constructivists and *social constructivists* have much in common, but they differ noticeably in one key area—the extent and type of involvement of both students and teachers. Although each model requires effort and responsibility on the part of both, *social constructivists* stress the organization of "communities of learners" in which "more expert" adults or peers provide assistance to the less skilled learners. *Cognitive constructivists,* on the other hand, describe a learner-centered environment where the making of knowledge is carried out by individual students in a fashion that supports their interests and needs. For cognitive constructivists, learning is primarily an individualistic venture.

WHAT IS COGNITIVE CONSTRUCTIVISM?

You have read in Chapter 6 that constructivists fundamentally agree that learning can be most reasonably explained as an active process that Piaget referred to as *equilibration.* This term describes a path of action by which students try to make sense of the world either by fitting new experiences into an existing schema (*assimilation*) or by revising an existing schema as a result of a new experience (*accommodation*). In this perspective, learning is always driven by the learner as she or he moves to assimilate or accommodate new experiences into existing schemata. Students learn by fitting, or attempting to fit, new information into what they already know. Although they agree on those principles, constructivists are split into two camps on their views of how constructive activity should take place in the social studies classroom. You will recall that the social constructivist camp (Vygotsky) claims that learning is embedded in *social situations.* The cognitive constructivists, on the other hand, explain learning from the perspective of the *individual.* A social constructivist would describe a sociable mind that prefers to pull out beyond the limits of one's body into her or his social environs, while a cognitive constructivist would depict the mind as being more solitary, confining its sphere of learning to an individual's head.

To a large extent, the cognitive constructivist approach presumes that development is a natural biological process that is essentially the same for all individuals regardless of gender, class, race, or the social or cultural context in which learning is taking place. Internal development is the focus of teaching, and the social context is somewhat minimized.

Instead of taking on the role of "collaborator" who assists students as they construct concepts or skills, the cognitive constructivist teacher functions as a "facilitator" who either waits for or provides something meaty for the children to sink their teeth into and then sits back to support their efforts. Facilitators do not check the teacher's manual to find out what to do next; they go to where the action is. Only one thing matters: The teacher must be tuned into the interests and curiosities of the students. Mutual understanding and respect between teacher and student frees the student to develop and exercise autonomy.

Perhaps the most important role for the teacher is to provide an environment in which the student can address problems through exploration and investigation. The classroom should be filled with authentic activity, tasks have real-world relevance and utility. The students should be given the freedom to construct meaning at their own pace while participating in these authentic activities with the idea that errors will be made and solutions will be found.

> Even as he emphasized the student's central role in learning, Piaget made it clear that the classroom should not be considered a free-for-all of student initiated activity where they are given unlimited freedom to work on their own. He viewed the teacher's role as one of active intervention—teachers have a responsibility to organize situations that provide useful problems:
>
> It is important that teachers present children with materials and situations and occasions that allow them to move forward. It is not a matter of just allowing children to do anything. It is a matter of presenting to the children situations which offer new problems, problems that follow on from one another. You need a mixture of direction and freedom. (Quoted in Evans, 1973, p. 53)

WHAT IS PROBLEM-CENTERED INSTRUCTION?

Since cognitive constructivism centers on *problem-centered learning*, it would be unwise to go any further unless we have a general idea of what problem-centered learning is. Various writers have used the term to describe what social scientists do, from putting puzzles together to dreaming up solutions for everything from war to famine. However, no description of problem-centered instruction has had more impact on elementary school social studies instruction than the one expressed by John Dewey (1916) during the early part of the 20th century. At that time, Dewey proposed that problems can be thought of as anything that creates doubt and uncertainty in learners. Because Dewey's description has maintained acceptance over the years, it will serve to guide our discussion. Problem-centered instruction, therefore, will be defined as anything that creates doubt and uncertainty in the minds of learners.

Making the Transition to Problem-Centered Instruction

If students are entering you classroom from traditional classrooms, you must make sure that the more student-centered course of action in problem-solving classrooms does not run against the grain of that which they are most familiar. As with cooperative learning, there must be a transition period during which students change over from teacher direction to more independence. Student-centered learning does not emerge spontaneously in elementary school classrooms; it is a product of helping youngsters work together in new ways. It may take several weeks or months to reach the point where you and your students can work together while investigating problems productively. I have heard teachers give up after only one unsuccessful try, saying, "I knew it! These kids just can't think for themselves!" and go through the rest of the year doing the children's thinking for them. But I doubt that these teachers would every say, "These children cannot add and subtract by themselves," and thereafter remove any further opportunity for them to learn those important skills the rest of the school year.

Before you make the same mistake and insist, "Bring back the textbook! Give me back my worksheets! This business of problem-centered learning just doesn't work!" remember that children must move slowly. They need loads of opportunities to grow and learn. The skills needed for problem solving will not materialize after a single exposure to the process. The presence of any new element in a classroom is potentially distracting. Introducing new expectancies all at once produces a situation in which the children's cognitive systems collapse under an overload of input. Time, patience, and your belief in the importance of student-directed learning are the key ingredients of a successful transition.

Teachers help students on the road to self-directed learning by offering early hands-on, problem-based experiences that incorporate the following elements: (1) designing captivating classroom displays (mini-museums), (2) discussing the displays, and (3) encouraging children's questions.

Classroom Displays (Mini-Museums)

Classroom displays, or what I like to call *mini-museums* (others have variously called them *interest areas*, *curiosity centers*, and *theme tables*), are essentially exhibit areas in your classroom designed to inspire children to explore, question, think, and talk. Today's exhibit might be origami, a Chilean rain stick, foreign coins, a butter churn, a powder horn, shark's teeth, campaign buttons, a tape recording of city sounds, or a sombrero. Whatever items you select for the mini-museum, they should be treated like exhibits in the best public, child-oriented museums—not with a "hands-off" policy, but with a policy that invites touching, exploration, and investigation.

Most elementary school students have visited museums during a school trip or with their families (if they haven't, you should take them), so they will have many ideas on how to create a museum in their classroom. Even upper-grade and middle school students enjoy designing exhibits and sharing interesting collections of objects. It is important to remember, though, that these collections should be neither haphazardly displayed nor briefly shared and then put on a shelf and forgotten. Monhardt and Monhardt (1997) suggest that the best place to start is to have the children share their past museum experiences. The authors suggest a discussion guided by questions such as these:

- "What are some different museums you've visited?"
- "What museums were most interesting?"
- "What made them so?"
- "What is involved in setting up a museum display?"
- "How can we find out more about museums?"

Introduce the idea of a social studies mini-museum to your class. One teacher modeled the process by placing an apparently odd object on a table—a stiff brush used by dog groomers. On the wall above the table was a sign that read, *Classroom Mini-Museum*. Almost instantly the children began looking at the brush, touching it, and talking about what it might be. The teacher watched and listened, occasionally asking open-ended questions and making comments to stimulate the children to think more deeply about the object. One child tried to use the brush on her own hair. She was surprised to see just how stiff the bristles were. Naturally, the other children had to try, too.

Rosa eventually identified the object. Her mother was a veterinarian and Rosa often helped around the office. She was obviously thrilled to share her knowledge with the class; their interest became much stronger as they listened to the knowledgeable description by their friend. To capitalize on this growing fascination with the brush and what veterinarians do, the teacher invited Rosa's mother to visit the class to talk about her profession.

You can see from this example that it is a good idea to plan what you display at the mini-museum rather than select items in hit-or-miss fashion. You want something to happen at the center—interests to grow and concepts to deepen as the activity extends in the direction of the children's interests.

Discussing the Displays   Rather than making the mini-museum an informal observation/conversation place, as Rosa's teacher did, some teachers prefer to introduce the mini-museum during planned meeting times that can involve a small group or the entire class. The following dialogue illustrates one teacher's initial meeting. That teacher, Roland Comegys, opens the meeting by calling the students' attention to a large study print of an archaeologist examining some artifacts.

Mr. Comegys: Today we're going to discover some fascinating things at our social studies mini-museum. First, look carefully at this photo. The person you see is called an *archaeologist*. Have you ever heard that word? (Mr. Comegys holds up a word card for *archaeologist*.) This is how the word looks. What is it that archaeologists do?

Adam: She's looking at something.

Mr. Comegys:	Yes, she's looking at, or examining, something. What kinds of things do you suppose archaeologists examine?
Denise:	Fossils?
Tamara:	Yeah. To see what Earth was like a long time ago.
Mr. Comegys:	Yes, they examine old objects and use that information to describe what people were like very long ago. That's a good start. Does anyone else have an idea?
Patrick:	They dig for old tools and things . . . even bones.
Mr. Comegys:	Good, they might study fossils, bones, tools, paintings, clothes, furniture, and other objects. These things are called *artifacts*. Studying artifacts can help us understand the lives of people. Have you ever seen an archaeologist examine artifacts?
Nelson:	I saw a picture of an archaeologist in a museum. It was in an exhibit about China.
Lucinda:	On a TV show once, I saw some archaeologists looking in old pyramids for mummies.
Mr. Comegys:	Yes, archaeologists study many things to learn about the lives of people. Artifacts can tell about the games they play, the tools they use, and even the way they eat their meals. From now on, this table will be called the mini-museum. It is a place where you will come to discover things about the lives of people by doing some of the important jobs archaeologists do—examining them and keeping a record of observations. (Mr. Comegys brings out a cornhusk doll.) I've brought an artifact for you to examine today. Look at it carefully and see what kinds of discoveries you might make. Amour, what are some things you notice?
Amour:	It looks like a toy—a doll, maybe?
Mr. Comegys:	What makes you think it's a doll, Amour?
Amour:	It looks like it has arms and legs. The top is like a head.
Mr. Comegys:	It is shaped like a doll. What do you notice, Raphael?
Raphael:	I think it might be made out of corn. It feels and looks like the dried corn plants we put out at Halloween.
Mr. Comegys:	That part of a corn plant is called a husk. Here, look at this. It is a cornhusk before it was made into a doll. (Shows cornhusk.)
Moira:	How do people ever make dolls out of cornhusks?
Mr. Comegys:	Here, I'll show you. It's quite simple. (He takes a few minutes and demonstrates how to construct a cornhusk doll as the children follow his lead to make their own. Mr. Comegys is demonstrating that people can be a very important source of

information. He emphasizes the importance of checking other sources, too, calling the children's attention to a set of five books, each of which contains information about cornhusk dolls.) What does the doll tell you about the people who used it? (The craft activity continues for several more minutes.) You've been examining our artifact very carefully today. You made some interesting discoveries. Archaeologists don't stop with discoveries, though. They must keep careful records of everything they do so their findings can be shared with other people. We will use a special way of recording our discoveries—observation sheets. (Mr. Comegys passes out the observation sheets.) There's a place for your name and the date, and then the paper says, "What I Know About . . . " followed by a long blank. What words should I put in the blank?

Martha:	Cornhusk dolls!
Mr. Comegys:	That's right, Martha. There is also a big box on the paper for you to draw an illustration of what you examined. Please make a careful drawing there. Finally, at the bottom you will find some space to write. What are some things archaeologists might write about this cornhusk doll?
Denise:	The doll is made from dried cornhusks.
Amanda:	It was made in a place where people grew lots of corn.
Martin:	It could have been a gift for a boy or a girl.
Louise:	There weren't many stores around selling toys then. People had to make their toys from things around them. (The suggestions flow forth for several minutes. The children then complete their observation sheets. Figure 8–1 shows a completed observation sheet.)

Mr. Comegys explained to the class that he planned to display something in the mini-museum every few days and that it would be directly related to the thematic unit under study. The children were told that they would be using their skills of observing and recording to catalog information.

As important as they are, observational experiences by themselves do not guarantee the acquisition of problem-solving skills. As you have read, Mr. Comegys used carefully worded questions or comments to help children gain meaning from the mysteries that confronted them. Skillful guidance must be provided to help children make accurate observations during their initial investigative efforts. You can guide their investigation with questions like the following:

- "What do you see here?"
- "How do you suppose it is used?"

FIGURE 8–1
Completed Student Observation Sheet

"ARCHAEOLOGY ATTIC"
OBSERVATION SHEET

NAME __Jesse__ DATE __4/6/94__

WHAT I KNOW ABOUT __Corn husk dolls__

The doll was made from corn husks.
It is a toy for a young child. It
probably came from a place where corn
is plentyful, like Nebraska.

- "I wonder what would happen if . . . ?"
- "If we try it again, do you think the same thing will happen?"
- "Is this like anything you've ever (used, seen, tried out) before?"
- "How can we find out more about . . . ?"
- "Can we find out if we watch it carefully?"
- "What makes you think so?"

- "Who do you think might use this?"
- "Where do they live? What makes you think so?"
- "What can you tell about the people who use this?"
- "What do you think of the people who use this?"

Some of these questions and comments help children look for specific things. Others are more open and encourage higher thought processes such as predicting and discovering relationships. Through such experiences, children develop the rudimentary scientific observation skills required for more sophisticated data collection activities.

Encouraging Children's Questions   Making careful observations and talking about interesting things under the teacher's direction are two important components of early problem-centered learning and make an excellent transition from more teacher-directed instructional approaches. A third important component of this process is encouraging children to ask their own questions about the experience. Children often have a lot of questions of their own to ask. For example, Thomas Edison's last day in school came when he asked, "How can water run uphill?" after he noticed that a river in Ohio did just that. Young Tom was then expelled for expressing himself in ways that were unacceptable at the time. Children come to us with a strong need to ask questions. Respect that fact and guide them in exercising this childhood gift. Here are a few questions and comments I remember from working with children:

"I heard something pretty disgusting. I read in my book about a guy who chewded wood. And about a guy they found alive in a whale's stomach!"

"Are babies born with brains?"

"Where does the water go when I flush the toilet?"

"Why is there war?"

When children blurt out such comments, ask yourself, "Am I listening as carefully and sensitively as I am able?" When you listen, you communicate to the child that he or she is a worthwhile individual whose honest thoughts are valued. This is something children need to know, for question asking is an indispensable part of the problem-solving process.

The goal of these preliminary experiences is to help children acquire the skills needed for self-directed learning. Self-directed learning emerges when students are aware that a problem or question exists and attack it in a systematic, thorough manner by understanding what they need to know and devising strategies to find out what they don't. Self-directed learners have the ability to find out something by themselves by using these three questions whenever they encounter a perplexing problem or situation: (1) What do I already know about this? (2) What else do I need to find out? (3) Where can I find this information?

Students' learning is most productive when teachers are able to thoroughly engage their interests with well-planned observational experiences.

How Do Teachers Facilitate Inquiry and Problem Solving?

Problem-centered learning is a label that includes two teaching approaches generally considered appropriate for cognitive constructivist classrooms—*inquiry* and *creative problem solving*. Although each is characterized by its own set of distinctive processes, they share one important similarity—helping students solve problems. The reading material that follows will help you distinguish between these two approaches by addressing these important questions: What are the characteristics of inquiry and creative problem solving? How are these two strategies similar? How are they different? How do they contribute to learning? What roles do teachers and students undertake?

Inquiry Procedures

The term *inquiry* has achieved widespread popularity among social studies educators. For example, the influential publication, *Curriculum Standards for Social Studies* (NCSS, 1994), recommends that, "Teachers model seriousness of purpose and a thoughtful approach to inquiry and use instructional strategies designed to elicit and support similar qualities from students. . . . Teachers gradually move from providing considerable guidance . . . to a less directive role that encourages students to become independent and self-regulated learners (p. 12)." However, as inquiry has become discussed more frequently in the professional literature, so has confusion about its meaning. Some people consider inquiry to be an approach to instruction that is undeniably new. Others consider it to be at least as old as ancient Greece. They contend that it previously traveled under such names as the *Socratic method, problem solving, critical thinking, scholarly investigation,* and *scientific thinking.* Despite this uncertainty, the characteristic that sets inquiry apart from other teaching strategies is that it is the only strategy designed to teach students how to carry out independent investigations through a systematic process of gathering and analyzing data. Therefore, for the purposes of this text, inquiry will be considered a systematic process for carrying out independent investigations. Descriptions of the inquiry process vary from source to source, but the most common pattern in elementary school social studies classrooms seems to be the time-honored pattern recommended by John Dewey (1916):

1. The students identify a problem or question that can be investigated.
2. The students generate hypotheses, or tentative answers that can be verified.
3. The students collect data.
4. The students analyze the data and form generalizations that can be applied to this problem and to similar ones encountered in their lives.
5. The students share their results with an audience.

Do you remember learning about the scientific method of inquiry in elementary school or high school? Many who do have come away with the impression that social scientists never deal with a problem until they put on their horn-rimmed glasses, sharpen their pencils, pull out a pad listing the steps of the inquiry process, and precisely mark off each step as it is carried out. In the real world, however, social scientists don't always work that way. Sometimes they follow the scientific method unerringly, but often they work in a slightly more disorganized way, grubbing around and hunting for answers through trial-and-error strategies. Does this hit-or-miss process look like the way children approach problems, too? It is. Children, by their very nature, are curious about their world and love to search for answers until their questions are worked out—sometimes unsystematically and sometimes in a more organized manner, just like working social scientists. And, from a social scientist's perspective, inquiry-oriented classrooms engage students in the investigative nature of social studies.

Locating Problems or Questions

Students must initially encounter an attention-grabbing problem in order for inquiry to work. The problem should hold a high degree of mystery and appeal—children resist investigating if they do not care about the issue. I clearly recall one youngster's reaction to a teacher who passed out a list of 12 topics about the Civil War and required the students to select one for a research report. The girl and the class cared very little about it: "Social studies is so boring when the teacher makes you do reports on stuff you don't even care about!"

What are good social studies problems? Obviously, the best are those in which students are interested. Herein lies the real crux of inquiry: "How do I find out what actually interests my students?" First and foremost, students will be interested if they can attach themselves to the problem. They must be convinced that the problems they encounter are worth pondering. The problems must be clear, understandable, and meaningful, and involve a high degree of mystery. Additionally, the problems must lie within the students' range of ability, offering just the proper amount of mystery to challenge previously established ideas, but not so much that it is either unchallenging or too difficult to understand. If the problem is too complex, students will be intimidated by it; they have no experiential attachment to make sense of it. By contrast, if the problem can be quickly solved with what the students already know, it is obviously not a challenge and students will quickly lose interest.

When students have a meaningful stake in a problem, motivation soars. Teachers have a crucial role in sustaining this spirit. They act as models, thinking aloud with the students and practicing every behavior they want their students to use. They ask questions: "What's going on here? What do we need to know more about?" They coax and prompt students to ask similar questions as they assume responsibility for their own learning. They are open to new experiences. Students welcome teachers who reach out for the different and unusual, teachers who look at life with passion. Teachers stop, look, and listen; they feel, taste, and smell. They ask, "What is it? Where does it come from? What is it for?" They perform their own careful investigations and, through their passion for new discoveries, offer the greatest form of encouragement to their students. We must do our best in dynamic social studies programs to nurture curiosity for life. One of the best ways to do this is to be a teacher who responds to the world with a probing, wondering mind and regularly proposes, "Let's find out!" The discovery of solutions to problems is usually accompanied by a strong feeling of delight. This is what drives people to explore and investigate: It feels good!

The problem, often stated as a question, is the initial spark for further investigation. This first step of the inquiry process is critical, for only if the students experience a felt need to confront the problem, will they be stimulated to move on and search for a solution.

In general, there are two fundamental sources of problems to set off inquiry episodes in dynamic social studies classrooms: (1) problems proposed by the students, and (2) problems sparked by a teacher. You will see one example of each in the "Inside an Active Classroom" features that follow the discussion of the remaining elements of inquiry. For now, think back to our chapter opening classroom scene. Did the problem originate with the students or with the teacher?

Generating Hypotheses

Once students understand the problem and accept it as worthwhile, they are in business. The students are ready for action; it is now time to uncover a solution. I hesitate to use the word *hypothesis* to explain what is done during this component of the

Inquiry capitalizes on young social scientists' needs and desires to figure something out by themselves.

inquiry process because many future teachers seem to feel intimidated by such jargon, thinking that such a big word most certainly entails some sort of complicated activity. But, for elementary school students, the hypothesis is simply an "educated guess" or a "feeling," "hunch," or "suspicion" based on incomplete evidence. You can help students come up with a hypothesis by asking questions such as these: "What do you already know about this situation? What have you already learned that we might be able to use now? How could this information help us come up with an answer to our problem? What ideas can you suggest as a solution based on what we've just discussed?" The purpose of these questions is to help students attach information they already know to the problem.

Formulating hypotheses involves a certain amount of risk for students, so you must be especially careful to attach importance to each individual's input. It is easy for teachers to acknowledge hypotheses they might agree with or those they think might be "sensible." Students do not always interpret "truth" as adults do. A central aspect of cognitive constructivism is that "erroneous" ideas are necessary for the construction of intelligence. Students must use ideas that they will later judge "incorrect" to arrive at "correct" conclusions. However, responding to incomplete or unusual suggestions is not quite as easy. Remember that the students' ideas are nothing more than presumptions, so you don't want students to drop out of the rest of the process because they feel rejected. Dignify all responses by offering comments and/or questions such as these:

- "I heard you say. . . . "
- "What I believe you are telling me is. . . . "
- "That is a very interesting idea. I never thought of it that way."
- "You have an intriguing idea, but I'm a bit confused. Could you enlarge upon it a bit?"
- "What if I told you (add some information)? How would that change you hypothesis?"

Definitive solutions and opportunities to accept or reject hypotheses will come as students go on to gather and analyze data. The main purpose of making hypotheses is to steer the students as they enter into the next phase of the inquiry process, *data gathering.*

Gathering the Data

Contemporary society relies more and more on the collection and communication of data than ever before, so it has become even more important that elementary school students understand how data is collected and used. A primary focal point of elementary school inquiry is on the collection of data because acquiring data collection and interpretation skills helps students ultimately become better informed and more decisive citizens. During the data gathering phase, therefore, students become involved in an active search for data that helps find an answer for, solution to, or explanation about that which they are curious. The data collection process can take any of several forms, depending on the nature of the problem. In most elementary school classrooms, data are collected in one of three ways: *surveys, descriptive research,* and *historical research.*

Surveys   Surveys entail a systematic collection of data that helps explain some characteristic of a particular group of people (feelings, behaviors, attitudes, etc.). The first step in conducting a survey is to design precise questions that will yield the specific data required to confirm or not confirm the hypotheses. Initial attempts at conducting surveys should take advantage of student interests in things close to their lives, such as movies, food, clothing, games, music, sports, pets, television programs, toys, books, and animals. First, the students must settle on an interesting question to look into: What information would they like to find out about each other? Let us suppose your students want to find out about favorite pets.

Once the clear-cut question has been decided and hypotheses have been made, an actual survey instrument needs to be designed that could test the hypotheses. The first step in building the instrument is to clarify the problem the students want to solve. For our purposes, we will say that your class wants to find out what animal is the favorite pet among fourth graders in the school. The next step is to have the students offer their predictions about a likely end result: "I think fish are most popular. A lot

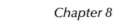

of my friends have aquariums in their house." Once the hypotheses have been shared, decide what categories of information would be most useful in testing them. Your students might write three to five categories of responses they think might be most frequently given across the top of a sheet of paper (see Figure 8–2.) A "favorite

FIGURE 8–2
Survey Instrument

FAVORITE PETS
MY SURVEY _____

CAT	DOG	BIRD	FISH	OTHER

pet" survey might include these categories: cat, dog, bird, fish, and other. Now that they are ready to interview other students, they need to decide the manner by which they will carry out that responsibility.

If the survey is to be taken from among their peers, will they need to question every child in the school? Should only a small portion of the student body be surveyed? Maybe they should interview just the students in their own classroom? Or would it be interesting to see if their classroom's results are the same as the other classrooms at the same grade level? Once your class decides on its preferred method of data collection, the students being interviewed will indicate their responses by signing their names in the appropriate columns on the survey sheets. While collecting data on a favorite pet, for example, it would probably not be necessary to poll every child in school. Your student investigators would be wise to select some type of sampling strategy. Perhaps they might interview every third child who moves through the lunch line at noon. They might want an equal boy/girl distribution; if so, they could alternate every third boy, every third girl, and so on. If none of those methods appeal to the investigators, they might want to randomly select 50 students from the general grade-level population by drawing names out of a hat. Whatever the choice, the students must do all they can to ensure that their survey data is gathered from a representative sample of the larger population.

When the surveys are completed, your students should organize the data from all survey sheets and summarize the data on a bar graph. They can do this by simply counting the names collected in each column and color in the correct number of spaces on a bar graph to match the survey results. It is best to use a different color for each graph column. See Figure 8–3.

Finally, your students should study the data by examining the bar graph and talking about the question, "What does our graph tell us?" To make the inquiry activity more authentic, it is desirable to share the results publicly in some manner. In this case, the students' findings can be published in a class newspaper under the heading, "Some Interesting Things We Discovered About Pets."

Descriptive Research   Of all options, *descriptive research* is probably the most frequently used of all data-gathering techniques in elementary school social studies classrooms. Descriptive research involves two major strategies: direct observation and indirect observation. *Direct observation* includes all the tangible, hands-on experiences that involve students in touching, handling, or trying out objects or events. Students gather information through observing and experiencing real people or objects. An outing to the commuter train station to observe the "crunch" of rush hour, a trip to the glass factory to see how molten glass is fashioned into pricey goblets, and a visit by the town's mayor to answer the students' concerns about the need for a traffic light near the school are all examples of ways data can be collected through direct observation.

Indirect observation makes use of information sources other than direct experiences. These resources often include library materials such as encyclopedias, informational books, computers, magazines, newspapers, pamphlets, almanacs, catalogs,

FIGURE 8–3

Graph of Survey Results

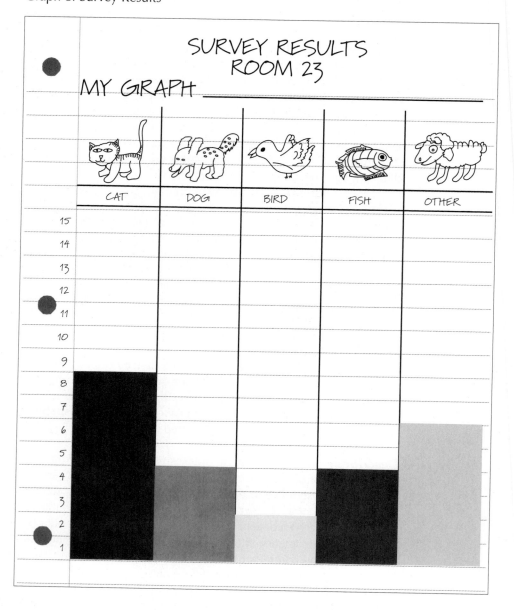

dictionaries, travel brochures, atlases, guides and timetables, posters, films, videos, photographs, and even the phone book. It must be emphasized that inquiry-oriented instruction does not preclude the use of textbooks as important information sources. Even textbooks can do much to excite the spirit of inquiry.

These students are gathering data from indirect and direct sources of information. Can you find examples of both sources in this photo?

Historical Research   When children delve into conditions of "long ago," they must gather and evaluate relevant traces of the past. These may include physical remains (artifacts, relics, and other "accidental survivors") and oral or written records (stories and documents). Historical research was treated with detail in Chapter 3; please refer back to that portion of the book if you need to refresh relevant understandings.

Organizing and Analyzing the Data

At this point in the inquiry process, students are faced with the challenge of organizing the information and deriving some meaning from it. In essence, they ask themselves, "What does all this data mean to me?" They have located data related to the problem they wanted to solve, and now they must examine and group the data based on shared relationships. They can do this by constructing a map or a graph, designing a chart, or creating some type of graphic organizer highlighting relationships among the data. (See Chapter 6 for more information on graphic organizers.) An effective method for helping students learn to complete these tasks is to model the process for them. For example, Bernard Schecter's sixth-graders had been studying the climate and topography of the Middle East when their interests focused on the camel, an animal that is almost perfectly adapted to the desert. That's all it took for Mr. Schecter's class to launch itself on a camel inquiry expedition. They searched a variety of references and found a wealth of fascinating camel facts. They filled their individual research notebooks with their facts and jointly listed everything they uncovered on the chalkboard, eliminating any duplicates. When they had filled the chalkboard with their facts, Mr. Schecter helped them organize their data into a web to highlight the relationships. He used timely questions and prompts to help them categorize facts related to food, location, size, body parts, strength, and other interesting information. Working from these main categories, the students plotted a fact web as shown in Figure 8–4.

This next-to-final stage of the inquiry process is a time for reflection—looking back at the problem or question, revisiting the hypotheses, studying the data gathering effort, and making observations: "Has a solution or an answer been found? Have

FIGURE 8–4
Camel Fact Web

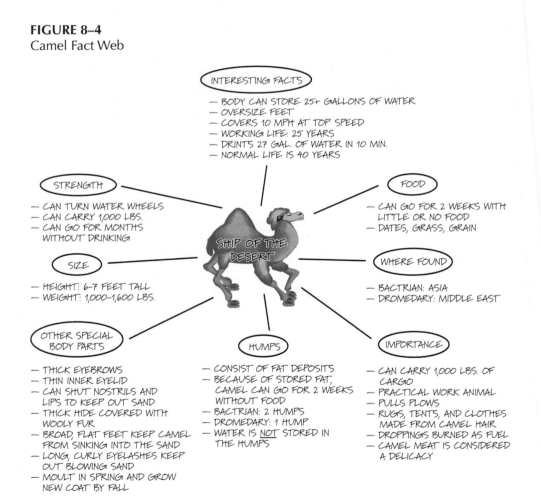

INTERESTING FACTS
— BODY CAN STORE 25+ GALLONS OF WATER
— OVERSIZE FEET
— COVERS 10 MPH AT TOP SPEED
— WORKING LIFE: 25 YEARS
— DRINKS 27 GAL. OF WATER IN 10 MIN.
— NORMAL LIFE IS 40 YEARS

STRENGTH
— CAN TURN WATER WHEELS
— CAN CARRY 1,000 LBS.
— CAN GO FOR MONTHS WITHOUT DRINKING

FOOD
— CAN GO FOR 2 WEEKS WITH LITTLE OR NO FOOD
— DATES, GRASS, GRAIN

SIZE
— HEIGHT: 6-7 FEET TALL
— WEIGHT: 1,000-1,600 LBS.

SHIP OF THE DESERT

WHERE FOUND
— BACTRIAN: ASIA
— DROMEDARY: MIDDLE EAST

OTHER SPECIAL BODY PARTS
— THICK EYEBROWS
— THIN INNER EYELID
— CAN SHUT NOSTRILS AND LIPS TO KEEP OUT SAND
— THICK HIDE COVERED WITH WOOLY FUR
— BROAD, FLAT FEET KEEP CAMEL FROM SINKING INTO THE SAND
— LONG, CURLY EYELASHES KEEP OUT BLOWING SAND
— MOULT IN SPRING AND GROW NEW COAT BY FALL

HUMPS
— CONSIST OF FAT DEPOSITS
— BECAUSE OF STORED FAT, CAMEL CAN GO FOR 2 WEEKS WITHOUT FOOD
— BACTRIAN: 2 HUMPS
— DROMEDARY: 1 HUMP
— WATER IS NOT STORED IN THE HUMPS

IMPORTANCE
— CAN CARRY 1,000 LBS. OF CARGO
— PRACTICAL WORK ANIMAL
— PULLS PLOWS
— RUGS, TENTS, AND CLOTHES MADE FROM CAMEL HAIR
— DROPPINGS BURNED AS FUEL
— CAMEL MEAT IS CONSIDERED A DELICACY

new questions come to light?" This is a major task of the inquiry process and teachers must be prepared to help the students through it.

Sharing Results

The final step of an inquiry episode is sharing the results with an authentic audience through appropriate vehicles of communication. In the adult world, much of the reward gained from research comes from having an impact on desired audiences. Professors of education take great pride in receiving the approval of their peers after delivering a speech about their research into a revolutionary new instructional approach, and medical researchers value the recognition they receive from other health care professionals after publishing a paper about a new treatment for some difficult-to-control disease. These professionals appreciate the respect for their research efforts and develop great personal satisfaction for their accomplishments.

Likewise, young learners take pleasure and pride in the recognition they receive after sharing the results of their research with an authentic audience. In the case of Mr. Schecter's class, for example, the student researchers were divided into collaborative author/illustrator teams, each of which wrote a short illustrated paragraph on one of the categories from their camel web. The paragraphs were later sequenced and bound together into a picture storybook entitled, "The Ship of the Desert." And, since most elementary school students take great pleasure in reading aloud what they have written, they happily shared what they had written with an authentic audience—students from all the third-grade classrooms in their school.

Keep in mind that sharing authentic research goes beyond the traditional formal written report by engaging children in varieties of communication possibilities—oral presentations, graphic representations, photographs, audio- or videotapes, debates, dramatic skits, bulletin board displays, and a variety of other forms. Lifelong learners get their start in elementary social studies classrooms as teachers arouse curiosity for stimulating problems and propel their students into research to obtain answers or solutions. The resulting outcomes lead to the intellectual independence we so often find in lifelong learners.

Two examples of inquiry-oriented learning are featured in the "Inside an Active Classroom" vignettes that follow. Examine each carefully, for they represent the diverse ways teachers practice inquiry. The first example is launched from a problem initiated by the students. The second emerges from a contrived situation planned by the teacher. Notice that the first vignette illustrates a spontaneous, less formal approach to inquiry while the second follows the steps of the inquiry process much more deliberately. These examples illustrate the point that sometimes a question will arise from the class and the teacher must be alert and sensitive to seize such opportunities when they occur. Other opportunities for carefully planned, full-scale inquiry lessons can be planned by teachers to get the inquiry process rolling. Both approaches are important components of quality social studies programs for, beyond their ability to provoke curiosity and wonder, they each do much to help students understand how knowledge is produced.

Inside an Active Classroom

Problem Proposed by the Students

The Clarksville Senior Center has a serene new flower garden—thanks to Debra Wood's fifth graders. While visiting the center in early autumn to bring gift of potted chrysanthemums they had started from seeds as a science project a few weeks earlier, the students noticed that an area between the main building and a shed looked desolate and depressing. When they returned to the classroom, the students asked Ms. Wood if they could do something to improve the area. After much discussion, the class eventually decided on a flower garden.

"A garden is so restful and peaceful," explained Jana.

"Yeah," added Vance, "a garden could even bring back memories of World War II victory gardens."

Ms. Wood is an avid gardener and the president of the largest local garden club. She invited several members of the club to visit the class to recommend plants that would need a minimum amount of upkeep in their hot and dry climate. The garden club donated the flowers for the children's project and offered advice to the children as they cleaned up the area and planted the flowers. A parent who owned a landscaping company wanted to help, too, so the students dressed the flower area with his donated mulch. The class then solicited other local businesses for help; several chipped in to help as the garden expanded beyond their wildest dreams. A retired carpenter volunteered his time and expertise to make benches. A local lumberyard supplied the gravel and decorative block for a patio where the beautiful wooden benches now rest. An individual donor contributed a birdbath and feeder. In addition, the students took up a collection for a butterfly bush that added to the overall ambiance of the garden.

The garden is wheelchair accessible, a definite plus for seniors with restricted mobility. The senior adults are now responsible for the general upkeep of the garden and have passionately accepted that responsibility. "It gives them something to take pride in," explains Ms. Wood. "Some senior adults like the tranquility of the garden and will sit on the benches reminiscing. Others find the garden a great place to socialize. I'm so glad the students thought of this wonderful idea."

One child's response to this project is shown in Figure 8–5. Buoyed by the success of their flower garden project, Ms. Wood's students tackled new opportunities for community volunteerism with boundless enthusiasm and energy. They adopted a local park and pledged to keep it clean, packed breakfasts for the homeless as part of a Martin Luther King Day community service project, collected funds for the March of Dimes, made placemats and took them to a local nursing home to be placed on meal trays on Valentine's Day, and raised $200 for a classmate's family whose house was destroyed by fire. Through their incredible thirst for involvement, Ms. Wood's young inquirers took their first ambitious steps into the realm of real-life learning.

FIGURE 8–5
Student's Reaction Letter

It was cool seeing all the beautiful flowers everywhere. It was fun when we got to plant and water the flowers.

I learned it can be fun to do stuff for the community. I never thought planting flowers could be fun but it is. It made the center look very pretty. I hope we keep up with the project and plant new flowers next spring.

Billy

Inside an *Active Classroom*

Problem Sparked by a Teacher

Michael Wang's sixth-grade class had been working at the sand table (borrowed from the kindergarten classroom) digging up and brushing off replicas of artifacts their teacher had hidden beneath the soil he had substituted for the kindergartners' sand. Acting as "apprentice archaeologists," the students divided the surface of the site into squares with grids made from yarn. Then they carefully removed the soil from their own section, layer by layer, to dig up the remains from an unknown past civilization. As they dug, students carefully recorded the exact location of everything they found. Jenny uncovered what looked like an old coin. She examined it closely and searched for any information that might tell her where the coin might have been from. She observed what she thought was a likeness of a Roman emperor wearing a laurel crown. The word AUGUSTUS was printed above the likeness. "Hmmm," reflected Jenny, "Where could this coin be from?"

"That's it! I'll prove to Mr. Wang that this mystery coin is from ancient Rome!" The excitement in Jenny's voice was as clear as the pleasure reflected in her face. She saw what she believed to be a Roman emperor wearing a head decoration that looked like leaves. Based on this observation, Jenny guessed that the coin could have come from ancient Rome. Jenny deftly formulated a reasonable hypothesis while observing the coin and deliberately searching for any clues that she might associate with previous experiences.

Jenny next used an indirect observation strategy to gather data for the purpose of testing her hypothesis. She searched through a series of reference books arranged beforehand by her teacher and learned about the history of Roman coins. She also consulted an electronic encyclopedia available on the classroom computer. She found that Roman coins were decorated with the likeness of the emperor in power at the time. She also discovered that laurel crowns were used to adorn emperors and also that the title AUGUSTUS was given to the popular Roman leader Octavian when he succeeded Julius Caesar following his death at the hands of Brutus. There was no date on the coin, but Jenny compared her information about Roman coins and emperors with what was on the coin she uncovered and made an educated guess that this coin was made in Rome between 31 B.C. and A.D.14.

Jenny was somewhat sure her research evidence supported her initial hypothesis about the Roman coin but, working with an open mind, she stood ready to alter her initial feelings should further evidence demand it. She compared the artifact she uncovered in the soil with something found by a classmate, Russell. He had dug up a miniature banner with the letters SPQR. Russell's research indicated that these were the initials for Latin words translated, "The senate and the people of Rome." Together, Jenny and Russell concluded that they had enough corroborating evidence to substantiate a contention that these items were from ancient Rome. The question was whether these artifacts from Rome had been left behind in foreign lands as the result of trade, travel, war, or migration. They would await the findings of their classmates before making a definitive conclusion.

Inquiry is but one important variation of problem-centered learning. Another problem-centered model challenges students to explore problems and to generate novel, creative solutions, rather than conclusions based on hard data. We will refer to this model as *creative problem solving*.

Creative Problem Solving (CPS)

We once saw a tyrannosaurus.
And we feared he'd end our lives faurus.

TEXT SET 13

Theme: The Roman Empire

Linda Honan's **Spend the Day in Ancient Rome: Projects and Activities That Bring the Past to Life, Ages 8–12** (Wiley) transports children to Rome at the peak of its empire during the summer of the year A.D. 125. Children join 10-year-old Marcus and his family in the celebration of the annual Roman Games, a two-week civic festival in tribute to the god Jupiter. And as they are in Rome, they do as the Romans do—joining a parade, participating in gladiator games, tunic weaving, coin making, draping a toga to making a legionnaire's helmet and shield, learning to write in Latin, and making a Roman emperor's feast. The book is a distinctive, hands-on peek into a remarkable civilization.

Laurie Carlson's **Classical Kids: An Activity Guide to Life in Ancient Greece and Rome** (Chicago Review) invites the children to travel back in time to experience life in ancient Greece and Rome. Divided into two parts, one for each civilization, the book contains a wealth of hands-on activities from the worlds of art, math, cooking, science, and geography. The undemanding one- or two-paragraph historical blurbs about each activity establishes important background knowledge.

John Green's and William Kaufman's **Life in Ancient Rome** (Dover) is a useful coloring book containing 41 finely detailed illustrations and informative captions. The book begins with the defeat of Germanic invaders (c. 108 B.C.) and moves through events like the crushing of a slave revolt (71 B.C.) and the assassination of Julius Caesar (44 B.C.) until it ends in the first century A.D. The drawings and captions are based on solid historical and archaeological evidence; they describe Roman cultural life, major landmarks, leaders and daily activities.

Simon James's **Ancient Rome** (DK, Eyewitness Books) is a great reference containing interesting, informative text combined with lots of great color photos. That wonderful combination brings the Roman Empire to life and can literally be thought of as a museum between the covers of a book. Readers will learn about numerous aspects of life in Rome, and outstanding photographs depict the objects people used every day.

TRY THIS

Obtain a teacher's guide for a social studies textbook program at a grade level that treats the subject of the Roman Empire (usually grade 6). Carefully read the student material and suggestions for the teacher. Now select one of the books in this list and develop a plan of instruction that applies one or more of the suggestions from the guide.

But, "Look!" said my friend,
"He's rubber, can bend!"
Then we realized we were in Toysaurus.

My son Jeff wrote this limerick in elementary school as part of an integrated thematic unit on dinosaurs. His teacher sent the poem home along with a note telling us that she felt the limerick was remarkably creative. Of course, Jeff's "impartial" parents thought likewise and displayed it proudly in the middle of the refrigerator door. What do you think of Jeff's limerick? Would you judge it to be creative? If so, what makes it creative? If not, you've just failed this course (only kidding)!

Creative Thinking

What do we mean by *creativity*? Like other inner-directed, deeply personal phenomena such as love, patriotism, or intelligence, the term *creativity* means different things to different people and is virtually impossible to define precisely. However, most definitions of creativity include two major components:

- *Novel or original behavior.*   Behavior that has not been learned from anyone else; it is fresh, novel, and unique.
- *An appropriate and productive result.*   Coming up with a suitable or worthwhile product or an effective solution to a problem.

How does Jeff's poem reflect these two components? Is it fresh and original, or did he get the idea from somewhere else? Is it an appropriate response to the teacher's assignment to write a limerick about the dinosaurs they had been studying?

What prompts some children to create in such engaging ways, while others struggle to move beyond the ordinary? Although a certain degree of intelligence is required, something more is needed. In Jeff's case, that "something more" was the ability to "play" with ideas—to see things in a new way. Identifying what that something more might be has been debated over the years, but consensus seems to exist that an individual's level of creativity is influenced by the combination of four cognitive traits: fluency, flexibility, originality, and elaboration.

- *Fluency* is the ability to produce a large number of ideas. The child who responds to the question, "What things are crops?" with "Wheat, corn, beans, peas, and tomatoes" is more fluent than the child who responds, "Wheat and corn."
- *Flexibility* is the ability to produce a number of different categories of responses. The child who responds to the question, "What things are crops?" with "Wheat, tomatoes, apples, peanuts, and tobacco" is a more flexible thinker than the child who responds "Wheat, rye, oats, and barley" (all grains).
- *Originality* is the ability to produce unusual or clever responses. The child who responds to the question, "What can you do with an empty cereal box?" with "Make a snowshoe out of it" is more original than the child who says "Store things in it." Originality is usually determined statistically; the response can be considered original if it is offered by less than 10 percent of those responding.
- *Elaboration* is the ability to expand on a simple idea to make it richer. The child who responds to a teacher's request to draw a picture of the geographical

area where the Sioux lived with a simple landscape drawing shows less elaboration than the child who includes buffalo, tipis, and Sioux farmers working in the fields.

If we hope to help students enhance their creativity in dynamic social studies classrooms, we need to examine the kinds of classroom activities and practices that support creativity. Certainly, a major responsibility of social studies instruction is teaching the content and, up to now in this text, we have examined various ways to challenge students to explore and discover new information. However, creativity takes knowledge a step further; it "puts knowledge to work." What that means is that creative acts allow students to express what they know in unique ways.

People who are creative are creative within a discipline they know, so a skills and knowledge base are essential components of coming up with new ideas. If content knowledge and skills are essential to creativity, then social studies teachers must teach in ways that allow students the opportunity to work in the same manner as those who are creative in social studies. They must approach social studies with a thinking focus—seeing things from a unique point of view. The remainder of this chapter examines how the content of social studies relates to creativity and the processes of thinking creatively.

CPS in Dynamic Social Studies Classrooms

Perhaps the oldest and most widely practiced technique to encourage creative thinking in social studies classrooms is the creative problem solving (CPS) method developed by Alex Osborn (1963) and Sidney J. Parnes (1981). To understand CPS, it would be instructive to contrast it with inquiry. It is important to remember that the goal of inquiry is to systematically search for facts and information that answer questions or solve problems. Some students do this well; they sort out the clues, pull them together, look for patterns, and deliberately arrive at valid conclusions. Others, however, attack problems in quite different ways. This variation of a well-known story helps illustrate the difference between the two:

An engineering major and an elementary education major were hiking in the woods when they came across a grizzly bear. Both were terrified and quickly began to search for an escape route, each in her/his own way.

The engineering major logged onto his laptop computer and quickly calculated the mathematical differential between his speed and the bear's. His face turned ashen as he stared at the results.

The elementary education major simply took off her hiking boots, opened her backpack, slipped on a pair of jogging shoes, and took off.

"Boy, you are STUPID," the engineering major yelled to the elementary education major as she sprinted down the trail. "My calculations show you can't outrun a grizzly bear!"

"I don't have to," the elementary education major hollered back. "I only have to outrun YOU!"

This story demonstrates how two people can respond differently to the same problem. The two response categories in this example are generally referred to as

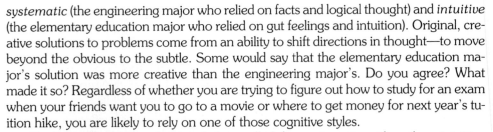

systematic (the engineering major who relied on facts and logical thought) and *intuitive* (the elementary education major who relied on gut feelings and intuition). Original, creative solutions to problems come from an ability to shift directions in thought—to move beyond the obvious to the subtle. Some would say that the elementary education major's solution was more creative than the engineering major's. Do you agree? What made it so? Regardless of whether you are trying to figure out how to study for an exam when your friends want you to go to a movie or where to get money for next year's tuition hike, you are likely to rely on one of those cognitive styles.

Traditionally, most schoolwork has called for systematic rather than intuitive thinking, so we find that schools tend to overemphasize logic skills at the expense of intuitive skills, giving our children an apparently "lopsided" education. Teaching for creativity does not minimize the importance of a solid background of information, however, for creativity in social studies is more likely to occur when students have mastered the content. Neither interesting problems nor their solutions often pop up without having substantial background knowledge. Teresa M. Amabile (1989) emphasizes this partnership in her acclaimed model of creativity. Her model has three components; in order for creativity to occur, all three must be in place:

1. *Domain knowledge and skills.* This component includes the technical skills and content needed to solve a given problem. A student who is to design a creative problem or make a creative contribution in geography, for example, will need to know something about geography. Creative ideas do not spring forth from a vacuum.

2. *Creative thinking and working skills.* Knowledge is but one component of creative thinking, but is not sufficient in itself. Creative thinking and working skills add that "something extra" that forms the creative personality. The four cognitive traits of creativity described earlier help explain the kinds of thinking abilities that help students take new perspectives on problems and come up with unusual ideas. These are required for creative performance.

3. *Intrinsic motivation.* Intrinsic motivation comes from within the person, not from an outside source. Intrinsically motivated students enjoy the pleasure and satisfaction of the work itself, not the external recognition or reward.

The Creative Problem Solving Model

The original CPS model is by and large described as consisting of six steps, each driving the creative process. That model works well with high school students and adults, but I prefer a simplified three-step method for elementary school students. A unique feature is that each of these steps, in turn, involves both a divergent phase during which students generate lots of ideas and a convergent phase during which they select only the most promising idea(s) for further exploration.

The divergent phase of each CPS step makes use of brainstorming strategies. *Brainstorming* is an appropriate strategy when you want to generate a large number of ideas, particularly new and original ones. In traditional brainstorming, students work in groups of three to five members with a recorder to keep track of ideas and an encourager to monitor the rules. Some basic ground rules help students be more effective as they brainstorm during each CPS stage. You (and your students) should become familiar with these ground rules so they will be second nature to all during CPS.

1. *Produce a large number of ideas.* The goal of brainstorming is to generate as many ideas as possible, for a large number of ideas seems more likely to bring into being a good idea. Don't worry about quality yet; that will be considered during the convergent phase of each step.

2. *Criticism is taboo.* Acknowledge every idea offered, no matter how strange or impractical it may seem at first glance. To create an atmosphere necessary for uninhibited thinking, one cannot criticize another's thoughts. You may later discover that a seemingly preposterous idea can lead to a fascinating, imaginative solution. No idea, then, is to be subject to judgment until all ideas have been presented. All forms of verbal and nonverbal criticism, including eye rolling, face making, and derisive smiles, are ruled out.

3. *Combine and improve ideas.* Don't be afraid to be a "hitchhiker." Piggybacking onto ideas of others can often originate exciting, new ideas as one idea inspires the next. Combining ideas with someone else's helps form new possibilities that are more intriguing than either by itself.

4. *Stretch yourself.* Many students will exert only minimal effort and then proclaim, "I just can't think of anything else." However, effective problem solvers make a strong effort to extend themselves beyond this point of "idea exhaustion." New and original ideas, however, seem to pop out after people think they have done all they can.

Let's consider the three steps of CPS along with an example of how they might be implemented in a dynamic social studies classroom.

The Mess This step involves saying all that can be said about a problem situation—factual statements as well as feelings. For example, Lalitha Imani created a simulated community environmental situation as shown in Figure 8–6. She divided her class into five-member groups and asked each group to line up in front of charts that were taped at even intervals around the room. The first student in line was to write a word, short phrase, or statement about the "mess" in which the community found itself. These could be factual statements or feelings about the issue. Basically, the students were advised not to hold back, for everything about the problem should be said whether they thought it fit or not. In turn, the rest of the students rotated to the chart, writing as quickly as they could the things they knew, felt, or thought about the "mess." Some groups wrote in excess of 20 entries in the 5 minutes allotted for this task.

Using each list, Ms. Imani directed the students to talk together and select one item that "bugs" them most or seems to capture the situation best. Each group then rewrote the selection as a problem statement. The Osborn/Parnes model suggests that the problem statement begin with an "IWWMW . . . ?" phrase, or "In what ways might we . . . ?" For example, if a concern about the unspoiled magnificence of the forestland was the most troublesome aspect for one group, its problem statement might read, "In

FIGURE 8–6
Environmental Pollution Problem

> Timberland is a small village in rural Forest County with a population of just over 5,000. It is a friendly place to live with characteristics common to most villages—homes, stores, places to worship, restaurants, a movie theater, service stations, schools, government, and a few miscellaneous businesses. People are genuinely happy with their lives in Timberland, but a problem of great concern has surfaced recently and has grown in scope during the past year.
>
> The problem is how to capture what the village residents describe as a "new breed of vermin"—illegal garbage dumpers. Village officials have identified 17 illegal dumpsites in the 85,000-acre forest that surrounds Timberland. They have noticed rubbish and junk accumulating along the roadsides, stream banks, and hollows.
>
> The problem has grown in part because communities surrounding Timberland have grown in size the past few years and there is more and more rubbish to dispose of. The Departments of Sanitation of these communities have been overworked and the local landfill is nearly filled to capacity, so each household is limited to the removal of two trash containers per week.
>
> Hoping to help solve the problem, the local Unspoiled Forest Club organized a campaign that prompted the village government to post signs threatening fines or possible arrests for those caught dumping junk illegally. The junk piles kept spreading, however, and the forest faces the danger of becoming an unhealthy eyesore.
>
> The condition of the forest is a topic of daily conversation among the residents of Timberland. Some have suggested that more drastic actions be taken toward the solution of their problem.

what ways might we control the junk that is being dumped in the forest?" If health concerns were the most worrisome facet for another group, it might write, "In what ways might we avoid infestation by dangerous vermin and avoid contagious diseases?"

Idea Finding   This step involves brainstorming dozens of possible remedies for the problem. What are all the possible ways to address the problem statement? Using a clean sheet of chart paper and employing the same "relay" strategy as they used in the previous section, Ms. Imani encouraged the students to write whatever came to mind, even if it seemed to have nothing to do with a solution at this time. No idea would be critiqued until after all ideas had been written down. The students then looked over their lists and determined which one or two might best be made into an interesting solution. The students considered all possible ways that the tentative solution might be elaborated on or improved. The convergent phase of this step required the groups to restate the problem and narrow down lists of suggestions by addressing such concerns as, "Will this idea actually solve the problem? Will it create new problems? What are the chances it will work? Is it practical? Will we be able to use it in the near future? What are the strengths and weaknesses? Can any of the ideas be combined into one useful solution?" After narrowing their lists, each group worked toward an agreed-upon decision. The ultimate choice might contain one idea or a combination of ideas.

Ms. Imani prodded the students' thinking with thought-provoking questions such as those that follow:

- New Ideas

    Can it be used in new ways as it is?

    Can it be put to other uses if it is changed in some way?

- Adaptation

    What else is like this?

    What other idea does this make us think of?

    What new twist could we add to the idea?

    Could we change the color, shape, sound, or odor?

- Enlargement

    What can we add?

    Should we make it longer, wider, heavier, faster, more numerous, or thicker?

- Condensation

    What can we take away?

    Should we make it smaller, shorter, narrower, lighter, slower, or thinner?

- Substitution

    What else can we use to do the same thing?

    What other materials or ingredients might we use?

One group suggested making big signs such as "*Spruce* Up Around Here!" (*Spruce* was their play on words!) Another thought it would be constructive to establish a community cleanup "festival." Still a third announced that it would install surveillance video cameras in secret locations throughout the affected areas with the goal of identifying and prosecuting violators and forcing them to pay fines or spend time in jail.

Action Planning   This step involves expanding the interesting idea or combining interesting ideas into a statement that outlines an action plan that details the steps necessary to implement the solution: What course of action will we take? Does this plan depend on someone else's approval or support? What steps are needed? Who will do what? When must the steps be completed? The video camera group, for example, suggested that its program would need to be approved by the village council and could be paid for with a grant from the state Department of Environmental Protection.

Three major benefits result when students are involved in CPS in dynamic social studies classrooms: (1) higher feelings of self-confidence, self-esteem, and compassion result; (2) wider exploration of traditional content subjects and skills are undertaken; and (3) students use higher levels of creative invention in content and skills. Therefore, our classrooms must encourage not only the systematic problem-centered efforts associated with inquiry, but also the inventive, intuitive thinking associated with creative problem solving.

Creative problems differ from inquiry problems in that they call for divergent thinking as opposed to convergent thinking as students search for solutions to problems. Both types of problems, however, are crucial to today's dynamic social studies classrooms in that they encourage children to dig into things, turn over ideas in their minds, try out alternative solutions, search for new relationships, and struggle for new knowledge.

AFTERWORD

It often happens that when the word *research* is mentioned to college students, groans and steely glares accompany the predictable questions, "How long does the paper have to be? How many references do we need? What's the topic?" Exposing students exclusively to this type of forced research often builds negative attitudes toward the processes of problem solving and inquiry. Written reports on teacher-determined topics using secondary sources not only produce negative attitudes in students but also present an unrealistic view of research in the real world. While this kind of research has a place, to present it as the only form of research does students a disservice. We cannot limit elementary school research to such practices either; remember that most elementary school youngsters are natural problem finders. They take pleasure in investigating the mysteries of their world. On their own, they deftly uncover problems of interest—the important first step of research: "Why do farmers cut off the corn and leave the lower part of the plants behind?" "How many ears of corn grow on each corn plant?" What students need at school is to learn the methods through which these questions can be explored. While all the particular problems children bring to school may not be particularly significant, the processes they go through and the feelings they gain about themselves as capable researchers are. Therefore, authentic research associated with creative problem solving and inquiry processes teaches students that they have the skill and ability to pursue knowledge in a meaningful way and that their efforts have real value now and in the future.

REFERENCES

Amabile, T. M. (1989). *Growing up creative*. New York: Crown.

Dewey, J. (1916). *Democracy and education*. New York: Free Press.

Evans, R. (1973). *Jean Piaget: The man and his ideas*. New York: E. P. Dutton.

Monhardt, R. M., & Monhardt, L. (1997). Kids as curators. *Science & Children, 35,* 29–32; 80.

National Council for the Social Studies (1994). *Curriculum standards for social studies: Expectations for excellence* (Bulletin 89). Washington, DC: Author.

Osborn, A. F. (1963). *Applied imagination: Principles and procedures of creative problem-solving.* New York: Charles Scribner's Sons.

Parnes, S. J. (1981). *The magic of your mind.* Buffalo, NY: Creative Education Foundation and Bearly Limited.

Instructional Planning:
The Basis of Successful Teaching

WHAT DOES INSTRUCTIONAL PLANNING LOOK LIKE?

Marge Feeney, a student teacher eager to spread her professional wings, had spent her first two weeks in Mr. Willmore's fourth-grade classroom impatiently observing the daily routine, correcting papers, taking lunch count, assisting individuals in need of special help, and getting to know the children. At last, the day she had been longing for had arrived. Marge's cooperating teacher assigned her to teach her first lesson—a social studies lesson! The class had been involved in a cross-curricular study of Russia, and the students were having a wonderful time discovering some of the unique aspects of Russian culture. To enrich their understandings, Marge's job was to prepare a lesson about Russian currency. In a twinkling of an eye, her eager anticipation turned to sudden alarm. "Russian currency?" Marge's mind shrieked silently. "Why, I don't know anything about Russian currency! How does Mr. Willmore expect me to teach something I don't have a clue about? Even worse, what kind of activity can I possibly use to teach information I don't know anything about?" Trying to maintain a coolness that wouldn't betray her inner panic, Marge swallowed hard and choked out the words, "I'd love to teach tomorrow's lesson about Russian currency!"

Marge was jolted into a sudden realization that dynamic social studies teachers need a lot of information—much more than they can store in their minds. She learned that to be effective, she must be ready to say many times a day, "I don't know. I'll look it up." Marge went back to her college library, sat down at a computer, and found a useful site with the information she needed for her lesson.

When Marge felt comfortable with the content for her lesson, she took on the next challenge—finding a developmentally suitable instructional strategy. Knowing she had only 40 minutes for the entire lesson, Marge needed to employ a time-efficient model. Therefore, she decided to begin with a short explanation of Russian currency, followed by a game designed to reinforce the concept.

Mr. Willmore required his student teachers to write detailed daily plans. "With a plan in place," he advised, "you'll feel better prepared to face the students." Therefore, Marge set to work writing a rough draft detailing the content as well as the step-by-step procedures she intended to carry out during the lesson. After an hour of jotting down and organizing ideas, a lesson finally took shape (see Figure 9–1).

Now Marge needed only one extra hour to put together the needed game materials and assemble all the other essential supplies "Who said teaching was easy?" joked Marge.

FIGURE 9–1
Marge Feeney's Lesson Plan

Theme: Russia

Grade: 4

Teacher: Marge Feeney

Goal
The children will understand the Russian monetary system.

Objectives
1. The student will identify Russian coins and state their value.
2. The student will solve problems that require the regrouping of kopeks into rubles.

Materials
1. Duplicate for each of five groups: 1 game card; ten 1-kopek coins, ten 10-kopek coins, and one ruble.
2. One die for each group.
3. A set of four small toys such as a plastic car, box of crayons, ball, and spinning top.

Procedure
1. Divide the class into five groups of four students each.
2. Give each group an envelope containing Russian coin cards and ask them to empty the contents on their table.
3. Ask: "Does anyone know the country these coins are from?" "What are they called?" Have them examine the coin cards, calling special attention to the Cyrillic letters.
4. Explain that the coins depicted on the cards are from Russia and that a ruble is much like the dollar in the United States, a 10-kopek coin is like a dime, and a 1-kopek coin is like a penny. (There are also 2-, 3-, 5-, 15-, 20-, and 50-kopek coins and 3-, 5-, 10-, 25-, and 100-ruble bills.)

5. Invite the students to examine the money for a short period of time. Then introduce them to the Kopek/Ruble Game. In each group:

a. Players take turns rolling the dice.

b. Count the sum of the dice and ask for the amount in kopeks.

c. Take the designated amount of kopeks and place them on the kopek section of the game board.

d. When a group has 10 kopeks in the first column, it must exchange them for a 10-kopek coin and place it in the second column. When a group has ten 10-kopek coins, it exchanges them for a ruble.

e. See which team can be first to trade ten 10-kopek coins for a ruble.

6. To bring closure, tell the students that you will show them a small toy and the price of the toy in Russian money. Each child in the group numbers off from one to four. Assign each child a toy and ask him or her to select the duplicated coins necessary to buy the assigned toy. Ask, "What are the important Russian coins and bills?"

Assessment

1. Observe the students during the game to see if they are selecting the appropriate coins and whether the coins have been correctly regrouped.

2. Check to see if each student has selected the correct Russian coins to pay for his or her toy.

3. Students write in their journals about Russian money.

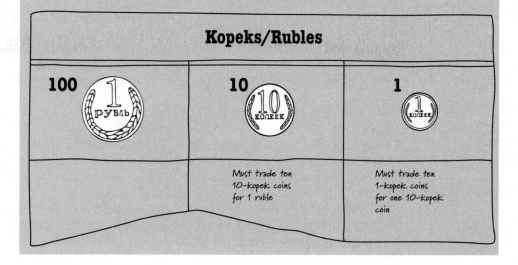

One could easily see that the growth in confidence Marge experienced from carrying out such a demanding professional challenge far outweighed the hard work she found herself caught up in. "I can do it," acknowledged Marge, "It's not easy, but like 'The Little Engine That Could,' I think I can . . . I think I can do it."

"It worked!" Marge bellowed to no one in particular as she returned from school the next day. "The lesson actually went well. It wasn't perfect, but it went well. I lost my train of thought once or twice, but the lesson plan kept me on track. I had the children explore Russian currency on a website (*www.masterrussian.com/blcoins. shtml*) and they learned all about kopeks and rubles. We played the Kopek/Ruble game and they loved it. When they got excited and I told them to calm down, they actually did. I feel like a real teacher, like I'm ready to step in and take over my own classroom. After all the course work, and all the worries, and all the dreaming, I think I'm ready to take the next step."

WHY IS PLANNING IMPORTANT?

Can you imagine a lawyer going to court without a legal summary (brief) of the case? How about a football coach going into the Super Bowl without a game plan? Would you allow a builder to assemble your house without the help of a set of blueprints? And, what kind of epicurean delight can you anticipate from a chef who cooks without a recipe? I think you would agree that the results in each case would be disastrous. Yet whenever the topic of planning for instruction comes up in my methods course, students are likely to whine, complain, gripe, and mutter their most melancholic complaint: "Do we *have* to write plans?"

I have found that one of the reasons why so many pre-service teachers underestimate the value of careful planning is that a great portion of their lives has been spent as students in classrooms. From this student-oriented perspective, teaching can look so smooth and effortless that the hours of background preparation and planning are undetectable. However, effective teaching is not a hit-or-miss process; teachers do plan ahead—formally or informally—to create an environment that sets learning in motion. Careful planning brings about such a command of content and mastery of teaching strategies that a well-prepared teacher's actions appear instinctive. This message comes across loud and clear to skeptics who stand in front of the classroom for the first time. They are often shocked to realize that when the spotlight is on them, the classroom, which they saw previously as an orderly domain, suddenly starts spinning with confusion and turmoil lurking at every turn.

Luckily, Marge Feeney realized that the framework on which successful social studies teaching rests is deliberate planning. After she experienced just how much the planning process contributed to the success of her Russian currency lesson, active planning became a high-priority in Marge's professional life. "Plans help keep me on course just like a roadmap for a trip, plotting out a sound route to a destination," explains Marge. "A friend of mine went into a lesson stone cold and the whole thing ended up a joke. The kids were bored and confused, and he kept wandering off track. I know my friend learned his lesson. I'm not so naïve to think that a plan in itself guarantees success, but it does give you a good guide for instruction and serves as a record of what should be kept for the future and what should be improved on next time."

To be fair, planning can be a tiring and time-consuming process; however, all good social studies teachers plan their daily lessons. Although experienced teachers will not spend the time and energy writing out the step-by-step formal plans that you will at this early stage of your career, they nevertheless understand the importance of planning. They think deeply about what needs to be done, even though their efforts may seem unsystematic (for example, jotting down their ideas on a note pad or in the small squares of large weekly planning books). They can record their lesson plans like this because their experience has helped them sense what methods and materials work best in certain situations. You do not yet have these experiences; therefore, you must be much more deliberate in outlining step-by-step plans.

Effective social studies teachers do not teach day to day, but their planning starts at the beginning of the school year when they examine what is expected to be taught during the entire year. They open up the textbook and examine the important topics to be covered. They examine the district curriculum guide for an idea of the concepts and skills that must be mastered. They become familiar with professional, state, and local standards that specify what students should know, understand, and be able to do. These sources are like a steering wheel on a car; they maneuver teachers in the right direction and guide the planning process. The planning process itself is carried out on two different levels. On one level, we have long-range plans called *unit plans* that usually last for about two to three weeks. *Lesson plans* spell out how daily instruction will be carried out. Unit plans describe long-term plans; lesson plans outline short-term, or daily plans.

HOW ARE UNIT PLANS CONSTRUCTED?

Unit plans are comprehensive outlines for instruction created by teachers around a central idea. They contain an orderly sequence of lessons that provide a sense of cohesiveness, or unity, to social studies instruction. The actual design of a unit plan varies from teacher to teacher. Some units are merely a chapter from the textbook supplemented with a few additional activities jotted down in the margins of the teacher's guide, but others are detailed written outlines for instruction incorporating content and processes from across subject lines, including math, science, literature, creative writing, music, and art. A five-step format provides the structure upon which most unit plans are built:

1. Select a topic for study.
2. Formulate goals and objectives.

3. Organize the content.

4. Select a rich variety of learning experiences.

5. Assess the degree to which the goals and objectives have been met.

Select the Topic for Study

Although it may appear deceptively simple on the surface, topic selection is one of the most delicate of all responsibilities associated with unit planning. The amount of freedom teachers have to select topics for study varies from district to district, so it is possible to encounter any number of freedoms and constraints. Consider the following examples:

- School district A has developed a districtwide, textbook-based social studies curriculum in its effort to meet state standards. It expects every teacher to follow the curriculum so closely that all teachers must be on the same page of the book at the same date; at times a subject area supervisor may check plan books to see that this is being done. There is little room for individual planning; the district contends that the textbook alone most effectively ensures achievement of state standards.

- School district B supplies a comprehensive curriculum guide and a set of textbooks for each teacher. Teachers are permitted to extend and enrich the specific topics as long as the basic subject matter and sequence of topics do not change. Conformity to specific content among all teachers is considered the most effective way to achieve state standards.

- School district C furnishes a curriculum guide and textbook program, but considers these more as guides for attaining standards than as the final word. Standards guide the curriculum, but the formality associated with a text-based program is missing. Topics and instructional strategies are modified as growing interests and needs dictate. This is a middle-of-the-road approach, moving away from textbook-dominated instruction, although not yet completely.

- School district D has developed a philosophy that the social studies curriculum should be planned by the teacher in response to state standards, but content is guided by student interests and backgrounds. Based on the standards, teachers formulate their own goals and objectives, learning activities, and assessment strategies. However, a great deal of emphasis is placed on integrating the curriculum and on the use of a variety of instructional resources, including individualized instruction, learning centers, self-paced materials, learning packets, and specialized research projects.

Should you have the good fortune to plan at least one special unit, the most important consideration is that the topic should have a high interest factor. What trips have you taken? What are you enthusiastic about? What do you enjoy reading about or watching on television? Do you have a rich knowledge of a particular culture? Likewise, what are your students excited about? What are some of their favorite stories, movies, television shows, and things to talk about? What questions do they ask? What are their ethnic/cultural backgrounds? In addition to interest, make sure that the topic is rich in literature, both fiction and nonfiction, and that it has natural links to other areas of the curriculum.

A lot of a teacher's energy and time go into selecting a topic, much more than first meets the eye. Nonetheless, the value of a personalized social studies program is obvious: It is chosen with your children in mind. And who knows your children better—you or the developers of a textbook series or curriculum guide?

Take Nina Zook, for example. She developed a fifth-grade thematic unit, *Great Inventors and Their Inventions,* for five good reasons. (1) "Inventors" was a required topic of study in her school district's fifth-grade curriculum. (2) The textbook treatment of inventors by itself was sketchy and needed to be enhanced. (3) She visited Washington, D. C., last summer and was fascinated by the presentations and exhibits at the Lemelson Center for the Study of Invention and Innovation at the Smithsonian Institution's National Museum of American History. She was impressed with the Center's mission to document, interpret, and disseminate information about invention and innovation; to encourage inventive creativity in young people; and to foster an appreciation for the central role invention and innovation play in the history of the United States. (4) She had collected assorted souvenirs, photos, videos, and print materials during her visit to the Smithsonian. (5) Her students were enthusiastic learners and had a keen interest in inventions and enjoyed expressing their inventive creativity.

One helpful way to think of actual unit construction is to imagine yourself as a tour guide and your students as passengers. You are about to escort this group as they embark on a most thrilling journey, a delightful excursion to exciting new worlds. Choosing a unit topic for a thematic unit answers the question, "Where are we going?" It provides you and your "passengers" with a general destination: "We're going to visit the creative world of inventors!"

Formulate Goals and Objectives

A tour guide and passengers cannot expect to embark on a pleasurable journey without having a good understanding of the trip's purpose: "We're going to visit the creative world of inventors? Great! But, what are we going to do when we get there?" If we do not take time to answer this question, we can run the risk of flitting about from one activity to another without getting much out of any, or of spending so much time on one or two things that we run out of interest, time, and energy. Coming up with a sequence of learning goals and objectives helps you avoid those problems by pinpointing precisely what you want to accomplish from the unit, and helps prevent the instructional sequence from wandering aimlessly or from becoming stalled in one place too long.

Goals

Goals, first of all, are broad, general statements of intended educational outcomes; in fact, they are such wide-ranging statements that most cannot be realized during the unit or even during the school year. Rather, students often work toward achieving some goals throughout all 12 years of schooling, and maybe throughout their entire lives. An appropriate goal statement, for example, is, "The students shall acquire understandings about the human experience from the past." An inappropriate goal statement is, "The students shall be able to select and defend their ten greatest inventions of all time." Can you see how the second statement defines specific understandings that are essentially limited to a single unit while the first is broader and more sweeping, appropriate for any number of units? Because goals are so wide-ranging, expecting to address more than three or four in any unit can become an exercise in futility.

For the sake of illustration, let us look at the goals Nina Zook wrote for the sample social studies unit, Great Inventors and Inventions:

1. The students will understand that every change, every invention, begins with the recognition of a problem or opportunity that somebody finds meaningful.

2. The students will understand that everyone has problems and challenges that need to be addressed and that most of them can be overcome using a simple, focused program of invention.

Objectives

The goals you have just read provide a general direction of the path we will take with the unit topic, but they are much too general for us to become aware of what will be specifically going on in the classroom. To extend our trip analogy, the tour director might inform us that we will be visiting the "Land of Great Inventors and Their Inventions," but that destination by itself does not tell us much about whom we will be meeting or what we will be doing. For that reason, our unit planning duties now move to identifying the expected outcomes with clearly stated objectives.

Writing objectives helps us inform. Objectives are statements that target the specific outcomes students will accomplish as a result of experiencing the unit of instruction. There are many recommended formats for writing unit objectives, but Norman Gronlund (1991) developed a style that seems particularly useful for our purposes. Gronlund's approach, or adaptations of it, is perhaps the most popular among curriculum writers and teachers today. In this text, I have chosen to use Gronlund's approach, which starts with writing a general goal and then clearly breaking the goal down into its specific objectives. To illustrate, one of the goals for Nina Zook's unit, Great Inventors and Their Inventions, is more precisely detailed as follows:

Goal

The students will understand that everyone has problems and challenges that need to be addressed and that most of them can be overcome using a simple, focused program of invention.

Objectives

1. The students shall understand that an inventor is someone who works hard to solve problems.

2. The students shall understand that some inventions are inspired by the desire to help people, others to make money.

Much as physicians translate physiological knowledge into medical practice, goals and objectives help teachers translate into educational practice.

3. *The students shall learn about the world's great inventors and their amazing creations.*
4. *The students shall be challenged to think like an inventor and dream up their own inventions.*
5. *The students shall understand and apply strategies to market their inventions.*

It is beyond the scope of this book to break down the remaining goal in Ms. Zook's unit plan, but the same process would be used. Although this course of action is time consuming, it is important to begin your unit plan with carefully selected and clearly articulated educational goals and objectives. These statements pinpoint what students should be able to know or do as a result of taking part in the unit and also serve as handy guides as teachers begin to organize the content, select instructional activities and materials, and assess the effectiveness of instruction.

Organize the Content

After stating the goals and objectives, the process of building a unit of instruction continues with a thorough search of the content required to help accomplish the targeted goals and objectives. Each unit has so much conceivable content that beginning teachers often become frustrated as they try to decide what information should be included and what should be left for another time. I find that they often try to include too much; as a result the unit quickly becomes unmanageable. The goals and objectives prevent this from happening by offering a clear idea of where to focus your content search.

Factstorming

A helpful technique to select and organize the unit content is called *factstorming*. Virtually any unit topic can be factstormed by a group or an individual. All that you need to get started is to think about what you already know. Begin by asking questions about the topic (for example, "What are considered to be the greatest inventions of all time?"). Repeat the process with each potential subtopic ("What are the steps to inventing?"). Most teachers do not know enough about the topic at this time to plan a good unit. But that's not the overall purpose of this activity; it is designed to simply help you realize what more needs to be done.

Expanding the Content

Once you exhaust what you already know about the topic, you will want to learn more in order to enlarge it. Toward that goal, you must have access to a variety of resources (the computer and a wide variety of print sources are good places to start). Check with your school or public librarian for references on a topic you wish to pursue. You should find yourself saying, "I'll look it up," many times a day.

The background material you unearth should be extensive. You will not use all of it, but when you teach elementary school children, it's best to learn all you can find out about a subject. As they progress through the unit, children will ask many questions. It certainly is ok to reply, "I don't know. Let's find out together," to some of the children's questions, but teachers who can answer a great many questions are the ones who gain their students' confidence and respect.

This important unit content should be outlined in a section at the beginning of your unit. The content outline is usually preceded by a short summary paragraph, like this one that will be used in Ms. Zook's sample unit, *Great Inventors and Their Inventions:*

Summary Paragraph

This is a thematic unit based on knowledge of inventors and their inventions. The lessons will introduce students to famous inventors, their inventions, and the process of formulating an invention. It is a learner-centered experience designed to motivate students to build on their knowledge of inventors, their inventions, and the invention process to create their own inventions. Emphasis will be placed on the problem solving and analytical skills involved in inventing. The culminating event will be an Invention Convention, where students will display their inventions for other students and their parents.

Immediately following the summary paragraph, you will need to organize an outline of the content. For the content outline, it helps to record the primary concepts and then list the key facts below each. Again, it is beyond the scope of this book to outline all the content appropriate for this unit, but the following example illustrates how the content outline for one concept (marketing) central to Ms. Zook's unit, *Great Inventors and Their Inventions,* could be outlined:

Content Outline

Concept: Marketing an Invention (Advertising techniques commonly used to persuade a buyer to purchase a product)

- ***Bandwagon*** *an appeal to follow the crowd*
- ***Buzz Words*** *words that have suddenly become popular with consumers (like "low-carb" or "natural")*
- ***Testimonial*** *someone you admire or respect endorses the product (like Tiger Woods endorsing a certain brand of clothing)*
- ***Snob Appeal*** *an attempt to convince buyers that owning a certain product is a status symbol*
- ***Facts and Figures*** *trying to convince a buyer that "nine out of ten families" prefer a certain product (without telling you who those families are)*
- ***Plain Folks*** *a suggestion that the product is a good value for ordinary people (such as an automobile manufacturer showing an ordinary family piling into a minivan)*
- ***Wit and Humor*** *giving customers a reason to laugh or to be entertained by clever use of visuals or language*
- ***Patriotism*** *the suggestion that purchasing this product shows your love of country (a company brags about its product being made in the United States by American workers)*
- ***Demonstration*** *simply showing the product in action*
- ***Problems*** *the product can help the buyer solve a problem (like cleaning out the rain gutters)*

Select the Learning Experiences

Once teachers target and outline the content for a unit, they face the next big challenge: "How can my students most effectively learn this content?" Learning experiences are the instructional activities we employ to achieve content goals and objectives, the actual experiences that involve children in puzzling, wondering, exploring, experimenting, finding out, and thinking. Not all learning experiences need to be new or unique; highest priority should be placed on balance and variety. Do not choose activities because they are "cute" or gimmicky; select them because they stand the best chance of accomplishing your goals and objectives.

This is often the section of a unit plan that creates a great deal of confusion for preservice teachers. Some instructional models require teachers to involve the entire class in the same experiences at the same time. Other models invite students to actively pursue individual interests. Which model works best? That is a question that has baffled educators since the onset of formal education, and one that has not yet been convincingly answered. After examining the pros and cons of all the models, however, Jarolimek and Foster (1997) offered some perceptive advice on the issue: "The act of teaching is so complex that it is nearly impossible to demonstrate that a specific way of teaching is superior to other ways for all purposes, with all teachers, with all children, for all times, and in all circumstances. . . . We are forced to conclude that there are many good ways to teach" (p. 146).

The nature of dynamic social studies calls for flexible, adaptable teachers. You may be surprised to know that not all contemporary teaching methods are original; most are adaptations or reworked versions of older, more traditional methods. The crux of successful teaching lies not in whether a method is new or old, but in flexibility; the younger the children, the greater the variety should be:

- Sometimes you will lecture to your children, but rarely; the younger the child, the less you should talk.
- Sometimes you will use good questioning and discussion techniques to hold instructional conversations with the entire class or with small groups.
- Sometimes you will lead whole-group learning experiences from the textbook or another common source of information; such experiences offer balance and proportion to the program.
- Sometimes you will bring to class objects such as jewelry, clothing, dolls, toys, books, catalogs, containers, tools, and other realia. These items help to form classroom connections to other people, times, and places.
- Sometimes you will choose books, computer applications, videos, slides, tapes, filmstrips, records, pictures, bulletin boards, and other learning aids to provide a variety of essential learning materials.
- Sometimes you will encourage children to solve problems and search for answers to their own questions; an independent quest for information is a lifelong asset.
- Sometimes children will work alone; meeting personal interests and needs must assume high priority in all classrooms. At other times you will encourage children to work together cooperatively; children learn a great deal from one another.

Plan the Learning Experiences

There are many ways to organize the learning experiences for a unit; the outline that follows is only a suggested guide. It should be adapted or restyled to suit your personal preferences and the needs of your students.

Regardless of the specific strategy employed, the challenge for dynamic social studies teachers is to create intellectually and socially active methods of instructions.

Phase One: Introductory Activities

Establishing classroom conditions that motivate children to learn is a major mission during this initial portion of the unit. What kind of "bait" can you cast out to "hook" students on the topic so they will participate as eager and involved learners? Usually encompassing the first day or two of instruction, the "hook" for a social studies unit can be cast out in a number of ways.

There are many good introductory experiences (field trips, community visitors, videos, realia, and the like); however, in my opinion, one of the most important ingredients is a good book or a well-told story. I call stories, either read or told, that are used during the introductory phases of social studies units *literacy launchers*. Their purpose is to sweep up the students and carry them off into the captivating, enchanting unit. As powerful as they are for this purpose, however, good stories should not be limited only as the introductory experiences. They are also powerful instructional tools when used at strategic points throughout the unit. A good unit is rich in litera-ture, both fiction and nonfiction.

Phase Two: Developmental Experiences

Following the introductory activities, you enter into what is often described as the "brass tacks" of the unit. Activities may be done independently, in small groups, or by the whole class, but what really matters is that you stay within the periphery of the children's interests. You must choose worthwhile experiences that are neither mere entertainment nor busywork, but are rich and powerful in potential learning. You must be constantly ready and eager to reach out and seize the most gripping experi-ences available. As you set this phase in motion, the students go to work; you may retreat a bit, since your initial teaching responsibilities as a stimulator and arranger are now over. You will have more teaching to do, but in other ways; you must now analyze the unit objectives and ask, "What learning experiences will most effectively help me achieve the unit's objectives?"

The developmental experiences, then, offer students opportunities to wrestle with real problems. The whole point is to help them comprehend the interrelation-ships among phenomena that can make this nation and the world better places to live. We do this not only from social studies alone, but by using experiences that cut across all subject lines.

Phase Three: Culminating Activity

While the preceding phases of the unit were content or process specific, the culmi-nating activity allows students to review, summarize, or bring closure to the topic. This concluding portion of the unit usually takes the form of a whole-class project that gives students an opportunity to apply or extend what they have learned. The cul-mination might be a time during which group projects are shared; a festival where dance performances, creative skits, and cultural meals are enjoyed; a "readers' fo-rum" where written reports are read; or a construction project, such as a model com-munity, where children represent the major concepts learned.

Sometimes a unit that follows is such a natural transition that neither a culmi-nating activity for the first unit nor an introductory experience for the second is nec-essary. If one unit deals with "The First Americans" (Native Americans), for example, and is followed by "Settling the Land" (early settlers), continuity from one unit to the next need not be broken.

You must carefully orchestrate the three major phases of activities, because each activity flows from preceding experiences and furnishes the foundation for those that follow. Think of the entire collection of activities as being much like a beautiful sym-phony that is made up of separate movements which, when woven together, shape a grand masterpiece.

Teachers usually describe the specific learning activities they have selected for the unit using either or a combination of two formats: *unit blueprints* and *daily lesson plans*. A unit blueprint gives a brief description, in paragraph form, of the daily ac-tivities a teacher intends to provide throughout the unit. Daily lesson plans, by contrast, are much more detailed; they expand on the blueprint's brief description by clearly and comprehensively detailing how things will be done. The following material describes Ms. Zook's blueprint. Any of the descriptive paragraphs can be easily expanded into a lesson plan, a process that will be detailed in the next section.

Phase One: Introductory Experiences

1.   Prepare an "Invention Box" with several unusual items that reflect both traditional and contemporary life, such as a "buttoneer" (gadget that replaces buttons in seconds) or a fake soda pop can that has secret storage for valuables. Obtain inexpensive items from friends, parents, restaurants, gift shops, or specialty stores. Wrap the box in brown wrapping paper and address it to the class. Ask a colleague or staff member to deliver the box to your classroom at a designated time. Looking surprised, bring the students to your group conversation area and say, "What do you suppose is in this special delivery package? Where did it come from?" Examine the box together for clues. Open the box and use these questions as you share each item: "What is it? How do you think it is used?"

Establish the point that an invention doesn't have to be something radically new or historically important. Even the simplest or more unusual items have an impact on our lives. Divide the class into groups of four. Ask the groups to think of all the appliances, medicines, and conveniences that have made a difference in their lives. Have all the groups contribute to a large class list of important inventions on the chalkboard. Then each group should rank the 10 they feel are most important in their lives. Did all the groups agree?

2.   Share Maynard Frank Wolfe's book, *Rube Goldberg: Inventions* (Simon & Schuster). Rube Goldberg is famous for producing ingenious cartoons that show the most complicated ways you can think of to complete the most ordinary tasks such as "Golf Inventions," "Simple Orange-Squeezing Machine" and "Idea for Dodging Bill Collector." Wheels, gears, handles, balls, and paddles are set in motion by canaries, boots, brooms, and shears to perform simple tasks like closing a window in case it starts to rain before you get home. Anyone who has played "Mousetrap" has witnessed a Goldberg invention. Goldberg's inventions appeared in newspapers every day from 1914 to 1964 as a single panel of drawings with an explanatory caption. The inventions were a tongue-in-cheek commentary on the Machine Age in which Goldberg lived as well as on the strong interest Americans displayed toward inventions and inventors of the time. The book presents a collection of Goldberg's inventions, comic strips, editorial cartoons, and sketches and provides a biography of Goldberg. A sample is shown in Figure 9–2. If the book is unavailable, you can sample some of Goldberg's clever inventions online (www.rube-goldberg.com).

3.   Gather containers full of various recycled objects such as dominoes, magnets, balls, cardboard tubes, funnels, yarn, thread, popsicle sticks,

FIGURE 9–2
Rube Goldberg Cartoon

balloons, glue, paper plates, bottle caps, empty thread spools, tape, cupcake paper tins—basically anything that could be found laying around the house or garage or in a junk box! Then show the class a Rube Goldberg Machine that you invented the night before from items that were lying around the house. Give a bag of "stuff" to each group. Invite them to use the materials to create their own Rube Goldberg invention that might turn the page of a book, drop a coin in a bank, pop a balloon, or perform some other common task in a complicated way.

After the inventions have been made, have the students gather for an informal get-together where they will exhibit their inventions and demonstrate how they work. The Rube Goldberg inventions will remain on display in the classroom throughout the entire unit.

Phase Two: Developmental Experiences

1. Read to your students from the book, Mistakes That Worked by Charlotte Foltz Jones (Doubleday). The 40 stories in this book portray inventions made by mistake. For example, Ruth Wakefield invented the "Toll House" (chocolate chip) cookie while running a Toll House Inn in New Bedford, Massachusetts. Having an imaginative touch, Mrs. Wakefield thought it would be interesting to make a special kind of cookie for her customers. She broke apart a chocolate candy bar and dropped the pieces into regular cookie batter. As the cookies were baking, Mrs. Wakefield thought the pieces would melt and marble into the cookie. However, when she bit into a finished cookie, Mrs. Wakefield was amazed that the chocolate chips were still intact, just a little softened. By accident, a delicious new cookie had been invented and quickly became a "Toll House" favorite.

After discussing the story of the Toll House cookie, divide your class into small groups. Challenge them to invent their own special cookies. The students must agree what special new ingredient (à la the chocolate chips)

will be in their cookie, what shape their cookie will take after it is baked, and what to name it. They should draw an illustration of their new invention. Finally, the groups should share their cookie inventions with each other. Display the illustrations in the room throughout the invention unit.
2.   Now that the students have had a "fun" introduction to the inventing process, they will be motivated to spend time learning about various inventors. It is time for the students to research the lives of inventors and prepare presentations for each. Organize a text set of books about great inventors (see Text Set 14). Assign groups of four students to separate titles from the text set. As they read, the students should uncover the following information:

- When the inventor lived
- The inventor's most famous invention
- Why she or he invented it
- The details of the invention
- Other interesting inventions by the inventor (if there were any)
- An explanation of the significance of the invention

Make a large chart with the headings related to the categories of information researched. Have each group fill in a summary of the data it uncovered. Discuss the results.

The students in each group should work together to design a costume that one member might wear to share information with the rest of the class. Did he have a moustache? Then the speaker should have one, too. Did she wear a hat? So should the speaker. The children should use their creativity to find items either at school or at home that would help them look like their inventor. They should try to act just like the inventor. In addition to looking and acting like the inventor, the students should try to use some type of aid in describing the invention. Would a large illustration work? What about a model or the actual invention?
3.   Involve the students in the actual steps of inventing something in response to a problem. First, lead a brainstorming session during which small groups identify as many problems as they can about their home, school, neighborhood, or any other location. Then, the students should narrow their lists to three. Next, they should examine these three problems and focus on one that bugs them the most. Centering on that problem, students should brainstorm ideas for an invention that could solve it. For example, one group may decide that they become quite uncomfortable playing outdoors on cold winter days. After scampering around for awhile, their noses inevitably begin to run. It is not easy for them to sort through layers of coats and sweaters to find a tissue or handkerchief. After considering several alternatives, including a handkerchief that could be attached temporarily to a coat sleeve and used to swipe away the drops (and removed to wash), the group suggested an invention called the "Stop

Theme: Great Inventors and Their Inventions

Russell Freedman's biography of Orville and Wilbur Wright, **The Wright Brothers: How They Invented the Airplane** (Holiday House), is an excellent resource for 9- to 12-year-olds. This biography tells the story of the lives of the Wright brothers, from the time they were little boys tinkering with toys to when they finally sold their marvelous invention to the United States government. This book shows how the airplane started out as a glider and developed into a plane that eventually stayed in the air for an hour and 13 minutes. The book is illustrated with a large number of photographs, many taken by the Wright Brothers themselves.

Laurie Carlson's **Boss of the Plains: The Hat That Won the West** (DK Publishing), is a story of how John Batterson Stetson invented the "ten-gallon hat." As a boy, John Stetson dreamed of going west. When at last he went, he found that everyone wore whatever hats they'd worn back home: knit caps, wool derbies, straw sombreros. Stetson found that the sun blistered his face because his derby did not provide enough protection, so the young hat maker invented the wide-brimmed "Boss of the Plains." Others struck gold or blazed trails through unknown territory, but John Stetson made his mark with a hat.

Catherine Thimmesh's **Girls Think of Everything: Stories of Ingenious Inventions by Women** (Houghton Mifflin) is a compilation of inspiring stories of successful women and girl inventors. Students will learn about what inspired these women and girls and how they turned their ideas into reality.

Dripping Mitten." The mitten carried a supply of tissues inside a dispenser built into its palm.

4.   Next, the students must plan and design their inventions. Distribute large sheets of drawing paper that could be used to sketch their designs. The students should draw the plans clearly and completely so that they could be easily understood by someone who would be interested in making the device. The drawings should show every feature of the inventions. It would be instructive to show students examples of actual sketches of inventions made by their inventors. If your students can do it, they might be interested in using the guidelines for making patent sketches. There are regulations for the size of the paper and the format, the color of the drawings, their proportion, the system for numbering and reference, and their inclusion in the patent application. You can find the specific guidelines on the official website of the United States Patent and Trademark Office (www.uspto.gov/web/offices/pac/design/index.html#drawings). Sample

Eva Moore's **The Story of George Washington Carver** (Scholastic) is a biography of one of the most distinguished individuals of our time. Born into slavery, he grew up to become a world-famous scientist and inventor. Carver is best known for his invention of hundreds of ways to use peanuts and sweet potatoes.

Keith Elliot's **Steven Jobs & Stephen Wozniak: Creating the Apple Computer** (Blackbirch Marketing Partners Series) highlights the importance of cooperation and teamwork in the invention process. The book tells the story of two contemporary inventors who were daring leaders in the personal computer revolution.

Bruce Koscielniak's **Johann Gutenberg and the Amazing Printing Press** (Houghton Mifflin) is a fact-filled book that starts out by explaining how books were handmade and individually penned to order in 15th-century Europe. After this overview, Gutenberg's revolutionary idea for a printing press is introduced and the story of this famous printer's successes and difficulties is told.

TRY THIS

Teachers are responsible for locating text sets of picture books and chapter books to incorporate in social studies thematic units. Some will be read aloud to students, others will be read independently, and a few will be read during guided reading time. Together, these books will comprise the text set for any topic. Working in groups of three, choose a grade level and select an appropriate social studies theme. Collect six books that you would use to build a text set and explain which would be read aloud, read independently, and read during guided reading time.

illustrations drawn by actual inventors can be found on various other sites as well. They serve as effective models for the students.

5.   After the groups have planned and designed their inventions, they have the opportunity of giving them a name. Students should not underestimate the importance of coming up with a good name, for the name has a very important purpose: It helps sell the product. A good product name will help get attention, especially if it is catchy, easy-to-remember, or clever. When students have created a name, they should make sure it will do all it can to bring attention to the product:

- *Does the name adequately describe the product?*
- *Will the name project the idea you want people to get?*
- *Is the name easy to remember?*

The next step in the invention process entails applying for a patent. A patent is an agreement between the U.S. government and an inventor that protects anyone from stealing the inventor's idea. Again, the specific guidelines can be found on the official website of the U.S. Patent and Trademark Office. For the purposes of this unit, however, group members will file a joint "application" for their inventions, a simplified version that asks them to name their inventions, describe them, explain the things they feel are unique and useful, attach the sketches, and verify that the works are theirs by placing their signatures in the spaces provided: "We, the undersigned, affirm that we are the original and first inventors of the _____." Of course, like the real patent application, the inventors must obtain signatures from two witnesses who can substantiate their claims.

When the applications are complete, they are sent to the Commissioner of Patents and Trademarks at the U.S. Patent Office (the teacher) who will check them to see if everything is complete and done according to the rules. The teacher will sign the applications, issue the inventions official patent serial numbers, and stamp them with the official acceptance date.

6.   No one is going to come knocking at the door of our new patent holders to buy their new inventions unless they promote them. If they expect to make money from their inventions, our young inventors must get people to buy them. One way to find potential buyers is to advertise the product, and one of the best ways to advertise it is to examine newspaper or magazine ads to find items that are similar to theirs. Then, using the advertising techniques described earlier in this chapter, the students should find examples of persuasive techniques. Discuss the ads with these prompts:

- Does the ad attract attention?
- Does it show the benefits of buying the product?
- Does it create a desire to buy the product?

To make students aware of the power advertising has in the success of a new product, have each group select one technique that they think will help make their product successful. Then have them design and display their own advertisements.

Phase Three: Culminating Experiences

Make known to others the products of the students' ingenuity by holding an "Invention Convention," a display of student-generated inventions. Both the Rube Goldberg-style and patent-awarded inventions, along with related activities, are organized on tables in different areas of the classroom. Parents enjoy seeing what can happen when their children's creative juices really get flowing. Send a note home cordially inviting parents to attend the Invention Convention. At the end of the event, award an Invention Convention certificate of achievement to each young inventor. The students will enjoy the pats on the back and encouragement that will pour their way on this big day!

Drama is a pleasurable vehicle that can be used successfully to integrate and apply social studies concepts and skills.

Unit blueprints describe the general flow of the unit activities; the lesson plans shed light on the explicit way those activities will be carried out. Figure 9–3 shows the lesson plan Ms. Zook wrote to outline the way she planned to carry out the Rube Goldberg Invention activity.

Assess Learning and Teaching

The final section of a unit plan describes the course of action you will take to gather information and provide feedback about student progress. This function, called *assessment,* is the process by which teachers collect clear, timely, and focused data on how well their students are meeting intended instructional outcomes in light of state and national standards. The purpose of assessment is to supply teachers and students with information and insights essential for improving learning quality and teaching effectiveness.

Knowing what and how well students learn has been and continues to be an important part of educational practice in social studies and a catalyst for strengthening and improving instruction. Standardized tests have been the customary measuring tool for gauging student growth and are considered to be among the most reliable and objective ways to measure academic performance. If used properly, standardized

FIGURE 9–3
"Rube Goldberg Inventions" Lesson Plan

Topic: Rube Goldberg Invention

Grade: 5

Teacher: Nina Zook

Goal

The students will understand that every change, every invention, is the result of someone's imagination and creativity.

Objectives

1. The students shall use their ingenuity and creativity to build their own Rube Goldberg machine.

2. The students shall understand the basic steps involved in the invention process.

Materials

Gather items from the junk drawer, garage, schoolroom, or home: cardboard tubes, string, old play figurines, jar lids, paper cups, rubber bands, thread spools, wire, small wheels, any junk.

Procedure

1. Review the information about Rube Goldberg, especially examples of his "real" Rube Goldberg machines depicted in his wacky cartoons.

2. Divide the class into groups of three and give each group a "junk" box ("Inventor's Kit").

3. Tell the students that they will use the materials in their Inventor's Kits to create a distinctive Rube Goldberg machine that will burst a balloon (the last step of the machine). Their inventions should consist of six actions in a chain of events; the last event is the burst balloon. The Rube Goldberg project rules are:
   - There must be six events.
   - The events must be clearly visible.
   - The goal is to burst a balloon.
   - Safety is important. Fire is prohibited. Any pointed objects such as a dart, nail, or pin cannot travel a distance of more than a foot.

4. Encourage the students to play with the things in their boxes. Can a toy car bump into something and knock it down? Can a string pull something up or knock it down? Can a ball roll down a ramp to set something else in motion? Use your creativity!

5. The students should sketch their ideas on a piece of drawing paper. Draw simple pictures of things that seem to work well so they won't be forgotten. Is there a theme that might be used (perhaps some toy military figures can be central to a battlefield scene or a toy tractor and toy cow can be part of a farm theme?) Start building the machine. Don't overlook a major element of Rube Goldberg's inventions—wackiness!

6. The students should remember what they have been learning in science class—levers, inclined planes, and other simple machines. They should also be reminded that many ideas they come up with might not be used and that they will change their minds quite a bit in the beginning.

7. Creativity cannot be forced out in a short time. The students may need two or three class periods to complete this project.

8. After the inventions are completed, have the students gather for an informal get-together where they will exhibit their inventions and demonstrate how they work. The Rube Goldberg inventions will remain on display on a table in the classroom throughout the entire unit.

Assessment

1. Observe students during the invention activity to determine the degree to which they are achieving the lesson objectives.

2. Use a rubric to assess the effectiveness of the invention: Is it unique? Does it have the right number of events? Does it work consistently? Have all the conditions been met?

tests provide teachers with evidence of academic growth. They can be used to compare the achievement of students in a school district, reveal how students in one school district compare to students across the state or nation, indicate the degree to which a school is meeting standards of instruction, provide support for grouping and placement decisions, help identify students in need of special services, and aid teachers in making curricular decisions.

When test results are used improperly or accepted as the singular evaluative tool, however, the consequences can be damaging. To clarify, it is acknowledged that a disconcerting misuse of standardized tests has resulted in a phenomenon known as *high-stakes testing*. High-stakes tests are standardized tests tied to major educational decisions such as whether a student will advance to the next grade, enter a preferred program, or receive a high school diploma. High-stakes tests could also be tied to district or school funding, teachers' and administrators' salaries, or even the accreditation of schools. Teachers in schools that perform well on the standardized tests may get cash bonuses, while poor student performance may result in sanctions so extreme that the operation of a school can be taken over by the state.

When test scores have such serious consequences—and they often do—teachers are forced to teach to the test, glumly realizing that this kind of instruction devalues good classroom instruction and undercuts the authenticity of scores as measures of what children really know or can do. Test generated instruction often leads to repeated drill-and-practice activities bolstered by mounds of worksheets because teachers feel pressured to cram as much knowledge into the student's minds in as little time as possible. One first-year teacher expressed the resultant stress: "I was petrified that my class would do so poorly that I wouldn't be back next year. So I taught what the other teachers recommended to get them ready for the test. After the test I started teaching, good teaching. The class enjoyed it, and I think they learned more the last three weeks of school than they did the first six months, because I was more relaxed, the students were more relaxed, and I was able to hone in on those areas where they needed help" (Livingston, Castle, & Nations, 1989, p. 24).

Such reactions only help to support the contention that "what gets tested gets taught"; that is, the system of assessment dictates the system of instruction. The National Council for the Social Studies (2003) took a firm stance on the role of high-stakes testing as it affects social studies instruction: "NCSS does not support the practice of using student assessment results to evaluate teachers and to rank schools, purposes for which the assessments were not designed" (p. 1).

NCSS does affirm that some standards may be most appropriately assessed with standardized tests. Knowledge, for example, is a necessary and valued outcome of social studies instruction for it underlies critical thinking and civic decision-making. Other outcomes, however, lend themselves to multiple assessments that require higher-order thinking, writing, and connecting social studies knowledge to applications in the world outside of school. To that end, NCSS recommends *performance assessments* that are intended to reflect real-life situations, including open-ended test questions, portfolios, essays, presentations, exhibitions, and large projects carried out over a period of time. Compared to standardized tests, says NCSS, performance assessments provide a more accurate gauge of student achievement.

Performance assessment in social studies is designed to further the goal of preparing students to become active citizens in a democratic society, making informed and reasoned decisions as citizens of a democratic society in an interdependent world. In the global world of the 21st century, students need not only know the basics but also must think creatively, critically, inferentially, and analytically. Educators and parents alike have recognized that the basics are no longer good enough and are calling for a closer match between what students learn in school and what they will need to know or be able to do as adults in a democratic society. As a result, performance assessment is evolving into a process that goes beyond the results of standardized tests to an examination of skills and understandings applicable in real-life, or *authentic situations*.

Authentic Assessment

Authentic assessment, another term for *performance assessment*, is a form of assessment where students are asked to perform tasks that demonstrate meaningful application of targeted knowledge and skills. The tasks involve students in challenging situations where they must use social studies knowledge and/or skills to produce effective and creative exhibits or presentations. To offer a trite analogy, let us suppose that I was your university's head basketball coach and had just opened a preseason tryout camp where I will be evaluating candidates for a possible place on the team. Naturally, I am interested in finding out whether the aspirants have a good understanding of the game as well as the skills necessary to perform at a high level on the basketball court. Would it be wiser for me to assess their knowledge and abilities by administering a multiple-choice test or by observing them perform on the hardwood? Although a coach's decision is obvious when it comes to judging athletic talent, teachers find that they, too, are better able to assess learning in school subjects if they ask their students to perform authentic tasks. A variety of approaches are possible for authentic assessment in social studies classrooms, but the following steps are considered necessary components of any design: (1) target the learning outcomes, (2) match the assessment practice, (3) specify performance criteria, and (4) use the results wisely.

Target the Learning Outcomes   To begin the assessment process, you must first pinpoint the desired learning outcomes: "What should my students know or be able to do after they have completed this lesson or unit?" You have clearly identified those outcomes in the goals and objectives for the unit, and should use them as a measuring stick to select assessment options. However, in recent years, the authentic assessment movement has assigned state or professional standards a more prominent place than goals and objectives as a guide for assessment design. Thus, high-quality authentic assessment usually begins with a set of standards in mind. Standards are important because they set reasonable expectations for what teachers need to teach and students need to learn. Clear social studies standards inform parents and teachers what is expected of their students and offer a guide for measuring each student's performance and achievement.

Connecticut has become a leader in the use of diversified assessments to assess social studies instruction. Its assessment plan is driven by a carefully articulated vision of learning, *Connecticut's Common Core of Learning (CCL),* a standards document which sets forth what students should know and be able to do as they prepare for productive adult life and responsible citizenship (*www.state.ct.us/sde/dtl/curriculum/ currkey2.htm*). Based on the standards contained in its *Common Core of Learning,* the Connecticut State Department of Education has initiated a multifaceted assessment program designed to measure outcomes delineated in the *Core*—a new model that includes, in addition to formal tests, authentic measures such as exhibitions, hands-on performance experiences, student portfolios, and other tasks that require students to demonstrate knowledge-in-use.

It is important for teachers to be aware of the standards established by NCSS or their respective state educational agencies so that assessment can be effectively based on the purpose for learning. For example, if a content standard specifies an outcome such as, *"Students will demonstrate knowledge of how the U.S. system of government works,"* then a written test might be a time efficient alternative. On the other hand, a standard such as, *"Students will use geographic tools to explain the interactions of humans,"* requires students to demonstrate their knowledge and skills in more complex ways. Clearly stated outcomes help teachers match the assessment method to the target of instruction.

Match the Assessment Practice   As has been previously stated, the type of assessment you choose must be related to learning outcomes as contained in state and professional standards documents. And, in an effort to provide better information about student academic growth, educators are transforming assessments from traditional paper-and-pencil tasks to more performance-oriented approaches. For example, the way to find out if Lamont can meet a targeted objective of reciting the *Pledge of Allegiance* is to have him recite it. And, if a lesson objective is to teach children how to fill out a patent application, then having the student fill out one would be considered an appropriate assessment strategy. If you want to find out whether Belinda understands the steps of the invention process, it would be appropriate to watch her during a class activity to see if she can carry out the process. By gathering information from situations and contexts like those in which students normally learn, the results may be more meaningful to you, to them, and to their families.

Performance-based or authentic assessment tasks are those which engage students in real-world tasks. Examples of performance assessments include:

- *Group projects*   enabling a number of students to work together on a problem that requires planning, research, collaboration, and group presentation.
- *Writing tasks*   reflecting students' understanding of social studies content through description, analysis, or summary.
- *Portfolios*   allowing students to provide a broad portrait of their performance through files that contain collections of work assembled over time.

Group Projects

As assessment tools, group projects allow for both the examination of content outcomes and for the evaluation of students' ability to function as a group member. Social studies projects that involve making a product and/or delivering an oral report provide especially worthwhile contexts for authentic assessment.

The teacher and other students can evaluate the performance and contribution of each group member during project presentations. Groups may be organized informally—random pairs of students helping one another learn—or formed to carry out a well-defined task. Before groups begin their work, however, you must make sure that students are not only skilled at working collaboratively but that they also have clear guidelines for their projects and presentations. You must inform them of the purpose of the group activity as well as the criteria that will be used for assessment. Students can then use the assessment criteria to help them develop the product or presentation. (See the next section for an elaboration of this point.)

Projects can take many forms, from designing posters and pamphlets to building models and displays. While projects and presentations function as important assessment tools, they also invite students to connect with important knowledge and processes as they construct new ideas.

Inside an Active Classroom

Aba Oshodi took his fifth grade students on a field trip to an Igbo Arts exhibit at a local cultural museum. The exhibit displayed more than 100 objects produced by the Igbo (or Ibo) people of southeastern Nigeria. The items at the exhibit included wooden totemic sculptures, pottery, textiles, examples of painting and body adornment, and a variety of masks. Though wood predominated, as it does in most African art, the exhibit also included objects fashioned from bronze, iron, and ivory.

The purpose of the visit was to stimulate interest in the Igbo through the beauty of their creative work. Mr. Oshodi's goal appeared to have been achieved as the students returned full of questions ripe for investigation: "Why are the small totemic figures important to the Igbo?" "What was the purpose of those intricate masks on display?" Mr. Oshodi capitalized on the strong spontaneous interest and established research groups that ventured into the world of the Igbo through visits to Internet sites, informational books, newspapers, and other references including informational pamphlets from the exhibit.

A whole new world opened up to Mr. Oshodi's students—they learned that Igbo art forms were a direct expression of their culture. For example, the small, wooden totemic figures (*ikenga*) symbolized traditionally masculine attributes such as strength, courage, and aggressiveness. These carved figures were kept in the men's meetinghouse. Among women, body jewelry such as ivory and brass anklets symbolized prestige and social satisfaction. The masks played a major role in the Igbo's masquerades in which male performers acted out various aspects of their spiritual beliefs.

The Igbo culture became more clearly understood and appreciated each day as its rich heritage and creativity came alive in the classroom. After the children had amassed sufficient information to fulfill their curiosities, Mr. Oshodi suggested a number of tasks that the groups might use to share what they had uncovered. The goal-directed tasks would serve as assessment tools because they required the students to use the information they had uncovered and interpret it in a meaningful way. One group created jewelry for a mini-display; another made a model of an Igbo mask; a third designed calabashes with intricate geometric designs; a fourth assembled a replica *ikenga*. Each group was responsible for addressing these questions:

- What is the item?
- From what is it made?
- How is it used?
- What do we have in our culture that compares to this item?

Each group demonstrated and described its item to the class. At the conclusion of the experience, Mr. Oshodi asked his students what they had learned about the Igbo culture from the items they researched. Through the group assessment tasks, the children became creators of original art forms that communicated the discoveries they made as captivated learners.

Writing Tasks

Writing tasks have long been used to assess a student's understanding of social studies through a written description, analysis, explanation, or summary. Writing tasks can readily demonstrate how well a student uses facts in context, expresses her or his ideas in creative ways, or structures a clear argument or discussion. Most writing tasks are expository in nature and can be easily assessed with observational checklists and rubrics that describe levels of content focus and writing mechanics. However, many opportunities for expressive (creative) writing are also found in social studies.

For example, Julia Blumenreich extended the study of African tribal societies by introducing *persona* as a writing technique. The fifth graders had learned that people in many African tribal societies have a "bush soul" that can take the form of something from nature—an animal, tree, rock, cloud, or any other object that might give someone strength and courage. Ms. Blumenreich used this understanding as the basis for a creative writing activity.

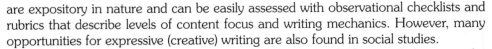

Inside an Active Classroom

Ms. Blumenreich started the lesson by displaying a large wall poster showing a young African woman adorned in ceremonial attire gazing thoughtfully across the tropical savanna into a brilliant sunset. Ms. Blumenreich asked her students to close their eyes and try to imagine for a moment to be this young woman. Then the students were asked questions about their transformation: "Who are you?," "What are you doing?" "How do you feel?" "What is it like to be you?" and "What are some of the things you've experienced in your young life?"

Ms. Blumenreich wrote their responses on the chalkboard and then organized several as a free form poem on the chalkboard:

> There was a young woman,
> Adorned with jewels,
> And painted with earthen ashes.
> It seemed like only yesterday
> When she skipped freely among the trees and grasses.
> Now she prepares for her wedding day.
> What lies ahead is invisible.

The group-generated model was kept in full view as Ms. Blumenreich distributed to the students individual photos of African tribal village life cut from old *National Geographic* magazines. The students were asked to compose their own persona poetry from these photos using the strategies from the model writing experience. Once completed, the poems were read aloud and mounted on a bulletin board where they were displayed for all to enjoy.

Diagnosing learning is an ongoing process throughout all such writing activities in social studies classrooms. Whether you choose to engage students in composing poetry, biographies, diaries, stories, or any other written product, continuous assessment of their strengths and weaknesses must be a priority. Student written products are far more useful than are scores from formal tests in gaining information about their social studies knowledge and abilities.

Portfolios

Portfolios have come to the forefront as a valued authentic assessment alternative. Paulson, Paulson, and Meyer (1991) describe a portfolio as "a purposeful collection of student work that exhibits the student's efforts, progress, and achievements in one or more areas. The collection must include student participation in selecting contents, the criteria for selection, the criteria for judging merit, and evidence of student self-reflection" (p. 60). There is no single list of items recommended for portfolios. They may include items such as student writings, art products, photographs, independent research reports, projects, favorite books, and other work samples from the social studies.

Nina Zook liked the idea of using portfolios to assess her students' progress in the unit, *Great Inventors and Their Inventions*, but felt they required a model before they were able to put together their own. So she used a special introductory plan.

Inside an Active Classroom

Ms. Zook wrote the word *portfolio* on the chalkboard. She asked if anyone had an idea of what a portfolio might be. Anticipating that not many would have a clue, Ms. Zook brought out a box containing items that, in effect, created a biographical sketch. She informed her students that portfolios tell a story and that she chose objects that helped tell a story about herself as a person.

The first item in Ms. Zook's portfolio was a photograph of her family. "I love my family," she announced proudly and showed that her husband and young children were in the picture (along with Barkley and Betty Basset Hound, the family pets). Next came her college diploma: "I was the first person in my family to graduate from college," she said proudly. Several ribbons followed—they were awarded to her as a youngster for winning several swimming championships. Ms. Zook then held up a favorite book and explained, "In my spare time, I enjoy reading." The most fascinating items came next—a photo of Ms. Zook taken when she was a fifth grader and her report card from the same grade. "I wanted to show you the best report card I ever received," she explained. "I had a fabulous fifth-grade teacher." The last article she removed from the box was a children's book, *The Little Engine That Could*. "This is one of my favorite books. From the first time my parents read it to me as a child, I loved it. It taught me that a person could accomplish almost anything if he or she tried hard enough."

Comparing her collection of personal memorabilia to a social studies portfolio, Ms. Zook asked the class what might be included in their portfolios for the unit. She received several suggestions: daily assignments, drawings, illustrated plans, their writings and reports, group projects, individual projects, journal entries, oral reports, and so on. The class then discussed the format of a good portfolio. They decided it should be housed in a suitable container—boxes, file folders, or binders. File folder "Inventor's Portfolios," all agreed, made excellent containers. The class also decided the portfolio should be neat and include a table of contents. Furthermore, each item should have with it a short personal statement about why it was important to the learner. Following this discussion, Ms. Zook gave her students two days to organize their portfolios.

There are countless ways to organize portfolios; the important consideration is that the students take an active role in selecting material for and maintaining them. Of course, the portfolios must address instructional standards and objectives. When students create their portfolios, their exhibits become a means through which you may provide evaluative feedback and monitor progress. You should hold individual conferences with the students during which you guide portfolio review with such questions as the following:

- "How has your work in social studies changed since last year (or last month)?"
- "What do you now know about _____ that you didn't know before?"
- "What are the special items in your portfolio?"
- "What would you most like me to understand about your portfolio?"
- "How did you decide to organize the items?"
- "What are the strengths as displayed in the portfolio? What needs improvement?"

The conference should focus not just on subject-matter accomplishments, but also on planning strategies, personal reflections, and evidence of progress. Adams and Hamm (1992) address this important aspect of portfolio use:

> Learning requires communication—with self, peers, and knowledgeable authorities. It also requires effort and meaningful assessments of these efforts. Since students need to be actively involved in evaluating and providing examples of their own learning, they must document the probing questions they are asking, identify what they are thinking, and reflect on their understandings. In this way students can create, evaluate, and act upon material that they and others value. Assuming active roles in the learning process and taking responsibility for what students are learning goes beyond simply recognizing that they have made a mistake to imagining why, getting feedback from others, and finding practical ways to do something about it. Portfolios provide a powerful way to link learning with assessment. They can provide evidence of performance that goes far beyond factual knowledge and offers a clear and understandable picture of student achievement. (p. 105)

Portfolios are a rich source for individual assessment in the social studies. They yield much concrete evidence that allows teachers to evaluate the progress their students are making. While this is important, however, the greatest asset of portfolios may be in self-evaluation. Portfolio assessment offers students the opportunity to set individual goals, select the items for evaluation, and reflect on their work. In this way it encourages pride in learning and helps students develop the motivation to improve.

An important point to remember about assessment is that no single instrument or technique can adequately measure the range of performances and behaviors in social studies. For this reason, educators today strongly favor using portfolios containing a variety of evidence. Despite these popular endorsements, some teachers have been slow to use portfolios in their classrooms. They are skeptical of whether the results justify the time required to evaluate multiple measures. Administrators must provide teachers with the time and support required to effectively evaluate student portfolios. School district and building administrators hold the key to helping teachers endorse this form of assessment. If teachers can see portfolios as manageable and rewarding, they will be inclined to add them to their already full workload and to evaluate them with enthusiasm.

Specify Performance Criteria In step one of our authentic assessment process, you pulled from the goals and objectives of your lesson and unit as well as from standards statements to identify what you want your students to know and be able to do. In step two, you selected the tasks students would perform or produce to demonstrate that they have met the goals, objectives, or standards. For step three, you will want to make sure that the criteria for judging student performance on the tasks are as specific as possible: "What knowledge or behavior can I expect to see in the students' performance?" and "How will I know if the students have done a good job?" In answering those questions you will be identifying the *criteria* for performance on the tasks.

Suppose you designed this assessment task to address an objective from Ms. Zook's invention unit: *Write a letter to a friend describing the steps you followed while creating your new invention.* Since the purpose of this assessment task is to find out whether or not students understand the invention process, you must establish criteria to measure that understanding. That is, you must clearly list the specific information students must include if their letters are to be considered either excellent, acceptable, or poor. For example, Ms. Zook decided that these points must be included in each letter:

- Define the problem
- Brainstorm ideas
- Plan and design it
- Name it
- Patent it
- Market it

This responsibility is important because the criteria form your basis for assessment—your expectations for an excellent letter may be that students must include each of the six elements listed. With such specific criteria, you can be more consistent when comparing one student with another. However, because authentic assessment invites students to personalize the way they present the information, end results need not all look alike. This does not mean, however, that students aren't responsible for including accurate facts and information as they complete the assessment task. Should a student's letter, for example, ramble on about how much fun the invention activity was without getting into the specifics of the invention process, there would be a concern about whether the student mastered the intended content. By contrast, references to the six elements, along with clear examples, indicate a strong mastery of the material.

Because a student's proficiency on any authentic assessment task is often judged by matching the student's performance against a set of criteria, we refer to the assessment tasks as criterion-referenced measures. Teachers usually select from among several different types of criterion-referenced scales that contain the essential criteria for the task and appropriate levels of performance for each criterion. Some of the most common are *observation checklists* and *rubrics*.

Observation Checklists

Observation checklists offer social studies teachers one of the most versatile and time-efficient tools in their authentic assessment repertoire. A carefully constructed observation checklist or rating scale should be used during observations of students as they are involved in performances related to the objectives for the lesson. Because they are relatively easy to construct and use, many teachers find it convenient to employ observation checklists for these purposes. Observations checklists are particularly helpful when you want to determine the degree to which students have demonstrated specific skills, behaviors, or competencies. To construct an observation checklist, first list the specific outcomes to be assessed and then record the occurrences of each. A sample observation checklist for behaviors considered important for cooperative learning is shown in Figure 9–4.

Rubrics

Teachers often use rubrics to identify important strengths and weaknesses in student learning. Rubrics consist of two primary components: *performance criteria* and

FIGURE 9–4
Observation Checkilst for Cooperative Learning Skills

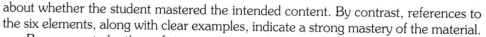

	Sometimes Present	Mastered
Assists co-workers when needed		
Follows group-established rules		
Does fair share of group work		
Respects group decisions		
Shares materials willingly		

Directions:

(√) Place a check in the "Sometimes Present" column if the characteristic is occasionally observed.

(+) Place a plus in the "Mastered" column if the characteristic occurs habitually.

( ) Make no mark if the characteristic is observed seldom or not at all.

level of performance. They are constructed by listing the behaviors associated with an assessment task and describing various qualities of those behaviors. The criteria, or characteristics of performance, are usually listed in the left-hand column of a rubric. A number or other indicator of the quality of work is often placed at the top of the rubric. To design a rubric, a teacher would include at least two criteria and at least two levels of performance.

The rubric shown in Figure 9–5 may give you a sense of one way rubrics are used to assess written reports. It was created online at RubiStar, a free Internet site supported by a grant from the U.S. Department of Education (*www.rubistar.4teachers.org*).

What to Do With the Results   After you carry out authentic assessment tasks, it is critical to examine the results and, if appropriate, make changes in classroom instruction. In other words, if you are not going to use the results, then don't require the students to perform the assessment task. Assessment results have important implications for instruction, for just as authentic assessment measures student learning it also influences the nature of instruction.

The primary aim of authentic assessment is to promote worthwhile social studies instruction for all students. To that end, our nation's schools have used assessment results to determine how well they are meeting instructional standards and to alter instructional practices so that standards can be better addressed. But unless the assessment practices match what is taught and how it is taught, the results are meaningless.

The skills to carry out effective authentic assessments are quite difficult to master. Because judgments of quality can be somewhat personal, you must make every effort to be fair and objective. For that reason, it is important to establish clear criteria and precise standards of behavior.

The assessment section brings to an end our discussion of unit and lesson planning. Planning at both levels is a crucial element of dynamic social studies instruction. Planning, either formally or informally, is a continuous process for everyone, for there is a constant need to keep materials, activities, and techniques up to date. As a new teacher, you will work hard to accumulate a rich teaching repertoire; ideas can be found in magazines and journals, and ready-made file cabinets (virtual file cabinets) are out there on the Internet, free for the taking. So, dive into the planning process, examine the many planning sources that are regularly popping up, and experience the joy and satisfaction of creating a plan for a topic that has held your fascination. Perhaps you will make an important professional contribution that will become a rich source for future generations of teachers and students in your school district to enjoy.

AFTERWORD

Creative teachers clearly demonstrate a key ingredient of first-rate instruction—a characteristic I call "stick-with-it-ness." This is a persistent, intense commitment to what they are doing. Teachers with stick-with-it-ness are thrilled with their professional responsibilities. Teaching is more than their job—it is their passion. It leaves them virtually starry-eyed and eager to devise experiences that activate children for

FIGURE 9–5
Rubric for Written Research Report

CATEGORY	4	3	2	1
Organization	Information is very organized with well-constructed paragraphs and subheadings.	Information is organized with well-constructed paragraphs.	Information is organized, but paragraphs are not well constructed.	The information appears to be disorganized.
Quality of Information	Information clearly relates to the main topic. It includes several supporting details and/or examples.	Information clearly relates to the main topic. It provides 1–2 supporting details and/or examples.	Information clearly relates to the main topic. No details and/or examples are given.	Information has little or nothing to do with the main topic.
Sources	All sources (information and graphics) are accurately documented in the desired format.	All sources (information and graphics) are accurately documented, but a few are not in the desired format.	All sources (information and graphics) are accurately documented, but many are not in the desired format.	Some sources are not accurately documented.
Internet Use	Successfully uses suggested Internet links to find information and navigates within these sites easily without assistance.	Usually able to use suggested Internet links to find information and navigates within these sites easily without assistance.	Occasionally able to use suggested Internet links to find information and navigates within these sites easily without assistance.	Needs assistance or supervision to use suggested Internet links and/or to navigate within these sites.
Paragraph Construction	All paragraphs include introductory sentence, explanations or details, and concluding sentence.	Most paragraphs include introductory sentence, explanations or details, and concluding sentence.	Paragraphs included related information but were typically not constructed well.	Paragraphing structure was not clear, and sentences were not typically related within the paragraphs.
Mechanics	No grammatical, spelling, or punctuation errors.	Almost no grammatical, spelling, or punctuation errors.	A few grammatical, spelling, or punctuation errors.	Many grammatical, spelling, or punctuation errors.
Diagrams & Illustrations	Diagrams and illustrations are neat, accurate and add to the reader's understanding of the topic.	Diagrams and illustrations are accurate and add to the reader's understanding of the topic.	Diagrams and illustrations are neat and accurate and sometimes add to the reader's understanding of the topic.	Diagrams and illustrations are not accurate OR do not add to the reader's understanding of the topic.

learning. All children must believe that their teachers are captivated by what they are doing in the classroom. In social studies, this means that teachers view their world with fascination and inspire their children to accept theirs as a never-ending mystery. To do this, teachers must plan significant learning situations in which there is a little mystery, a bit of magic, and a dash of magnificence to confront the children. Elementary school children respond to these situations; that is what makes their classrooms different from those for any other age.

Teachers achieve magic in the elementary school social studies program when they help each child become challenged by the activities and emotionally involved in the subject matter. They deliver the best for each youngster and make the most of their time every day. Teachers adapt instruction to meet the special needs and interests of all their students; they fully understand and are willing to work toward fulfilling the principles and assumptions that underlie learning carried out by small groups or individuals. Teachers use a large variety of learning tasks to meet their students' needs. Although thematic planning has become extremely popular in recent years, many elementary school social studies teachers continue to use a number of techniques that have been a part of the educational scene for years. We will learn more about these techniques and about the kinds of activities most appropriate for individual pursuits in the following chapter.

REFERENCES

Adams, D. M., & Hamm, M. E. (1992). Portfolio assessment and social studies: Collecting, selecting, and reflecting on what is significant. *Social Education, 56*, 105.

Gronlund, N. (1991). *How to write and use instructional objectives.* New York: Macmillan.

Jarolimek, J., & Foster, C. D., Sr. (1997). *Teaching and learning in the elementary school.* Upper Saddle River, NJ: Prentice Hall.

Livingston, C., Castle, S., & Nations, J. (1989). Testing and curriculum reform: One school's experience. *Educational Leadership, 46*, 24.

National Council for the Social Studies. (1994). *Curriculum standards for social studies: Expectations of excellence* (Bulletin 89). Washington, DC: Author.

National Council for the Social Studies (2003). Promoting fair and equitable assessment, [Online] Available http://www.socialstudies.org/positions/assessment/, January 5, 2005.

National Education Goals Report. (1995). Washington, DC: U.S. Government Printing Office.

Orlich, D. C., Harder, R. J., Callahan, R. C., Kauchak, D. P., Pendergrass, R. A., Keogh, A. J., & Gibson, H. (1990). *Teaching strategies: A guide to better instruction.* Lexington, MA: D.C. Heath.

Paulson, F. L., Paulson, P. R., & Meyer, C. A. (1991). What makes a portfolio a portfolio? *Educational Leadership, 48*, 60.

Ryan, K., Burkholder, S., & Phillips, D. H. (1983). *The workbook.* Upper Saddle River, NJ: Merrill/Prentice Hall.

Shepard, L. A. (1989). Why we need better assessment. *Educational Leadership, 46*, 5.

Key Instructional Resources:
Going Beyond the Ordinary

WHAT DO KEY INSTRUCTIONAL RESOURCES LOOK LIKE?

Econ is a friendly toy spider who dangles from an elasticized string while helping children learn all about their world by integrating language arts, mathematics, art, music, and economics. "Econ" rules the Land of Economics and invites the children to journey to his kingdom. The kingdom consists of 26 towns, each with an economic alphabet letter name. Producers, whose occupations begin with the town letter, live in each town. *A-Town* is the home of artists, actors, and advertising executives; *B-Town* houses barbers, bankers, and butchers; in *C-Town* live chefs, carpenters, and coal miners. Several days are spent in each town, where children learn about occupations starting with that letter. Vera Dunbar invites parents to class to talk about their occupations—for example, Isaiah's mother, a landscaper, visited during *L-Town* week. Parents become members of the VIP (Very Important Parent) Club, and all are encouraged to visit during the weekly studies.

Mrs. Dunbar must stretch the limits of her creativity while trying to ensure that each occupation has only one VIP visitor (if there are two truck drivers ready to come to the classroom, for example, one would be the "truck driver" and the other a "delivery person"). VIPs are classified as either producers of goods or providers of services. Appropriate storybooks, videos, field trips, and other sources of information help fill in the content while students visit a specific town; creative dramatics, art projects, writing activities, and reinforcement games supplement instruction and provide for information processing and enrichment.

As the journey through the economic alphabet comes to an end, usually during the busy holiday weeks in December, Econ welcomes the children to a beautiful shopping mall, unfortunately not completely constructed because of an untimely strike. Econ leads the children in a discussion of some of the causes and effects of strikes. Even though the strike has now been settled, it will take more workers to complete the mall in time for the holiday shoppers. Econ asks the children to work for him.

Children work and plan the shopping center with Econ's help. He hires them to staff the shops, paying them in play money for their "labor" in completing the mall. Finally, they become eager consumers at the luxurious new shopping center. One day, half of the class is assigned to work in the shops while the other students are consumers. The next day, the groups reverse roles.

The shopping center includes a bank where students deposit and withdraw the play money they earn in class. Stores include a restaurant, a card and gift shop, a travel agency, a bank, a flower shop, a fast food service, a shopping market, a jewelry store, an electronics boutique, a shoe store, and a clothing shop. The story of a pizza shop illustrates how one business was created.

After a field trip to a local pizza shop, the children are ready to transform an unoccupied store space into their own pizza restaurant. Their first task in setting up the restaurant focused on arranging the tables and chairs for the customers and making sure the "kitchen" was ready to begin producing pizzas. Once that was accomplished, others thought some special touches were needed: flowers for the tables, pictures on the walls, a telephone for reservations, and even wallpaper to brighten up the space. Crews went to work on each project, taping up their own artwork for pictures, getting the play telephone from the dramatic play center, using sponge printing to create several sheets of patterned "wallpaper," learning from Mrs. Dunbar how to make flowers out of pipe cleaners and tissue paper, and selecting easy-listening music for the diners.

Next, the children concentrated on a name for the restaurant as well as signs, menus, a logo, and order taking. They decided that "Pizza World" would be a fine name for their restaurant. Mrs. Dunbar provided paint and a long sheet of butcher paper for the children to make a large sign. They decided to use a pizza slice as a logo and painted one next to the name. Other groups made "restroom," "no smoking," "exit," "open/closed," and "please wait to be seated" signs.

After carefully inspecting the sample menu from the pizza restaurant they visited, the children decided to use it as a model for their pizza menu. They looked through old magazines for pictures, but ended up drawing their own and putting the prices next to an illustration of each food and drink item. Mrs. Dunbar cut some sponges into the shape of their logo, and the children stamped the logo onto the menu, plain white napkins, take-out boxes, place mats, and order pads.

Now the children used their pizza restaurant to dramatize the roles of producers and consumers. Some were customers and sat at the table ("Do you take credit cards?"). Others put on aprons to take orders ("Hello. My name is Christopher. What can I get for you?"). No one seemed to notice that most of the orders were taken down in scribble writing. Two children donned chef's hats and pretended to flip and spin pizza crusts.

The pizza restaurant is but one example of the kinds of projects you would find if you visited Mrs. Dunbar's mixed kindergarten/first-grade social studies classroom. As a matter of fact, Mrs. Dunbar's children began another project immediately after their interest shifted from the pizza restaurant to Gerald, who came to school with a new pair of eyeglasses. You guessed it—a trip to the ophthalmologist and the construction of an eye care facility was next, complete with an eye chart that helped some children learn the alphabet to a section that displayed pipe cleaner "designer frames."

The restaurant was one area that the children came back to visit over and over again. As they added the eye care center and other stores, they took great pride in giving tours to parents, other classes, and building visitors. It became the catalyst and context for the study of neighborhoods and communities throughout the year.

Mrs. Dunbar was an extraordinary teacher with many years of experience when I met her during my first year of teaching. A model professional, Mrs. Dunbar had a tremendous influence on my teaching career. This remarkable woman motivated children to do great things. She encouraged them to be curious, active, and persistent in finding answers to life's mysteries. If you were lucky, somewhere along the line you would have had a Mrs. Dunbar. Someone who made the sun come up. Someone who smiled and was patient. Someone who wouldn't let you quit. Someone who told you that all things really are possible. Someone who motivated you to fulfill your potential.

The Mrs. Dunbars of our world realize that the goal of dynamic social studies education is to develop informed, caring citizens who will one day make a difference in our country and world. To help achieve this goal, our Mrs. Dunbars make social studies a subject that drives children to want to learn more by reading them fascinating stories of Alaska's untamed frontiers, helping them write with Chinese *ideograms*, making special Pueblo paper-thin *piki* bread, creating a salt-and-flour relief map of the United States, or searching through the Internet to uncover fascinating information about coal mining.

William Webster (1993) had his Mrs. Dunbar, too—a special teacher who evoked similar memories. His Mrs. Dunbar was named Miss Monroe. While a little boy in Miss Monroe's room, Webster first learned what a fascinating world he lived in:

When we studied the Colonial era, we visited Philiplse Manor, the home of an early Dutch patroon. We danced the minuet and made candles. We also wrote stories, created plays, and learned our arithmetic by preparing Colonial food and building sets for our dramas.

That year we also studied Brazil and the great Amazon River, and it sparked in me a lifelong desire to go see the river, the rubber trees, and how tapioca grew. . . . My mother came to school and helped my teacher, Miss Monroe, cook the tapioca, something we

TEXT SET 15

Inspirational Books About Teachers

Jack Canfield's, Mark Victor Hansen's, and Sharon Wohlmuth's **Chicken Soup for the Soul Celebrates Teachers** (HCI) offers an inspirational collection of stories and photographs that celebrates the influential teachers in our lives. This photo essay illuminates the teacher-student bond and helps readers recall that special teacher who inspired them to greatness.

Jack Canfield's and Mark Victor Hansen's **Chicken Soup for the Teacher's Soul: Stories to Open the Hearts and Rekindle the Spirit of Educators** (HCI) contains nearly 400 pages filled with dozens of humorous and heartwarming true stories from the archives of actual teachers' memories. This should be required reading for all students who are considering teaching as a career.

Patricia Polacco's **Thank You, Mr. Falker** (Philomel) is a children's picture book in which little Trisha (Patricia Polacco herself) is elated at the thought of starting school and learning how to read. But when she looks at a book, all the letters and numbers just wiggle around on the page. Her classmates make matters worse by laughing at her and calling her "dumb." This all changes after her family moves across country and she meets Mr. Falker (actually George Felker), a stylish new teacher who recognizes Trisha's exceptional artistic ability and her learning problem.

now call parental involvement. My classmates and I constructed a native village using papier-mâché for the rubber trees and weeds for thatch-roofed houses. The richest girl in the class was the daughter of a ship captain who had been to Belem. Her father came and told us about the city, which we now label "using community resources." (p. 45)

As a result of his involvement in these splendid activities, Webster developed a lifelong infatuation with Brazil and the Amazon River. He had a powerful dream to travel there. Decades later, Webster's little-boy dream came true; he visited Brazil and traveled the Amazon, living everything he had learned about in Miss Monroe's class. Webster was fortunate to have a teacher who brought such life to her social studies program that she was able to inspire lifelong dreams within her students. However, Webster laments that an overwhelming emphasis on meeting standards and achieving high scores on standardized tests are cheating many of today's social studies teachers of their dream-building time. Has the quest for inspiration been squelched by a sanitized and bland school curriculum? Have we seen the last of our Mrs. Dunbars and Miss Monroes?

When your first class comes eagerly marching into your classroom, whom will they face as their teacher? Will you take your place among the Mrs. Dunbars and Miss Monroes of educational history? Or, will you be satisfied to be counted among the ordinary? Some of your children, like Webster, will only need to have their natural enthusiasm for learning kept alive, while a number of unlucky others will need to have it revitalized. Fortunately, you can reach both groups by offering learning materials

Gloria Houston's **My Great Aunt Arizona** (HarperTrophy) is another inspirational children's picture book about a gifted teacher. As she grows up, Arizona longs to visit the faraway places she reads about, but her mother dies while she is still young and is forced to take on family responsibilities. Despite all the obstacles facing her, Arizona becomes a teacher and, for 57 years, influences the lives of generation after generation of students in her one-room schoolhouse.

Ellen Kindt McKenzie's **Stargone John** (Henry Holt) is a children's novel about John, a child who uses his senses in creative ways to experience things most people don't. He and his invisible friend, the Meesong, travel to places only John can imagine. John attends a rural, one-room school where his teacher punishes him cruelly for his outward lack of interest. Fortunately, his sister takes him to visit an ex-teacher who is sightless because of cataracts and allegedly a little strange. She turns out to be the liberator in John's life; soon he is learning—in his own special way.

TRY THIS

I am especially grateful to all the wonderful teachers who have shared their lives with me. Think of one who has been especially important in your life. Share that teacher's story with your classmates.

that fascinate children and capture their interest. Sometimes you will use textbooks and workbooks, but not all the time; these will be but one kind of teaching tool. A true test of your skill lies in how well you choose all other materials for instruction. What will work best today: trade book, textbook, video, computer, slides, filmstrip, pictures, overhead transparency, cooking, singing, dancing, field trip, or guest speaker? Sometimes the children will need to sit, but most of the time they will be up and moving, performing tasks and investigating Earth's mysteries.

Everyone sitting in your classroom, including you, has a teacher to thank. You've all had that special person in your lives who you could count on, a special teacher who was able to find that delicate balance between fun and seriousness that was the key to unlocking your world. Find the time to let that once-in-a-lifetime individual know just how much she or he mattered. As a final Text Set for this book, I've decided to honor the spirit of all excellent teachers by presenting a collection of books not specifically for children, but for you. These books tell the inspirational stories of teachers who have made a difference. If you read one book, you'll want to read them all!

DOING SOMETHING REAL

Because children of all ages learn best when involved in experiences where they can actually do something, the first job of all dynamic social studies teachers is to challenge them with fascinating materials and rich inspiration. Direct involvement in real experiences like making fabric dyes from berries or designing petroglyphs (early Native American cave drawings) not only deepens their understandings, but also widens their interests. Social studies teachers around the country have developed significant learning situations in which their students are actively and directly involved in doing something real:

- Designing an Egyptian-style calendar, creating numbers the ancient Egyptian way.
- Decorating Ukrainian Easter eggs, called *pysanky*.
- Preparing and eating Russian pancakes, called *bliny* (blee-NEE).
- Celebrating "Juneteenth," a slang combination of "June" and "nineteenth." Food, music, and dance commemorate the day in 1865 when the slaves discovered the Civil War had ended.
- Reciting this prayer chant, to the slow beat of a drum, that was used by the Navajo people:

  May I walk in beauty before me.
  May I walk in beauty behind me.
  May I walk in beauty below me.
  May I walk in beauty above me.
  With beauty all around me, may I walk.

- Folding paper in the Japanese origami tradition.
- Playing "Marble Bridge," a game German children like to play.

Realia

Hands-on learning has become a familiar phrase in social studies education, but like many other recurrent terms and phrases, there are discrepancies about what *hands-on-learning* means. Rather than enter into a debate about the issue, we will simply operate with the idea that hands-on learning generally refers to any activities that use real materials (realia). Hands-on learning, however, does not simply have to do with handling things; it is using realia to engage students in absorbing inquiries with objects and drawing meaning and understanding from their experiences. As students develop effective investigative techniques, they learn the *what, how, when,* and *why* of things and people. A hands-on approach requires students to play an active part in the learning process rather than passively read a textbook, listen to a lecture, or watch a video. Field trips and resource persons are traditional sources of hands-on experiences in social studies, but hands-on includes having students manipulate and maneuver the things they are studying—a Nigerian calabash, Chinese tangram, Korean 1,000-won note or 50-won coin, and a genuine Navajo rug. Students should also have many opportunities to handle instruments of investigation: maps, globes, compasses, computers, timelines, charts, graphs, timing devices, cameras, and calculators. Social studies must be experienced to be understood. The concept of hands-on social studies is based on the belief that children should learn with the methods of natural exploration they naturally use while trying to make sense of the world around them.

Inside an Active Classroom

Hisham Barradah had been experimenting with a variety of ways to teach social studies for the first year-and-a-half of his teaching career. Most of what he tried was confined by the safety of his textbook, and each resulted in a reasonable amount of success. But he was not satisfied. He wasn't sure what it was, but the feeling lurked in the back of his mind that something was missing. Mr. Barradah began to tire of doing essentially the same thing with his students, so he started to talk with other teachers, read professional magazines, and take graduate courses that could help him discover new strategies to enliven his social studies program. Throughout all his inquiries, one major theme seemed to stand out—*active learning.* Mr. Barradah was fascinated by the possibilities of active learning in which students are given the opportunity to use hands-on materials, participate in real experiences, and employ other meaningful resources in their quest to understand a problem or topic of instruction. With the time that remained in the school year, Mr. Barradah decided he would create one special unit that required student initiative and active participation.

To begin the special unit of study on Japan, Mr. Barradah prepared a "cultural box" with items that reflected many aspects of both Japanese traditional and contemporary life. He borrowed items from parents and friends who travel, located some free items in Japanese restaurants, and bought a few things from gift shops and a local import store. He purchased the "cultural box," a large, hand-woven bamboo "hitsu," or kimono storage chest. Mr. Barradah opened the antique brass hinged box and used these questions as he pulled out each item: "What is it? How do you think it is used? What do we have in our culture that compares to this?" The last item he pulled out was a manila envelope containing a round-trip "airline ticket" to Tokyo for each child. Mr. Barradah challenged students to find Japan on a large world map. He asked them to name the ways people might travel to Japan, tracing the various routes on the globe. He had the students prepare for their trip by filling out "passports" (samples are available at local post offices).

A Japanese *kamishibai* storyteller (Mr. Barradah, in costume) was the first person the children met on their visit to Tokyo. Kamishibai, a unique form of Japanese street storytelling, is an authentic folktale strategy. The kamishibai storyteller, who was also a candy seller, rode from neighborhood to neighborhood on a bicycle equipped with a small stage for showing story cards. He entered a neighborhood striking together two wooden clappers, and everyone knew it was story time. The children ran from their homes so they could buy candy—those who did were able to sit closest to the stage. The storyteller illustrated his stories with 12 to 16 story cards, on the back of which were written the corresponding parts of the story. He was sure not to read all the cards during one visit, for he wanted to capture enough intrigue by reading only three or four to entice the children to come back again. Mr. Barradah used a number of illustrated kamishibai cards to tell a traditional folktale, *The Tongue-Cut Sparrow.* [Authentic kamishibai cards can be ordered from: Kamishibai for Kids, P.O. Box 20069, Park West Station, New York, NY 10025-1510; telephone and fax, (212) 662-5836.]

Another activity started with Mr. Barradah's oral reading of *Tree of Cranes* by Allen Say. It is a tender story of a young Japanese boy who recovers from a bad chill after falling into an ice-cold pond. His mother gives him a hot bath and sends him straight to bed, seemingly ignoring the confused boy. However, as he sleeps, his mother is busily folding origami paper into delicate silver cranes in preparation for the boy's very first Christmas, just as she celebrated Christmas in California, where she grew up. Since a large part of the plot had to do with paper cranes symbolizing love, peace, and sharing, the children enjoyed learning how to make authentic origami cranes from folded paper, a centuries-old art form in Japan.

Next, Mr. Barradah thought it would be instructive to simulate a day in the lives of Japanese schoolchildren. He assumed the role of a Japanese teacher (*sensei*) who taught the children some basic school-related information, such as Japanese writing and numeral characters.

Mr. Barradah began this simulated school day by having the students greet him in traditional Japanese style. The students stood behind their chairs and bowed to Mr. Barradah (*sensei*), offering the greeting, "O-hayo gozaimasu," which means, "Good morning."

Mr. Barradah informed the students that they would be making a well-known Japanese folk toy that has been treasured for generations since the sixth century. He displayed the sample *Daruma doll* that had been contained in the cultural box and explained that these dolls are named for a Buddhist priest who traveled to China, Japan, India, and other countries. He was an Indian Buddhist named Bodhidharma who is purported to be the founder of Zen Buddhism. Zen is actually a way of life rather than a religion. It requires meditation, inner serenity, and a balanced and orderly way of life. The Daruma doll's form portrays a highly stylized seated figure without arms or legs. The Buddhist priest is said to have lost the use of his arms and legs by sitting for nine years with them crossed in meditation. See Figure 10–1.

In some parts of Japan, the dolls are used to bring good luck. Mr. Barradah introduced the idea of making a wish for something good to happen and asked them to recall some of the things they associated with good luck—rabbit's foot, four-leaf clovers, wishing well, and lucky penny. He informed the students that children in Japan make wishes with the Daruma doll. The Daruma doll is constructed much like "roly-poly" dolls in the United States. No matter how hard it is pushed over, it bobs right back up. It has become the symbol of "never give up, keep trying."

Mr. Barradah helped the students make their own Daruma dolls by giving each student a blown egg with an enlarged hole at the bottom. The children put a small fishing sinker (sand works well, too) into the hole and covered the hole with masking tape. Next, they coated their eggs with four layers of papier-mâché strips. After the strips dried, the students painted on the clothes. The clothes could be painted in many colors, but the most traditional is red, symbolizing the priest's red robe. Next, they colored in the face, leaving the eyeballs blank. The dolls are given to someone who is trying something new. When that person sets a goal, one eye is painted in; when the goal is accomplished, the other eye is painted in.

Mr. Barradah invited the students to set two goals for the remainder of the school year. After one goal is accomplished, they should add one eye. When the other goal

FIGURE 10–1
Daruma Doll

Procedure

1. Review the previous lesson by having the students greet the teacher in traditional Japanese style.

2. Review the Japanese kanji figures from the previous day. Inform the students that they will experience a sample craft lesson today; they will be making a toy that has been appreciated for generations in Japan. Discuss some of their favorite toys. Are any of their toys like the ones their parents enjoyed as children?

3. Display the souvenir Daruma-san dolls. Explain that legend has it that these dolls are named for a Buddhist priest (*san* means "mister," a title of respect) who sat in a red robe with his arms and legs crossed for 9 years while contemplating serious problems. A roly-poly doll that, no matter how it is tipped, bobs back upright represents Daruma-san. Traditional Daruma-san dolls (popularly called "roly-polies" in the United States) are painted red with a face having no eyes. The dolls are given to someone who is trying something new. When that person sets a goal, one eye is painted in; when the goal is accomplished, the other eye is completed.

4. Help the students make their own Daruma-san dolls. To make the dolls, give each student a blown egg with an enlarged hole. The children put a small fishing sinker through the hole and cover the hole with masking tape. Next, they coat their eggs with four layers of overlapping papier-mâché strips. After they dry, the students can paint on a face, leaving off the eyes. The clothes could be painted in many colors, but the most traditional is red (symbolizing a red robe).

5. Encourage the students to set two goals for the remainder of the school year. After one goal is accomplished, they should add one eye. When the other goal is accomplished, the remaining eye should be colored.

6. Discuss the patience and determination it takes to reach an important goal.

is accomplished, the remaining eye should be painted in. He and the students discussed the patience and determination it takes to reach an important goal.

Several other activities immersed Mr. Barradah's students in Japanese culture, but one they enjoyed very much was built around Japanese food. To begin, Mr. Barradah read the book *How My Parents Learned to Eat* by Ina R. Freedman. The class discussed the similar and dissimilar eating habits of Japanese and American cultures. To immerse them in the Japanese culture, Mr. Barradah gave each child a set of chopsticks, a free item he got from a Japanese restaurant. He demonstrated how to use the chopsticks: hold one like a pencil; slip the other chopstick under the first one, leaning it against your third finger; move the second chopstick up and down to pick up crumpled pieces of paper. The students practiced with the chopsticks and crumpled paper for awhile.

The next day, Mr. Barradah showed the students pictures of food enjoyed in Japan and pictures of authentic Japanese restaurants. The students were then escorted to the multipurpose room where, with parental help, Mr. Barradah had set up a mock-up Japanese restaurant with a low table, pillows for sitting, menus, and kimonos for wait staff. Simple Japanese food such as kiwi fruit, vegetable tempura, noodles, rice balls, and rice cakes were served. Although contemporary Japanese children enjoy such varied fare as spaghetti, hamburgers, and Korean BBQ, the experience of tasting the traditional items was essential. Japanese people distinguish traditional Japanese-style dishes as "Washoku" (*Wa* means "Japanese-style" and *shoku* means "food") as opposed to Western foods, which are generally called "Yo-shoku" (*Yo* means "western-style"). Traditional Japanese music played in the background as the children dined in elegance.

Active learning is student-centered because students become actively involved with the material being learned; it is a hands-on, experiential approach.

Field Trips

Field trips are first-rate learning adventures for any age—kindergartners, upper-graders, high school or college students, and adults. Who doesn't learn best when taken to a firsthand source of information? Good field trips for elementary school youngsters involve students as active participants. A trip to the automobile museum during which children are lectured at by a guide or required to be silent onlookers is not as good as a trip that allows them to get into an automobile, sit in the driver's seat, talk to the owner, listen to the engine roar, and possibly even be taken on a short ride on a protected course. A trip to the bakery where the children can only watch something being made is not as good as a trip that allows them to measure and mix the ingredients for a batch of muffins that they will devour later. A good field trip must envelop elementary school children in opportunities for direct, meaningful involvement.

Inside an Active Classroom

At no time was this point clearer than when Erika Ziegler heard a discussion about firefighters among a small group of her first graders as they were looking at a book in the library corner. Because she was planning to introduce firefighters as part of their year-long study of community workers, she listened as the children talked excitedly about the big rubber boots and hard red hats the firefighters wore in the pictures. Seizing the moment, she suggested that it might soon be fun to visit some firefighters at the fire station near their school. "We could really go there?" asked Chin-Jen. "Wow, that would be fun!" exclaimed Sarah. Ms. Ziegler had no doubt that interest was high, so she called the fire department to ask if the class could visit. She was told that not only was such a visit possible, but that arrangements could be made for two firefighters to take them for a short ride on a truck.

On the day of the trip, the children eagerly got off the school bus when it arrived at the fire station. Their anticipation grew into excitement as they peered in at the bright red and silver truck parked in the garage. Keeping the children well in control, Ms. Ziegler reminded them to stay behind her and the parent volunteers until the firefighters explained what to do. When two firefighters invited them to enter, the children gingerly approached the vehicle. The firefighters showed the children all their paraphernalia and explained their jobs. "The truck is so shiny," remarked Rebecca. "Yeah, and look at all those big hoses!" shouted Ben. "That fireman is a lady. Wow, a lady fireman!" shouted Denise, all agog. "Do you have to go to college to learn how to be a firefighter?" asked Caio. The children watched, listened, commented, and asked questions as they tried on the hard hats and floppy boots, stared at the dazzling lights, and listened to the firefighters talk. The most adventurous youngsters even accepted an invitation to climb up into the cab and sit in the fire truck. All this wonderful activity culminated in a well-supervised short trip around the parking lot on the back of the truck.

Ms. Ziegler was rewarded by the fact that the children thoroughly enjoyed this learning experience and learned a great deal about a valuable community service.

When they returned to school, Ms. Ziegler brought the children together as a group to talk about their experiences at the fire station. They then drew pictures and wrote about their favorite experiences (see Figure 10–2). Later that day, the children dictated a thank-you note that was mailed to the firehouse.

Ms. Ziegler's field trip was successful because she always followed a set of specific guidelines whenever she planned field trips for her students. She learned that appropriate field trips include the responsibilities as shown in Figure 10–3.

Resource Persons

Resource persons are individuals from the world outside of school who come into your classroom to share some skill or knowledge with students. They serve the same

FIGURE 10–2
A Student's Response to a Field Trip

Jennifer   10-10-97

I saw a

fire truck it

was coll

FIGURE 10–3
Field Trip Checklist

1. Address logistical concerns associated with the trip:
   - Have you taken the trip beforehand?
   - Have you made all necessary arrangements at the field trip site—what time you will arrive, where the restrooms are located, accommodations for children with special needs, places for lunch and snack?
   - Are there any special rules or regulations that must be followed at the site?
   - Have parental permission slips been signed (even if the school uses a blanket permission form)? Do not take children who haven't returned them.
   - Has transportation been arranged? (For liability reasons, a school bus is much better than a private car.)
   - If private cars are to be used, have you verified that each driver has adequate insurance and a valid driver's license? Have you provided each driver with a map and precise directions?
   - Have you planned proper supervision? (I always felt a 4:1 child-adult ratio was maximum.)
   - Are chaperones informed about what you expect of them? Do they know the behaviors expected of the children?
   - Do parents understand what clothing is appropriate for their children?
   - Do the students understand the expected standards of conduct? (Children respond better when they have a voice in determining these.)

2. Establish a clear purpose for the trip; be sure the children understand clearly why they are going ("What are we looking for?" "What do we want to find out?"):
   - Read books, share brochures or posters, and talk about what to expect at the site. Give the children an idea of what to expect.
   - Involve children in planning the trip.

3. Prepare for the trip:
   - Use name tags (including the school name and teacher's name). This helps if a child gets lost, as well as assisting volunteers when they need to call a child by name.
   - Assign a partner, or buddy, for each child. Explain why it is important to stick together.
   - Divide the class into groups. Give each student a specific responsibility (recorder, photographer or illustrator, organizer, and so on).
   - Show the students how they will record information from the trip (worksheet or guidesheet).

4. Take the trip:
   - Be sure to take roll when you leave and each time you depart or return to the bus.
   - Take along a basic first-aid kit (or nurse). Several wash cloths or paper towels will be needed if a child gets sick on the bus.
   - Arrive on time.
   - Keep the children who will need your attention close to you.
   - Introduce your class (but not each individual child) to your guide, if there is one.
   - Enjoy the experience!

5. After the trip:
   - Have the children write (or dictate) thank-you notes, or draw pictures expressing their appreciation to volunteers and field site personnel.
   - Talk with the class about what they liked best.
   - Provide enrichment activities—draw pictures, write stories or poems, create a dramatic skit, make a map, or conduct any related activity to help the children deepen their understanding of the trip.
   - Have the students evaluate the trip: Did they accomplish the purposes identified at the beginning of the trip?

purpose as field trips, but resource persons bring the action to school. As with field trips, the resource person should not be a talker putting on a demonstration while the children serve as a captive audience. The children must be involved in the action.

Although interacting with a resource person is not as intrinsically motivating as going somewhere, children nevertheless enjoy contact with outside visitors and the interesting ideas and materials they share. You might invite people who provide goods or services in your community: police officers, firefighters, farmers, delivery people, construction workers, doctors, nurses, newspersons, bakers, industrial workers, store workers, crafts persons, lawyers, bankers, clergy, and government officials. Visitors can help break down stereotypes, such as senior citizens with special skills or hobbies, women carpenters, or male nurses.

Care must be exercised in the way guests are selected, however. The safest approach seems to be getting recommendations from other teachers, involved parents, and other school personnel. In this way, you will be able to select speakers who will appropriately inform and motivate your children. You and your students will benefit the most if you send your visitor a list of helpful suggestions similar to the following:

1. *Think young.*   Remember that you are speaking to young children, so be especially careful of your vocabulary. Also, limit your talk to the attention level of the children—about 20 minutes for K–2 children and 30 minutes for grades 3 and up.

2. *Bring something.*   Real, touchable objects that relate to your area of expertise help children understand your life and work. For example, a construction worker recently visited our class and brought along a hard hat, small tools, and a lunch box.

3. *Move around.*   As you speak, try to move to various sections of the classroom so the children will feel personally involved. It helps to ask them questions once in a while, too.

4. *Share personal stories.*   Is there something that happened during your childhood that motivated you to do what you're now doing?

5. *Allow time for student questions.*   When students ask you questions, repeat them back to the class so all can hear.

6. *If possible, leave the children a memento.*   You might bring something small to leave with the children (a florist brought a small flower for each child, an artist left an autographed print, and a flight attendant gave out some "wings"). If you can't leave a small souvenir, you might want to create something (the construction worker helped the children build a structure with blocks).

Depictions of Reality

When it is impossible to provide realia, a field trip, or resource person, it is wise to use various sources of secondary experiences. These experiences cannot inform and educate quite as effectively as direct experiences, but they offer excellent sources of information when direct experiences are impractical.

Digital and VHS Cameras

Although audiovisual resources, such as movies or slide and filmstrip presentations, have been and continue to be popular educational resources in classrooms around the country, they are rapidly being supplemented with (and in many instances replaced by) digital still cameras and digital or VHS video cameras. These electronic gadgets are among the hottest items in teaching today, and with good reason. They're fun, easy to use, and produce speedy results.

While many digital cameras look just like regular film cameras, they don't use film. Instead they record an image on a small photoelectric semiconductor (CCD) that turns it into tiny electronic dots, or pixels, which are stored on the camera's memory card. Most digital cameras display the picture on an LCD screen, and, if it is unsatisfactory, the photo can be erased and shot again. In a few seconds, the selected images can be transferred to a computer and edited as desired. In one class, for example, faces of famous historical figures were replaced with the faces of each fifth grader at the conclusion of a biographical study of famous Americans.

The main tip for using a digital camera in your social studies program is to be adventurous. I've found that teachers who are unsure about how to use a digital camera do best by handing it over to one of their more technologically savvy students. These students never have a problem figuring out how to use it and love to teach the teacher and their peers how to do something new. If you like to experiment with new technology, take a few minutes to become familiar with the camera and how it operates. Push the buttons and find out what they do. Certainly, you will want to examine the handbook that comes with your camera, but it is important to get your hands on the camera and use it as soon as you can. Remember that experience is the best teacher!

A related tip is to be creative and encourage your students to offer input when planning digital camera projects. Teachers are just beginning to realize the potential of digital photography in the social studies classroom. They have used their pictures in PowerPoint, Microsoft Word, and TimeLiner programs, or in desktop publishing software like Print Shop. Pictures have been formatted as slide shows, PowerPoint presentations, newsletters, greeting cards, booklets, brochures, photo essays, electronic timelines, and virtual tours. Successful teachers are not afraid to use their imaginations. Sit down and brainstorm ideas with your students and fellow teachers. Try out ideas, assess your efforts, and then try again.

Kristen Bronstein's first experience with a digital camera, for example, involved taking digital pictures of a field trip. Ms. Bronstein and her students took many pictures of their class involved in different activities. When they returned to the classroom, they imported their pictures into a word processing document and worked in pairs to write captions to tell the story of their field trip. The students displayed the images and captions at full screen size in slide show format for other classrooms, rotating the pictures at any speed they chose.

Along with digital still cameras, digital and VHS camcorders have now become a favored medium for recording and storing all kinds of information. A digital or VHS camera with all the bells and whistles, however, is not going to be of much value if it's difficult to use, so select one that the students can operate by themselves. Be sure that the camera fits easily in their hands and the controls are accessible and workable. In addition, the camera should be easy to mount to and disconnect from a tripod. Many newer digital cameras can take still pictures, storing them on mini-memory cards of the type used in digital still cameras. Video camera use in social studies classrooms is limited only by a teacher's creativity; among the most popular applications include documenting field trips, interviewing people, making a photo essay, using photos to add meaning to a timeline, recording student projects to share with a wider audience, and documenting student work in electronic portfolios.

In Doug McGee's fourth-grade classroom, for example, the students use a digital video camera to produce a special weekly television show in a music/news/talk format: "My name is Farrell Pelensky, and this is television station WOW right here in Cedar Elementary School. I hope you're having a great day and are ready to listen to the top tune of the week as voted on by the fourth graders of Cedar Elementary. Here it goes!" (Changing the host weekly generates most interest.)

Once the song (accompanied by relevant images at full-screen size in slide show format) is over, Mr. McGee's students provide a teletype background for the news. They found that an old electric typewriter does fine. News items range from actual current events to announcements of school proceedings, special student accomplishments, or other local happenings. Commercials are often interjected to promote items such as a school band concert, the school store, and so on. Some children enjoy creating parodies of actual television commercials. The talk show format may conclude with the host interviewing a teacher who has taken an interesting trip, a student who has won a special prize, or other notable happening. Throughout the telecast, appropriate still images and video clips help bring to life important events and ideas.

In addition to producing original video programming, students learn from commercially prepared CDs and videotapes. What are the benefits of these resources? First, they involve action. When action is essential to a concept being taught, a good video or CD will get the idea across. And, if stop-frame, time-lapse, or slow motion can help clarify a point, the VCR or DVD player is ready to respond. Second, the video or CD can transport students to other times and places too difficult to reach in any other way. A trip back to the Battle of Gettysburg or a voyage on the Mayflower is as easy as the click of a few controls. Third, the video or CD adds interest and variety to teaching. Through music and excellent camera work, the viewer becomes immersed in the mood of educationally significant times and places.

Some videos or CDs are interesting when they are viewed a second time. The second viewing can occur the same day if the program is short, but if it is long-lasting, the second viewing should be done the next day. As the program is shown the second time, you could ask the students to narrate the action as the sound is turned all the way down.

In short, there are hundreds of ways digital still or video cameras can be used in dynamic social studies classrooms. Think about the many ways they can enhance any project that you would normally use photographs or any other special visual aids.

Pictures and Study Prints

A rich storehouse of social studies content can be uncovered in the countless pictures found in such sources as posters, literature books, textbooks, prints, newspapers, travel brochures, calendars, and magazines. Pictures help children envision people, places, events, or feelings that are difficult to perceive in other ways, proving the truth of the old expression, "One picture is worth a thousand words."

As you display and discuss pictures, remember that children vary in their ability to read and interpret them, much as they vary in their ability to read and interpret words. Some children may function only at the *literal level,* being able to simply name, list, and describe specific details about items being observed. Most, however, extend their skills to the *inferential level,* where they can speculate about such things as character traits, missing details or elements, or cause-and-effect relationships. Very few students will be found at the *critical level,* where they are able to interpret feelings and values.

You should attempt to structure picture discussions with questions of varying degree of difficulty, giving children of different abilities the chance for success at their individual levels and exposing less-mature students to the higher-level thinking expressed by their more mature peers. Sample questions follow.

- *Literal Questions*
  "Tell me what you see."
  "How many _____?"
  "Describe the _____."
  "What color (size, distance, and so on) is the _____?"
  "What is this person wearing?"

- *Inferential Questions*
  "Where (or when) does this take place?"
  "What will happen next?"
  "What are the _____ doing?"
  "How is (this) the same as (different from) _____?"
  "What kind of a person do you think _____ is?"

- *Critical Questions*

"Why did _____ happen?"

"Do the people like one another? How do you know?"

"What do (don't) you like about the picture?"

"What conclusions could you make about _____?"

"How might the information in this picture be used?"

INTEGRATING THE ARTS

Teachers around the country are being encouraged to view the world from a perspective that integrates social studies with the expressive arts—literature, music, drama, dance, and visual arts. This expanded viewpoint calls for exciting new partnerships, such as history and music, geography and art, creative dramatics and political science. The overall aim is to help students gain a sense of a culture's human spirit by examining the great works of arts of its people. That idea is simple, but the harsh truth is that arts education is denied to most children in our elementary school classrooms today. It seems that many people think of the arts (for young children at least) as having little value other than being something to put on the refrigerator door. That perception of the arts can never compete adequately for time in the social studies program. Fowler (1989) offers this forceful reaction to our failure to tender a role for the expressive arts in our schools, particularly as it relates to social studies:

> By denying children the arts, we starve our civilization. We produce children who are more fitted for an age of barbarism than the advanced civilization of the information age. . . . But equally important, we fail these children educationally by depriving them of the insights that the arts afford. The arts provide windows to other worlds. . . . The arts illuminate life in all its mystery, misery, delight, pity, and wonder. Encounters with the arts invite us to explore realms of meaning that, according to an old Persian proverb, lie next to the curtain that has never been drawn aside. (p. 62)

It can be said that the social sciences give us the content and processes; the arts give us the emotion. The arts tell us about people—how they feel and what they value. Isadora Duncan, a renowned dancer, was said to have once commented, "If I could tell you what I meant, there would be no point in dancing." Through dance, Duncan was able to communicate feeling as few dancers had done before her. She accomplished this using a special "language" comprised of a series of graceful, elegant movements. If Duncan were not able to express her message through dance, whatever she wished to convey would have been lost forever. (The story of this talented dancer is portrayed in Rachel Isadora's splendid book, *Isadora Dances* [Viking].) Thus, the social sciences inform us while the arts impassion us.

Fowler (1994) argues in support of connecting the social sciences and the arts in dynamic social studies instruction:

> We need every possible way to represent, interpret, and convey our world for a very simple but powerful reason: No one of these ways offers a full picture. Individually. . . history

[and the social sciences] convey only part of the reality of the world. Nor do the arts alone suffice. A multiplicity of symbol systems are [sic] required to provide a more complete picture and a more comprehensive education. . . . Both views are valid. Both contribute to understanding. . . . The British aesthetician and critic Herbert Read once said, "Art is the representation, science the explanation—of the same reality." (pp. 5–8)

The social sciences supply insight and wisdom; the arts reflect the spirit of the people. Every child should have the opportunity to explore the expressive arts as "language of civilization," for the arts may well be the most telling feature of any society.

INVOLVEMENT IN THE ARTS

Students must be exposed to a wide range of artistic encounters. Elementary school children must experience original art (concerts, museums, and performances) and be presented opportunities to enjoy reproduced art (records or CDs, CD-ROMs, videos, posters, and the like). These valuable firsthand encounters help students understand the place of the arts in people's lives. The arts that are meaningful to children are not the same as "great art," but children must gain a sense of art in their own lives before they can be expected to value artistic achievements from the past or from other cultures.

Exposure to the arts must not stop at examining and responding. You should give children opportunities to re-create what they observe as an extension or enrichment of the topic under study. Because the process of re-creating an expressive arts product is intended to reinforce specific understandings, authenticity and accuracy of the representation are primary considerations. Few valid understandings about early dances in Colonial America could be expected, for example, if students were allowed to move freely to the music instead of duplicating the specific steps of a minuet. The designated purpose of the activity dictates the amount of conformity you expect. If the purpose of an activity is to "deepen understandings of Kachina dolls as religious educational objects of the Hopis," then you must use accurate details, colors, and distinctive symbols. For example, a rain-cloud design on each cheek of the Kachina is a symbol with specific meaning. The children should use this symbol only if they intend to communicate that meaning, as the Hopis have done. Likewise, other special symbols, shapes, and colors convey specific messages to the Hopis. Experiences with Kachinas, then, must begin with solid information. By examining a Kachina doll or its representation, you must help the students understand where, why, how, and by whom it was made. Then, give students the opportunity to apply what they had learned to constructing an accurate reproduction of Kachinas. Experiences in re-creating a culture's art must be authentic; these projects lead children to deepened interest in academic pursuits and strengthen their understanding of culture.

Since a major aim of the arts is to maximize creative potential, teachers should not stop with examining and reproducing art but take the third step of promoting original products. To return to the Kachina doll example, suppose that you have approached the project in a way similar to our recommendations—(1) learning about real Kachinas followed by (2) having students construct an accurate reproduction or model. Now

The arts offer children a valuable way to express what they have learned.

you wish to encourage children to personalize the information more deeply by having them create original symbols for Kachina dolls. Therefore, you inform your students that there are more than 200 actual Kachinas and that new ones are often invented. You might approach the creative phase of the experience by creating new symbols to represent a spirit that's important to them individually or to the class as a whole.

John Dewey once made a clear connection between the complementary aspects of the arts when he said, "A beholder must create his own experience." Children must be given opportunities to enrich and express what they learn about the arts through as many expressive experiences as possible, for students who study the arts are also more likely to display originality and creativity in all of their social studies work.

Select activities not because they appear to be "fun" or "cute," but because they contribute directly to students' understanding and appreciation of a culture. What rationale, for example, could you use to support making log cabins with pretzel sticks and peanut butter or constructing tipis with painted construction paper cones? These activities commonly appear in idea resource books, but they create a weak connection between the experience and an understanding of early colonial or Native American cultures. This word of caution is not meant to stifle your eagerness for a hands-on approach to social studies instruction, but rather to point out your responsibility to organize and coordinate meaningful knowledge through the visual arts to channel students' imagination and enthusiasm into creations that reflect accurate understandings of a culture.

The Visual Arts

Dynamic social studies teachers believe that immersing students in a culture means the visual arts must play a significant role in instruction. As students explore the art of Africa, for example, they will be eager to try their hands at tie-dye, weaving, mask construction, or sculpture. You help enhance the study of Greece by having students create plaster reliefs or signature seals. Enliven a lesson on medieval Europe by having children study and re-create coats of arms, stained glass, and castle designs. You can use the arts of Gyokatu (fish printing), block printing, kite making, batiks, and folded-paper design to introduce students to Asian cultures. Native American sand paintings, blankets, Kachina dolls, and totem poles help students learn about the earliest cultures in North America. Pysanky (intricately designed Easter eggs) and flax (straw) dolls bring to life important aspects of Ukrainian culture. The potential is unlimited for integrating the visual arts and social studies. Mildred Spriggs, for example, enriched her fifth graders' study of prehistoric life by engaging them in a study of ancient cave paintings. Displaying large study prints of actual cave paintings and those found in art books available from the library, Ms. Spriggs directed the students through a discussion of what was important in the life of prehistoric humans, as depicted by their art. Then, making paint from grass and berries, and using homemade brushes of sticks and reeds, students created designs on large rocks illustrating subjects important to them.

When children become aware of art as something valuable that people do in real life to communicate ideas and feelings, they are inspired to create their own.

Illustrations

Although dynamic social studies programs offer countless opportunities to involve children in standard art experiences such as dioramas, murals, mosaics, and collages, the most popular art procedure used in elementary social studies classrooms seems to be illustrations. You may have primary-grade children replicate the collage technique as modeled by Eric Carle, make a picture book of animals common to the tropical rainforest, draw a product map of China, or paint a scene showing the landscape of the high Andes Mountains. There are literally hundreds of possibilities.

The Drawing/Writing Partnership Starting with the youngest, teachers routinely ask children to record what they have learned on paper in a variety of ways—most often with simple drawings accompanied by printed words. When their teacher offers a piece of drawing paper or primary-grade writing paper, most kindergartners and first graders will draw a picture of something important to them and then talk about it. The teacher can write their words, or they might like to try writing on their own. The drawing/writing partnership is illustrated clearly in the classroom example drawn from the experiences of Avilda Breen.

Inside an Active Classroom

When Ms. Breen's first graders came back to school at the close of winter break, they were excited to share all the interesting things that happened to them while they were on vacation. Hands flew into the air during sharing time in eager anticipation of who would be the first to talk. Teri's words exploded as she told about helping her father shovel the driveway after a heavy winter snowstorm. Agostino's eyes sparkled with pride as he described the new furniture that arrived at his house a week ago ("A beautiful yellow sofa, just beautiful!"). Wendy sadly recounted her family's heavyhearted task of saying good-bye to their 10-year-old beagle, who was struck down by a speeding car. Kun Hwan happily described his seventh birthday party, and Kyle told of his family's trip to the state aquarium.

After they shared orally, Ms. Breen passed out drawing paper and asked each child to draw a picture of his or her special event. After the children finished their drawings, Ms. Breen directed them to print their "stories" in the space below each drawing. Figure 10–4 is Kyle's story about his family's trip to the state aquarium. Kyle

FIGURE 10–4
The Drawing/Writing Connection

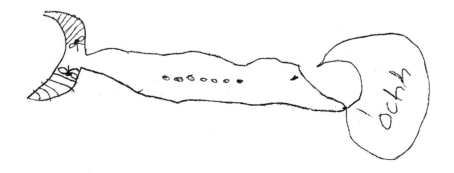

was particularly interested in the dolphins; when asked about his written piece, Kyle explained that the dolphin was saying, "Ouch!" Then he read what he had written above the drawing: "Animals should definitely not wear clothing because a dolphin might have trouble with its fin."

Ms. Breen explains the importance of these early drawing/writing experiences: "As the blank pages come alive with drawings and words telling of their experiences, I could see these children were showing me what they knew as well as what they needed to know."

Music

People have sent messages across distances by pounding on drums. People have marched off to war to inspiring music and walked down the aisle to the joyful strains of a wedding march. People have raised their voices in national anthems. People have sung work songs or chants to keep their work rhythm straight as they pulled in nets or pried rails back into line. People have sung songs of worship in camp meetings and cathedrals, and they have welcomed harvests with celebratory dances. People have expressed their grief in tender ballads and rocked their babies to sleep with gentle lullabies. Wherever and whenever possible, people have expressed sadness, grief, love, satisfaction, and joy in making music for themselves and for others.

How can you help children to understand all of this? Certainly, young social scientists must have experiences with many kinds of music. Different people and faraway places may be abstract notions for some children, but they can be made more concrete by forging a relationship with music and social studies. Of all types of music, exposure to folk music is one of the most fitting mediums for teaching about various cultural groups. Folk music can be defined as the traditional music created by people as part of their everyday existence and handed down from one generation to another. It reflects a group's cultural heritage and traditions.

Inside an Active Classroom

Leona Boreski sought to enrich her unit on the state of Hawaii by including its folk music. She realized that for the music to have a constructive role in the unit, she must be sure to know a great deal about it. After hours of intensive library research, Ms. Boreski discovered that the early Hawaiians created their musical instruments from objects found in the island's natural environment—the low wail of the conch shell, the resonating rattle of hollowed-out gourds filled with pebbles, the clack of split bamboo, the hollow tock of hardwood sticks, and the click of smooth stones tapped lightly together. From such sounds created by common objects found in the sea, forest, garden, and river, Hawaiian musical instruments first accompanied chants called *olis* and dances called *hulas.*

Since there were no written records from ancient Hawaii, the history of its culture was often told through and passed on by *olis* and *hulas.* Some *olis* and *hulas* were used for entertainment and others only for religious ceremonies. Ms. Boreski was able to display several native instruments for the children to observe as she played recorded songs and chants for them. She was careful to use appropriate language labels as she introduced the instruments—*ili-ili* (smooth oval pebbles), *kalaau* (hardwood sticks), and *ipu* (large hollow gourds filled with pebbles). Ms. Boreski emphasized that times have changed in Hawaii, as they have in any location that has been modernized. But even today, original instruments still accompany programs or other special pageantry of the islands. Ms. Boreski then shared a brief video clip of a performance of the "*Va Nani O Nuuanu*" ("Pebble Dance").

Listening to and appreciating the unique and fascinating music of the folk song tradition is an important way children learn about cultures, but a learner's experiences in music should also include opportunities to reproduce the music by singing songs, moving to rhythm, or trying out musical instruments. After Ms. Boreski's students learned of the early music of the Hawaiian people as described previously, she introduced them to "*Kauiki,*" an old song about a dormant volcano that juts out into the sea. Background music for "*Kauiki*" is a ukulele accompanied by *ipu* beats. Ms. Boreski was able to obtain a few ukuleles on loan from parents, and brought in her own *ipu.* Volunteers strummed the ukuleles (the strings were tuned to the proper chords) and beat the *ipu* while the rest of the class sang the lyrics in both Hawaiian and English.

Creative Movement and Dance

Dance is an art form in which the human body is used as a vehicle of expression. Dance has existed since the beginning of humankind, before verbal and written communication was developed. It was the first form of communication used by humans to communicate and to make meaning of their world. Likewise, moving rhythmically seems to be innate in young children and seems to help them better understand themselves and the world in which they live. Because movement as a form of self-expression seems to be fundamental to our existence as human beings, dance should be considered an important part of a dynamic social studies program. Dance helps young social scientists use movement to creatively uncover and come to understand and appreciate diverse cultures. As students examine the role of dance in different cultures, they learn to connect with other people and respect their diversity.

Until recently, dance was taught mainly as an activity included in the physical education curriculum. It is now recognized as an art form comparable to music, drama, and the visual arts, and equally worthy of inclusion in the social studies curriculum.

Inside an Active Classroom

Returning to Leona Boreski's classroom, for example, the students made Hawaiian grass skirts (to represent the authentic ti-leaf skirts used on the island for performances) and leis. The girls wore the grass skirts while the boys dressed in clam diggers or shorts and Hawaiian pattern shirts; both boys and girls were bedecked in flowers and leis. Ms. Boreski, dressed in a lovely muumuu with flowers in her hair, played a recording of the traditional Hawaiian chant *Ka Hana Kamalii* (*What Children Should Do*). The chant was composed for Queen Emma of Hawaii and recited by children to demonstrate to the queen that they had learned the lessons in personal hygiene that the missionaries had taught them—to wash with soap and to use mirrors to see that they were clean. Their words were accompanied by a hula dance to show what they should do and how they should do it. Ms. Boreski taught the chant to the children and demonstrated the hula routine. Throughout the entire experience, one child beat an *ipu* (hollow gourd) in a steady rhythm. After the class finished the hula, they proudly ended with a *pau* (bow).

To be sure children acquire accurate concepts of a culture, it would be helpful to invite resource people who can demonstrate dance movements into the classroom to share their talents with the children. Ms. Boreski knew the hula basics, so she was able to demonstrate the movements to the children. If you are unfamiliar with the specific movements of a particular dance, it would be important to invite someone into the classroom who has that knowledge or seek information that will help you learn (a gym teacher or dance school instructor can help). Capitalizing on the value of dance and movement in the social studies program demonstrates to children that all forms of music are integral parts of people's lives rather than a form of expression for only a talented few.

Drama

Like music, people have used drama to reveal their innermost feelings of conflict, despair, truth, beauty, hope, and faith since the dawn of civilization. Drama brings out the essence of a culture clearly before one's eyes and is an excellent vehicle to challenge students to think about and appreciate diverse cultures. Drama is a vital aspect of a culture; by its very nature, drama is an important kind of social communication. For primitive humans, it was a ritualistic effort to communicate with magical spirits; through ceremonial rituals, while dressed in masks and skins, groups would try to seek cooperation with the spirits to control certain events (a good hunt, the power of thunder, fertility). As humans began to settle in regular communities and rely more on agriculture, their greatest fears became bitter weather and a failed harvest, so special dances and rituals were created to appeal to the controlling spirits. From these early forms, drama developed into a stylized form of communication with intricate dialogue, disguises, and symbolism.

By nature, children are born to create. As it applies to drama, they create in a joyfully daring way. They are confident and expressive in their actions and improvise freely by making up dialogue and actions. Such informal dramatic experience is important to the social studies curriculum. Informal classroom drama is an activity in which students invent and enact dramatic situations for themselves, rather than for an outside audience. This unrehearsed activity is spontaneously spawned by the students who assume the dual tasks of inventing and performing their parts as the drama unfolds.

The best play for younger children is informal dramatic play. A dramatic play center housing equipment for play is usually set up as a separate area of many kindergarten and first-grade classrooms. Children enjoy recreating life experiences in the center, using child-size furniture to enact family experiences and activities. As their horizons widen and they become exposed to new experiences, children will begin assuming the roles of doctor, nurse, gas station attendant, firefighter, police officer, construction worker, taxi cab driver, pilot, or dentist. Children normally enjoy dramatizing occupations where people are active rather than deskbound. A lawyer or bookkeeper, for example, holds little appeal for dramatic play. Some early grade social studies teachers like to set up specific creative dramatic play centers after the children have gone on a field trip. An "ice cream store" with scoops, empty cartons, white aprons and caps, and a table with chairs works well. So does a "hospital" with a doctor's bag, stethoscope, bandages, doctor and nurse uniform, crutches, and cot. Children love to imitate what they experience; imitation is a great way to clarify and refine concepts as well as to explore and experiment with solutions to real problems.

In addition to informal dramatic play, formalized drama in the social studies classroom is often represented through three major forms: *pantomime, improvised skits,* and *dramatizations.*

Pantomime

Children of all ages enjoy using body movements to convey ideas without words, and this is a good technique for introducing more formalized creative dramatics in your classroom. Use your imagination to concoct stimulating situations for pantomime. One possibility is the popular "What Am I Doing?" or "Who Am I?" game. Many social studies concepts have to do with people making or doing something and children like to challenge their classmates to guess who they are: pilgrims landing at Plymouth Rock, the first landing on the moon, Ben Franklin's kite-flying escapade, Barry Bonds' record-breaking home run, or the type of work people do at home or in the community.

As each child or small group shares its pantomime with the class, it is important to lead a follow-up discussion: "Who is represented in the action? What helped you recognize this person? Where do you think the action took place? What helped you think this? What do you think the people were talking about? What are some of the feelings you think the characters experienced? From what you know about the actual situation, do you think the actors accurately portrayed what really happened? What feelings did you have as you watched the action? What would you have done if you were any one of the characters in the same situation? Can you predict what might happen to the people after what was shown in the pantomime?"

Improvised Skits A charming characteristic of young children is their ability to use their creative imaginations in improvisations—unplanned situations where dialogue is necessary but there are no learned lines, no costumes, and no sophisticated scenery. Many of the situations described for pantomiming activities are also suitable for improvisation experiences—just add words. Begin the initial improvisation experiences with simple situations. As the children gain confidence, they can attempt more challenging material.

Inside an *Active Classroom*

Alberta Yakob was itching to try something new to deepen her students' understanding of and interest in Japan. She read them Eleanor Coerr's (1977) book, *Sadako and the Thousand Paper Cranes,* a story based on the life of a real girl who lived in Japan from 1943 to 1955. Sadako Sasaki was only two when the United States dropped an atom bomb on Hiroshima in an effort to end World War II. Ten years later she died from leukemia as a result of radiation from the bomb.

The morning after she was diagnosed with leukemia, Sadako woke up in the hospital and hoped the day before was just a bad dream. It wasn't long before she was jolted with the realization that everything was indeed real. That afternoon, Chizuko, Sadako's friend, was her first visitor. Chizuko brought a square piece of gold paper that she folded over and over until it turned into a beautiful crane. She told Sadako, "If a sick person folds one thousand paper cranes, the gods will grant her wish and make her healthy again." Chizuko handed the crane to Sadako and said, "Here's your first one."

Sadako folded 644 cranes before she died. They hung above her bed on strings. Her classmates folded the rest. Today, Sadako is a hero to the children of Japan, who visit her memorial in the Hiroshima Peace Park to leave paper cranes they make in her honor.

Ms. Yakob's students found Sadako's story to be unforgettable and were touched by her life. Because the story was written tenderly, it was neither morbid nor weepy. The children were touched, but not crushed or brokenhearted. Therefore, Ms. Yakob chose to review the events of the story as well as promote creative thinking by using a role playing strategy called *character interview.*

To prepare the class, Ms. Yakob announced, "Today we are going to pretend to be somebody else, and we are going to do that by using our imaginations. We have just finished reading the story of Sadako Sasaki, and I would like for some of you to share with us what you learned about her life. You will do that by pretending to be Sadako."

Ms. Yakob continued, "I've made this cardboard name sign with a string loop that will fit over your head and hang around your neck. The name sign has the name *Sadako Sasaki* on it. One of you will come up here and put the sign around your neck. You will then become Sadako. Of course, we know that Sadako is no longer alive, but through the use of our imaginations, we will have an opportunity to hear her innermost thoughts. The rest of the class will ask questions about Sadako's life."

Ms. Yakob's final directions were, "We are going to use our imaginations. When Tara puts on the sign, we won't see Tara anymore; instead we will see her as Sadako Sasaki." Once Tara placed the sign around her neck and the transformation occurred, the class interviewed the character. Ms. Yakob took the lead: "Welcome, Sadako. We are very honored to have you here today. What questions do we have for Sadako, class? What things might she share that she may have never said before? What dreams did she have? What are we curious to know more about?"

After several questions, Ms. Yakob checked to see if the student playing Sadako seemed uncomfortable. When she sensed that the student was struggling with answers, she simply thanked the character, removed the sign, and had the student face the class for applause. Ms. Yakob then went on, "Now, who else would like to be Sadako Sasaki?"

Dramatization

Many times, children like to extend informal dramatics by putting on a formal play with script, costumes, and scenery. The most effective type of formal play is one in which the children are responsible for most of the planning. Your role in the process is to guide the students as they write the different scenes. While the children plan and write their script, ask them, "What are the most important things to tell? What are the people really like? What kind of place do they live in? What do the people do to make their lives interesting? How will you stage your play?"

Dramatizations should emerge from the social studies content. The students' concern for elaborate scenery and costumes should not take precedence over the concepts or ideas the play is designed to convey, however. Simple objects can effectively represent more intricate items; for example, a mural or bulletin board can serve as a backdrop; a branch in a big can filled with dirt makes an excellent tree or bush; your desk becomes a cave; chairs placed in a straight line can be seats on a train or airplane; a pencil can become a hand-held microphone. The following example describes a highly appealing and successful dramatic skit composed by Chandra Venna's fifth graders following a reading of an African Cinderella variant, *Mufaro's Beautiful Daughters* (Lothrop). At the end of the book, the main characters, Nyoka and Nyasha, are married. The children, understanding the importance of babies to African village life, wanted to continue the story by creating an authentic naming ceremony for the couple's first baby. Spurred on by the authentic opening scenes to the movie *Lion King*, Ms. Venna helped her students obtain information about African naming ceremonies from a local African American society and used the information to develop the following skit.

Inside an *Active Classroom*

African villagers celebrate the birth of babies with great pride. Babies are an important part of African life; the African baby belongs not only to its mother and father, but to everyone in the village. Everyone in the village loves the baby and is responsible for giving it protection and direction in life.

SCENE:	People are milling about the village. Nyoka and Nyasha are sitting and holding their baby. Traditional African music is playing in the background.
Nyoka:	With pride and joy, we announce that on this special day our child is to be named.
Nyasha:	Come be our guests at this joyous celebration.
SCENE:	Everyone comes together. All guests sit in a circle with Nyoka and Nyasha. The ceremony begins when the oldest living member of the family recites the family history.
Elder:	Welcome to all who join us to bless and honor the child of Nyoka and Nyasha. Out of deep respect for their ancestors, we begin the ceremony with a short family history.

The baby's mother is Nyasha, who is the most worthy and most beautiful daughter in the land. Nyasha's father is Mufaro. Mufaro is very rich because he has two most beautiful daughters, Nyasha and Manyara. Mufaro is known for his great wisdom and patience. Dayo (DAH-YO) is Nyasha's mother. She can sing so sweetly about the land! It is said that she composed a song for each cow in a herd of a thousand. This is Nyasha's gift from Dayo—a voice as sweet as honey.

The baby's father is Nyoka. He has the special power to appear as all living things. Nyoka's father is Olu (OH-LOO). Olu had a large family, all of whom were fearless warriors. Olu is the one who built the great city. As an adventurous young man, Olu spent much time in the tropical forest by himself. Olu learned many new things from the beasts and serpents he befriended. Olu was a great king. He was handsome, tall, and strong. Olu had a son and named him Nyoka. Olu taught Nyoka all that he had learned in the tropical forest. That is the reason Nyoka now has the power to appear as all living things.

Now, everyone will join together to introduce this child to the nature of life.

Friend 1:	I offer a few drops of wine to the baby because the wine ensures the child a full and fruitful life.
Friend 2:	I splash a few drops of water on the baby's forehead and put a drop or two into its mouth when it cries. This is a way of show-

ing that water is important for all living things. It also tells me if the baby is alert.

Friend 3:   I drop a bit of honey onto the baby's tongue. This is to show the child that life is sweet.

Friend 4:   I place a pinch of pepper on the baby's lips to represent the spice of life. Although we have learned that life is sweet, we must also know that life is exciting.

Friend 5:   I lay a dab of salt on the baby's lips. The salt stands for the liveliness and zest of life.

Oldest: The baby of Nyoka and Nyasha will be rich in its pursuit of life.

SCENE: Everyone, including Nyoka and Nyasha, must give the baby a name. Girls are named on the seventh day after birth; boys are named on the eighth.

Oldest: On this joyful _____ th day after birth, all who are present are invited to offer a chosen name for the baby of Nyoka and Nyasha.

[The rest of the group uses the sentence pattern shown below to offer a name for the child.]

Child: I have picked the name NAYO because it means we have joy. This child brings much happiness to Nyoka and Nyasha.

Oldest: The ceremony is now complete. May Nyoka and Nyasha have many beautiful days with their lovely new child.

TEXTBOOKS AND TRADE BOOKS

Lately, there has been significant disagreement over whether textbooks or trade books should serve as the principal resource for teaching social studies in our elementary schools. Goodman (1988), for example, argues that textbooks are written too unimaginatively for young children; their shortened sentences and controlled vocabulary result in dull, impersonal reading. On the other hand, Wixson (1991) replies that the content and instructional design of textbooks help the student learn. Texts, for example, have a logical flow of information, and the unity in the focus of texts helps the students acquire big ideas. Instructional supports in the texts, such as headings, graphics, and charts, relate important information in a way that guides learning. To further muddy the waters, Tompkins (1997) suggests that there is a place for both trade books and textbooks in social studies. She explains that textbooks are especially important for beginning teachers who "often rely on [textbooks] and move toward incorporating trade books in their [social studies] programs as they gain confidence in their teaching abilities. . . ." (p. 203).

Literature is a valued part of social studies programs because it educates while it entertains.

What should teachers of dynamic social studies do—use trade books only, textbooks only, or a combination of both? The point of view of dynamic social studies is that students need a wide variety of reading materials in their social studies program, including both well-written textbooks and quality trade books. Each has the potential to extend and enrich learning, if used properly.

Textbooks

Social studies textbooks are graded sets of reading materials traditionally used by social studies teachers as a major source of planning and instruction. Typically published as a sequential series from kindergarten through grades 6 or 8, textbooks are developed by large publishing companies under the direction of a senior author who is usually a respected name in social studies education. Most social studies textbook programs contain an array of instructional materials, including student books and teacher's manuals.

Oftentimes, when teachers are asked to describe their social studies curriculum, they will tell you all about their textbooks. Principals regularly introduce new teachers to the school's social studies curriculum by informing them, "Here's the textbook. You should get to know it; it will be your best friend." I would estimate that 90 percent of all classroom instruction in social studies is regulated by textbooks. Most educators agree that textbooks are important tools of instruction but that textbooks should not dominate everything that goes on in the social studies program. They should be considered only one of many useful teaching tools.

Textbooks can be used to survey a topic; trade books can add depth and passion. Beginning teachers often rely on textbooks and their accompanying teacher's guides to gain confidence in the classroom; as their teaching abilities grow, they rapidly move toward using trade books. Many experienced teachers, especially those using an integrated approach to social studies instruction, incorporate reading from a variety of sources, including textbooks and the rich treasures of children's literature.

Benefits of Textbooks

Because most social studies textbooks are easy to use and offer a convenient instructional package as well as a carefully researched, systematized body of content, they are the predominant source of information in most classrooms. Such general acceptance by social studies teachers is not hard to understand. When elementary school teachers are required to use developmentally appropriate strategies and activities in all school subjects, including math, reading, spelling, writing, and science, the thought of having specially "packaged" help in social studies greatly reduces the pressure and anxiety of daily planning. In addition, textbooks provide extensive treatment of subject matter that is organized sequentially from one grade level to the next. Each teacher from kindergarten through grade 8 knows what was done in earlier grades and what will be expected in later grades, thereby minimizing gaps or repetition. Finally, school districts and teachers appreciate the carefully researched, comprehensive nature of the teacher's manuals, which come complete with goals, objectives, lesson plans, suggestions for activities, and tests. Teachers at all levels of experience acknowledge the utility of textbook programs, but beginning teachers find them especially attractive. Jarolimek and Parker (1993) explain:

> Beginning teachers are usually most comfortable starting with [textbooks]. The teaching environment can be controlled sufficiently well to reduce management concerns to a minimum, the objectives can be made specific, the children's study materials can be preselected by the teacher, and the process can be entirely teacher directed. . . . This initial [textbook experience relies heavily] on the suggestions presented in the teacher's manual that accompanies the book. (pp. 30–31)

Although textbooks virtually take teachers "by the hand" and guide them through the instructional process, teachers must plan and execute specialized instructional strategies that help students think and learn with text.

Problems With Textbooks

Although textbooks have many beneficial features, they are not without their problems. Critics, for example, complain that textbooks are often used as the curriculum, the only source of learning in the classroom. In surveying the reactions of a dozen teachers to the question, "What do you associate with social studies teaching that is clearly not creative in the elementary school?" Solomon (1989) discovered that viewing textbooks as divinely inspired canons was a common response:

> In these classrooms, wrote one of the teachers surveyed, the "teaching [is] only from the textbook. . . . Students answer questions from the textbook or [do] nothing but worksheets, worksheets, worksheets." Another responded, the teacher is "following each page and paragraph within a textbook—giving the same emphasis to every paragraph and calling for learning." All twelve respondents had the same message: Teachers in these classrooms allow one textbook to determine what they teach, with students simply expected to learn the material in it. (p. 3)

On another note, Sewall (1988) inquired into the features of social studies textbooks that make them ill disposed for elementary school classrooms. His findings suggest that:

1. The physical size and weight of textbooks discourage enthusiasm for their contents. Reviewers stressed that young children would not be drawn to "curl up and read" the social studies texts mainly because of their bulk.

2. The prose style of most textbooks is bland and voiceless. Even though quality varied from publisher to publisher, reviewers thought that the overall literary style of the texts fell well short of the mark: "Reviewers found textbooks generally to be more catalogues of factual material. . . , not sagas peopled with heroic and remarkable individuals engaged in exciting and momentous events" (p. 35).

3. Excessive coverage makes textbooks boring. Many textbooks are most effective as almanacs, encyclopedias, or reference guides; names and dates seem to dart past like telephone poles seen from the window of a swiftly moving train.

4. Textbook formats and graphics diminish the style and coherence of the running text. To be competitive with television and other mass media, textbooks have lost the narrative content that made up 90 percent of their pages just a generation ago, and now substitute "endless photographs, diagrams, charts, boxes, subunits, [and] study exercises. . . especially in lower-grade-level textbooks" (p. 35).

To be fair, it must be emphasized that most of these criticisms cannot be directed to the textbooks themselves as much as to the ways teachers use them. Textbook publishers encourage teachers to supplement and enrich their materials with auxiliary literature sources, information books, videos, field trips, realia, computer programs, and other instructional resources. Textbooks are not meant to furnish the total social studies experience, but to serve as a single resource among an array of possibilities. However, I'm sure your personal experiences as a student have helped you visualize the stereotyped textbook-bound teacher following the rigid routine of assigning a section to read and calling on students to answer questions.

Trade Books

Disenchanted by the dryness that has often been associated with the "assign-and-answer" approach to textbook-driven instruction, more teachers than ever before are using a variety of print sources in social studies. Although these texts may include such sources as newspapers, magazines, diaries, primary resources, and a number of other print learning tools we have examined throughout this book, this section will focus on the use of trade books.

Most of us have shared our childhood with a menagerie of trade book buddies. We remember many with special delight. Their adventures and misadventures were sources of great enjoyment, and the thoughts of missing out on the likes of Winnie-the-Pooh, Strega Nona, Tom Sawyer, Laura Ingalls Wilder, or Johnny Appleseed is unthinkable. Zinsser (1990) notes that "[n]o kind of writing lodges itself so deeply in our memory, echoing there for the rest of our lives, as the books that we met in our childhood" (p. 3). First and foremost, then, good literature brings delight and enjoyment to childhood. But literature can educate at the same time it entertains. Huck, Hepler, and Hickman (1993) explain:

> The experiences children have with literature give them new perspective on the world. Good writing can transport the reader to other places and other times and expand his life space. The reader feels connected to the lives of others as he enters an imagined situation with his emotions tuned to those of the story. . . .
>
> How better can we feel and experience history than through a well-told story of the lives of its people and times?. . . A history textbook tells; a quality piece of imaginative writing has the power to make the reader feel, to transport him to the deck of a slave ship and force him into the hold until he chokes on the very horror of it. (p. 11)

Trade books, both fiction and nonfiction, contribute much to the social studies program; they present information about people, places, events, and times in inspiring, memorable, and relevant ways. But implementing a trade book-based social studies program means that teachers must be familiar with the books that can help students explore a theme or topic. The range of trade books is enormous, spanning all types of topics. But three genres of books are especially useful in dynamic social studies classrooms: historical fiction, biographies, and folk literature.

Informational Books

A good informational book informs. Informational books support social studies instruction by supplying facts, concepts, and ideas for children's own investigations and projects. Informational books also serve as strong models for children's expository writing projects, such as reports. Informational books are not designed to entertain; they deal exclusively with factual material. Many have stereotyped informational books as being dry and dull; however, scores of informational books adhere to finer literary standards and catch our eyes and hold our interests just like a good novel. As Darigan, Tunnell, and Jacobs (2002) state, "The writer of compelling [informational books] does not simply collect and display facts but weaves information and details into a vision that reveals the subject in a way readers find irresistible" (p. 330).

How do you know which informational books tend to spark interest and curiosity in elementary school students? Qualifications of the authors and illustrators are highly important. The credentials of the author and illustrator should be carefully inspected. They bear responsibility for accuracy of material.

Organization and scope are also considerations in evaluating informational books. Organization includes features such as chapters, headings and subheadings, provision of a table of contents, glossary, and indexes; these are important organizational features of informational books.

Including suggestions for activities beyond the book and suggested reading lists can enlarge the value of an informational book. However, be sure the author supplies a list of materials, recommends safety rules to follow, and suggests whether there is a need for adult supervision. Examples include cookbooks and how-to books.

Informational books should supply an ample amount of facts for children to understand the concepts presented, but not be so intricate that they are frustrating for children of the intended grade level. A necessary quality of good informational books is correct information. Because some informational books may have been published before new facts were discovered, the copyright date is important in making a classroom selection. The goal should be to enlighten, not confuse.

A good informational book should provide factual information in an interesting and instructive way. One rule of thumb is to examine the cover and sample pages from the beginning, middle, and end of the book. Does it appear to be dull and lifeless? If it does, it will be even more boring to a child; children will reject books if they do not catch the eye. Illustrations and photographs should clarify the text as accurately and realistically as possible. Advanced technology has made it possible to fill informational books with helpful graphics. Be careful with this graphics element, though. An over-abundance of graphics may divert children's attention from the written text.

Authors and illustrators should also avoid stereotypes in informational books. All books should feature both children and adults of different racial and ethnic backgrounds.

Inside an Active Classroom

While studying the Native American Indians of the Great Plains, Maurice Tatum organized daily learning experiences around such motivating questions as "What would it be like to eat a meal with a Cheyenne friend of the past?" (food gathering and consumption) and "What games would you play if you visited the home of a Sioux friend of long ago?" (leisure, recreation, and education). Today's question of intrigue was, "How did the Plains Indians teach history to their children?"

Mr. Tatum selected the Sioux as the focus of exploration to answer that question. He informed the students that, like all native North Americans, the Sioux of the Great Plains had no written language. Mr. Tatum explained that stories and history were passed down from one generation to the next in the oral tradition. To set the scene, Mr. Tatum sat together with his students on the floor and shared multiple copies of two informational books, Ann McGovern's *If You Lived With the Sioux Indians* (Scholastic) and Marie Sandez's *These Were the Sioux* (University of Nebraska Press). The students were searching for several pieces of important information, but were especially interested in learning about one way that the Sioux wise men recalled the major events of passing years—the "winter count."

Each year a tribal artist would depict a special event, drawing it on bison hides that the women had stretched and dried in the sun on drying racks. Mr. Tatum showed an example of one event, the story of which was centered on a drawing of a horse. He explained that about 250 years ago the Sioux got horses from the Spanish and that these horses had both positive and negative influences on the lives of the Sioux. Horses allowed the Sioux to hunt bison more skillfully, but they also caused them to stop growing their own food. By drawing a single picture to remember an important event, the wise storyteller could remember enough to retell the history of the tribe to its youngsters, such as the introduction of horses to the Sioux.

Mr. Tatum encouraged his students to retell some of the important events they had been learning about from their informational books by making their own "winter counts" following these steps:

1. Cut a long sheet of brown butcher paper (8 by 15 inches) or a section of a grocery bag. Tear it into the shape of a bison hide.
2. Crumple the sheet into a ball and dip it into a container of water until it is thoroughly soaked.
3. Press out the sheets on newspaper and let them dry.
4. Recount important events in the lives of the Sioux.
5. As the students select events to depict, draw them on the sheets with crayon (press hard with the crayon).
6. Place the sheets between two pages of newsprint and press with a warm iron. The colors will darken and the "winter count" will have a weathered appearance.

There are many opportunities to use a variety of print sources in dynamic social studies programs. Teachers familiar with the concept of "literacy across the curriculum" know that they must supplement their basic textbook with some of the many superb print sources available today. Information books, historical fiction, folklore, biographies, and poetry collections, as well as newspapers, add depth and substance to any topic under study.

NEWSPAPERS

Amendment 1—United States Constitution

Congress shall make no law respecting an establishment of religion, or prohibiting the free exercise thereof, or abridging freedom of speech, or of the press; or the right of a free people to peaceably assemble, and to petition the Government for a redress of grievances.

People over the centuries have argued that a free press (not only newspapers, but all broadcast media) is the keystone of a democracy and have predicted that without it our democratic form of government would fail. Likewise, it has been argued that a free education is the keystone of a democracy. Combining these two popular sentiments, we find that neither a free press nor an informed citizenry could exist without each other. The free press ensures the public's right to know; our schools have a responsibility to prepare able and interested citizens to understand the issues involved in their lives. With important issues changing as rapidly as they do in contemporary society, the matter of being well informed is now more important than ever. The foundation for developing informed citizens should be established in the elementary grades as you establish an effective newspaper-based current affairs program.

Perhaps the best place to begin an effective current affairs program is to teach children how to read a newspaper. Children should learn to examine the various sections of the newspaper (world news, sports, community events, and so on) with special attention directed toward the sources of material for these sections (wire services, local writers, and syndicated columns). Children can understand that a good news article answers four basic questions—who, what, where, and when—in the first paragraph or two and then should go on to state why and how. Lead the children through the literal interpretation of news articles by making copies of a news article, distributing it to each child, allowing him or her sufficient time to read it (for a purpose, of course), and then guiding the interpretation:

- "Who is the story about?"
- "What did the person do?"
- "When did the event take place?"
- "Where did the event take place?"
- "Why did the event come about?"
- "How can this event be extended (be prevented from happening again, teach us a lesson, and so on)?"

News stories are objective; they present the facts with an absence of personal reaction. Encourage the children to share their feelings regarding any particular news article with questions such as the following:

- "How did you feel about the situation?"
- "What would you have done?"
- "Would you be willing to do the same thing?"
- "Do you agree with the central character?"
- "Is there any information you can add to the article?"
- "Do you think the story was written fairly (accurately)?"

Teachers can and should use newspapers in creative ways. The following are some guidelines you might find helpful with your students:

- Fictionalize a story about what happened just before and just after the moment captured in a selected newspaper picture.
- Give students a newspaper headline and ask them to write their own news story based on it.

- Take a student survey to find out what part of the newspaper interests them most. Divide the class into groups, each with a variety of interests. Each week, assign a group to report to the class. Urge "reporters" to read all they can find in the newspaper each day concerning their field. Each "reporter" then reads to the class one especially interesting item each week.

- Read only the first paragraph of a news article, and then make up the rest. Be original! Compare your story with the original article if you want.

- Have each student study newspaper articles about different well-known personalities and pantomime personality sketches as other students try to guess who is being portrayed. As students become skilled in mime techniques, have them scan the newspaper for simple situations to play out in pairs or small groups. Other students will enjoy guessing the actions.

- Have a student assume the personality of a person in the news and have classmates interview him or her. Remember, the student who assumes the character's personality must answer questions using the character's observed speech and other mannerisms.

- Have students take a favorite nursery rhyme and write it up as a news story, giving it an appropriate headline; for example, Mr. Egg Fractures Skull.

- Let your students be advice columnists. Have them read letters to a popular advice columnist. Pupils then write their own advice on real problems affecting playground behaviors, classroom problems, and other sources of conflict.

- Clip headlines from stories, but keep one newspaper intact. Have students read news stories and write their own headlines. Did students discover the main idea of the story expressed in the headline? Compare student headlines with the headlines in the uncut issue.

- After identifying the main topic of an editorial, scan the paper to locate stories related to the topic and read them. Study how the editorial was developed and then have students write their own editorials on the same issue.

Electronic Newspapers

Knowing what is going on in the world creates better citizens. One of the major goals of elementary school social studies programs is to help children acquire a lifelong interest in newspapers so they can keep in touch with what is going on in the world. However, when teachers try to interest children in current events, they often assign a child to bring in a newspaper article the next day. What normally happens is that, just at bed time, the child realizes that she needs a current events article for tomorrow and a parent frantically searches the front page to clip out something the child can take to school. Or, even worse, the child informs a parent just before he goes to sleep that he needs a specific current events article on Tasmania. The newspaper has probably been discarded, but even if it hasn't, did anything newsworthy happen in Tasmania that day? The value of such hit-or-miss newspaper programs is questionable.

An option currently being carried out by many elementary school teachers is on-line newspapers. They have selected this option for several reasons. One that stands out is immediacy—the newspaper that is discussed in school at 9:00 A.M. does not include the important stories that broke at 8:00 A.M. Online news fills the gap, keeping the class informed creates links between what is in the newspaper and what is happening right now. In addition to immediacy, the multimedia presentation of on-line newspapers is impressive. Video clips, sound, and full-color images accompany online news stories. In addition, should a particular story capture the interest of the class, online newspapers allow them to search the story by key word and access a rich storehouse of related news. Students can incorporate all of these sources into their own multimedia packages, properly cited, creating a customized newspaper.

Several online sources offer colorful, easy-to-read newspapers. *The Christian Science Monitor* is one of the most useful (*http://csmonitor.com*). Others include CNN Interactive (*http://www.cnn.com*), MSNBC (*http://msnbc.com*), and USA Today Online (*http://usatoday.com*). Several local newspapers have online versions, too, so check to see what is available.

None of these online newspaper sources is meant to replace the daily newspaper; newspapers are here to stay. However, online newspapers can augment the use of classroom newspapers by serving as an alternative that many people believe will be the dominant source for delivering information in the future.

Current Affairs Periodicals

Teachers often rely on commercially produced current events magazines or newspapers such as *Weekly Reader* for most of their program in current affairs. This approach has both advantages and disadvantages.

Some teachers become too dependent on a formal reading–reciting technique when using periodicals, but they can be an important educational tool for several reasons. First, these periodicals can motivate. They are written especially for children, and even reluctant readers respond positively to the nontext format and the comfortable reading levels. Second, the periodicals select interesting, contemporary topics. This week's big news, a special TV presentation, or the latest technological breakthrough helps to make the classroom more current. Finally, comprehensive teacher's guides that describe creative teaching strategies accompany periodicals. Periodicals are used in thousands of schools around the country and are a valuable resource material.

COMPUTERS

With the advent of classroom technology, students can now participate in a nontraditional form of hands-on education through the use of computers. When computers were first introduced into elementary schools during the late 1970s and early 1980s, they were used primarily as "electronic workbooks," providing drill-and-practice exercises much like conventional workbooks. Students were presented problems and entered their responses; the computer would send a graphic reward (smiley face or explosion, for example) for the right answer. This use clearly concerned many educators, for they envisioned computer terminals as centers of "busy work" with the same potential for abuse as regular worksheets and workbooks.

Although software companies continue to produce drill-and-practice programs, educators everywhere are convinced that the singular electronic workbook role of computers is long gone. The evolution of tutorials and simulations quickly joined the drill-and-practice programs as powerful tools for teaching content and skills. Some, like *Oregon Trail* (MECC), remain among the most popular programs in elementary school social studies classrooms. Now educators everywhere are trying to figure out ways to enhance learning in elementary school classrooms with computers. "I see the computer as an irreplaceable tool in my classroom," comments Ms. Kathy Nell, a fourth-grade teacher from Philadelphia. "I don't see it as a workbook, but a skylight— a skylight that opens up so many new opportunities for my students. The computer is pretty much my ally."

Ms. Nell concurs that some drill-and-practice computer programs are excellent aids for practicing certain skills and learning specific facts, but also realizes that an expanded variety of sophisticated educational software gives more attention to higher-level thinking processes. Overall, the programs can be classified according to the following types: (1) tutorial, (2) problem-solving, (3) simulation, (4) word processing and database, (5) telecommunications, and (6) hypermedia presentations.

Tutorial Software

Tutorial programs focus on the reinforcement of knowledge and skills, as well as the introduction of new concepts and skills. One example of a tutorial program is *Nigel's World* (Lawrence Productions), a fascinating world of adventures and learning experiences for children of all ages. Nigel is a fearless Scot who takes on the world, camera in hand, in search of a photograph that will earn him first place in a photography contest. As he journeys to the ends of the Earth snapping pictures, Nigel calls for the help of the students to make decisions involving geography and basic map skills.

Problem-Solving Software

Problem-solving programs often present highly complex situations where students face a dilemma, are put in a position of choosing from a number of possible alternatives, and come up with a solution. The computer program encourages active exploration and discovery. One extremely popular problem-solving program for children in grades 3 to 8 is the *Where in the World Is Carmen Sandiego?* series (available from Broderbund Software). Students become crime fighters as they search the world for Carmen Sandiego (an ex-secret agent turned thief) and her gang of criminals, who are out to steal our most precious natural treasures. The venture starts with 1 of the 16 thieves hiding in a city and leaving a trail of clues for student "detectives" to decipher. The students read descriptions of various cities, visit clue locations, and check possible destinations, all the while using their problem-solving and analytical skills. Along the same principle, the program developer has added other adventures.

Simulation Software

Computerized instruction may take the form of simulations, reproductions of something real. Simulation programs place students into situations that are as authentic as possible to real-life conditions. Social studies teachers employ simulations because they invite many modes of thought—conceptualization, problem solving, and varied opportunities to apply knowledge and skills. One of the most noteworthy simulations available for upper-grade elementary school classrooms is *The New Oregon Trail* (available from Minnesota Educational Computer Consortium). It presents a series of decisions that pioneers faced in 1847 as they set out in wagon trains to find new homes in the Oregon Territory. They stock up with provisions at the beginning of the 5- to 6-month journey, but heavy rains, wagon breakdowns, illness, and robberies eventually deplete their supplies. Children must make decisions along the way, but if they choose to hunt for food or stop at a fort, for example, they lose precious time and could suffer starvation or illness, or fail to pass the western mountains before the freeze and the blizzards. The computer mathematically determines the outcome of the children's decisions and gives the decision makers immediate feedback about the consequences of their choices. Although most simulations involve only one user per computer, *The New Oregon Trail* may involve a small-group approach by engaging a student family of four or five children to make the difficult decisions.

Another useful simulation for students in grades 4 to 8 is *Galleons of Glory: The Secret Voyage of Magellan* (available from Broderbund Software). The students imagine the world of 1519 by taking the place of Magellan and trying to sail a galleon around the globe. They are confronted with problems ranging from nature's fury to shipboard politics as they react to changing circumstances that arise during the voyage. Calm seas give way to vicious storms, and a frightened crew comes close to mutiny, challenging students to make decisions in situations representative of actual historical events.

Word Processing

Word processing systems are computer software programs designed to facilitate the efficient collecting, revising, storing, and printing of text. Word processing software has made it possible for elementary school students to type a first draft of a composition or report on a keyboard and simultaneously display it on a computer screen. By using a few quickly learned computer commands, the author can insert or delete text; combine sentences; "cut and paste" words, sentences, and paragraphs, moving them to new locations; change grammar and spelling errors; and print out the completed copy.

One type of word processing system helps students prepare neat, well-edited written pieces; another, called desktop publishing, combines graphics and text and allows users to produce other products such as signs, banners, greeting cards, newsletters, letterheads, travel brochures, and newspapers.

Across the country, children have developed a passionate and lasting love affair with the computer.

Telecommunications

In a small but growing number of classrooms, connections to the Internet are providing access to vast outside sources of information and creating new opportunities for collaborative learning. The Internet is often designated as a telecommunications service because it involves two-way communication via telephone lines. You are using a form of telecommunication when you chat with someone on the phone; a person who faxes a document from one fax machine to another transmits over telephone lines, too. In much the same way, we now find it possible to transfer data from one computer to another via telephone lines or high-speed cable connections. If your classroom and others have computers, it is possible to connect to one another through a modem or network and go online. This means that you are connected to a network of users who can exchange files, send and receive e-mail, conduct joint projects, share data, and even play educational games with one another.

As fascinating as the Internet world can be, it can also confront you with a few problems. Perhaps the greatest is the availability of material not suitable for children. The Telecommunications Act requires Internet services to keep such material away from children, but nothing substitutes for careful supervision. Online services provide controls that allow you to limit what your children can access. Software such as Cybersitter or Surfwatch lets you supervise visits to the Internet.

Some teachers hail the Internet as a new era in learning. Ms. Nell maintains that her online connection has revitalized her teaching and motivated and excited her students, who are learning much of the same information as in their textbooks, but in a more engaging way. According to Ms. Nell, this added motivation comes from the fact that her students have an immediate, authentic audience for their work; through planning and sharing with their online peers, they find that the information they exchange has meaning—an instantaneous and utilitarian motive. One of the greatest benefits cited by Ms. Nell is the capacity for collaborative research. She and her students have joined other classrooms around the country to investigate everything from the weather to prices for consumer goods. Ms. Nell's major complaint is that there just are not enough online classrooms to make a comprehensive exchange of projects and ideas possible.

For many teachers, it's a challenge to bridge the gap between traditional instruction and technology. However, as many teachers have learned, tapping into the Internet helps children benefit from a rich source of new ideas, friends, and experts. Blagojevic (1997) describes several categories of project ideas that were carried out in classrooms using the Internet:

- *To make new friends.*   Using electronic mail, children from Maine exchanged letters with Icelandic children.

- *To extend the curriculum.*   After listing favorite storybook characters, children from Sacramento and Baltimore initiated a "story swap." Each group created and e-mailed original stories to the other.

- *To build cross-cultural comparisons.*   Children from Oregon worked with children from Florida, Arizona, Japan, Russia, and South Africa on a collaborative book. Each location responded to the question "How do you like to play?" The children assembled a How We Play book of stories and drawings.

- *To produce information.*   After a bee stung young Ted on the leg one day, his classmates suggested they build a Web page that would educate people about bees. They researched bees and added their own drawings to the informational pages.

- *To learn more.*   A week after creating their Web page, the class received an e-mail message from a bee expert. He pointed out that their bee was actually a yellowjacket wasp and explained the difference between bees and wasps. The children used this information to correct their page.

- *To meet new people.*   While they were studying penguins, a group of children electronically "met" a class of second graders from Dunedin, New Zealand. They were awed to learn that their New Zealand friends could walk a half mile down the road to see penguins in the bay.

- *To explore the world.*   The Internet allows children to break out of the walls of their classroom to interact with people all over the world.

Hypermedia (Presentation Software)

A special area of interest that has contributed greatly to social studies programs today has been the use of hypermedia, a communications tool that combines video, graphics, animation, and text. Known as *presentation software,* hypermedia authoring programs enable students to organize and communicate information in innovative and thought-provoking ways, accessing and integrating information from such diverse sources as the Internet, sounds or clip art pulled from public domain software, photographs from a digital camera or scanner, and clips from a video camera or CD-ROM. Three widely used presentation software programs are *HyperStudio, ClarisWorks,* and, especially for the younger set, the *SlideShow* portion of *KidPix.* These are not the only hypermedia tools available to teachers and students, but they are excellent examples of how such programs work.

Inside an Active Classroom

I once heard a computer expert say, "To be truly literate, one must learn to communicate in the dominant system of a culture." At no other time was this truism clearer to me than when I visited an elementary school "History Fair" and examined all of the wonderful projects. Every display attracted a great deal of attention, but one stood out above all the others. I was made aware of this special display by a neighbor who turned to me and asked, "Can you believe what Michael did on the computer?" I walked over to Michael's space and was met with eye-popping graphics, clear text, dazzling animation, and breathtaking audio. Telling about the life of Harriet Tubman, Michael's project gave every impression of a professional presentation. Scanned photos from literature sources, spoken text that highlighted the key events in Harriet Tubman's life, recorded spirituals, and the culminating video clip of Martin Luther King, Jr.'s "I Have a Dream" speech made the presentation a special occurrence. The "flash" was not the priority in Michael's presentation; the message was certainly the important element. However, the presentation software added much more to Michael's research than if he had simply put together an oral or written report.

Some presentation software systems contain special "buttons" that allow the user to immediately access another part of the presentation by clicking on a prompt. For example, Michael's presentation included a button at the point in Harriet's life when she gave slaves secret directions on how to flee to the North. By using the mouse to click the button, the user could listen to the song "Follow the Drinking Gourd" while looking at an illustration of the Big Dipper.

Speaking of presentation software, Muir (1994) comments that if students find learning more interesting and engaging as a result of creating an interactive project (perhaps one that makes information pop up on the screen when you click a button), "then computers have served their purpose. If students become more enthusiastic about research—because they know that their final report is going to look good and be fully interactive—then computers have made a valuable contribution to the educational process" (p. 32).

Presentation software is available, relatively inexpensive, and not difficult to use. Teachers should use this practical technology application and demonstrate modern, effective communication techniques to their students.

AFTERWORD

The heart of dynamic social studies instruction is balance and proportion. These elements do not normally emerge as part of a teaching personality during a student's undergraduate certification program, during student teaching, or even after a year on the job. They often emerge after repeated successes with textbook-based instruction. You will not rely on textbooks to guide you throughout your entire teaching career; a feeling of unrest and a strong desire to "spread your wings" will begin to entice you to expand your repertoire and experiment with varied instructional materials and activities during your earliest years of teaching. Katz (1972) describes this professional evolution as a stage-related process:

- *Stage One:*   You are preoccupied with survival. You ask yourself questions such as, "Can I get through the day in one piece? Without losing a child? Can I make it until the end of the week? Until the next vacation? Can I really do this kind of work day after day? Will I be accepted by my colleagues?" Textbooks are useful tools that help teachers gain the confidence necessary to manage the routines causing most of the anxiety during this stage. (First year)

- *Stage Two:*   You decide you can survive. You begin to focus on individual children who pose problems and on troublesome situations, and you ask yourself these kinds of questions: "How can I help the shy child? How can I help a child who does not seem to be learning? What more can I do for children with special needs?" (Second year)

- *Stage Three:*   You begin to tire of doing the same things with the children. You like to meet with other teachers, scan magazines, and search through other sources of information to discover new projects and activities for the children. You ask questions about new developments in the field: "Who is doing what? Where? What are some of the new materials, techniques, approaches, and ideas? How can I make social studies (or any other subject) more powerful?" (Third and fourth years)

According to Katz's developmental theory, then, new teachers should not expect to move away from a deliberate textbook-based routine until sometime during the third year of teaching. At first, you will feel more comfortable teaching with the help of textbooks and with ideas learned from others. The need to grow and learn will become evident as an inner drive gives you no other choice but to branch out. You should then begin to formulate and refine a personal philosophy of instruction that will serve as a foundation to undergird all professional decisions in the future. The difference between teachers who are good "technicians" and those who are educational leaders appears to be their willingness to constantly think about and work toward methods based on a sound personalized philosophy of teaching and learning.

You will use textbooks, and they will contribute immeasurably to your social studies program. But the emphasis of your instruction should be on variety. Continually confront youngsters with significant experiences so they get to know our world and build the qualities that help them become constructive, active citizens. The kinds of citizens our boys and girls grow up to be is determined to a great extent by the ways they live and grow in school.

REFERENCES

Alliance for Arts Education. (1985). *Performing together: The arts in education.* Arlington, VA: Author.

Blagojevic, B. (1997). Internet interactions. *Scholastic Early Childhood Today, 11,* 47–48.

Brandt, R. (1995). Future shock is here. *Educational Leadership, 53,* 5.

Coerr, E. (1977). *Sadako and the thousand paper cranes.* New York: Dell.

Darigan, D. L., Tunnell, M. O., & Jacobs, J. S. (2002). *Children's literature: Engaging teachers and children in good books.* Upper Saddle River, NJ: Merrill/Prentice Hall.

Fowler, C. (1989). The arts are essential to education. *Educational Leadership, 47,* 62.

Fowler, C. (1994). Strong arts, strong schools. *Educational Leadership, 52,* 4–9.

Goodman, K. S. (1988). Look what they've done to Judy Blume!: The "bazalation" of children's literature. *The New Advocate, 1,* 29–41.

Huck, C. S., Heppler, S., & Hickman, J. (1993). *Children's literature in the elementary school.* Fort Worth, TX: Harcourt Brace Jovanovich.

Jarolimek, J., & Parker, W. C. (1993). *Social studies in elementary education.* New York: Macmillan.

Joint Committee of the National Council of Teachers of English and the Children's Theatre Association. (1983). Forum: Informal classroom drama. *Language Arts, 60,* 370–372.

Katz, L. G. (1972). Developmental stages of preschool teachers. *Elementary School Journal, 73,* 50–54.

Lapp, D., Flood, J., & Farnan, N. (1992). Basal readers and literature: A tight fit or a mismatch? In K. D. Wood & A. Moss (Eds.), *Exploring literature in the classroom: Contents and methods* (pp. 35–57). Norwood, MA: Christopher Gordon.

Muir, M. (1994). Putting computer projects at the heart of the curriculum. *Educational Leadership, 51,* 30–32.

Sewall, G. (1988). Literary lackluster. *American Educator, 12,* 35.

Solomon, W. (1989). Teaching social studies creatively. *Social Studies and the Young Learner, 2,* 3–5.

Starr, J. (1989). The great textbook war. In H. Holz, I. Marcus, J. Dougherty, J. Michaels, & R. Peduzzi (Eds.), *Education and the American dream; Conservatives, liberals, and radicals debate the future of education.* Grandy, MA: Bergin and Garvey.

Steptoe, J. (1987). *Mufaro's beautiful daughters: An African tale.* New York: Lothrop, Lee & Shepard.

Tompkins, G. E. (1997). *Literacy for the 21st century: A balanced approach.* Upper Saddle River, NJ: Merrill/Prentice Hall.

Webster, W. (1993). Thank you, Miss Monroe. *Educational Leadership, 50,* 45.

Wixson, K. K. (1991). *Houghton Mifflin social studies (Teacher's Edition for a message of ancient days).* Boston: Houghton Mifflin.

Zinsser, W. (Ed.). (1990). *Worlds of childhood: The art and craft of writing for children.* Boston: Houghton Mifflin.

Author Index

Subject Index